Court and Country

Court and Country 1688–1702

Dennis Rubini

Rupert Hart-Davis LONDON 1967

Rupert Hart-Davis Ltd
3 Upper James Street, Golden Square, London W1

Printed in Great Britain by
Western Printing Services Ltd
Bristol

SBN : 246. 64477. X

Acknowledgments

I should like to thank Professor J. H. Plumb for originally suggesting the topic; Dr J. B. Owen for bravely reading through so many drafts; G. V. Bennett, W. A. Speck, D. C. M. Platt, H. G. Horwitz, D. Jacobs, H. C. Beaufort-Bashford and M. R. Williams for their kind advice; and especially J. Steven Watson and Professor L. P. Curtis for their consistent encouragement. I hope that the archivists and owners of papers mentioned directly or indirectly in the manuscript bibliography will accept this totally inadequate acknowledgment of their help and hospitality.

Contents

Abbreviations

Standard abbreviations have been employed and only some of the following might not be apparent:

B.M.	British Museum
Bodl.	Bodleian Library
Cal. S.P. Dom.	*Calendar of State Papers, Domestic*
Chic. Univ. Lib.	Chicago University Library
H.C.J.	*Journals of the House of Commons*
H.L.J.	*Journals of the House of Lords*
N.L.W.	National Library of Wales
N.U.L.	Nottingham University Library
P.R.O.	Public Record Office
R.O.	Record Office (preceded by county or other abbreviation)
T.C.D.	Trinity College, Dublin

ONE

Introduction

With the dissolution of the Oxford parliament in 1681, hopes of legally excluding the Roman Catholic successor to the English throne came to an end. Subsequent assassination attempts only re-buttressed the prerogative and aided in the quiet remodelling of the corporations. When James called his first parliament in 1685 he found not above forty members whom he would not have chosen himself. Monmouth's abortive uprising in the West aided in suppressing dissent, serving as it did loosely to identify opposition with treason. Nevertheless, if no new constitutional limitations were placed upon the prerogative, the second session was as stormy as it was brief. That parliament was soon prorogued and was not to meet again. Within a year of James's accession, England faced a revolution from on high in the form of an arbitrary Roman Catholic monarch apparently bent on Romanizing and centralizing most things characteristically English. Alienating one source of support after another by his unpopular use of the royal prerogative to suspend or dispense with statutes, James was soon aware that he had little chance of success, but continued with determination apparently desiring the honours of martyrdom and sainthood. Before the eyes of a bewildered establishment the prognostications of the most rabid whig pamphleteers of the exclusion crisis were coming to pass. When in June of 1688 the queen unexpectedly gave birth to a son, many cried that he was supposititious, having been brought in by papists in a warming pan. Supposititious or not, the political nation had seen enough.

The 'immortal seven', seven Englishmen of considerable importance representing a fair spectrum of political opinion, signed an invitation requesting William of Orange to invade England and secure English liberties by calling a free parliament. William's subsequent landing at Torbay on 5 November 1688 has generally been called the glorious revolution. Recently an American historian has called it the respectable revolution,[1] and Russian historians agree in not even considering it a revolution at all, but simply a palace coup. Today most socialists scorn what made it so glorious to the whig historians, namely the decentralizing tendencies which made later reforms so difficult. As G. M. Trevelyan has pointed out, the effect of the revolution was the success of the outside against the middle, the country against the court. While conservatives applaud William's refusal to lead a class war in either Holland or England, perhaps neither scorn nor applause is called for; William simply followed the most practical course of action to gain his ends. In not becoming another Cromwell he avoided Cromwell's problems. Few practical politicians would become demagogues if they could be kings.

Even the most legitimate of sovereigns have problems, however, and William was little better than a usurper. If Charles I was his maternal grandfather, and his wife Mary James's eldest daughter, no equivocations by the gentlemen of the long gown could obscure the compulsory nature of James's 'self-imposed' exile. When at last the new parliament met, it was only with considerable reluctance that plans for a regency were rejected, as were those for making Mary sole sovereign. While at length James was said to have abdicated, the throne declared vacant and William and Mary made joint sovereigns with the executive power to reside in the king, many concurred only with considerable reluctance and because of their desire to avoid civil war. Many remained suspicious of the new sovereign, perhaps less on account of the usurpation than of his remaining indisputably both a foreigner and a warrior. Throughout his life, William's heart lay in the Netherlands. The attempts of the convention parliament to secure his resignation as Dutch stadtholder were unsuccessful while by contrast on several subsequent occasions he did speak of giving up the English throne. His chief advisers, favourites and receivers of prodigious royal magnanimity were Dutchmen. During the war, the king's second self was thought to be Hans Willem Bentinck, lord of Drummelin and now earl of Portland; later it would

---

[1] Lucile Pinkham, *William III and the Respectable Revolution* (Cambridge, Mass., 1954).

be the young Arnout Joost van Keppel, whom he created first earl of Albemarle. William corresponded and took advice from the Dutch Pensionary Heinsius before most of his English advisers. For some years the commanders of the English troops in the field remained foreigners, while the king strove to maintain his Dutch guards about him in England.

The new king's foreign policy was in the Dutch interest. Certainly it was in the Dutch interest for William to secure the English settlement as he did; as his most recent biographer freely admits, one reason William came to England was to guard against the birth of a commonwealth.[2] Such an event the Dutch regarded with utter horror. Indeed, how could they forget the effects of a rival commonwealth dedicated to commerce, and more particularly the devastating effects of the navigation laws. Nor was it William's politics alone which were Dutch. His failure ever truly to master the English language was exemplary of his Dutch nature, as was his lack of sympathy with the English way of thinking and its emphasis upon civilized tastes and virtues.

William's domestic life also presented difficulties. While Mary was docile enough, Princess Anne detested the Dutchman and all but established a rival court with the help of John and Sarah Churchill. While Churchill gained an earldom for coming over at an opportune time during the revolution, he wished for a dukedom and the garter if not more. When he did not get them he was soon involved in conspiracy. In addition, William's sex life had Dutch overtones. Although his wife was English, his extreme intimacy with Bentinck and more especially the beautiful young Keppel has been the subject of much busy speculation from that time until the present day. Whether or not the accusations are true is of concern here only in so far as they were believed true to the prejudice of his affairs. While certainly even the most rustic members of parliament must have become acquainted with the rumours, it is not at all certain that they believed them; people with strong moral views are often incredulous of immoral behaviour—and at the least, William was discreet. While then, there are innuendos in a few speeches, one suspects that what irked most Englishmen was not whether his favourites were male rather than female, but rather that they were Dutch and hideously expensive.[3]

Despite or perhaps because of such difficulties, William was amongst the bravest and personally most reckless warriors of his age. His military

---

[2] S. B. Baxter, *William III* (1966), p. 231.   [3] See Chapter 7

courage and skills had made him the redeemer of the Netherlands and were to win him the admiration of the sun king. Certainly it was his image as a successful general which secured his invitation to England and brought over many uncommitted adherents. While it would be untrue to say that he had gained the throne by right of conquest, his force was very different from Monmouth's ragged band, and his was highly clever and successful strategy. William thought in terms of war—a war against France. The estates general had allowed him to leave in the hope that he would ally England firmly and irrevocably to their cause and he was not to disappoint them; it was even said that he simply took England on his way to France. William thought of his life as a great battle and his ideas as a warrior pervaded his ideas as a politician. If William succeeded in Holland, England, Ireland and Scotland without shedding blood with his own hands, most of those who did so on his behalf were not punished but rewarded.[4] If his plotting to secure the English throne did not begin in earnest until the birth of the pretender, the favours shown Monmouth until Charles's death seem to indicate that his subsequent caution was wise rather than laudable.[5] William simply employed the same scientific approach to politics that he applied to war; a wise commander expends neither himself nor his troops on the ramparts if capitulation can be obtained by simply holding siege. William's caution and moderation then did not make him any less a danger to English liberties.

Was there any danger that the new king, encouraged by evil counsellors and aided by foreign mercenaries, might become as absolute as any of his predecessors? If William had in effect aided in deposing an arbitrary Roman Catholic monarch largely to further the fight against another Roman Catholic monarch, was there any reason to suppose that the saviour of Protestant Europe did not wish to become its absolute ruler as well? And why only Protestant Europe? William's aesthetic taste, as exemplified in the decorations of his palaces, was largely inspired by Versailles. His toleration and employment in Holland of Roman Catholics, as well as the general non-enforcement of the penal laws in England, leads one to suppose that if given the opportunity, he would not find any European subjects distasteful or in need of conversion. This is not to imply that William spent his nights dreaming of a Europe controlled by the House of Orange. He probably hoped for little more than stopping the growth of French power—a laudable

---

[4] Baxter, *William III*, p. 274.   [5] *Ibid.*, pp. 168, 192, 197 and 231–2.

enough ambition by almost any Englishman's reckoning. The problem was, however, the uncertainty of what would follow; if he did succeed, what would he do next? How much should Englishmen sacrifice to stop French ambition? How much must be paid to secure a good peace? Must parliament grant all the supplies requested for the war? What proportion of the burden should the English bear in comparison to that of the allies? If they sacrificed too many liberties to aid in the war effort, in the end might they not find that they had made Esau's bargain?

To outward appearances, parliament had few liberties to spare. The royal prerogative remained almost as unfettered as at the closing of the first session of the long parliament: Charles II sacrificed a strong foreign policy and avoided making any considerable concessions to obtain a large supply; James would have been legally bound by additional limitations if the opposition had not demanded exclusion, or if the subsequent attempts at assassination and rebellion had not served to identify opposition with treason—a fine device employed by monarchs of all ages. If during the convention parliament the suspending power was declared illegal and the dispensing power put under parliamentary control, this limitation was not certain to endure nor was it a death blow even if it did.

COURT FACTIONS

William appeared determined neither to allow a further diminution of the prerogative nor to falter in an aggressive anti-French foreign policy. He wished his court to be above party and his ministers to do his bidding as readily as his officers in battle. His problem was, of course, that while the leaders of an English faction might be taught to assume military regularity in the performance of their duties, they had to be shown that his battles were their battles. While, moreover, one faction might support part of his plan, it might oppose another. His policy of great supplies for an aggressive foreign policy was best obtained from the whigs, but then the tories at first seemed better able to maintain the cherished prerogative. While William wished for both, in the event he was forced to choose. He chose great supplies with a concomitant diminution of the royal prerogative and within a few years he was forced to become something of a whig king. Or rather a *new whig* king, for he was not the puppet king, arbitrary only in proscribing tories, which the red-eyed extremists of the convention would have had to be sure, for most of these whigs were forced to compromise their aims too and generally came to support the court. If for some whigs it meant the shame of changing their coats, to others it was the long-awaited opportunity to show their true colours and make the royal court a whig court.

The change was not only necessary but desirable and from the days of the civil wars they had tried to shed their radical country allies and all that silky talk of English liberties, cheap government and ministerial responsibility to parliament. If only William could be brought to see himself in his domestic role as they did—as their own little hook-nosed Dutch doge, let us say,—then all would be well and they might appear in the resplendent despotic garb of Venetian oligarchs. Indeed their day came and lasted a hundred years. But it did not come at once and for the next quarter century it was sometimes a question whether an indignant squirearchy might not hang them for their efforts. In the years which concern us, whig setbacks were almost as great as advances and it is always a mistake to think of a trend as a *fait accompli*. If there was an unmistakable movement towards oligarchy, William did not become a mere doge of Venice. He did not think of himself as a whig king and his English friends remained tories. Still there is little surprising in this; to this day, many think with the radicals and dine with the conservatives. The former tory ministers were nicer people; more liberal, more cosmopolitan and at least less openly ravenous in seeking favours. Still, William was forced to come to the painful realization that while the tories were supporters of the king, to many tories he was not really their king—at least so long as he continued in his desire for an active and expensive war against France.

It would, however, be wrong to think completely or even largely in whig and tory terms save in reference to the ministry and even here the king tried to minimize the dominance of any one party as much as he could. The real battles took place in the commons and there the frame of reference was not usually whig and tory but court and country. It seems obvious that as most divisions were over matters favourable or unfavourable to the court, this was the important division, as even such whig and tory historians as Macaulay and Feiling freely admit. Robert Walcott has argued that politics in William's reign are best seen in the light not of a two-party, but something of a four-party system, in which court and country form the north and south poles, while whig and tory form the east and west. One might thus see a full circle of political opinion, in which there is court, court-tory, tory, country-tory, country, country-whig, whig, court-whig, and so back to court, thus making a full circle of political opinion, allowing for a wide variety of alliances.[6] While all combinations were possible, events showed that only a few were probable. Owing to the war and the foreign nature of the court, the court-country dichotomy predominated. Admittedly, when it came to questions of religion, or men rather than measures, then whig-tory factionalism played a dominant role. Owing to the war, however, contemporaries did not see these issues occupying the centre of the stage during most of William's reign. Still, Walcott is correct in seeing that to carry out the court programme William wished to rely upon whig and tory factions as little as possible. He wished rather for the moderates of either or preferably both factions to unite with his own parliamentary following in an effort to retain the initiative and to push his programme past any country opposition.

During the convention parliament, this policy may be said to have had only a modicum of success. While his first minister, Halifax, was the very embodiment of the beloved bipartisan qualities, he was, for similar reasons, repugnant to the extremists: the whigs would not forgive his opposition to exclusion despite his later fall from office; the tories could not abide the extremity of such whig actions as proposing to make William sole sovereign, while opposing the tory oath of allegiance recognizing William as only a *de facto* monarch. Neither faction liked his policy of a mixed ministry, and both combined in a series of heated attacks which ensured his resignation as lord privy seal at the dissolution. In retrospect one sees that the whigs were the real losers. As Professor J. H. Plumb has argued, the convention parliament was much less whig than commonly supposed.[7] While Professor Allen Simpson buttresses the traditional view, he does so in a rather untraditional way, admitting that the whigs were occasionally divided amongst themselves, and even when united were but the strongest of several factions. The whigs by no means had an absolute majority. The loss of the comprehension bill illustrates the first point, for only some whigs supported comprehension. Simpson argues that the loss of the indemnity bill was, in fact, a whig victory as the tories had succeeded

---

[6] Robert Walcott, 'The Idea of Party in the Writing of Stuart History', *Journ. Brit. Stud.* (1962), i, 54–62.

[7] The elections are discussed in considerable detail in Professor Plumb's 'Elections to the House of Commons in the Reign of William III' (Ph.D., Cantab., 1936), part ii, ff. 165 and following, esp. f. 262.

in making it exclude only a very few. This seems, however, far more a defensive tactical success, for the whigs had displayed their inability to proscribe a larger number. In this case the effect of both courtiers and moderates seems apparent, as it does with the progress of the corporation bill which would have restored the municipal charters forfeited during the past two reigns. In a poorly attended house, the whigs introduced the much vaunted Sacheverell clause which would exclude from municipal offices all involved in the surrender of the charters for a period of seven years. Coupled with this blatant attempt to proscribe their rivals was a threat to block the court's financial programme unless the king assented when the bill came before him. In the event, William was not forced to signify his pleasure, the clause being thrown out by eleven votes with many tories still to come up. While Simpson finds that the whigs showed considerable strength in mustering almost two hundred votes to retain the measure, he notes that the opposition contained not only tories, but courtiers and moderates.[8] This, of course, serves to give added credence to the aforementioned four-party analysis even during the convention. Still, if only because of the sense of crisis and unstable nature of the new court, there is some justification in talking largely in whig and tory terms at this time. If the whigs had passed the proposal perhaps the king would have been forced to capitulate. In fact, however, they failed and in failing the strength of their appetites had left an even greater impression than their teeth. William also came to question their counsel. It was with the advice of the republican Hampden that he had given up the unpopular but highly profitable hearth money tax, and then they had failed to provide suitable alternative funds. Indeed, the extremists' attacks upon Halifax and now their failure to carry the Sacheverell clause made the whigs appear not as commonwealthmen but, what was worse, ineffectual commonwealthmen. Probably the king did not regret the subsequent resignations from the ministry of such inveterate whigs as Delamere, Mordaunt, now earl of Monmouth, and Sir Henry Capel.

The tories had done all they could to ensure a dissolution. Sir Thomas Osborne, earl of Danby, now marquis of Carmarthen, was at the fore of such designs. During the convention he had received the position of lord president when he had hoped to become lord treasurer. Certainly

[8] 'The Convention Parliament, December 1688–February 1690' (D.Phil., Oxon, 1939), ff. 29–36. 10 January 1689/90. *H.C.J.*, x, 329. H. C. Foxcroft, *Life and Letters of Sir George Savile, 1st Marquis of Halifax* (1878), ii, 343.

William was indebted to him and Carmarthen was not one to under-value his services. If he had opposed exclusion, he was anti-papist and pro-Orange; he had arranged William's marriage to James's daughter, Mary, and demonstrated a willingness to take a leading part in the revolution. His earlier experience as lord treasurer made William value him much, although less for his advice than for his management of the court's financial programme in parliament. To William this was of the utmost importance and the task he set was not an easy one. The War of the League of Augsburg was primarily a war of sieges. Perhaps this was necessary. Perhaps the best way of stopping French ambition was to show the utmost in tenacity and willingness to expend huge sums for insignificant, not to say negative results. Needless to say, this was a rather unpleasant picture to present to representatives of even the more remote provinces of the Dutch Republic. But what would result if it was proposed to an English parliament thinking itself more removed from the European hostilities than the American congress in 1939? Carmarthen had no intention of finding out. Proceeding less by presenting powerful arguments than by the employment of trickery and stealth, he was highly sophisticated and spoke of church and tory in-terests as one. A skilful manipulator who proceeded by finesse, he would employ almost any method so long as it was effectual, and if it were not for the fact that he identified with both his family and party, one might be completely blinded by such dazzling qualifications. Still, he was able to overcome the handicap of having more mouths to feed than such childless rivals as Halifax by being not only an industrious shopper for office but a thrifty one; leaving the prime cuts to others, he filled his basket with scraps and offal which were soon transformed into tasty Yorkshire patronage pies. The problem of party principle cast more ominous shadows. Indeed, there was little to be done, although his pleas for expediency and moderation perhaps forestalled his in-evitable eclipse.

The other leading member of the old administration who stayed in office, Daniel Finch, second earl of Nottingham, seldom employed such terms as expediency or moderation. The very embodiment of the church party, Nottingham led a godly, righteous and sober life, directing his brood of over a score upon similar lines. While breaking with James over the use of the suspending power in his attack upon the church, he had fiercely opposed the whig concept of a vacancy in the succession and recognized William as only a *de facto* monarch. Still, William found him to be an honest man and even such inveterate whigs as Bishop

Burnet admitted that his appointment as secretary of the northern department was essential to ensure tory acceptance of the revolution settlement. One tory who did not immediately reappear was Laurence Hyde, created earl of Rochester during the exclusion crisis. Politically, he followed much the same course in choosing sides. Perhaps it was because he was related to both James and Mary that he felt he could burn his political candle at both ends. He continued in his office as lord treasurer until 1687 and did not really come over to William's cause until it was unwise not to do so. William found him combining the worst features of both Carmarthen and Nottingham, drawing upon the unscrupulousness of the former and the more prejudiced high church sentiments of the latter. Not surprisingly, he did not gain admission to the privy council until the tory ascendancy in the spring of 1692.

William was in fact searching for men less attached to party and strong sentiments than to the simple business of administration. Sidney Lord Godolphin was one of these archetypes of the professional civil servant. Unobtrusive and yet indispensable in Charles's reign, he had supported exclusion and still was continued in office by James, if relegated from his post as first lord of the treasury to the modest household position of queen's chamberlain. He returned to the treasury board on William's accession but subsequently resigned, apparently owing to difficulties with Carmarthen. In mid-November 1690, however, William persuaded him to return as first lord. During this interim period his place had been filled by Sir John Lowther of Lowther. A whig in both the exclusion crisis and revolution, Lowther soon fulfilled Carmarthen's expectations that he could adjust to being a good court tory, although his failure to be a competent lord treasurer was something of a disappointment. In the spring of 1692 he was dropped from the treasury board altogether and returned to his less exalted, if increasingly important, duties of directing the court's business in the commons.

If Godolphin was a professional treasurer, Robert Spencer, second earl of Sunderland, was a professional adviser and, to most Englishmen, the very embodiment of evil counsel. While holding office under Charles II and supporting exclusion for various dark motives, he subsequently became and remained one of James's most trusted and indispensable advisers, making a timely conversion to Roman Catholicism. After a brief exile following the revolution and demonstrating an almost unrivalled capacity to condemn what he once applauded, he soon had William's ear—and William listened. Aided by his henchman, the elderly but nimble Henry Guy, Sunderland acquiesced in the tories' ascendancy, then advised William to bring in the whigs, then call back the tories, and finally bring back the whigs—although not before he had given their enemies advice on how to secure their impeachments and hang them 'in a garret'. Considering the circumstances, Sunderland usually offered sound advice, and while William was wise in taking it and even in giving him the post of lord chamberlain for a time, there can be little doubt that Sunderland's presence in or behind the ministry increased parliamentary uncertainty of royal plans.

Charles Talbot, twelfth earl of Shrewsbury, provides a sharp contrast to the opportunist Sunderland. Although born a Roman Catholic, he became an Anglican during the exclusion crisis and was the youngest of the immortal seven, signing the invitation at the age of twenty-eight. His good looks, bachelor status and general popularity made him known as the 'king of hearts'. William eagerly sought his presence in the ministry to gain both popular support and confidence in his good intentions. Despite his youth, however, Shrewsbury's very bad health and very good conscience made him a reluctant officeholder. At first he was balanced against Nottingham as secretary of the southern department, and indeed it was probably his urgings which kept William from dissolving the convention parliament earlier than he did. Soon after the first session of the new parliament Shrewsbury resigned, leaving Nottingham as sole secretary. While he disliked the principles of Carmarthen's administration, he came to distrust the new whigs, who at first eagerly sought him as their patron. Only reluctantly, and seemingly at the price of the king's acceptance of new constitutional limitations upon the prerogative, did he resume the secretarial office in the spring of 1694. Even then he stated his disillusionment with the ethics of his friends in office, generally known as the court or junto whigs.

They were led by Sir John Somers, Edward Russell, Charles Montague and the Hon. Thomas Wharton. While included amongst those who first attacked the Carmarthen ministry out of 'different principles and different ends' they were thought to be fundamentally different from the country opposition, for all held places and were obviously in search of greater ones. Opposition leaders suspected them of being 'men of trick' and 'playing a double game', willing to gain important places by either assistance or obstruction. They attacked men in office because they wanted their offices, not because they wanted reform. By 1694, with the acceptance of important offices, these whigs clearly became court whigs. Here were the whigs William really brought in.

Although continuing to maintain an aggressive anti-French foreign policy, they generally assumed the tories' position as defenders of the prerogative. The junto whigs showed their efficacy in opposition and yet appeared less intent on party vengeance than the whigs of the convention. It appeared, moreover, that unlike some tories who were bought off earlier, the whigs could bring many of their followers with them; that they could be as effective 'in' as they were 'out'.

Only Somers was not of a noble family with extensive land holdings and electoral influence; he amply compensated for this failing with his legal knowledge and services as the workhorse of the coalition. He was born in Worcestershire, followed his father's profession of barrister and during James's reign served as counsel to the seven bishops, putting forth the case against the suspending power. He became solicitor general in the spring of 1689 and was knighted the following October. Russell was a cousin of the whig martyr, Lord William, and nephew and son-in-law to the earl of Bedford, elevated to a dukedom in 1694. In the spring of 1688 he was sent to The Hague to negotiate with William and subsequently signed the invitation. During the first year of the reign he was made a privy councillor and treasurer to the navy. Charles Montague was made clerk to the privy council in 1689 and became the junto's financial expert; a task for which he had had considerable experience, having been an auditor of the exchequer since 1679 (although not holding a parliamentary seat). Montague was similar to Russell, both in being born to a great whig family and being the younger son of a younger son. Both were expected to make their own way and both amply fulfilled all expectations.

Wharton was the most extreme. He had been a member of parliament since 1673 and witnessed the failure of exclusion and the subsequent royalist vengeance. Joining William shortly after his landing, he was subsequently sworn of the privy council and made comptroller of the household. He had by far the most extensive electoral influence of the four and in William's last parliament Walcott ascribes twenty-five members to his following, the junto as a whole having about sixty-four seats.[9] Dr. E. L. Ellis has challenged Walcott's estimate, saying that the junto was at once far larger and yet far more brittle than indicated. That is, while many uncommitted members would support them on some measures, many even of what Walcott describes as their

[9] R. Walcott, *English Politics in the Early Eighteenth Century* (1956), p. 200.

closest following would desert them on others.[10] They might, for example, gain considerable support on ministerial questions and find their numbers sadly depleted when they attempted to uphold the prerogative. It was in such instances that those whigs who remained in opposition regarded the junto whigs as apostates, having forsaken their former views regarding English liberties. Many would not accept the contention that the prerogative must be maintained in wartime and that the king and the new whig ministry could be trusted not to abuse it; for if the threat from monarchy was diminished, oligarchy presented new dangers. By the time of the Peace of Ryswick in 1697, the junto ministers had definitely proved their value to the king as war ministers. William was to view the peace as little better than an armed truce and for a time seemed determined, if not to keep the junto ministers in, to keep the tory ministers out; for he associated their programme with a peace policy. Only slowly was he forced to allow a tory ministry to come into being and it had scarcely lasted a session before he was planning a return to the junto.

COUNTRY FACTIONS

As the king's chief support came from those who held places, the logical leaders of the opposition were those who did not; country, as opposed to court. While, admittedly, some were in opposition even while holding office, usually this occurred only while the ministry was in a state of transition; that is, either while they were trying to gain greater places and were demonstrating their danger in opposition, or alternatively, when they were apparently about to be forced from office. The junto's action against the Carmarthen ministry serves to exemplify the former exception, while the subsequent court-tory obstructionism during the period of transition to the whigs demonstrates the latter.

The concept of a conflict between court and country is scarcely new. It was this problem to which many members tacitly referred when they said things had not been right since Elizabeth's time. If they had looked back with a critical eye they would have seen that things had not been right then either. Still, the deterioration of the relationship had certainly become more apparent since the accession of the Stuarts, being marked by the execution of one king and the forced abdication of another. The

---

[10] E. L. Ellis, 'The Whig Junto from its inception until 1714' (D.Phil., Oxon., 1961), ff. vii–viii.

country party now sought to keep this from happening again by defining the constitutional relationships between king, lords and commons,
by ensuring some commons' control of the use of public funds and by
enforcing ministerial responsibility to parliament. These aims were, of
course, fundamental to the opposition throughout the seventeenth century. But if one can hear echoes from the speeches of Coke, Pym,
Cromwell or Shaftesbury, it must be noted that they were not cited as
authorities—and this was not simply because they would have been
forced to substitute 'Holland' for 'France' as the secret enemy in so
doing. Such precedents as the country party employed were based far
more upon interpretations of acts passed by reigning sovereigns. The
radical nature of the reforms was minimized and, indeed, even in looking at the private correspondence of the members concerned with
making them, one might still suppose that they had completely for-
gotten what happened from the prorogation of the long parliament's
first session until the restoration, as well as during the exclusion crisis.
After the glorious revolution then, the country party saw itself safe-
guarding English liberties primarily against the dangers of monarchy
and oligarchy inherent in the Dutch warrior king and the war ministry.
At the same time, however, many knew that they had to be cautious,
for if they went too far there was a danger of so weakening the government as to invite foreign invasion—or to allow for the re-emergence of
troubles from below. While then, the convention parliament ensured
that the king was limited by statute, the bill of rights was but a pale
shadow of the robust measure hammered down in committee. So too a
mutiny bill was passed providing for the summary trial of military
personnel before a court martial while the habeas corpus act was sus-
pended.[11] In part, of course, this was due to court influence. Nevertheless, in passing these measures, the commons had indirectly ensured
annual sessions, for both acts required an annual review for their continuance. Nor had the commons given up its right to make subsequent
reforms. In William's reign, largely because of the sense of crisis, individual problems were met with as they arose. There was not one all-
encompassing act, but rather a series, and these were not passed in one
session, but rather over a period of thirteen years. By proceeding in
this way they maintained a government which was neither arbitrary nor
ineffectual. While some might say that the country party went too far,

---

[11] See C. C. Crawford, 'The Suspension of the Habeas Corpus Act and the
Revolution of 1689', *Eng. Hist. Rev.* (1915), xxx, 613–30.

and undoubtedly many country party members would have gone further if they could, there can be no doubt that the final solution was far from disastrous to the English nation, as both the treaties of Ryswick and Utrecht bear witness.

The country party was largely negative in character; it knew more what it did not want than what it did. In part, this was due to its very nature, for it seldom had any positive programme save in regard to constitutional reform, and even here there might be disputes over both timing and degree. Usually the country party only opposed or acquiesced in the court's programme. They did not propose to tell the king what he should do, but rather what he should not. In defining the composition of the country party one is again forced to resort to negatives.

The king in his early trimming policy employed a mixed ministry; so too the opposition was an alliance—an alliance of mutually distrustful men. Although this hindered the development of a positive programme, when they coalesced for an attack there was formidable breadth. Amongst the various factions which made up the country party, the most valued were those who, though offered places or at least acceptable to those in office, yet chose to remain in opposition. From the time of the junto ascendancy this group was largely restricted to whigs. Those who were proponents of exclusion, or had favoured the whig Sacheverell clause in the convention, constituted the very heart of the country party throughout most of the reign. Without their support, opposition would have been far more easily identifiable with treason, and it is their presence which best justifies the usage of the term 'country party' rather than 'tory party'. They were exemplified by such Presbyterian moderates as Sir Edward Harley, who had risked much in opposing the arbitrary practices of not only Charles I and the protector, but the royal brothers and now William III. They were not simply against the government because they were not of it, but because it posed a threat to English liberties as they knew them. Even during the convention parliament Sir Edward was feeling his way towards an alliance with his former opponents, although his son Robert came in with strong whig patronage and indeed, in an election petition to the 1690 parliament, was supported by two of the junto leaders themselves.[12] During the

---

[12] Sir Edward wrote: 'A Gent you know, hast worn a bullet above 40 years was not displeased to find it gilded in the debate by Some [who] were then his prisoners.' To R. Harley, 29 January 1688/9. B.M. Add. MSS. 40,

junto ascendancy, however, Robert stayed in opposition despite being
offered some of the most considerable offices at a very young age.[13]
Admittedly, in Anne's reign, Harley became lord treasurer and was
created earl of Oxford and Earl Mortimer. At that time, the circumstances were, however, quite different. As Angus McInnes argues, the
threat to English liberties then came from the war party rather than the
sovereign.[14]

Harley was thoroughly country in nature. He thought of his family
and estate at Brampton Bryan in Herefordshire seemingly first and foremost. He had a puritanical upbringing and remained to his dying days
provincial in temperament, if not in outlook. Financially, the family
estate was of a middling size. The Harleys were richer than mere gentry,
if not substantial squires, and Robert was both able and forced to be
diligent in the pursuit of his parliamentary duties. Harley was related
by marriage to Paul Foley, who serves as another exemplar of the ideal
country leader. The son of a great Stourbridge ironmonger, Foley was
heir to a considerable estate with concomitant influence about Worcestershire. He too had a Presbyterian background and was a big fish in
a lesser pond. When in the spring of 1695 the court-tory Speaker Sir
John Trevor, was expelled for bribery, Foley was elected in his place.
It is worth comparing him with his predecessor. In one respect they
were alike for both had always worn only one coat; Foley's was country,
Trevor's court. That the court had changed and their principles had
not, makes their consistency the more remarkable. In their attitudes to
local and court interests they were utterly dissimilar. Trevor showed
complete disdain for local interests. In six parliaments he represented
as many constituencies in three different counties. Foley sat in five parliaments for the same constituency[15] and never accepted a place. Trevor
assumed the former Speaker's position as master of the rolls soon after

---

621, f. 7. E. Harley to Sir E. Harley, 20 November 1960. *H.M.C. Portland*,
iii, 451.

[13] Harley states that from January 1691, when he was first brought into
the king's confidence, he was several times pressed to come into his service
'... particularly on occasion of several vacancys, to be secretary of state.' The
first subsequent instance occurred in March 1692 when Nottingham became
sole secretary. B.M. Portland loan 29/163/3 ('Account of Robert Harley's
conduct with reference to the Revolution and succession').

[14] 'The Political Ideas of Robert Harley', *History* (1965), l, 319.

[15] Littleton, who was to succeed him in 1698, had admittedly sat for one
seat since the convention, but this was the pocket borough of Woodstock.
Harley was to change his constituency only once.

being elected to the chair, while also being made first commissioner of the great seal. Foley, on the other hand, had an impeccable record in opposition. As early as the reign of Charles II he had been described by Roger North as the most industrious among those busy '...in ferreting the musty old repositries with design to produce in parliament what they thought fit, to the prejudice of the crown and its just prerogatives.'[16] During James's reign, while Trevor was Speaker, Foley was noticeably absent from parliament and listed as one thought eminent in opposition in the country.[17] After the revolution, Foley frequently spoke against court proposals and was active on parliamentary commissions of inquiry.

Harley soon began to overshadow Foley as leader of the country opposition. In part this was due to Foley's age and the death of a large number of possible rivals,[18] although it is somewhat misleading to think of rivalries for the leadership of the country party. Harley did not deceive himself into believing that he was the head of a large number of often fiercely independent country squires in anything approaching the same sense that William was leader of the court party, or even, like Wharton, in being the patronage chief of a large coalition. The personal following which Harley did have was shared largely with the Foleys, and the number which Professor Walcott accords the coalition in William's last parliament was but twenty, few of whom were related by blood. This estimate is not only generous, but would be ridiculous if it implied that even that number would follow Harley if he chose some unusual course of action which conflicted with country principles. If, for example, he had voted with the court in hope of a place as, in fact, one of the Foleys did earlier, the others would probably not have joined him.

One comes to suspect then that the 250 members of the court and aristocratic connections might also be somewhat more loosely joined than Professor Walcott has supposed. Professor Plumb, Dr Ellis and others have voraciously attacked Walcott for employing inaccurate methods which placed so high a premium on geneaology and the scanty division lists of the period; Professor Walcott himself has admitted the need for some adjustment along these lines. The new division lists

---

[16] Roger North, *Lives of the Norths* (1890), i, 194.

[17] The latter list is printed and explained in A. Browning, *Thomas Osborne, Earl of Danby* (Glasgow, 1944–51), vol. iii, appendix iv.

[18] About sixteen eminent old whigs had died by 1700. For a list of their names see Walcott, *English Politics*, p. 86.

which have come to light tend to confirm the suspicion of many historians that Walcott has either said too much or too little. There is at
times the factionalism he indicates but at other times considerable
cohesion, depending on not only the issue in question and the state of
national sentiment, but a host of surrounding circumstances.[19] Still,
even if one assumed that Walcott was correct, there would still be a
numerical majority of uncommitted members. It was these men from
whom the country party was largely composed, and of whom Harley
was leader only in the sense that a lead wolf leads the pack (an analogy
he employed).[20] If he had acted otherwise he would have found himself all but alone, for to most members Harley had little to offer. Indeed,
he does not even appear to have given any considerable help to his
friends in elections.

It is, of course, difficult, if not impossible, to discuss the country
party following in any detail. This is most unfortunate and the lack of
political correspondence in surviving estate papers makes it seem unlikely that very much will ever be learned about them. Probably they
wrote few letters, but this does not mean that they did not discuss
politics when they gathered: 'You were not much mistaken,' one opposition leader wrote, 'when you Apprehended I was not very fond of
scribbling but I make a much better returne when I come in person.'[21]
One is thus forced to make random generalizations which are often
misleading. Macaulay condemned the country members as ignorant;
Professor Plumb on the other hand believes that many were rather well
educated. Certainly Plumb's view would tend to be substantiated by the
presence in opposition of Narcissus Lutterell, whose education shines
through not only his diary, but his copious abstract of the debates for
two sessions which remains unpublished.[22] Even those country members
of little education who were returned as knights of the shire might
claim with considerable justification to know England's interest better
than any placeman. In the elections for these more open constituencies,
considerable correspondence does survive. And there were many con-

---

[19] See appendix A.

[20] See, for example, his letter to Godolphin of 10 September 1707 in which
he states his willingness to 'howl with the wolves'. *H.M.C. Bath*, i, 181.

[21] Sir Edward Seymour to Col. James Grahme at Levens. 14 n.m. 1700.
Levens, Bagot MSS.

[22] Narcissus Luttrell, 'An Abstract of the Debates, Orders and Resolutions
In the House of Commons wch are not printed in their votes' is in two vols.:
Codrington Library (All Souls) MSS. 158a and b. Hereafter cited as Luttrell,
Abstract MSS. i (ii).

tests: as Professor Plumb points out, the years 1689–1715 witnessed '...more general elections, and more contests at these elections than for the rest of the eighteenth century'.[23] While there are dangers in generalizing from contests for only the more open constituencies, there is considerable evidence that at times their voting influenced and reflected that of parliament as a whole.[24] Perhaps it was because their provincial accents and rustic clothes only made them all the more certain that they were on the side of the angels. These were the men Harley appealed to with his strong reasons and few words.

The country party was an amalgam of interests. If such as the Harleys and Foleys had a genuine distrust of almost any central government, another group led in the commons by Sir Thomas Clarges, Sir Christopher Musgrave and (usually) Sir Edward Seymour owed their obstructionist principles more to William's particular government and the continental war policy it pursued. The prestige and speaking ability of these venerable tory gentlemen greatly aided the country cause. Pillars of church and squirearchy, they were not Jacobites. While all three stood against making William and Mary king and queen and earlier had both opposed exclusion and held minor offices, they also opposed James's extensive use of the prerogative and romanizing policy. Clarges, brother-in-law to General Monk, duke of Albemarle, had been knighted at Breda after taking part in negotiations between king and parliament. He had sat in every parliament since 1656 and continued to play an active role until his death in 1695.

Less scrupulous was Sir Edward, eldest member of the ducal family of Seymour (Somerset), who was the unquestioned first commoner of the land and a leader of the South-West squirearchy. In 1692, however, he accepted office for a period of about two years, but neither he nor the king could have found this a very pleasant experience. Seymour could not bring over any considerable support and yet tarnished his integrity as an opposition leader—an indignity he made up for by subsequent increased virulence in opposition. The lesson was not lost on others. Musgrave was more canny and if, as was rumoured, he was not above accepting bribes to expedite a supply bill, he did not accept a place. The Musgraves had been passionate opponents of the Lowther families for generations and perhaps his opposition was assured by the

---

[23] *The Growth of Political Stability in England, 1675–1725* (1967), p. xv.
[24] In three divisions in the year following the disclosure of the assassination plot (February 1695/6) the voting of the knights of the shire deviated from the average by only a few per cent towards the opposition. See p. 261 n.

latter's adhesion to the court. There can be little doubt that the tories formed the more extreme parts of the opposition and if the Jacobites had controlled a faction within the country party this obviously would have been it; but they had little influence over English politics in William's lifetime. Admittedly, many of these tories were Jacobite fellow travellers, but while such men might cause breaches in security they did not alter country principles. Few in parliament had any place for the restoration of an arbitrary Roman Catholic monarch and the *quo warranto* proceedings likely to accompany him; to vote for a regency or against abjuration oaths was not to vote for that. Even some who were said to be self-confessed Jacobites probably loved neither James's politics, religion nor person, but simply wished to make some sign of obedience to fool their inferiors into thinking that no revolution could be respectable. Kneeling to drink to the king over the water might serve the dual function of expiating for their sins of omission (or down-right commission) in putting him there and imply that somehow, some-how—the divine right theory of kings might live on in a divine right theory of squires.

A third faction were the buff friends; the dissatisfied self-seekers from any faction who spoke against the government simply because they were not of it at the time. Sir Edward Seymour, as mentioned, was a marginal member of this group, but it should not be thought that it was confined to tories alone. Three Sacheverell whigs, Jack Smith, Jack Howe and Sir John Thompson, provide examples of those who changed their coats at least once during the war. Those who sought places by making a name in opposition might follow the lead of such embittered former placemen as Seymour or Howe. The court found this last group as objectionable as they were dangerous, for they knew the court as only courtiers could. By their virulence they tried to allay the suspicion that while in the country party they were not of it; the suspicion that they would become courtiers again if offered a suitable reward.

While the first group had the best claim to the country banner, all were united in owning it and usually attempts to distinguish them from their speeches or even private correspondence requires divine guidance; the hypocrite can often outplay the saint. Without the added strength of the more suspect elements, the fears of the country party may well have been realized.

THE COURT'S ADVANTAGE

It would at first seem unlikely from the large number of country members that the court party could have ever succeeded in matters generally opposed to the country interest. That this was not the case is written throughout the Journals. One reason, of course, was that the king retained his prerogative to veto distasteful bills if, indeed, they ever reached him; for the lords also were often employed as a government defence against unfavourable measures. As the peerage was largely a Stuart creation, the court's successes need a word of explanation. Two reasons may be ventured. Firstly, while William did not tamper with the peerage as a whole, the ecclesiastical bench was a different matter; in 1691, owing largely to the vacancies of the non-jurors, 15 new bishops were appointed and 3 translated. Although there were over 150 peers, owing to extensive absences the bishops' votes had considerable importance. These absences are a second reason for court successes, for on average only 71, or less than half the peers were present.[25] While then the peerage as a whole might not have supported the king on many critical measures, those who participated often did, as becomes increasingly apparent following the peace of Ryswick in 1697.[26]

When the country majority in the commons was determined, both obstacles usually gave way, for whatever other constitutional principles escaped their control in 1688, the all-important power of the purse had not. The court thus resorted to either panacea only in an extremity. Aside from providing only temporary relief, both had ugly side effects: to employ the royal veto was to sour the session; the lords' opposition '...united the commons like a burning glass.'[27] Little wonder then that the court so ardently sought to effect its wishes in the lower house.

A court memorandum of 1690 makes it clear that direct pressure was applied to placemen to secure support for court measures:

The king will speake to the commissioners of the Treasury, to desire all such Members as have Imployments in The Customes,

---

[25] Computed from the tables in A. Browning, *English Historical Documents* (1953), vol. viii, appendix iii.

[26] See A. S. Turberville, *The House of Lords in the Reign of William III* (Oxford, 1913), pp. 13–30 and 196–224. See too, Dr G. V. Bennett's excellent essay, 'King William III and the Episcopate', in G. V. Bennett and J. D. Walsh, eds., *Essays in Modern English Church History* (1965), pp. 104–31.

[27] Robert Harley ton. n., 24 February 1705. B.M. Portland loan 29/9. Indebtedness is acknowledged for this reference to Dr B. W. Hill.

Excise or that are Officers of the Revenue or that have Pentions or
have Advantages under the Crown to forward the king's supply.[28]

Not only lobby fodder but spokesmen, their oratory might win over the
uncertain. And as to the advantages for placemen–well, offices provided the high road to power, urbane friends, a town house and a
stately family mansion in the country: '...courtiers must venter their
fortune,' one wrote, 'and they can have noe better lottery than our
House to push their fortunes in.'[29] Probably the lures of places and
pensions were the 'strongest arguments' which various ministers agreed
upon as '...the best means of persuading them [the members of parlia-
ment] to be reasonable...'[30] One might say with a fair degree of certainty that not only did the majority of members have their price but
that this price was often modest.[31]

How many placemen were there? As no crown office lists were published at this time (an ominous fact in itself) the deficiency must be met
with unofficial estimates: a court clerk includes 103 placemen in 1692;
a year later the country leader, Robert Harley, finds 97; in 1694 the
non-juror, Samuel Grascombe lists 136; an anonymous pamphlet of
1698 mentions 95. In William's last parliament, Professor Walcott notes
113.[32] Receivers of unreported crown pensions or bribes must be added
as well as those supporting the court with a view to future reward. The

---

[28] P. R. O. S.P. Dom., King William's Chest, 8/26 f. 52r. Unprinted in the
Calendar which prints most of the placemen's names save that Mr Guy is
listed therein as Mr Gray and Mr Harboard is deleted. *Cal. S.P. Dom.*, 1690,
p. 211.

[29] Peregrine Bertie, writing to his brother, the earl of Lindsey, 29 November
1694, *H.M.C. Ancaster*, p. 437. The Berties provide several examples of those
who held places and yet frequently voted against the court. Places, however,
probably mitigated their opposition, and without them they might well have
become more outspoken.

[30] Sunderland to Portland, 2 May 1693. N(ottingham) U(niversity)
L(ibrary), PwA 1212 (Portland Papers).

[31] In his list of placemen and pensioners, Samuel Grascombe noted several
selling their votes for £20. 'A list of such Members as are Become Pensioners or Dependents of State...' Bodl. Rawl. MSS. D.864. The pamphlet
was written *c.* 1693 and subsequently revised.

[93] A. Browning, *Danby*, iii, 184–7; B.M. Portland loan 29/206, ff. 171–2;
'A List of such Members as are Become Pensioners or Dependents of State...'
Bodl. Rawl. MSS. D.846, ff. 5–6; Cobbett, vol. v, app. clxxi; *English Politics*,
p. 171. Eight held higher offices in the treasury, twenty-three had administra-
tive offices, seventeen held legal positions, eight were military governors,
two were government contractors and fifty-five had household posts, sinecures, part-time offices or pensions. *Ibid.*

total number was then a matter of conjecture and led to airy estimates
by opposition pamphleteers. In 1695 Grascombe wrote: '...there are
pensioners to the number of two hundred nynety and nine...'[33] and
another pamphleteer subsequently said there to be '...three hundred
who all had places at the king's pleasure...who united with those who
had secret pension, future hopes or other private engagements.'[34] Undoubtedly these inflated figures were designed to incite fear, envy or
hatred among members not holding office. Indeed, some placeholders
dared vote against the court on a number of issues while other would-be
placemen sought office by making a name in opposition. There is,
nonetheless, a grain of truth behind the hyperbole, for there must certainly have *seemed* as if there were three hundred: the disciplined placemen were said to resemble regular troops; country gentlemen but an
unskilled militia.[35] Grascombe stated that while seldom two thirds of
the house was present, the placemen were '...always attending the
service, unanimous in their votes, arts and in their persons...' Owing to
influence, tricks and intrigues, they convened the house when they
pleased, '...and thus they in effect are the Parliament...'[36] In stating
this he is not far wrong. Although in the most heavily attended division
of the session almost three quarters of the members might cast their
votes, on the average there were less than half.[37] The real power of the
court acting in conjunction with allied factions may then be compared
to that of a large shareholder who has something approaching controlling
interest in a present-day corporation which does not allow proxies.
While he does not control proceedings if most of the others care to
attend, he can usually come near to doing so owing to absenteeism and
the disunity of those present. During William's reign divisions were
sometimes so close as to require the Speaker's casting vote. In 1700
Robert Harley wrote that one vote gave the great turn of the previous

[33] 'A List of such Members as are Become Pensioners or Dependents of
State...' Bodl. Rawl. MSS. D.846, f. 3v. Grascombe estimated their expenses
at two million pounds which came from the secret service money.
[34] James Drake, *The History of the Last Parliament* (1702), p. 83–4.
[35] *Considerations upon the choice of a Speaker* (1698). French dispatch, 20
February/2 March 1698/9. P. Grimblot, ed., *Letters of William III and Louis
XIV and of their Ministers...1697–1700* (1848), ii, 292.
[36] 'A List of such Members as are Become Pensioners or Dependents of
State...' Bodl. Rawl. MSS. D.864, f. 3r.
[37] The highest attendance each session averaged 381, the average 238 (including the four tellers and the speaker). Computed from the tables in
A. Browning, *English Historical Documents*, vol. viii, app. iii.

session, and yet as there were four such divisions[38] it is something of a mystery as to which it was. A year later the court candidate for the Speakership failed to be elected by only four votes.[39]

Probably the court would have had even more control if placeholders felt as obliged as the bishop of Exeter who, after his brother received a favour from William, swore a courtier's allegiance: '...In a word my Lord, I am a person where my mouth and heart goes together.'[40] If the king not infrequently found a placeman's mouth bigger than his heart and all the placemen did not serve the court on all occasions, most did, especially in matters of supply when constitutional issues were not involved, and they received some of what they voted as their reward. Although it certainly did not amount to the millions of pounds suggested in Grascombe's pamphlet,[41] it did justify the country party's indignation and led one member to declare it '...harsh that the same men should be both givers and receivers of the revenue.'[42] Although placemen might argue that the government needed strengthening,[43] might not government supporters be returned who did not hold office? Indeed, their candidacies but added to the reluctance of honest country gentlemen to incur the expenses involved in contesting elections, and increased the likelihood that those who posed as anti-placemen were really would-be placemen. Halifax was led to remark that '...a member of parliament of all others ought least to be exempted from the rule that no man should serve two masters.'[44]

Those who served two masters were far more likely to attend the bell at Westminster than those who served only one. There were a

[38] Robert Harley to J. Brydges, 5 December 1700. Noted by G. Davies and M. Tinling, eds., 'Correspondence of James Brydges and Robert Harley...', *Hunt. Lib. Quart.* (San Marino, Calif., 1938), i, 459. Note too, the small size of the court majorities even in what were thought to be considerable victories during the 1695–8 parliament. See appendix A.

[39] *H.C.J.*, xiii, 645.

[40] To Portland, 22 April (*c.* 1697). Perhaps, however, even the bishop was not telling the whole truth, for he wrote the letter because his allegiance to the court was questioned. N.U.L., PwA 1405.

[41] 'A List of such Members as are Become Pensioners or Dependents of State...', *passim.*

[42] Stated by Sir Charles Sedley in a debate over the place bill during December 1692. Cobbett, *Parliamentary History of England* (1809) v, 745.

[43] See for example Lord Cutts, 'Reflections Upon the Government of the Isle of Wight, with Regard to the Civil Power' (1693). *H.M.C. Frankland-Russell-Astley*, p. 77.

[44] Quoted in Betty Kemp, *King and Commons, 1660–1832* (1957), p. 53.

number of reasons for the poor attendance which plagued the country party. Country gentlemen certainly must have found parliament's location in Westminster inhospitable both collectively and as individuals. The court, by pandering to the various London interests, could bring considerable pressure to bear from out-of-doors; a mob might occasionally go so far as to bang on the very doors of the commons itself and threaten recalcitrants. London's unfriendliness fell heavily upon provincials, while its soot and smog were breathed by all, driving the weak-lunged coughing in search of less polluted air; the king to Kensington, Paul Foley to Hampstead.[45]

In contrast to the placeman's rewards for good attendance, a country member was penalized by possible loss of income through absence from estate or business and the uncompensated expense of living in London.[46] Country whips were, by the very character of the party, amateurish in nature. One country member was told that until he and the other members came up '...we are like to have no sport';[47] another simply '...to add another country gentleman'.[48] Because of diminishing attendance, it was only during the first few months of a session that the court usually had much difficulty in directing the proceedings.[49] During the court successes of July 1698, Robert Price noted sarcastically that '...the house of Commons is dwindled into a Committee'.[50] It was little wonder. As spring passed into summer, the increased financial strain of lengthy sessions fell even harder upon members with agricultural interests. As the heat warmed garbage and sewerage, the resulting stench became a rather powerful adjunct to the court's power, driving the country

---

[45] S. B. Baxter, *William III*, p. 248. Paul Foley to Sir E. Harley, 30 October 1699. B.M. Portland loan 29/75/2.

[46] See R. C. Latham, 'Payment of Parliamentary Wages—the Last Phase' *Eng. Hist. Rev.*, lxvi (1951), 27–50. Latham notes that wages continued in a very few constituencies where the competition for seats was limited to a small circle of civic office holders. The end of payment is said to have occurred about 1695.

[47] From Robert Jennens, 16 November 1699. *H.M.C. Cowper*, ii. 393.

[48] Owen Wynne to Sir Robert Owen, M.P. Carnarvon, 25 October 1962. N(ational) L(ibrary) (of) W(ales), Brogyntyn MSS. W/1063.

[49] Tallard, the French envoy, wrote that William would become master of the proceedings in the month of April or May, owing to the regular attendance of the court party. French dispatch 20 February/2 March 1698/9. Grimblot, *Letters*, ii, 292. Sir John Banks noted the thin house '...that has soe great concerns in hand at the end of a session'. To Heneage Finch, 18 June 1698, Chatsworth, Finch-Halifax MSS., box 3.

[50] To the duke of Beaufort, 2 July 1698. Bodl. Carte MSS. 130 f. 391.

members who were not compelled to attend back to the clean air of the
countryside. St Stephen's chapel with '...the evil smells descending
from the small apartments adjoining to the speaker's chamber, which
come down into the House with irresistible force when the weather is
hot...' made some look back upon summer sessions with nostalgic
nausea.[51]

COURT–COUNTRY CONFLICTS

Despite the court's advantages, the country party did succeed in
effecting much of its programme, if with considerable delays and revisions. Macaulay in his masterly *History of England from the Accession of
James II* has provided a narrative of events of William's reign which is
unlikely ever to leave the study of the serious student of the period.
Still, Macaulay candidly admitted that he could have said far more
against his work than even his fiercest critics. What he would have said
is not certain but it has been pointed out that the real criticism comes
from the new contributions to the same period. Recently a number of
biographies have been written upon the leading personalities, but while
the men have been studied in depth, the political history of the conflicts
between court and country beyond the convention parliament seems to
have been somewhat neglected. This book is primarily a study of these
conflicts, with special emphasis given to a neglected opposition and
their programme; the tight little island programme with which
Macaulay and others have shown very little sympathy and apparently
thought best to ignore. To do this is neither to approve nor to condemn
their policy, but merely to affirm that ignorance of either side of a given
conflict is not a virtue.

It is, of course, a question whether the country party really had a
programme. Perhaps, indeed, it can be seen only in retrospect, and certainly individual problems were dealt with separately as they arose.
Still, it seems that there was some method in their actions and, if only
for the sake of convenience, the study may be divided into several parts.
Most important to the country party was the constitutional settlement,

---

[51] Charles Davenant to Thomas Coke, 14 December 1700. *H.M.C. Cowper*,
ii, 411. Davenant, reminiscing over the jubilee of stench (over the space of
almost sixteen years when member for St Ives, Cornwall, in 1685), added that he
would rather be in Derbyshire in the winter than the commons in the summer.

particularly the nature of monarchy, and especially the commons' attempts
to reduce the crown's influence over parliamentary proceedings through
such means as placemen, long parliaments, or a court-nominated
Speaker.[52] The need to safeguard the rights of the subject against court
influence in judicial proceedings was deemed no less important, as becomes increasingly apparent during the period of the junto ascendancy.[53]
The country concept of the constitution was a largely pre-Tudor one
that its proponents revered as 'ancient and Gothic'. It was to be lucidly
described by Montesquieu and later embodied in the American constitution with its rigid separation of executive, legislative and judicial
powers; a solution, of course, which has worked to the detriment of the
executive, leaving, as it does, considerable power to congress and the
individual states. Today, this principle usually defended and maintained
in America by conservatives, especially southern conservatives, is
known as 'states rights'. It was not without reason, then, that one
finds the gentry and squirearchy who formed the backbone of the
country party usually referring to their counties as countries. They saw
the revolution as by no means complete with the passage of the bill of
rights and were to echo Sir Edward Seymour's cry in the convention:
'What care I for what is done abroad, if we must be slaves in England,
in this or in that man's power.'[54]

Another common ground for country party support was the desire
to ensure that the king would have insufficient funds to govern in
either peace or war without frequent and probably annual support from
parliament. Even after the junto ascendancy this principle did not
change, although country party attempts to minimize developments
enlarging the war interest were singularly unsuccessful. Still, in achiev-
ing the former aim, the commons did succeed in inserting itself between the king and the critical workings of his administration, guaranteeing a parliamentary review of at least the broader outlines of crown
policy. In so doing, the king was forced to accept a parliamentary interpretation of the constitution.[55]

The final study deals with the maintenance of civil liberties by radically reducing the armed forces in peacetime,[56] while keeping those
responsible for the war policy on the defensive, principally by attacks

---

[52] See chapters 4 and 8.   [53] See chapters 5 and 8.
[54] W. Cobbett, *Parliamentary History of England* (1809), v, 56.
[55] See chapter 3.
[56] See chapter 6.

upon foreign favourites,[57] by placing additional constitutional limitations upon the prerogative[58] and by bringing occasional impeachment
proceedings against the old war ministry.[59] In this last effort the country
party was by no means united, but country members were forced to
come to a decision as to whether or not to combine an attack on measures
with an attack on men. The next chapter will be a study of the rise of
these men and their attempt to identify opposition with treason.

---

[57] Chapter 7.   [58] Chapter 8.   [59] Chapters 9–11.

TWO

Opposition and Treason

THE TORY DILEMMA

Tory hopes of truly dominating the government were all but stillborn, the general election of 1690 having provided neither victory nor unity. While printing a list of those who favoured the Sacheverell clause, the whigs effectively countered with one of 'Jacobites' opposed to creating William and Mary king and queen.

Although historians have paid substantial lip service to the lists, no one seems to have analysed them in relation to the personnel of the subsequent parliament. When one does, the tories do not appear to have done better than the whigs as might be assumed, but on the contrary, slightly worse: 46 of the 150 'Jacobites' listed failed to be re-elected as compared to only 43 of the 146 supporters of the Sacheverell clause.[1] Thus a little under a third of both partisan groups were not returned, about the same proportion as that of all the members. This is not to say that there were not tory gains, for more of the new members may have been tories than whigs. Indeed, London turned out four whigs and replaced them with four tories; Westminster also returned two tories[2]

---

[1] It would be less correct to say voted for or against, as the lists contain many inaccuracies, as Professor Walcott points out in 'Division Lists of the House of Commons, 1689–1715', *Bul. Inst. Hist. Res.* (1936–7), xiv, 25. The division lists are reprinted in A. Browning, *Danby*, iii, 164–72.

[2] Narcissus Luttrell, *A Brief Historical Relation of State Affairs* (Oxford, 1857), ii, 19. Note Harley's concern. To Sir E. Harley, 22 and 25 February. *H.M.C. Portland*, iii, 444. The position of the four London members to the right of the Speaker undoubtedly served to enhance their importance.

by a majority of over seven hundred votes.[3] The outspoken republican, John Hampden, was to be conspicuous by his absence. Still, as Dr E. L. Ellis has shown at some length, the whigs did considerably better than has generally been supposed and the tories less well.[4]

Despite the work of such as Sir Edward Seymour, who swore he was sparing neither '...purse nor paynes to get good men chose,'[5] the tory campaign was generally thought uninspiring. Many tory candidates were unwilling to stand,[6] despite vivid memories of the Sacheverell clause.[7] Some thought the timing poor, believing that the war in Ireland should have been concluded before the election.[8] Carmarthen put considerable blame upon the whig postmaster, Sir John Wildman, who was said to look '...into all letters now, to find what interests are making for Elections, and stops all such as he dislikes from going to the Corporations.'[9]

With not infrequent majorities of one, even modest changes must not be ignored. Moreover when the members met one observer believed there to be not two parties but rather four: 'Tories, Whigs, Court Whigs, and Tory Whigs,'[10] As many of the last group will be seen not generally to have cared who the ministers were, the recognition the ministerial tories received by 1692 might have fairly represented their support if only they had enough strength to rid themselves successfully of the Jacobite stigma. Although they succeeded in complimenting the king for favourable changes in the London lieutenancies, a stiff abjuration bill obliging officeholders to abjure King James was defeated by only twenty-three votes.[11] Subsequently, moreover, Carmarthen was shown to have insufficient support to override the Wharton-led whigs,

---

[3] N.n. to Visc. Weymouth, 12 March 1689/90. Longleat, Thynne Papers, xiv/95.

[4] 'The Whig Junto in Relation to the Development of Party Politics and Party Organisation, from its inception to 1714' (D.Phil. Oxon., 1961), i, f. 169.

[5] Sir E. Seymour to Visc. Weymouth [February 1689/90]. Longleat, Thynne Papers, xii/95.

[6] Carmarthen to [Abingdon], 15 February 1689/90. Shrops. R.O., Attingham Collection, 112/3. [Dr] R. Taylor to Dr Charlett, 4 March 1689/90. Bodl. Ballard MSS. 35, f. 48.

[7] Sr. Jos. Broderick to s., 8 February. *Ibid.*, xi, f. 185.

[8] *Ibid.*

[9] Carmarthen to [Abingdon], 15 February. Shrops. R.O., Attingham Collection 112/3.

[10] J. D. Colt to Robert Harley, 22 March. *H.M.C. Portland*, iii, 446.

[11] The vote was 192 to 165, 25 April 1690. *H.C.J.*, x, 391.

and to obtain a more moderate oath.[12] One might well disagree with
Professor Browning's assertion that this was but a small failure;[13] allegations of Jacobitism were to prove the ministerial tories' Achilles heel.

Still, the new parliament began auspiciously. Sir John Trevor's unopposed election as speaker aided in the development and direction of
the court party in the commons.[14] The consciences of the non-juring
bishops allowed for a remodelling of the ecclesiastical bench in the
lords.[15] Subsequent votes of supply both satisfied the king[16] and greatly
increased his reputation abroad,[17] while the mixed ministry enjoyed
surprising success.

For several sessions the ministry went unscathed. Attacks upon
Carmarthen never quite came off. When the time came for an assault
during the first session, one ardent whig noted that '...nobody spoake
a word about it, and so those of the other side laughed at them, for
some were absent, and some had been spoake to, and some were false.'[18]
Robert Harley became increasingly unenthusiastic about such inter-
party conflicts which could so easily work to the benefit of the court.[19]
Carmarthen's timely direction of confessions[20] and disclosures not only
thwarted attacks upon himself both from within the ministry and without, but so disconcerted the opposition that even supply was more
easily voted.[21]

---

[12] Luttrell, *Brief Relation*, ii, 35. Such compromise tests were ridiculed in
what must have been junto-inspired lampoons. One was entitled 'A New
Nothing': 'I [William] have a new Test which neither shall own myself to be
king, Nor King James to be none/And yet shall both empty and fill up the
Throne' (*c.* 1692). Chic(ago) Univ(ersity) Lib(rary), Misc. Eng. MSS.

[13] *Danby*, i, 472–3.

[14] See pp. 96–100.

[15] See A. S. Turberville, *The House of Lords in the Reign of William III*
(Oxford, 1913), pp. 19–30.

[16] 8 November 1690. Doctor Williams' Library, Roger Morrice, Entering
Book, iii, f. 217.

[17] Tho. Maule to Geo. Clarke, 14 October 1690. T(rinity) C(ollege)
D(ublin) MSS. 749/238 (Clarke Correspondence). *H.C.J.*, x, 8–13.

[18] Doctor Williams' Library, Roger Morrice, Entering Book, iii, f. 226.

[19] To Sir E. Harley, 30 December 1690, 1 and 3 January 1690/1. *H.M.C.
Portland*, iii, 456. Gilbert Burnet, *History of His Own Times* (Oxford, 1833),
iv, 121–2. Neither Harvey nor Foley participated in the debate of 7 November
regarding the mismanagement of the Fleet. Price to Beaufort, 10 November
1691. Bodl. Carte MSS. 130, ff. 326 v.–327.

[20] Browning, *Danby*, i, 494–7.

[21] To Sir Edward Harley., 5, 10 and 17 November 1691. *H.M.C. Portland*,
iii, 481–2.

Throughout the subsequent spring, the king indulged his prerogative with a build-up of tory ministers. In early March, Henry Sydney vacated his position as secretary for the northern department, thus allowing Nottingham to resume his role as sole secretary. Rochester and Seymour were both sworn of the privy council; all in accord with Sunderland's advice that most of the nation did not care who were ministers 'whether this man or that'.[22] Still, William was not wholly to abandon his trimming policy; Sydney became lord lieutenant of Ireland, Montague was given a place in the treasury, and Somers became attorney general, although in place of another whig, Sir George Treby. This was but a sop to the whigs, and the success of Sunderland's dictum depended on fair weather as he admitted but a year later. In the ensuing session, the court successfully opposed any significant constitutional reform. Country party agitation for the signed responsibility of privy councillors for their advice was easily moved off by encouraging whig and tory cross-accusations, which hopelessly entangled the proceedings; the movement against cabals and for the discussion of matters in full privy council was challenged as being most unwise because of the need for security in wartime.[23]

But clouds were gathering on the horizon. If considerable supplies were voted, the war's expenses were vast. The agitation for constitutional reform continued and the opposition received even wider support out of doors. While there was little if any mention of a court-country dichotomy in the 1690 general election, in November 1691 Robert Harley saw the election of Kent fought on this basis, finding 'Sr. Thomas Roberts set up by the Country Gentlemen, Mr Robt. Smith by the Courtiers'.[24] Although the ministerial frame of reference remained whig and tory, the terms 'court' and 'country' came increasingly to dominate political conversation.

The naval victory off La Hogue in May 1692 was the last important

---

[22] To Portland, 5 May 1692. N.U.L., PwA 1209.

[23] 14 May 1690, 23 November 1692. Cobbett, v, 731–2. See too below, p. 44. The reform was embodied in the act of settlement of 1700/1.

[24] To Elizabeth Harley, 17 November 1691. B.M. Portland loan 29/164/8. Harley noted that Roberts had a four to one majority. Although neither member sat before, Roberts, of Glassingbury, Kent, is said to have opposed the measures of James II (G.E.C., *Baronets*). He was re-elected for Kent in 1695 and appears to have tempered his opposition to the court, being included on the court side in the division lists of that parliament. Smith came in at that time for Andover, apparently under the influence of the junto adherents, the Powletts.

military success of the year, and even this was darkened by the failure to follow up with a descent upon France, or for that matter, even with effective pursuit of the routed French fleet. Namur was lost and William's army defeated at Steinkirk in late July. Nottingham and Carmarthen both believed a popular feat of arms essential to avoid the crushing effects of an outraged parliament which might seriously impede if not block supply.[25] When at the opening of the session in November it still had not come, Carmarthen, while still optimistic, became increasingly worried, fearing an alliance between those who would 'subvert the government' and others who would 'govern the king in it'. By this he probably meant the leaders of the country opposition and the junto, although his terminology in the first instance seems pejorative.[26] The alliance between the country party and the junto leaders was but a negative one and there were policy disagreements within the country party itself. As to the first point, it was not that the alliance between country and tory factions became firmer, as was soon to be suggested in one junto-inspired pamphlet,[27] but rather that the country party leadership had little desire to help the junto into office.

COURT AND COUNTRY WHIGS

The ministerial conflicts of the subsequent session saw the four positions of court, junto whig, country tory and country quite clearly defined. Certainly the difference between country and whig aims accounts for the subsequent loss of the abjuration bill.[28] The tories and the court

[25] Nottingham to Portland [27 August 1692]. H.M.C. 'Finch', iv, No. 794. Carmarthen to the king, 14 July and 9 September. *Cal. S.P. Dom.*, pp. 369–70 and 413.

[26] He believed that the court party could probably see the necessary measures through the session successfully. To the king, 9 September. *Cal. S.P. Dom.*, pp. 443–4.

[27] 'Your great P.F.—[Paul Foley] turns cadet and carries arms under the general of the West-Saxons [Seymour]; the two H—s [Harleys] are engineers under the late lieutenant of the Ordnance [Musgrave], and bomb any bill, which he hath once resolvid to reduce to ashes, though it were for Recognition [which would proscribe many tories], or anything else that is most necessary to our security...' *A Dialogue Between Whig and Tory, Alias Williamite and Jacobite* (1693), pp. 28–9.

[28] R. Price to the duke of Beaufort, 15 December 1692. The abjuration bill was thrown out by a vote of 200–175. 'The town says the Jacobites and Comonwealths men joynd together...'

were attacked at the opening: one observer noted that the opposition's
'...first Broadside was at the Lords of the Admiralty and their second
at forrin Generalls.'[29] On the second day Sir Thomas Clarges demanded to know why the victory at La Hogue was not properly followed
up and why the 'descent upon France...ended in a descent at Ostend...'[30]
In a later debate Harley openly condemned an unfulfilled promise of a
descent upon France the previous session as but a ruse to get money.[31]
Nevertheless, there was to be no true reform; while it was resolved
that all orders were to pass through the hands of the lord commissioners of the executive office of lord high admiral, the resolution
asking the king to '...constitute a Commission of the Admiralty of
such persons as are of experience in Maritime affairs' was lost 135–
112.

Luttrell noted that the opposition came from '...all the persons in
office and Generally the whigg party...wch was much wondered at.'[32]
In retrospect one might easily see that it was scarcely wondrous: the
junto whigs were not interested in reforming offices but simply in getting them. The whig attack aimed at the tory ministry, and more
specifically at the sole secretary of state, Nottingham, was the main
feature of the session.

In the attempt to condemn Nottingham as being little less than a
Jacobite,[33] the junto was only partially successful. While Foley moved
that the king employ only men of 'known ability and integrity', he did
not let it proceed to a vote of censure upon the secretary's office
itself, which such junto whigs as Goodwin Wharton would have. He
reiterated instead the country demand that privy councillors sign for
their advice, saying that until that was done parliament '...cannot tell
who to accuse for ill advice.'[34] Nevertheless in early December, by a
majority of one, the committee of advice passed a resolution con-

---

[29] Owen Wynne to Sir Robert Owen, M.P., 29 November [1692]. N.L.W.,
Brogyntyn MSS. W/1061.
[30] 11 November. Luttrell, Abstract MSS., ii, f. 12.
[31] 21 November. Cobbett, v, 726, See below pp. 77–8.
[32] 11 January 1692/3, *H.C.J.*, x, 775. Luttrell, Abstract MSS., ii, 263. The
court speaker also aided in the outcome of this division. See p. 99.
[33] Nottingham again played into his opponents' hands or at least his press
licenser, Edmund Bohun, had done so when he passed the pamphlet *King
William and Mary Conquerers* which advocated the *de facto* doctrine of which
Nottingham approved.
[34] 26 November 1692. Luttrell, Abstract MSS. ii, ff. 90–2. R. Harley to
Sir E. Harley, 26 November 1692. *H.M.C. Portland*, iii, 508.

demning the 'management of the descent',[35] a vote Harley considered to be expressly directed at the secretary.[35] Harley appears to have taken no part in the debate although Paul Foley spoke on the side of the whigs, perhaps believing that it was less a vote of censure upon Nottingham than one upon policy. Indeed, the court tories gained enough support to put aside the censure motion upon Nottingham and substitute one merely thanking Russell.[37] Certainly the court's success was partially due to country suspicions that the comptroller, Thomas Wharton, was simply trying to revive the censure motion because he wanted to become secretary himself.[38] Perhaps too, they had come to agree with Lowther that the king was unlikely to be '...false to his own interest.'[39] In any case, even the address thanking Russell became embroiled in an inter-house debate, each defending its own member.[40] After an involved dispute over conferences, the lords were not to agree.[41]

As the tories already overwhelmingly dominated the ministerial ranks there really could be no united attack upon the whigs. The commons' vote of thanks at the opening of the session made Russell largely invulnerable.[42] Still, Bishop Burnet provided a real target at least vaguely connected with the ministry, and the burning of his *Pastoral Letter* in January is said to have caused the king great concern.[43] Harley believed that it was only the act of indemnity which kept the bishop from joining the flames. [44]

---

[35] 5 December. Luttrell, Abstract MSS., ii, ff. 148–51. The vote was 156 to 155. Goodwin Wharton was majority teller.

[36] To Sir E. Harley, 6 and 8 December. *H.M.C. Portland*, iii, 509.

[37] 20 December. Luttrell, Abstract MSS., ii, 207–12.

[38] (Dykevelt) Dispatch, 23 December 1692 and 2 January 1693. *H.M.C. Denbigh*, iii, 211. Note Goodwin and comptroller Wharton's frequent speeches in the debates of 30 November 1692. Luttrell, Abstract MSS., ff. 106–17.

[39] 30 November 1692. *Ibid.*, ii, f. 113.

[40] It was argued in a letter from Peter Shakerley to Roger Kenyon, 21 December. *H.M.C. Kenyon*, p. 269. Seymour, in debate, said that Nottingham would be heard in another place.

[41] 29 December. Luttrell, Abstract MSS., ii, ff. 228–30. 29 and 30 December *H.M.C. Lords, 1692–3*, p. 185.

[42] 21 November. Cobbett, v, 723–5.

[43] Newsletter to Nottingham, 24 January. H.M.C. 'Finch' [MS. draft], vol. v, item 45.

[44] R. Harley to Sir Edward Harley, 21 January 1692/3. *H.M.C. Portland*, iii, 512.

The country tories aimed primarily at everything foreign. They proceeded from the half-hearted negative measures of the previous session, such as merely preventing thanks being voted to foreign generals,[45] to a dedicated policy of forthright attack. As much blame as possible was placed upon the Dutch for the losses. The commons was quick to censure the conduct of Count Solmes at Steinkirk, which led to a subsequent resolution that English officers be commanded by native Englishmen.[46] This was complemented in the lords by Halifax's motion that English officers take precedence over all foreigners of equal rank save those of crowned heads, a move aimed expressly at the Dutch.[47] The anti-Dutch sentiment continued, coming ever nearer the king when Captain Pitt moved to have foreigners excluded from the council.[48] The court replied that there was but one [Portland], who could do no harm as long as the majority was against him. Although the court was seemingly successful on this occasion, four days later in a supply debate Sir Thomas Clarges fanned the flames by finding that the reason England was paying a larger share for the war than the Dutch was '…occasioned by having one of the Dutch States in your Council'.[49] Subsequently Colonel Cornwall, supported by Clarges and Colonel Granville, moved that as it was dangerous for the Dutch to know too much about England's defences, in view of the history of past wars, no foreigner should be employed in the Tower of London, the garrisons, ordnance or stores. Sir John Lowther noted that only two thoroughly honest Dutchmen were so employed, and stated the obvious which might be applied not only to this resolution, but to all the aforemen-

---

[45] Col. Granville, assisted by Musgrave, objected to thanks being voted General Ginkle, claiming it was merely a 'colour' to advance him to the position of master of the ordnance. Although Ginkle was complimented, it was not done in the house and other officers were complimented as well. 4 January 1691/2. Luttrell, Abstract MSS., i, ff. 189–90.

[46] 21 November 1692. Cobbett, v, 722. Brandenburg Dispatch, 25 November/5 December. L. Von Ranke, *History of England Principally in the Seventeenth Century* (Oxford, 1875), vi, 186.

[47] H. C. Foxcroft, *The Life and Letters of Sir George Savile, bart., First Marquis of Halifax* (1878), i, 317.

[48] 7 December 1692. Luttrell, Abstract MSS., ii, f. 148. The opposition was of mixed party allegiances. Capt. Thomas Pitt, M.P., Salisbury, was thought to have supported the Sacheverell clause. The other three (named below) ardent proponents of the anti-Dutch measures were former tories; Clarges and Cornwall having voted against making William and Mary king and queen.

[49] 9 December 1692. *Ibid.*, f. 165.

tioned xenophobic measures, namely that it '...seems to reflect a little on the king...'[50]

Probably no one was really pleased with the ministerial aspects of the session. Country party suspicions that any changes would be simply of men rather than measures were confirmed when the junto whigs blocked the vote for the reform of offices. The largely tory ministry was so blemished by the virulence of the attacks upon mismanagement[51] and their inability to control proceedings, as witnessed by the virulent country tory campaign against Dutch influence, that the king had doubts as to both the popularity and power of his managers. But if the reputation of the country tories suffered a sharp decline, the junto whigs at first saw little reason to be overjoyed. In March, despite being thought the great victor at La Hogue, Russell was displaced with a largely tory admiralty commission while Nottingham remained in office. Edward Ward, another tory, was made attorney general. There were, however, important whig advances: Sir John Trenchard became secretary of the northern department and Somers was appointed lord keeper.

This would probably have been the extent of their success had it not been for the combined effects of a number of misfortunes. Not only was there no descent upon France, but the main excuse for the failure, namely the need for the fleet to convoy the Smyrna merchant ships, resulted in tragedy. The escort did not proceed with them far enough: shortly after being left fifty leagues southwest of Ushant, the fleet of four hundred strong was effectively intercepted by the French.[52] Even before this loss, Sunderland wrote to Portland that '...if people writ you truth, you will hear so much of the discontent, or rather rage, people are in concerning the fleets, the Admirals and the Ministers, that it is of no purpose to mention anything of it.' After the loss, he found talk both in the country and in parliament of '...taking the government into their own hands' and the universal opinion that '...the two millions given for the fleet had better have been thrown into the sea.'[53]

---

[50] 16 December. *Ibid.*, ij, ff. 198–9. It was argued that the two men, Meyster and Sir Martin Beckman, had served the nation well.

[51] Sunderland, in a memorandum to Portland of June 1693, noted that the dispute '...was managed very much to the prejudice of the K[ing's] affairs.' N.U.L. PwA 1219.

[52] J. Ehrman, *The Navy in the Reign of William III* (1953), pp. 491–3 and 500–2.

[53] To Portland, 20 June, 23 July and 14 August 1693. N.U.L. PwA 1217, 1223 and 1224.

Sunderland had now completely reversed his opinion of the previous year, believing that a thoroughly whig ministry was called for.[54] Despite the tory gathering convened by the duke of Somerset at Petworth, Sunderland's junto whig conference at Althorpe attracted the most attention.[55]

Perhaps the first heavy pamphlet campaign of the reign was launched from there. Many tory pamphlets had far too Jacobite a sound to them, which but tended to confirm the whig accusations that the tory ministers owed allegiance to France. One whig pamphlet entitled: *A Dialogue Betwixt Whig and Tory, Alias Williamite and Jacobite*, was noted by a tory as having '...gone for gospel among too many.'[56]

As early as late August, fear stalked the tory camp. John Isham of the secretary's office announced that he was henceforth a non-party man.[57] In mid-October, Nottingham was told that over 250 were ready to attack him in the commons.[58] He was dismissed the day before parliament met and there were subsequent fears that his friends would shortly follow.[59] Although Russell was restored to the head of the admiralty, the whigs did not immediately gain a second secretary of state.[60] Nor did they gain anything approaching domination of pro-

---

[54] He now believed ministerial changes might cure all: 'But it must not be by patching, but by a thorough good administration, and employing men firm to this government and thought to be so.' To Portland, 14 August. N.U.L. PwA 1224.

[55] Burnet. iv, 187–8. J. P. Kenyon, *Robert Spencer, Earl of Sunderland* (1958), pp. 254–6, See too, the letter of Gilbert Dolben to Nottingham, 3 September 1693. H.M.C. 'Finch' [MS draft], vol. v, item 383. Suderland's plan to replace Nottingham with himself is said to have gained little support save from the Whartons.

[56] Humphrey Prideaux, archdeacon of Suffolk, to John Ellis, under-secretary of state, 11 December 1693. E. M. Thompson, ed. *Letters of Humphrey Prideaux, sometime Dean of Norwich to John Ellis, sometime Under-Secretary of State.* (Camden Soc., 1875), p. 160.

[57] He wrote '...it is not proper for men in this post to declare themselves for a Party, Diligence, Fidelitye, and Zeal for the present Government [,] which will be approved by either party.' To Sir Justinian Isham, 29 August 1693. Northants. R.O., Isham MSS., xxiii/1487.

[58] Information by Richard Holland, 10–16 October 1693. H.M.C. 'Finch' [MS. draft], vol. v, items 411–12.

[59] Humphrey Prideaux wrote to the under-secretary, John Ellis, to this effect, urging him to temporize with the new administration. 27 November 1693. *Prideaux Corr.*, pp. 156–7. Nottingham was dismissed on 6 November.

[60] This was one of the three demands of the whigs at this time, the others dealing with tory local justices and the lieutenancies of London the king was substantially to comply with. 12/22 December. (Dykvelt) Dispatch, *H.M.C.*

ceedings in the ensuing session, although their remodelling of the London lieutenancies and local justices in apparent preparation for a general election was thought an important step to securing a parliament more of their mind.[61]

If Sir John Thompson's hope that the new office holders would not be '...so mollified with place as to betray their country' seems highly cynical, some most certainly betrayed their country principles.[62] Shrewsbury was not brought into the ministry because of his demands for constitutional reform.[63] Indeed, largely owing to junto abstentions or outright opposition, none of the great reforms was effected that session, and once again seemed useful only in obstructing the court's financial programme.

The court did not find the ensuing session as bad as at first expected, although it was not to be a great victory.[64] The king's success in turning the tables on the enemy at the battle of Landen in August,[65] his dismissal of Nottingham who, if only as patron of the tory admirals, outwardly appeared most responsible for the Smyrna losses,[66] and the promise in his opening speech to punish those at fault,[67] probably helped abate the expected storm of protest.[68] Whig and tory ministerial factions were most concerned in the subsequent investigations, and

---

Denbigh, iii, 218. Lord Bridgewater, although generally thought otherwise acceptable, was believed incompetent. *Ibid* Sunderland was apparently unacceptable to the whigs and Wharton to the king.

[61] Sir Henry Norris to Sancroft (d. 24 November 1693), n.d. Bodl. Tanner MSS. 27, f. 22. See Somers to [Portland], 20 June and 25 July 1693, as to the difficulties of removing the so-called disaffected. N.U.L. PwA 1171 and 1173. Harley was able to advise Somers in the selection of the local commissioners of Herefordshire. See his letter to Edward Harley, 24 April 1693. Brampton Bryan Estate Office MSS. Also his letter to Somers of 3 September 1693. Reigate Corp. R.O., Somers MSS. A/5.

[62] 14 November 1693. Estates General Dispatch, B.M. Add. MSS. 17677. PP., ff. 391–9. Thompson soon joined the court's ranks himself.

[63] See p. 109.

[64] See p. 81.

[65] Somers to Portland, 18/28 August 1693. N.U.L. PwA 1173. Carmarthen to (Wm. Blathwayt), 8 August. Browning, *Danby*, ii, 223.

[66] Dr H. G. Horwitz marshals his evidence to show that the fault did not lie at Nottingham's door. 'The Political Career of Daniel Finch, Second Earl of Nottingham' (D.Phil. Oxon., 1963), ff. 339–42.

[67] 7 November. *H.C.J.*, xi, 1.

[68] Mary said the king '...thought his case so bad that he was forced to part with Lord Nottingham to please a party who he cannot trust.' R. Doebner, ed., *Memoirs of Mary, Queen of England* (1866), p. 61.

the country party could only find cause for further disgust in a public
display of the court's dirty linen. The opposition's attack was marked
by party dissension. A statement from the commissioners of accounts
of money given and received by the navy during the war put considerable blame upon the lords of the treasury for not furnishing adequate
provisions.[69] The whigs, however, opposed this move and wished to
vote that the navy was adequately provided for to fulfil the require-
ments of a proper escort.[70] Their motives are not difficult to fathom,
for they did not wish to place blame upon the government, but simply
upon the tory admirals. In this they failed, for the vote of condemnation
was lost by a majority of ten.[71] This failure caused them considerable
chagrin and seems responsible for the subsequent rumour that Nottingham might even return to office.[72]

Such rumours proved false. The supplies voted were thought adequate and the junto whigs seemed to be securing their positions. The
end of the session was followed by more whig achievements. In March,
Shrewsbury became secretary of the northern department and Russell
first commissioner of the admiralty. In June, Somers was enthusiastically remodelling the customs and excise commission.[73] The moderate
Shrewsbury, however, was lukewarm about the changes[74] which Godolphin opposed, believing them made merely for the sake of party.[75]

The changes were in line with Sunderland's advice that the king
'...take care to make all his servants of a piece, and put his business into
a method.'[76] He added that when the government leaned to the whigs

---

[69] 16 November. *H.C.J.*, xi, 2, 4 and 9. The commission's report is found
in *H.M.C. Lords, 1693–4*, pp. 12–14. The treasury's answer follows it. *Ibid.*,
pp. 14–21. The commission's reply to these objections is found in the entry
for 5 December. *Ibid.*, pp. 22–9.

[70] On 27 November by a vote of 188 to 152 it was decided that there was
sufficient beer on board adequately to escort the convoy beyond the French
fleet. *H.C.J.*, xi, 13.

[71] (Dykvelt) Dispatch 8/18 December. *H.M.C. Denbigh*, iii, 217. 'Ils [the
admirals] gagnerent par 12[10] voix seulement sur 366[360] au grand deplasir
des Wigs qui ont deja perdu deux batailles contre les Torys sur l'affair des
admiraux.' The vote of 6 December was 185 to 175. *H.C.J.*, xi, 21.

[72] Prideaux to Ellis, 11 December. *Prideaux Corr.*, p. 162.

[73] Somers to the king, 15 June 1694. *Cal. S.P. Dom.*, p. 179.

[74] Shrewsbury to the king, 15 June. *Ibid.*, pp. 180–1.

[75] Godolphin to the king, 15 June [1694]. N.U.L., PwA 471. Somers in a
letter to Portland of 14 August admits that Godolphin was highly upset at
the alterations despite that fact that the others were pleased. *Ibid.*, no. 1175.

[76] To Portland, 13 July 1694. *Ibid.*, no. 1238.

it was 'strong' but when to the tories 'weak and despised'.[77] William was warned to avoid '...the great mistake that has been made for five years together...' which was to think the parties were '...equal in relation to this government, since the whole of one [the whigs] may be made for it and not a quarter of the other [the tories] ever can.'[78] In this last, Sunderland grossly overstates the case, for few of those in the convention parliament who opposed making William and Mary king and queen favoured a Jacobite restoration; many who supported the Sacheverell clause objected to a vast, expensive and long enduring continental war and were disturbed at the court's obstruction to the advance of constitutional liberties. Many of those who opposed each other in the convention parliament were united in constitutional opposition during the officers' parliament. It is an indication of the sinking of past differences that, by the last session of William's longest parliament, sixty-nine known convention extremists who are either listed as opposed to making William and Mary king and queen, or in favour of the Sacheverell clause, are included in the same opposition list in a not radically unequal three to two 'Jacobite'—'Republican' ratio.[79] If, however, by

---

[77] S. to s., 5 August. *Ibid.*, no. 1240.   [78] S. to s., 13 July. *Ibid.*, no. 1238.
[79] Berks. R.O., Trumbull Add. MSS. 13, f. 68. Those forty-two members listed in the opposition list who were thought to have voted against making William and Mary king and queen:

Cambridge: Sr. Robert Cotton [County]; Cornwall: Sr. Bourchier Wrey [Liskeard], Charles Godolphin [Helston], Sr. Joseph Tredenham [St Mawes]; Devon: Sr. Edw. Seymour [Exeter], Christopher Bale [Exeter], Henry (?) Seymour [Totnes?]; Dorset: Edward Nicholas [Shaftesbury]; Durham: William Lambton [County], George Morland [Durham]; Gloucester: William Cooke [Gloucester]; Kent: Caleb Banks [Rochester], Sr. John Banks [Queenborough]; Lancaster: Sr. Edward Chisenall [Preston]; Lincoln: Charles Bertie [Stamford]; Northampton: Gilbert Dolben [Peterborough]; Northumberland: Roger Fenwick [Morpeth], Sir Ralph Carre [Newcastle]; Oxford: Henry Bertie [Oxford]; Salop: Edward Kynaston [County], Hon. Andrew Newport [Shrews.], George Weld [Wenlock]; Somerset: John Sandford [Minehead], John Hunt [Ilchester]; Southampton: Sr. Benjamin Newland [Southampton], Earl (Richard) Ranelagh [Petersfield], Thomas Dore [New Lymington], Francis Gwyn, [Christ Church]; Suffolk: Henry Poley [Eye], Sr. Robert Davers [Bury St Edmunds], Sr. Henry Johnson [Aldeburgh], William Johnson [Aldeburgh]; Warwick: Lord Digby [Warwick]; Westmorland: Sr. Christopher Musgrave [County], William Cheyne [Appleby]; Wilts: Charles Fox [Cricklade], Sr. John Ernley [Marlborough]; York: Sr. Jonathan Jenings [Ripon], Christopher Tankard [Aldborough]; Denbigh: Sr. Richard Middleton [County], Edward Brereton [Denbigh]; Pembroke: Sr. William Wogan [Haverfordwest].

allegiance to the government, Sunderland meant whole-hearted support
of the war policy as dictated by king and junto, and if by 'the whole of
one [party]' he meant those who economically benefited from the war,
and by the three quarters of the other party, those who suffered, he was
probably not far from the truth. This division, however, was far less
whig and tory than it was court and country. It was from the court that
he wished all direction of affairs to originate, hoping, for example, that
all proposals of money '…should at least be intended to come from the
court and not from the country gentlemen.'[80] Harley, indeed, soon expressed his disgust that the ministerial changes were not resulting in a
change of measures and were made 'only to get men in'.[81] Even in
regard to constitutional reform this was to prove an ironic understate-
ment, for junto oligarch was to mean but king writ large.

THE QUEEN'S DEATH AND THE ELECTION OF 1695

The queen's death in late December, 1694, furthered the tories'
commitment to a country policy and drove the junto whigs into an even
more desperate court alliance. While the country party gained increased
tory support, as a corollary it was increasingly prone to accusations
of Jacobitism. Probably the court derived greater benefits from the new

---

Those twenty-seven members in the opposition list who were thought to
have voted for the Sacheverell clause:

Bucks: Sr. Thomas Lee [Aylesbury]; Cheshire: Sr. John Mainwaring [County],
Sr. Robert Cotton of Cheshire [County]; Gloucester: Sr. John Guise [County];
Hereford: John Howe [Cirencester], Paul Foley [Hereford], John Dutton
Colt [Leominster]; Worcester: Thomas Foley [County]; Hertford: Sir Will-
iam Cooper [Hertford]; Kent: Sir Thos. Taylor [Maidstone]; Norfolk:
George England [Gt Yarmouth], Sr. Rob. Howard [Castle Rising]; North-
umberland: Sr. Fran Blake [Berwick-on-Tweed]; Nottingham: Sr. Scrope
Howe [County]; Oxford: Sir Tho. Littleton [New Woodstock]; Southamp-
ton: Rt. Hon. Charles (Paulet), Marquis of Winchester [County], Lord William Paulet [Winchester]; Surrey: John Arnold [Southwark], Sir Rob. Clayton
[Bletchington], Tho[mas] Howard [Bletchington], Sir John Thompson [Gat-
ton]; Wilts: Maurice Bocland [Downton]; York: Sir William Strickland
[Malton], William Palmer [Malton]; Cinque Ports: Robert Austen [Win-
chelsea], Thomas Papillon [Dover]; Radnor: Robert Harley [Radnor].

[80] To Portland, 13 July 1694. N.U.L. PwA 1238.
[81] To Sir E. Harley, 20 November. *H.M.C. Portland*, iii, 560.

arrangement. Rochester's and Seymour's motions that parliament be dissolved upon the queen's death, for example, were poorly conceived.[82] Not only were the motions censured, but even if a dissolution were effected, the court party might well have gained: if the Jacobites were 'reckend very busy' by one observer,[83] it was probably because of their willingness to play very long odds; in many constituencies, the queen's death dampened the churchmen's electoral prospects.[84] William's successful reconciliation with the Princess Anne, and parliament's zealous and unanimous address that the king should take care of his person, were both indicative of the general unwillingness to jeopardize the revolution settlement.[85]

It was, nevertheless, the displaced ministerial tories who were providing the most ardent and eloquent vindications of country principles. The previous summer, Sunderland found that 'The Party in opposition do what they can to be popular, by pretending to be true Englishmen, equally against all strangers, against an army, against letting money go out of the nation, and in short to be of the confession of faith which was made in the House of Lords.'[86] The credo Sunderland refers to was not given by the whig leaders, and that winter Nottingham and Lord

---

[82] Estates General Dispatch, 29 January/8 February. B.M. Add. MSS. 17677 PP., ff. 137v.–138r. Chas. Hatton to Lord Hatton, 12 February 1694/5. B.M. Add. MSS. 29574, f. 379. See too the Jacobite pamphlet, *Whether the Parliament be not in Law dissolved by the Death of the Princess of Orange? And how the subjects ought and are to behave themselves in relation to those Papers emitted since by the Stile and Title of Acts.* The pamphlet argues that as Mary is dead, William is no longer king in the sense of the writs by which parliament was summoned. It is not executive power which brings parliaments into being, but rather sovereignty, and William does not have this power. To argue that he held the sovereign power by survivorship is said to be a paradox. By Mary's death, he lost all title to the crown for by right it passed on to Anne making him 'a Robber, an Usurper and a Traitor'.

[83] Michael Fleming to Daniel Fleming, 2 March 1694/5. West. R.O., DRy/4778 (Le Fleming papers).

[84] R. Richmond wrote that he hoped the present member, Brotherton, would be allowed to continue to sit. If the election was declared void '...wee church-men shall have but a melancholy prospect at Liverpoole...' for the sad news of the Queen's death 'dampens spirits'. To Roger Kenyon of Peel, 4 January 1694/5. Lancs. R.O., DDke/9/68/9 (Kenyon MSS.).

[85] Lexington to Portland, 26 January 1694/5. Japikse, *Correspondentie van Willem III en van Haus Willem Bentinck* (The Hague, 1927–37), ii, 185–6. G. Caldecott, ed., *Authentick Memoirs of the Life and Conduct of her Grace, Sarah, Late Duchess of Marlborough* (1744), pp. 127–8.

[86] To [Portland], 18 May 1694. N.U.L. PwA 1233.

Torrington directed a mighty broadside against the government's men and measures from the time of the former's dismissal.[87]

Little serves better to illustrate the growing divergence of purpose between court and country whigs than the inquiry into bribery and corrupt practices. While both groups participated, they did so for quite different ends: to the junto, it was an opportunity to frighten, displace and impeach the ministerial tories while replacing them with their own followers; to the country whigs, it was simply to encourage the others by making examples of those engaged in bad ministerial practices. While the court-tory Speaker, Sir John Trevor, was to be expelled for bribery, he was not replaced by the junto candidate, Sir Thomas Littleton. Rather, to court's chagrin, the country party succeeded in electing one of their leaders, Paul Foley, to the chair. Nor was the attempted impeachment of Carmarthen (now duke of Leeds) really a success. While the junto whigs succeeded in diminishing his influence in the ministry,[88] the court party as a whole suffered. To the king it must have seemed to be a renewal of the spirit of the Sacheverell clause, causing wounds which would be slow to heal.[89] It provided the opposition with almost unparalleled opportunities to obstruct the king's business,[90] and so bad were the effects on the session that the next autumn Shrewsbury wrote to the king that he must promote a bill '...against all sorts of bribery and corruption...[otherwise] the session will not be long enough to go through that one examination alone.'[91]

The common assertion that Harley and Foley left the whigs and joined the tories at this time thus seems both oversimplified and prejudicial. To say that they should have rejected the help of former ministerial tories would also be both unrealistic and unfair: unrealistic, because successful political groups almost always take help wherever they can find it—especially if, as in this case, it is unsolicited and calls for no

---

[87] Estates General Dispatch, 29 January/8 February 1694/5. B.M. Add. MSS. 17,677 PP., f. 138.

[88] Osborne was elevated to the last step of the peerage the previous March. For a discussion of his involvement and subsequent withdrawal from real influence, see Browning, *Danby*, i, 518–26.

[89] N. Johnston wrote to the earl of Huntingdon that it was fortunate that France had no design on England at the time '...for the divisions in the House since the bribery was inquired into hath made great changes in people's minds, and uneasiness.' 20 April 1695. *H.M.C. Hastings*, ii, 247.

[90] Thomas Norris, to Richard Norris, 20 April. *The Norris Papers*, T. Haywood, ed. (Chetham Soc., 1846), ix, 27.

[91] To Somers, 31 October/10 November 1695. *Shrewsbury Corr.*, pp. 399–400.

compromising of ideals; unfair, because it was the junto whigs who were forsaking their former country principles, thus leaving others to maintain the beliefs which they appeared to abandon.

The great question in William's mind at the end of the session was whether or not to call a new parliament. The present one was defended as having a favourable balance between parties, which would aid the king in his control of factions rather than the reverse.[92] Admittedly, the parliament had been good enough in regard to the essentials. Foley had led in the offer of £2,500,000 for army supplies[93] and there were promises '...to make good the next session wt they have given this last falls short.'[94] Such moderation, however, made it appear likely that the opposition simply feared an election. Foley's election to the Speakership was one sign of their growing strength in the old parliament, as was the triennial bill's uneventful passage. This act necessitated an election at the end of the next session in any case, and as the time neared, many placemen and would-be placemen who did not have safe seats would almost undoubtedly become more country in their voting. With the exception of Godolphin, 'our seven kings', as Harley scathingly termed the lords justices, were said to be heartily for a new parliament.[95] Francis Gwyn's belief that the decision would rest upon William's success or failure in his siege of Namur[96] was correct. Shortly after his victory, the king wrote to Shrewsbury assuring him of a new parliament.[97]

---

[92] See the representation in *Cal. S.P. Dom., 1694-5*, pp. 362–6.

[93] Brandenburg Dispatch, 4/14 December 1695 (in Feiling, *Tory Party*, p. 308).

[94] Robert Henly to Robert Harley, 20 July 1695. B.M. Portland loan 29/146/9.

[95] To Sir E. Harley, 20 August. *H.M.C. Portland*, iii, 565. See too, E. L. Ellis, 'The Whig Junto, from its inception to 1714' (D.Phil., Oxon. 1961), i, f. 267. Ellis disagrees with Professor Kenyon's surmise that Sunderland overcame Wharton's and Montague's hesitancy, believing it to be but hearsay in Wharton's case. Kenyon apparently bases his belief on the letter of Sunderland to Portland in which 15 (Wharton) and 23 (Montague) are said not to be so warm in it '... thinking they shall have less power in a new one.' 29 July 1695. N.U.L. PwA 1248. J. P. Kenyon, *Sunderland*, p. 274. Daniel Bret also employed the phrase 'our seven rulers' in a letter to the earl of Huntingdon, 13 July 1696. *H.M.C. Hastings*, ii, 265.

[96] F. Gwyn to R. Harley, 31 July 1695. B.M. Portland loan 29/188.

[97] 28 August and 16 September. *Shrewsbury Corr.*, pp. 103–4, 106. Although it would appear that this was done simply to take advantage of the current success of the war, Somers thought the king might have had a view to

The junto campaign was under way long before Namur was taken. The comptroller, Thomas Wharton, was said by Robert Price to have '...a list of 80 new members hee will bring into the next parliament wch shall entirely serve the court.'[98] While others thought it a question whether he did not have a proscription list (he might have had both), the country leaders were caused considerable worry, despite official denials.[99] Not without reason had the rumours flown '...as far as Musgrave in Westmorland'[100] for both there and in Cumberland the Lowthers and Musgraves contested a number of seats largely on court-country lines. As early as July, an agent of Sir John Lowther of White-haven was making preparations in Carlisle to keep the Musgraves from '...enlarging their foundations undisturbed...[owing to] the variable Temper of many of the voters, and the indefatigable industry by wch they will be *managed on the other side*.'[101] At first he thought Musgrave intended to offer his son as a candidate while he stood for Westmorland. Soon, however, it became apparent that Sir Christopher might be forced to offer himself at Carlisle as Sir John Lowther of Lowther now hoped to depose him in the county.[102] As his opponents brought pressure to bear on his supporters, Musgrave's electoral interest rapidly declined. One notes, for example, that Sir Daniel Fleming, a considerable figure in Northern politics, originally said that neither he nor his son would stand, and proceeded to support Musgrave.[103] Lowther, however, asked

---

avoiding a clearly defined party commitment. To Shrewsbury, 11 September. *Ibid.*, 397–9. Shrewsbury was in complete agreement with calling a new parliament. Shrewsbury to Portland, 6 September. *H.M.C. Buccleuch-Whitehall*, II, i, 222.

[98] To the duke of Beaufort, 18 May. Bodl. Carte MSS. 130 ff. 355–6. Some were said to make a jest of Wharton's list, saying that he would meet with considerable difficulty in Buckinghamshire himself. Guy to Portland, 12/22 July. N.U.L. PwA 508.

[99] Robert Henley to Robert Harley, 20 July. B.M. Portland loan 29/146/9. See too, the following: Musgrave to Harley, 20 June 1695. B.M. Portland loan 29/151/6; the charge to this effect in the East Grinstead election petition (below); Guy to Portland, 18/28 June; 5/15 and 12/22 July. N.U.L. PwA 504, 506 and 508.

[100] S. to s., 12/22 July. *Ibid.*

[101] W. Gilpin to [Sir John Lowther of Whitehaven], 20 July. Cumb. R.O., Lonsdale MSS., bound volume. His Italics. Gilpin expected that 'The Bp. and the whole Clergy (except the Chancellor) will (I doubt) be agt us, and so too will the Jacobite Interest.'

[102] S. to s., 25 July. *Ibid.*

[103] S. to s. 16 and 17 September. *Ibid.* Sir Christopher Musgrave to Col. James Grahme, 12 September. Levens, Bagot MSS.

for permission to contradict the 'rumours' of his support for one who '...openlie and zealoslie applied himself to the Non-Juring partie.' He asked for this neither on personal grounds nor to promote the Wharton interest, but rather because '...many now look upon this as a national question.' If Fleming did not see it this way, then Lowther would write to '...the Great Person to whom you obliged me to speak to,' stating his mistake in giving a good report of Fleming's character. He would, moreover, destroy any hopes of his children's interest with the court, '...to which some of them have very good Pretensions.'[104] By return of post, Fleming said he would support the candidacies of both his son and Musgrave and 'if that did not please' then he would not vote at all.[105] To Musgrave's chagrin, this last is just what he was forced to do. Despite claims of misrepresentation,[106] Musgrave had clearly refused to promise his support for all crown requests of supply, which, as the Estates-General envoy, L'Hermitage, wrote delightedly, bound many members returned in that election.[107] To the request, Musgrave answered that '...tho' never soe agreeable to his present Judgement he thinks such infringement of the liberty of a Commoner of England as noe man ought to agree to; that takes upon him the Service of his country in parliament.'[108] Despite the country spirit of the reply, the court's tactics

---

[104] Sir John Lowther (of Lowther, later Lord Lonsdale) to Sir Daniel Fleming, 15 September. West. R.O., DRy/4844. Incompletely calendared in *H.M.C. Le Fleming*, p. 337.

[105] 16 September. West. R.O., DRy/4845. Even Fleming's neutrality cost him a good deal of trouble in regard to his hopes of appointment to the land tax commission. W. Fleming to Sir D. Fleming, 26 January, and 13 February 1696/7. *H.M.C. Le Fleming*, p. 347. Also S. to s., 4 February (misdated 7 February in *ibid.*), West. R.O., DRy/5092 (Le Fleming MSS.).

[106] In letters to Robert Harley, Revd. Jackson and Sir Daniel Fleming, 14 September, *H.M.C. Portland*, iii, 567; 26 September, *H.M.C. Bagot*, p. 331; 19 October, *H.M.C. Le Fleming*, p. 338.

[107] 29 November. Estates General dispatch, B.M. Add. MSS. 17,677 PP., f. 430. See too, the letter of Roger Sloane to John Ellis, 30 October 1695. B.M. Add. MSS. 28,879, f. 258.

[108] Particulars of terms which Sir John Lowther and Sir Christopher Musgrave agree to sit together as members for Westmorland. West. R.O., DRy/4867a. The date suggested is February 1689/90 in *H.M.C. Le Fleming*, p. 338, which does not give the letter's contents but places it among the letters of October 1695 where it more probably belongs. This would seem confirmed by the letter from T. Banks to James Grahme in which the former states that the failure to unite Musgrave and Lowther was owing to Musgrave's refusal to vote, without disputing any supply demanded for the next year's war. 14 October 1695. *H.M.C. Bagot*, p. 331.

succeeded. Musgrave was so disheartened by '...one of his friends standing Neuter' that Francis Gwyn noted '...he intends to desist, tho wth great regret for the dishonour of it.'[109] Only with difficulty did friends convince him to stand anywhere at all and only with considerably more difficulty was he elected. He was not returned at Oxford, as Gwyn had hoped, nor at Carlisle; an important alderman of that city decided at the last minute to support the Lowthers' candidates '...because he thinks the Interest of the Government requires it.'[110] Far from enlarging his foundations as the Lowthers originally feared, Musgrave, his '...candidacy made a secrett till the day of Election,'[111] was reduced to coming in for the burgage borough of Appleby.[112]

Sir Edward Seymour was also forced to retreat from Exeter to his pocket borough, Totnes, and even then he encountered court tricks which delayed his coming up.[113] In Bristol, despite some clever trickery on the country side,[114] Robert Henley's fears that the court would carry it '...for whom they please,'[115] also proved correct. In Liverpool too, one frightened church candidate found '...the entire Presbyterian party to a man,...engaged against them.'[116] In Herefordshire, a firm country supporter, Colonel Cornwall, was said not to have stood long enough

---

[109] To the Hon. H. Finch, 7 October. Chatsworth, Finch-Halifax MSS., box 2.

[110] W. Gilpin to [Sir John Lowther of Whitehaven], 23 September. Cumb. R.O., Lonsdale MSS., bound volume.

[111] Sir John Lowther of Whitehaven was told that Aglionbie (evidently the Lowther candidate for Appleby) '...hath been treated with in the strangest manner in the World, and for Applebie Sr. Will Twisden [elected, and voted on the country side*] is publicklie Recommended and the other [Sir Christopher Musgrave] made a secrett till the day of Election, so that by all this way of proceeding and by conceding names and Days you Easilie see they apprehend they shall have no good Successe.' From S.T.L. [?], 28 October. Cumb. R.O., Lonsdale Misc. Unsorted Corr. *See appendix A.

[112] Walcott ascribes the general control of Appleby in 1701 to the earl of Thanet, although noting that Wharton had considerable power there as well. *English Politics*, p. 56.

[113] See p. 63.

[114] Lord Keeper Somers to Shrewsbury, 26 October. *H.M.C. Buccleuch-Whitehall*, II, i, 245. Somers wrote that the Quaker, William Penn, employed Shrewsbury's *laisser-passer* for the purpose of furthering the election of Sir John Knight. Sir Thomas Day and Robert Yate were returned and both voted consistently court. See appendix A.

[115] To Robert Harley, 20 July 1695. B.M. Portland loan, 29/146/9.

[116] Thomas Wilson to Roger Kenyon, 28 October. *H.M.C. Kenyon*, p. 385.

'...even to poll for it.'[117] Despite expectations of bipartisan support,[118] an opposition candidate at Cambridge University also found himself faced with Musgrave's problem—broken promises from frightened friends. John Isham wrote sadly that although he had more promises than either of the two successful candidates, '...I could not prevail wth them to perform what they had promised.'[119] In London and West-minster, in place of the tory candidates elected in 1690, five of the six new members apparently had junto support.[120]

The country party can scarcely be said to have had a campaign. The war's taxation gave the court the added advantage of making the heavily burdened gentry wary of electoral expenses. As Viscount Weymouth saw it, the great country problem was largely one of having gentlemen stand, for they were said to be '...unwilling and indeed cannot bear the expense polls require.'[121] Admittedly a few pamphlets exploited the junto's inept handling of treason trials in Lancashire and gave a few examples of the king's arbitrary practices in Holland, Scotland and Ireland.[122] On the whole, however, court and junto probably had the best of the pamphlet battle, successfully exploiting military victories and the corrupt practices of the ministerial tories.[123] Occasionally

---

[117] William Bridges to Marshall Bridges, 9 November. Herefordshire R.O., Brydges Corr. E31/61. Col. Cornwall's opponent was evidently Sir Herbert Croft, bart. who was to vote solidly court in the divisions of the ensuing parliament. The other successful candidate was Sir Edward Harley.

[118] H(enry) B(oyle) to Robert Harley, 17 October. *H.M.C. Portland*, iii, 571–2. Boyle noted that while he felt safe, there would be a contest between Dr Oxenden and John Isham. Isham was thought to have received the support of the Abp. of York, the Bp. of London, Ld. Nottingham and Montague.

[119] The votes were: Oxenden, 153; Boyle, 132 and Isham, 115. To Sir Justinian Isham, Northants. R.O., Isham Corr., xxiii/1529. Boyle, of course, voted solidly country, so he was probably trying to defeat Dr Oxenden. See appendix A.

[120] The exception was Sir John Fleet, an alderman, who voted against the court on one issue (the devaluation of guineas) and does not appear to have voted on the other recorded issues. See appendix A.

[121] To Halifax, 21 October. Althorpe, Halifax MSS., box 10.

[122] For the Lancashire trials, see chapter V. See too, *Galliennus Redivius* [*Gallienus Radivivus*]: *...being a true Account of the De-Witting of Glencoe, Gaffney, etc.*' (reprinted, 1695). *A Letter from a Gentleman in Scotland to his friend at London who desired a Particular Account of the Business of Glenco* (20 April 1692, reprinted, 1695).

[123] The junto employed at least three pamphlets in an attempt to exploit the investigations: *A Collection of the Debates and Proceedings in Parliament, in 1694 and 1695, Upon the Inquiry into the Late Briberies and Corrupt Practices*

pamphlets of this last type caused a backlash, as in Yorkshire where they were said to make '…the country Gentlemen…more in favour of Danby than formerly.'[124] Sometimes, too, apparent court successes soon proved to be qualified country victories. While Sir Christopher Musgrave lost the election at Oxford University, one of the successful candidates was Sir William Trumbull. Although Trumbull was secretary of state he proved anything but a consistent supporter of the junto programme.[125] Heneage Finch, Nottingham's brother and a fervent court opponent, was, moreover, unanimously returned as the other member.[126] In Derbyshire, while Devonshire's son and heir apparent was elected unopposed, so too was Sir Gilbert Clarke.[127] Although the latter was a devout court supporter for a few years earlier, it was believed that this would not be the case much longer. One country observer correctly noted that '…a better disposed man [to the government] might have been picked than Sir Gilbert.'[128]

There were a few signs of considerable determination on the part of the country party. After Wharton's defeat by the earl of Abingdon in a ferocious contest for control of the Oxford City mayoriality, the subsequent election of two ardent court opponents was assured.[129] In

---

(1695); *A Supplement to the Collection*…(1695); *A letter to a Member of Parliament Occasion'd by the Votes of the House of Commons Against their Late Speaker and Others* (1695). The victory at Namur received full publicity. See for example, *An Exact Journal of the Siege of Namur: Giving a Particular Account of the several sallies and attacks, and other most remarkable Passages from the first Investing of the Place. Together with the Articles of Capitulation, both for the surrendring the City and Castle* (1695).

[124] *A Letter sent from a Gentleman in Yorkshire to a Country Man in London*, (1695), p. 6.

[125] Trumbull voted inconsistently during the ensuing parliament and came to show a hatred for the junto during the subsequent trial of Sir John Fenwick. The junto virtually forced him from office. He vacated his post in December 1967.

[126] [L.] W. Finch at All Souls, to Hon. H. Finch, 28 September and 21 October 1695. Chatsworth, Finch-Halifax MSS., box 2. George Fleming to Sir Daniel Fleming, 22 September. *H.M.C. Le Fleming*, p. 338.

[127] Jos. Whildon to James Whildon [October 1695]. Chatsworth, Whildon Coll. B.V.10.

[128] A. Pye to Abigail Harley, 4 November 1695. *H.M.C. Portland*, iii, 573. Clarke even refused the voluntary association. See appendix A.

[129] George Fleming to Sir Daniel Fleming, 22 September 1695. *H.M.C. Le Fleming*, p. 338. 'Here [Oxford City] hath been the greatest canvasing for a new Mayor tht [there] hath been perhaps in the memory of man.' West. R.O., DRy 4852.

Cirencester, Jack and Richard Howe were returned after a determined struggle against the younger John Guise and Henry Ireton, who had gained fervent dissenter support.[130]

The most important part of the country campaign was defensive. The vast number of safe and relatively safe seats held by members from such country strongholds as Wales served to check court advances. In Denbighshire, for example, Sir Richard Middleton's agent told him that despite rumours of an election, he '...found none moving on the other side,...[and] thought it more decent to sitt still.'[131] From Wiltshire, Viscount Weymouth wrote that '...the elections in these parts will be much the same, not worse than the last.'[132] In Kent, too, there were doubts that the court would make any substantial gains.[133]

At the opening of the session, the king expressed his 'entire satisfaction' with the outcome of the elections.[134] If one were to accept a whig-tory frame of reference, at first sight the court might indeed appear to have achieved a considerable success. In the election of 1690, of the whig and tory convention extremists of the convention parliament who either voted for the Sacheverell clause or against making William and Mary king and queen, it has been seen that almost exactly the same proportion were returned of each group: 103 of the 146 whigs; 104 of the 150 tories.[135] In 1695, however, the whigs made a proportional gain; 84 whigs now being returned as opposed to 67 tories.[136] The change, if not large in itself, would seem highly significant if a similar change occurred among the other members. One would expect the convention tories and whigs to vote solidly against or for the court in divisions in which the junto programme was severely challenged. If, however, the

---

[130] (Paul Foley) to Robert Harley, 12 October 1695. *H.M.C. Portland*, iii, 571. H. Ireton to [Ld. Wharton], 6/16 September. Bodl. Carte MSS. 228 ff. 108–9. *Autobiography of Thomas Raymond and Memoirs of the Family of Guise of Elmore, Gloucestershire*, G. Davies, ed. (Camden Soc., 1917), p. 138.

[131] Robert Wynne to Sir Richard Middleton, M.P., Co. Denbigh. 19 October. N.L.W., Chirk Castle MSS. E.1048.

[132] To William, second Marquis of Halifax, 21 October 1695. Althorp, Halifax MSS., box 10.

[133] (Dr Richard Kingston) to Sir William Trumbull, 20 July 1695. *H.M.C. Downshire*, I, ii, 512.

[134] *H.L.J.*, xv, 599. Note the delight of L'Hermitage. Estates General dispatch, 25 October/4 November 1695. B.M. Add. MSS., 17,677. PP., f. 407.

[135] See above, p. 39.

[136] See appendix A. Edward Russell, elected for three constituencies, is counted only once.

convention tories were almost unanimous in their opposition[137] so too was a significant segment of the convention whigs. In three court-country divisions which took place *after* the rise in court fortunes following the disclosure of an assassination attempt upon the king's life, sixteen, or about a fifth of the whig group, voted consistently against the court. By adding five others who did not vote consistently for the court, one finds that about a quarter of the Sacheverell whigs may be said to have been at the least moderately country in their voting. This proportion becomes far more significant when one considers the political stature of these men. Not only were almost half of them knights of the shire, but the group as a whole dominated the opposition's participation in the debates.[138] Probably it was their outspoken support which made opposition respectable and kept the country party from becoming a routed tory fragment.

Even at the time of the election Burnet realized the limited nature of the court's success, finding that if the general trend of the elections was towards the whigs '...many of the sourer sort of whigs who were much alienated from the king, were chosen...'[139] In regard to the more general court supporters, there again appears to have been no spectacular additions: Foley supposed that there would be about 150 new members[140] and George Tollet, clerk to the commissioners of accounts, thought that if almost all of these new members were '...in the

---

[137] Only three convention tories voted consistently against the court, and but eight more voted inconsistently. See Appendix A.

[138] The following voted for Sacheverell clause, but in the 1695 parliament voted consistently country: William Duncombe [Co. Bedford], Thomas Lewes [Chipping Wycombe], Henry Boyle [Cambridge University], Sir Robert Cotton [Co. Chester], Sir William Drake [Honiton], John Howe [Cirencester], Sir Edward Harley [Co. Hereford], Paul Foley [(Speaker), Hereford], Sir Edward Hussey [Co. Lincoln], Sir William Ellis [Grantham], Philip Foley [Stafford], William Bromley [Co. Warwick], Thomas Pitt [Old Sarum], Sir Michael Warton [Beverley], Sir William Williams [Beaumaris], Robert Harley [New Radnor].

The following voted for the Sacheverell clause but voted inconsistently in the 1695 parliament: Thomas Freke [Co. Dorset], George England [Gt. Yarmouth], Sir Richard Onslow [Co. Surrey], John Lewknor [Midhurst], Thomas Foley [Co. Worcester]. The association is not deemed a division here.

See appendix A for a discussion of the issues involved.

[139] Burnet, *Own Times*, iv, 288.

[140] To Robert Harley, 26 October 1695. B.M. Portland loan, 29/188. This is corroborated by Narcissus Luttrell, *A Brief Relation of State Affairs...* (Oxford, 1857), iii, 548.

court interest, most of those in whose places those came were so too.'[141]

Only where the court could present a strong case for a given issue being one of national security could it be certain of overwhelming support; in more questionable constitutional and financial matters it would be forced to rely on the state of national sentiment and hopes of poor attendance.

If, as L'Hermitage noted, many members were charged to support requests for supply, many of these same members apparently had no intention of allowing crown interference with impartial parliamentary proceedings. During the general election some country members feared that the court might again propose Littleton for the Speakership. Seymour, writing to Harley from Exeter, deplored the fact that the sheriff of Devon had now postponed his election (evidently at his pocket borough, Totnes, where he had been forced to retreat). He believed one reason for the delay was to prevent his being up for the opening of the session. Hoping to aid in the opposition to Littleton, '...the man the [court] party have designed for the chair for my friend Paul', he even urged that all business be deferred until it could be ascertained which members were present.[142] With the embarrassing defeat of the previous spring in mind, however, the court decided not to risk provoking and possibly enlarging the opposition by a trial of strength over the Speakership. Foley was re-elected unopposed.[143]

Not only did the court not dare to challenge Foley's re-election as Speaker, but it soon became apparent that parliament had no intention of allowing the court to make the committee of elections their tool. Some whose elections were in doubt succeeded in mollifying the court through compromises which might have been less respectable had it not been for the outcome of the East Grinstead election petition. One observer called it the first great '...tryall of skill betwixt court and country', and it had resulted in a resounding country triumph. In their defence, the sitting members claimed that the contestation was groundless and simply the fulfilment of court intimidation: the borough had been told that if these old members or sixty others included on a blacklist were elected, they would be removed. Probably it was this

---

[141] George Tollet to Bp. King., 16 November 1695. T.C.D. MSS., 1122/477.

[142] 13 November B.M. Portland loan 29/156/6.

[143] 22 November. *H.C.J.*, xi, 334.

heavy-handed threat which resulted in the election being decided against 'the court party'.[144]

THE ASSASSINATION PLOT

Such modest country successes as had occurred over the Speakership and controverted elections were followed by some constitutional advances and the semblance of an opposition financial programme. But in late February 1696, with the disclosure of the abortive royal assassination attempt, a period followed during which the court carried all before it. For the event which caused their golden days, the junto was doubly grateful. Not only was William still alive, but they might exploit the plot to their advantage, dealing both a severe blow to the *de facto* school of tories, who were again challenging their monopoly of ministerial power,[145] and crippling the country opposition as a whole.[146] On 24 February, soon after the king's disclosure, Sir Rowland Gwyn moved that all members who would subscribe to an association which promised to 'revenge' an assassination also own him as 'rightful and lawful'. This wording was carried despite the voiced objections of Sir William Williams, Lowther, Musgrave, Finch and Seymour.[147] Undoubtedly a large part of this success was due to excellent timing, for only three days later tempers appear to have appreciably cooled. The association, which had not been introduced until this later date in the lords, required only the recognition of William as the lawful king and the abjuration of King James and the pretender.[148] In the commons,[149] Sir John Thompson's

---

[144] Sir John Bland to Roger Kenyon, 31 December 1695. *H.M.C. Kenyon*, pp. 386–7. See too, Robert Harley's detailed summary of the proceedings. B.M. Portland loan, 29/31/3. The sitting members were Sir Thomas Dyke and John Conyers; the challengers were Lord Orrery and Spencer Compton. 9 January 1695/6. *H.C.J.*, xi, 384.

[145] See the letters of C. Littleton to Ld. Hatton, 12 February 1696/7. B.M. Add. MSS., 17,677, QQ, ff. 285–6. R. Price to the duke of Beaufort, 11 February 1695/6. Bodl. Carte. MSS., 130 f. 359.

[146] See for example the court tract: *An Impartial Account of the Horrid and Detestable Conspiracy to Assassinate His Sacred Majesty, King William, Raise a Rebellion in England, Scotland, and Ireland, And to Encourage an Invasion from France* (1696).

[147] Daniel Bret to the earl of Huntingdon, 27 February 1695/6. *H.M.C. Hastings*, ii, 259.

[148] R. Price to [Viscount Weymouth], 27 February. Longleat, Thynne papers, xii, f. 113.   [149] *Ibid.*

motion, that all non-subscribers be expelled, failed at the same time. It was, however, ordered that all were either to subscribe or definitely reject it within the fortnight.[150] At least twenty refused in the lords[151] and between ninety and a hundred in the commons.[152]

The court had succeeded in both limiting and defining the opposition as almost never before. Of the hundred who initially refused, thirty had voted in the convention against making William and Mary king and queen, while only five had voted in favour of the Sacheverell clause.[153] None of the hundred voted on the court side in all the other recorded divisions of the session, and only eight had even occasionally done so.[154] It is little wonder then that the junto was to include the non-signers in a model proscription list.[155] Without doors the objections were outspoken and some '...termed it a trick.'[156] Robert Price noted that '...many subscribed for feare to my own knowledge.'[157]

The fears of the members soon proved well founded, for a trick it was indeed, exploited not only with almost unprecedented success in parliament, but out of doors as well. Often the associations subsequently circulated with such enthusiasm in the country were also inspired by fear. Many of the 28,000 signers of the petition in Lancaster would

---

[150] 27 February 1695/6. *H.C.J.*, xi, 470.

[151] *H.M.C. Lords, 1695–7*, ii, 206–12. Browning, *Danby*, iii, 188–94.

[152] *Ibid.*, pp. 194–213. It was noted at the time that about one quarter of the lawyers in the house refused to sign. John Freke and E[dward] C[larke] to John Locke, 27 February 1695/6. Bodl. MS. Locke C.8. f. 213.

[153] The five who supported the Sacheverell clause were Thomas Freke [Co. Dorset], John Howe [Cirencester], John Lewkenor [Midhurst], William Bromley [Co. Warwick] and Sir William Williams [Beaumaris]. See electoral appendix A.

[154] Richard, Lord Newport, [Co. Salop.] voted consistently court on two divisions. Thomas Freke and John Lewkenor had supported the Sacheverell clause. Both voted inconsistently, as did Robert Payne [Gloucester], Thomas Cartwright [Co. Northants.], Henry Holmes [Yarmouth], Sir Wm. Morley [Midhurst] and Sir Rice Rudd [Carmarthen]. See appendix A.

[155] See the court's pamphlet, *A Summary Account of the Proceedings upon the happy Discovery of the Jacobite Conspiracy, in a second Letter to a Devonshire Gentleman. H.M.C. Lords, 1695–7*, pp. 206–12. See Browning's remarks on the lists. *Danby*, iii, 187 and 194–213. Before the 1698 election, there were rumours that those who refused this voluntary association would be incapable of sitting, but the court appears not to have dared propose it. Vernon to Shrewsbury, 4 April 1698. Boughton, Shrewsbury Papers, ii, f. 5.

[156] John Verney to Visc. Hatton, 5 March 1695/6. *Hatton Corr.*, ii, 220–1.

[157] To [Viscount Weymouth], 27 February 1695/6. Longleat, Thynne Papers, ii, f. 113.

appear to have signed largely to prevent the abrogation of the privileges of the duchy.[158]

Not all the associations employed the strong parliamentary wording. In Norwich and the diocese of Carlisle, for example, the signers of the association promised only to 'punish' those responsible for the king's death rather than 'revenge' it.[159] To the moderate high-churchman, Humphrey Prideaux, the difference was scarcely semantic. By the later phrasing he feared that those favouring revenge '...would draw their swords and cut the throats of all the Jacobites', and that Jacobite might be interpreted to mean all '...whom the rabble shall think fit to plunder and abuse.'[160] Those favouring the word 'revenge', both in Norwich and Appleby, formed another association employing the parliamentary wording; principally, it would appear, to display their enthusiasm to the government. The Norwich weavers certainly had good reason to do so: they were told by one of the whig leaders of the county, that the more zeal they showed the more court support there would be for a bill prohibiting the import of Indian silks and Bengals.[161]

In some places, the junto's following made certain that only their friends would have an opportunity to sign any association at all. Such was said to be the case in Radnor, where Sir Rowland Gwyn apparently hoped to employ the list to aid in appointing a new commission of the peace in an attempt to overpower the Harley interest.[162] Similarly, county associations were occasionally managed in such a way that entire towns were omitted, causing frantic efforts to draw up new ones in a reasonable time.[163]

To all outward signs the junto's management of the association was a considerable success. The only blight occurred in April, when because of too much whig enthusiasm and perhaps tory foresight, the association became compulsory for office-holders and members of parlia-

---

[158] Rich. Edge to Roger Kenyon, 29 February 1695/6. *H.M.C. Kenyon*, p. 406.

[159] Humphrey Prideaux to John Ellis, 8 April 1696. *Prideaux-Ellis Corr.*, p. 167. Henry Fleming to Sir D. Fleming, 30 March 1696. *H.M.C. Le Fleming*, p. 342.

[160] To John Ellis, 15 April. *Prideaux-Ellis Corr.*, p. 168.

[161] S. to s., 8 April. *Ibid.* H. Fleming to Sr. D. Fleming, 30 March. *H.M.C. Le Fleming*, p. 342.

[162] Edw. Howarth to R. Harley, 15 March 1695/6. B.M. Portland loan 29/147/4.

[163] W. Gilpin to Sir John Lowther, 10 April 1696. Cumb. R.O., Lonsdale MSS., (bound volume). Gilpin noted examples throughout the nation.

ment.[164] Harley was overjoyed at this development, finding it easier to bring pressure to bear on his associates to sign under the principle of force and thus diminish the dangers of a snap election.[165] While this proved a deterrent to some of the junto's planned purges of such parliamentary bodies as the commission of accounts, they were not hindered by such legal niceties in other ways. In local elections that summer they employed the voluntary association to intimidate the opposition,[166] and their purge of crown offices was little less than 'thorough'. The recurring question found in the court's correspondence was how to remove as many 'disaffected' local justices and commissioners as possible. All who had refused even the voluntary association were to be displaced. The usually moderate Shrewsbury, moreover, added that since the purge went this far, it might as well extend to those who were simply *thought* to be disaffected.[167] Although the king appears not to have concurred in this last junto proposal, the changes were still extensive.[168]

The assassination plot was to divide court and country conflicts from 1690 until the Treaty of Ryswick like a watershed. Until that event, there were general country party encroachments upon the king's prerogative and at least some opposition to the court's monetary proposals. After the plot, the opposition showed a sharp decline; country strategy being seldom more than to effect successful retreats. Country initiative in financial matters was crushed and there were even constitutional setbacks. In many ways the situation paralleled that following both the Rye House plot and Monmouth's rebellion; once again the court benefited from the loose identification of opposition with treason.

---

[164] In 1701, Shaftesbury hoping for a voluntary abjuration oath in the ensuing parliament believed the tories had made the association compulsory '...by enforcing it and making it penall, so that the whole party came in on the purpose of force and constraint under a king *de facto*.' To Furley, 29 September 1701. T. Forster, *Original Letters of John Locke; Algernon Sydney and Anthony, Lord Shaftesbury* (1830), p. 156. Note, however, that Nottingham opposed the association in the lords. *H.M.C. Lords, 1695–7*, pp. 245–6.

[165] See p. 85.

[166] Humphrey Prideaux to John Ellis, 1 June 1696. *Prideaux-Ellis Corr.*, p. 175.

[167] To the king, 5/15 June. *Shrewsbury Corr.*, pp. 122–3.

[168] In July, for example, eighty-six justices and over a hundred deputy lieutenants were removed. Narcissus Luttrell, *Brief Relation*, iv, 91. See, for example, the list of Lancashire J.P.'s thought likely to be turned out. Guicciardini Wentworth to Roger Kenyon, 10 September. *H.M.C. Kenyon*, p. 411.

THREE

The Power of the Purse

If considerable supplies were eventually voted to fulfil the war's unprecedented expenses, the commons' monopoly of financial power, coupled with the development of an informed opposition leadership, increasingly secured acquiescence by both king and lords in measures that would otherwise have been found unacceptable. So implied Sir Thomas Clarges when he found it necessary to delay supply as the '...House hath nothing to get a good bill past but their money, wch when they have once parted with, they have no great power...'[1] Indeed, outright tacks were occasionally employed, for without such methods many country measures might have never been effected.

The financial historian, W. A. Shaw, believes that to represent these proceedings which led to parliamentary supremacy as a triumph of whig, constitutional or republican principles '...is simply moonshine', ascribing it instead to the chaotic debates and commons' lack of financial sense.[2] In coming to this conclusion, Shaw rejects the possibility that such chaos and obstruction was designed by the country leaders—that

---

[1] 18 February 1691/2. Luttrell, Abstract MSS., i, f. 331.

[2] W. A. Shaw wrote two introductions to the *Calendar of Treasury Books* for the years 1689–1702. Although in most ways excellent, the works present a very hostile view of the country party in general and the commission of accounts in particular. The first is in vol. IX, pt. i (1931), and covers the earlier period, from 1689–1695; the later period in the introduction to vols. ix–xviii (1935). They are cited as Shaw, *Earlier (Later) Treasury Introduction. Earlier Treasury Introduction*, p. lxxxv.

there may well have been method in their madness. It might otherwise have been most difficult indeed to stop the comparatively well organized court party from effecting even larger supplies by setting contending ministerial factions to bidding for the king's favour. One need not delve into the tangled proceedings of the convention parliament to grasp the significance of Sir William Williams's statement urging an ordinary revenue bill to last but a year and no longer. He said in defending the measure that laws were being provided '...against ill men, and for ill times and therefore it was thought convenient to put in the words "and no longer" '. It was not that the crown was to have no hereditary revenue. Williams believed that '...some part of the revenue follows the crown as the shadow the body; but to say, therefore, all the revenue does so is no consequence.'[3] Still, the revenue which was always to follow the king might cast but a pale shadow in the exchequer and provide for but little more than the royal state—if he avoided extravagance. By May 1690 only the temporary excise was granted for life while the customs was voted for but four years. Even this was largely mortgaged for war purposes,[4]—perhaps with good reason. The previous August, Halifax noted that the king said once his revenue was settled, 'he would take his measures'. Halifax supposed that such designs caused apprehensions in parliament.[5]

THE COMMISSION OF ACCOUNTS AND THE COURT'S REQUESTS

Parliament's apprehension did not dissolve with the convention. With unprecedented sums being voted for wartime expenditures, there were widespread fears that the king might misappropriate sizeable amounts for other purposes—including wholesale bribery of members from the secret service money. With the stated purpose of inquiry into government expenditures, the country party wished to establish a commission for examining, taking and stating the public accounts of the kingdom.

The idea of such a commission was not new. In 1667 after Charles had frustrated attempts of the previous session to effect a similar institution, the opposition achieved a qualified success. Although no member of the commons was to be a commissioner, the very creation of any commission has been considered one of the Clarendon administration's

---

[3] 17 December 1689. Cobbett, v, 490.
[4] Shaw, *Earlier Treasury Introduction*, pp. lxxxi–ii.
[5] Halifax Memo. of 4 August 1689. Foxcroft, *Halifax*, ii, 228.

great failures. Its subsequent discovery of widespread embezzlement
proved its danger to the court and value to the opposition. The next
year it was not revived.

The Carmarthen administration viewed the prospect of a revived
commission with considerable apprehension. To both court and country
it meant something quite different from what the innocuous name might
suggest. Not without reason has Shaw described it as '...the spearhead
of the country opposition'.[6] Certainly most commoners came to consider the body as guardians of parliamentary expenditure, and the commission, although a financial institution, soon came to be thought of as a
constitutional necessity, at least in wartime. The commissioners learned
where to look for ministerial mismanagement and aided the commons
in making advice informed advice. George Tollet, the commission's
first clerk, wrote that the execution of even that office would '...give a
man an insight into all the offices of accts. in England, wch has made
me so much to covet it.'[7] As few commoners understood government
finance as well as the commissioners, they became the logical counter-
parts to the treasury lords and were consequently prominent in the
highly important supply debates. Still, there can be little doubt either
of the commissioners' loyalty to the revolution settlement. Although the
'spearhead of the country opposition', it was anything but a gathering
of Jacobites: of the nineteen commissioners who acted during the war,
fifteen had sat in the convention parliament, and of these ten had voted
for the whig Sacheverell clause and only two against making William
and Mary king and queen.

The court sometimes claimed that there were omissions in the commission's annual reports. No one doubted the truth of such charges—or
that it was the court which deliberately refrained from making their
reports more complete and accurate. Such omissions would not cease
until the treasury became far more accountable to the commons; a
development by no means openly urged by the commissioners, but
the fulfilment of which was largely due to their work. Nor need one
look far to discover the cause of the secrecy surrounding the treasury's
books, for they were the king's books in a sense they would never be
again. William attended the treasury meetings about nineteen times a
year and unquestionably would have attended far more frequently had
he not been abroad for much of the time. The treasury was still almost

---

[6] *Later Treasury Introduction*, p. clv.
[7] To Wm. King, bishop of Derry, 24 January 1690/1. T.C.D. MSS.,
1122/174.

totally dependent on the crown, having little of the freedom that it was to enjoy even in Anne's reign.[8] The king considered the very challenge of the commission enough of a threat to keep placemen engaged in devising methods to obstruct its activities, hinder its renewal and harass the commissioners. In part for these reasons, few of the nineteen members who acted in the four commissions during the War of the League of Augsburg chose or were chosen to continue 'in office'; thirteen were elected only once, three twice, one three times, and only two, Robert Harley and Paul Foley, on all four occasions.

It would be difficult to overestimate the commission's value to the country party. Apart from being of critical importance in providing men with enough financial knowledge to criticize the course of foreign affairs, about which the king told them so little,[9] it both supplied the experience necessary even to attempt to initiate country monetary schemes and furnished the largest slices of the opposition's humble patronage pie.[10] With the heavy war taxation, it is difficult to conceive how the gentry could otherwise have spared the time from their estates or the additional expense concomitant with constant attendance and clerical assistance.

Only in the face of determined court opposition was the commission established,[11] and even when the commissioners met, it at first appeared that the Carmarthen administration might benefit from renewed whig-

---

[8] Doris M. Gill, 'The Treasury, 1660–1714', *Eng. Hist. Rev.* (1931), xli, 600–22.

[9] M. A. Thomson argues that the king told parliament only enough to secure supply during the War of the League of Augsburg. This is in sharp contrast to both his and Anne's later policy of keeping parliament generally informed of at least the broader outlines of the court's foreign policy. 'Parliament and Foreign Policy, 1689–1714'. *History* (1953–4), xxxviii, 234–54.

[10] George Tollet, one of the seekers of office, in writing to Bishop King stated that in his quest for the position of clerk, he had the support of seven of the nine commissioners. 24 January 1690/1. T.C.D. MSS. 1122/174.

[11] George Tollet believed that the prorogation of the first session which had interrupted the passage of the commission's enabling bill to be more than coincidence:

'But the Court not likeing, nor being provided against such an Inquisition, the K.[ing] adjourned the Parlimt the very day in wch this Bill shoud have pas'd, and afterward Prorogued them.'

The next session the commoners who, as Tollet noted, '...seldome let anything fall wch they have once taken up, have resumed the Bill and an Act is pas'd...' To Bp King, 24 January 1690/1. T.C.D. MSS. 1122/174.

tory factionalism. Indeed, Thomas Clarges and Sir Benjamin Newlands
were thought '...of a sense different from the rest of the commissioners'.[12] undoubtedly because of their tory sympathies. Both had
opposed making William and Mary king and queen, while the six
others who sat in the convention were supporters of the Sacheverell
clause.[13] These party differences, while prominent at the outset, were
not to remain so for long. Robert Harley wrote that on the day of the
first meeting there were 'hot words between some' but that it soon
calmed down, largely owing to Clarges 'worthy pains'.[14] Subsequently,
when the commissioners were taking an active part in an estimates
debate, Edward Harley wrote: 'Whigs and tories unite against the court
in endeavouring to be frugal by good management.'[15] By the end of the
year, Clarges, along with his old friend Musgrave, had gained the reputation of 'commonwealth men'.[16]

   As it was to turn out, the two placemen, Sir Robert Rich and Robert
Austen, both commissioners of the admiralty, were found to be the
ones truly different. The unsuccessful bill of the previous session would
have excluded all placemen, causing one commissioner to stand down.[17]
Probably it was but to gain court acquiescence that they were allowed,
for the next enabling act was effectively to exclude them by continuing the existing commission while disqualifying admiralty commissioners.

   The commissioners' work was to make a great impact in the eyes of
the courtiers. Within a year of its creation, the king was warned of the
design of 'a very great party' who wished the war to be managed by a
parliamentary committee. So imminent was the danger that a new parliament was thought advisable. Intelligence received of a planned
parliamentary usurpation of the king's authority seemed to be '...made
good by the manner of the proceedings of the Commissioners for
accounts who Act soe inimated [i.e., as if they were in agreement with
the plan] and in many things exceeding their pow'r that it seems plainly
to be a Method in order to such A design, and as formerly an Abjuration

---

[12] Roger Morrice, 'Entering Book', iii, f. 224.
[13] Sir Samuel Barnardiston did not sit in the convention, but is listed as
being prominent in the country in opposition to James II in 1685.
[14] To Sir E. Harley. 7 March 1690/91. *H.M.C. Portland*, iii, 459.
[15] To s., 10 November 1691. *Ibid.*, 481.
[16] S. to s., 17 November. *Ibid.*, 482.
[17] On 22 May 1690, Richard Kent (Chippenham), a placeman, was left out
and replaced by Thomas Coulson of London. *H.C.J.*, x. 422.

of any other Pow'r has been refusd this seems an Abjuration of your Matys.'[18]

The aforementioned warning was made even before the commissioners delivered their first report, for they had already shown their mettle in the session's supply debates. The reports appear, indeed, to be of comparatively little value in and of themselves: the first was less noted for its statement of incomes and issues than the accompanying list of outspoken grievances against the government; the five following reports were similar to those subsequently issued by the treasury. Still, even in their limited official capacity, the commissioners' work is of more value than W. A. Shaw's caustic remarks might lead one to suppose. In criticizing them, Shaw finds that their reports contained only what they requisitioned from the exchequer. Although this would appear to be quite true enough on the surface, what he believes follows from it seems a gross error in emphasis: 'They were *only* of use to the house of commons for the rough and ready purpose of debate on votes of supply.'[19] To the opposition, however, probably this purpose was thought to be the commission's most important function.[20] The reason for their figures being less accurate than the treasury's is that, as Shaw admits, the books of 'every branch of the government' were open owing to the financial year being incomplete. The later treasury report is thus said to put it 'out of court' and make it 'comparatively valueless'.[21] But might not the treasury's figures be 'comparatively valueless' to the opposition, coming as they did usually after, rather than before, debates of supply? Even if the commons ordered the treasury to draw up figures in time for the opening of a session as Shaw suggests,[22] they might well be fraudulent. Quite possibly the figures of both the commission and treasury might be grossly inaccurate if there was a second set of government books designed for the 'benefit' of the public. One is certainly led to ask why the commissioners were unable to demand information under oath, if the government had nothing to hide. It seems possible that the treasury's figures might have been quite different if there had

---

[18] Sir Robert Howard to the king, 31 July 1691. P.R.O., S.P. Dom. 8., King William's Chest, 9 f. 239. He said that he sent the letter on the approval of Godolphin. Howard was auditor of the exchequer and member for Castle Rising. He is listed as favouring the Sacheverell clause and is one of the placemen included in the opposition list of 1694 perhaps composed of those favouring the triennial bill. Incompletely paraphrased in *Cal. S.P. Dom., 1691*, p. 465.

[19] W. A. Shaw, *Later Treasury Introduction*, p. clxii, Italics added.

[20] *Ibid.*   [21] *Ibid.*, p. clxx.   [22] *Ibid.*

not been a parliamentary commission '...merely duplicating the work of the treasury.'

The commissioners' leadership of the country party in holding the line against the court's financial demands was, nevertheless, their more obvious and probably most significant function. They performed this unofficial task not only directly in debating questions of supply, but indirectly through the committee of ways and means. The effectual use of a ways and means committee often provided a second and often higher hurdle for 'the king's business' and became a most important part of opposition tactics. A bill for raising revenue in Ireland, leaving much to be raised by the Irish themselves, serves as but one example where a bill ostensibly of ways and means was in effect one for the diminution of supply.[23] Such bills usually resulted from the court's unsuccessful encounters with the opposition in debate: the country side usually arguing that the supplies voted were very large and that the means voted to raise them would probably provide more than intended; the court conversely urging that they were barely enough and that the means voted to fulfil them were inadequate and largely imaginary.[24]

It would be naive to suppose that this uncertainty was primarily due to the embryonic state of financial knowledge. Once again considerable divisions arose between court and country over what sort of tax should be employed and whether its executors should be appointed by the crown or parliament. Once again the court party took a position which tended to maximize revenue usually countered by a country position tending to minimize it. The government strove to make taxes pleasant, hidden and easily made permanent; the opposition to make them harsh, obvious and impossible to collect beyond the termination date fixed by parliament.

Of the £38,000,000 voted between the revolution and December 1695, less than one quarter was raised by long-term borrowing and none predated the first million bill of the fourth session.[25] Thus under the Carmarthen administration all but a small fraction of war expenditure was paid for out of the yearly revenue. It was not that the country party did not want it this way, for it clearly did, showing distaste for even the earlier short-term borrowing clauses. Such measures

[23] Note the debate of 13 February 1692/3 in which Lowther pleads for more funds to make up deficiencies. Luttrell, Abstract MSS., ii, f. 352–4.

[24] 8 February 1692/3. *Ibid.*, ii, ff. 338–40.

[25] 4 William and Mary, c. 3.

made the war taxation less of an immediate hardship and only postponed the day of reckoning—the day when the national debt and the usurious interest rates would have to be repaid largely by them and largely to the benefit of the war profiteers. Even when short-term borrowing clauses were inserted to guarantee the sum, these could often serve as occasion for further debate and delays.[26]

Of the various forms of taxation, the country gentlemen viewed the excise with considerable alarm and tried to keep this source of revenue to a minimum. Not only was it all too easily collected beyond the stated expiry date, but it allowed for the development of an army of government collectors. Despite highly significant regional inequalities in assessment,[27] the country party generally favoured a land tax to all other forms:[28] over half the revenue raised during the reign came from this source.[29] Founded upon the principle that whoever pays the piper calls the tune, it gave the landed interest considerable if undefined control over royal policy and served to unite gentry and squirearchy against any unnecessary war expenses which would obviously fall hardest upon them.

For the court, a land tax assessed by commissioners appointed by parliament provided the gravest uncertainty. After the close of the second session Russell wrote to the king, saying that '...if the Gentlemen in the Country do their duty, wee shall be well anuff provided...'[30] But

---

[26] In the debate of 10 February 1691/2, Harley and Bertie succeeded in keeping the court from including a loan clause in the poll bill, but later the clause was inserted despite protestations from Col. Cornwall, Bertie, and Bathurst. Luttrell, Abstract MSS., i, ff. 308 and 326. 3 William and Mary, c. 6, s. 31–2.

[27] H. J. Habakkuk in his study of Northamptonshire and Bedfordshire notes the devastating effects the taxes had upon the gentry and the static economic state of the squirearchy. While this was truer of the home counties than the more lightly assessed North and West, there was probably the same tendency in most areas. 'English Landownership, 1680–1740', *Econ. Hist. Rev.* (1940), x, 2–17.

[28] R. Longworth wrote Roger Kenyon that 'When money is given, if I had the casting vote it shold [should] be by a land tax, for certaynely [certainly] it is the safest and readyest way to raise money, and with the most equallity [equality]. 7 October 1690. *H.M.C. Kenyon*, pp. 247–8. It must be noted however, that both lived in lightly taxed Lancashire.

[29] During William's reign the land tax brought in £19,174,059. 8s. 3½d. the excise £13,649,328. 0s. 5¾d.; the poll tax £2,557, 649. 7s. 7½d. See the table in Cobbett, vol. V, p. ccxlii.

[30] 18 February 1690/91. P.R.O. S.P. Dom. 8, King William's Chest, 8 f. 177. *Cal. S.P. Dom.*, p. 268.

would they? Godolphin's letters in the spring and summer of 1692 are but a series of complaints as to the inadequacy of the land tax revenue.[31]

The effectual use of ways and means had also provided a method of restricting court and allied interests. At the opening of the first session William gave permission for loans to be placed against his ordinary revenue for war purposes,[32] although he probably did not anticipate the enthusiasm with which his words were to be taken; £1,000,000 being so voted in April 1690, almost twice as much as he apparently expected.[33] Indeed, until the last year of his reign, William's ordinary revenue was almost completely mortgaged for war purposes.[34] Crown officers' salaries were also subjected to taxation and attacks upon royal grants played an important part in country party policy after the peace.

An aptly named court tract appeared for the opening of the second session, entitled: *Mercurius Reformatus, or the New Observator in Giving Directions in the Matter of Money.* Clarges, Foley and Sir Peter Colleton (all of the commission) as well as Sir Charles Sedley and Sir Edward Seymour, roundly condemned the pamphlet as a breach of parliamentary privilege.[35] But although the printer and author received a parliamentary reprimand on their knees, this did not make the contents any less true a reflection of the opposition's resourcefulness in financial obstruction. With a number of opposition members having an increased knowledge of financial matters, the court found it increasingly difficult simply to force through bills of supply. Reasons were demanded for the court's requests—and good ones too. The opposition's attempts to reduce the court's military demands became so ingenious that two placemen stated that while in former sessions the house sat daily in such matters '…now 'tis a hard matter for the king's business to get one day.'[36]

At the opening of the supply debate, Paul Foley, supported by Clarges, attacked the past extravagance of the crown, thinking it incredible that eleven million should have been spent in three years, and expressed the view that no more than a third of that sum should be voted for the

[31] To the King. 25 March, 15 April and 13 May 1692. *Cal. S.P. Dom.*, pp. 199, 238 and 281.   [32] 21 March 1689/90. *H.L.J.*, xiv, 433–4.

[33] (Robert or Edward Harley) to Sir E. Harley, 3 April 1690. *H.M.C. Portland*, iii, 446.

[34] W. A. Shaw considers that parliament 'defrauded' the king of every last penny of his ordinary revenue during the war. *Earlier Treasury Introduction*, pp. lxv and lxxii–iii.

[35] 9 and 21 November 1691. *Ibid.*, i, ff. 9, 57 and 59. *H.C.J.*, x. 548 and 558. Richard Baldwin and Dr James Welwood were the printer and author.

[36] 18 November 1691. Luttrell, Abstract MSS., i, ff. 40–1.

ensuing year. Clarges and Musgrave said that there had been a smaller navy when England fought both France and Holland and argued that troops other than seamen might fill up the number voted. A court attempt to add four new ships to the list was defeated after it was noted that they could not be made serviceable that year.[37] A commons' committee inquiring into the court's estimates agreed to abate £180,000 of the £1,850,000 voted for the fleet.[38] This decision was subsequently confirmed, despite a last minute court attempt to add almost £25,000 which was successfully countered as being irregular.[39]

The next session it at first appeared that the court would be made to proceed only 'at their perill' as Foley put it,[40] especially in regard to supplies for the land army. Bathurst wished to know what sums were sent to the 'Beggarly Princes of Germany' and Clarges supported him in urging the commons to give the crown 'advice as well as your money'. Sir Robert Sawyer gave the principal speech, saying that while '...all agreed to have as good a fleet at sea as we can, [it is] not so for land forces.' The opposition, evidently finding its strength, reversed Foley's and Musgrave's earlier and more moderate motion for a select supply committee[41] and it soon appeared that the army estimates were going to be subjected to an unprecedented scrutiny before the whole house.

All was brought to an abrupt halt by a timely royal message delivered by Carmarthen's henchman, Sir Henry Goodricke: Goodricke informed the house that the king planned to keep but a minimal force in England and effect '...*a descent into France, or otherwhere to annoy the common enemy*;...'[42] If anything less than a descent had been promised it seems clear that the court would have found the outcome far more bleak. One well-informed observer noted that most members thought that little was necessary for England's security abroad: 'They [the members of parliament] talk of the taking of Charleroi, Namur, Liege and even Brussells and Ghent as matters of little importance. Only Ostend is considered to have any relation to the Thames.'[43] With a descent in view, however, it would be quite a different matter. Bonet, the Brandenburg envoy, firmly believed that if 80,000 troops had been asked for

---

[37] 14 November 1691. Luttrell, Abstract MSS., i, ff. 29–30.
[38] Robert Yard to George Clarke, 14 November 1691, T.C.D. MSS. 749/ 1330. R. Warre to s. s.d. *Ibid.*, 1332.
[39] 18 November. Luttrell, Abstract MSS., i, f. 42. *H.C.J.*, x, 555.
[40] To Robert Harley, 17 September 1692. B.M. Portland loan 29/135/7.
[41] Luttrell, Abstract MSS., i, ff. 43–5.   [42] *Ibid.*, f. 45. Italics added.
[43] (Dykevelt) Dispatch, 20/30 November 1691. *H.M.C. Denbigh*, iii, 207.

they would have been granted.[44] Another noted that some of the Western members, especially those from Cornwall, would even have supported a request for 100,000 men.[45]

Not all of the opposition were so credulous. Sir John Thompson complained that the projected war in France was merely 'a colour' to allow a standing army. Foley argued that the land army cost '...these 3 last years as much again as your fleet' and Clarges believed that £150,000 might be '...saved by good management...' Sir Charles Sedley warned against spending too much for a war which appeared likely to be of long duration just as one does not '...ride at the same rate for 100 miles as a Citizen does if he were going but to Islington;...'[46]

Apparently it was all to little avail. Goodricke's qualificatory closing to William's promise of a descent was perhaps scarcely heard by many members and certainly not remembered by such as Nottingham the next summer when he wrote that the court had broken '...thro' the rules and formes of parliament to add 12,000 men to the army.'[47] Nottingham hoped that a successful descent '...may cause a Revolution in France and put an end to the war.'[48] The promise of a descent was to be kept at all costs. He not only believed it better to spare troops from Holland and even to let Namur fall, but, on behalf of both himself and other lords, offered to aid in the endeavour with financial assistance. Although the other peers were not named, they almost certainly included Godolphin and Carmarthen, both ardent advocates.[49] The latter thought parliament's enthusiasm motivated by hopes of eventual savings. Even if a descent did not fulfil Nottingham's hopes of creating a revolution led by the Protestants, the army might subsist on its own or, at the least, be supplied from England and thus diminish the outflow of bullion.[50]

---

[44] Von Ranke, vi, 170.

[45] (Dykevelt) Dispatch, 20/30 November 1691. *H.M.C. Denbigh*, iii, 208.

[46] 30 November 1691. Luttrell, Abstract MSS., i, 90–5.

[47] To Portland, 14 June 1692. H.M.C. 'Finch' (galley proof), iv, no. 436.

[48] To Portland [27 August 1692]. *Ibid*. No. 794.

[49] S. to s., 14 June. *Ibid*., No. 436.

[50] Carmarthen to the king, 9 September. *Cal. S.P. Dom.*, p. 443. See too, Godolphin to the king, 13 July. *Ibid*., p. 366. One armchair strategist advocated the creation of fortifications along the French coast which could be lightly garrisoned and reinforced by marines. These would be self-sustaining as the might gain tribute money from the surrounding area and would also aid in a more practical and substantial descent. *The Descent Upon France Considered In a Letter to a Member of Parliament* (1693.)

Perhaps at the opening of the next session the court might have drawn some solace from the opposition's disunity. Policy disagreements gave Foley considerable alarm. Some preferred the past method of leaving the initiative to the court, simply holding the line on supply and fighting the excise. Others, however, wished to employ a maritime strategy; that is, to reduce the army while strengthening the fleet. Still others were thought to favour a descent upon France with the concomitant large army, despite its earlier lack of success.[51] Although the court was probably partially aware of these advantages at the outset, Carmarthen had considerable worries about the opposition's strategy, which he believed would be one not of direct attack but of 'division and opposition'.[52]

The court must have found the first days of the session unpropitious. After numerous delays,[53] the king apparently attempted to surprise the many country members who were not yet up by an unexpected opening in early November. His plan was at best only partially successful: in the session's first trial of strength, a motion for a six-day adjournment to allow time for members to arrive was 'carried clearly' for the country side despite court attempts to limit it to three.[54] The king in his speech had asked not only for assistance but advice. Although probably so doing with a view to deflecting criticism of his ministry, he was apparently ill advised, for as Sunderland noted later, it '...gave a handle to the P[arliament] which was well improved.'[55] When the commons met on 10 November, some even balked at pledging assistance, fearing that the court would use the vote to oblige them to come up to the highest estimate.[56] The court moved to promise the king supplies '...according to his occasions,' which one country member found '...a little too fast', believing it better to wait until the commission of accounts made its report '...to judge what is necessary.'[57] The commission appears to have

---

[51] To Robert Harley, 17 September 1692. B.M. Portland loan 29/135/7.

[52] To the king, 9 September. *Cal. S.P. Dom.*, p. 443.

[53] T. Foley to R. Harley, 24 September. *H.M.C. Portland*, iii, 501. T. Foley believed that the king was delaying the opening of parliament so that '...nothing may be done but give money.'

[54] 4 November. Luttrell, Abstract MSS., ii, f. 4.

[55] Memo of Sunderland to Portland, June 1693. N.U.L. PwA 1219.

[56] Geo. Tollet to Bishop King, 10 November 1692. T.C.D. MSS. 1122/242a.

[57] Luttrell, Abstract MSS., ii, f. 5. Thomas Neale spoke for the court. The country member was Sir John Darell.

amply justified the previous session's effort to extend their term of office; three of the commissioners, Clarges, Harley and Foley followed up Darell's motion, wishing to make inquiries before giving advice and assistance. Clarges proceeded to the offensive, asking to see all royal leagues and alliances. Still, the country party did not avert a vote of support. Lowther and Seymour succeeded in equating it with a vote of confidence in the king; the former minimizing any inherent vote of specific supply and the latter maximizing the need to lessen French hopes and aspirations.

Indeed, the court also succeeded in having the commons vote for the continuation of a vigorous war against France, although some, probably led by Foley, are noted to have opposed the inclusion of the word 'vigorous', apparently fearing escalation.[58] Foley led the fight a week later to keep three thousand men from being added to the navy, arguing that he could see no point '...to increase now when you beat your enemy the last year...'[59] On the committee's report, three of the nine heads were fiercely attacked by the country side which first accused the court of having 'particular men' bring in the supply bills and then found it guilty of irregular increases. The court dismissed the first argument as being irrelevant, and argued that the increases were necessitated by inflation.[60]

The next day, Sir Christopher Musgrave precipitated a crisis which might have fulfilled Carmarthen's gravest fears of the power of 'division and opposition' by leading the battle to separate naval from army supply. This procedure would take up at least a day as the house would have to agree on the committee's resolution. The court countered with another *deus ex machina*, not Goodricke again with more qualified promises of a descent, but Sir Edward Seymour, who told of vast French invasion plans which he claimed to have seen the previous night. This timely disclosure was so successful as to leave Musgrave and Sir John Knight alone in the division. Still undaunted, Musgrave attempted to reverse the court's success by resolving the house into an even more time-consuming committee of ways and means, saying that it was necessary to fulfil supply at once if time was so precious. In this he was assisted

---

[58] 22 November. Luttrell, Abstract MSS., ii, ff. 66–8.
[59] 29 November. *Ibid.*, ii, f. 99.
[60] I December. *Ibid.*, ii, 118–22. Harley, Foley, Sir Christopher Musgrave, Col. Granville, Sir John Knight (M.P., Bristol, who had voted against making William and Mary king and queen) and Theodore Bathurst (M.P., Richmond), led in the debate.

by extensive but insufficient country support, the motion not being carried.[61]

The next session, the aforementioned ministerial factionalism had a profound effect on matters of supply. Jack Howe stated on the court's behalf: 'As to the faults of the Fleet, one part lies upon one [party] and another upon another. Prop the building first, and then enquire where the defect is.'[62] The words fell seemingly on deaf ears. While a very brazen attempt to provide 'for the fleet alone', and lay aside the army in Flanders, did not get off the ground,[63] the Smyrna losses made the inquiry into the fleet's mismanagement the foremost consideration. Although the cross-purposes characterizing the attack kept any effectual action from being taken, the question of supply was delayed. And when it finally came on, the king's initial greediness put his managers in a very awkward position: William had requested 93,500 men, a number which Musgrave and Granville quickly seized upon and defended, wishing the sum to be voted in a lump; a move which would almost certainly fail. While this manoeuvre was lost by common cry and the question to proceed by degrees to keep the forces equal to those of the common enemies overwhelmingly carried,[64] the voracious attack undoubtedly left its mark. If after subsequent delays supplies were eventually voted, it was only in the face of strong tory opposition and fervent junto co-operation. And the junto was coming to demand a more considerable share in the government.

THE MEN FOR MONEY

The new junto managers' abilities to raise funds successfully was their greatest asset to the king, and from the establishment of their ascendancy until the peace, demands for war expenses encountered less

---

[61] Musgrave was assisted in the second debate by Palmer, Ld Eland, Clarges, Sir Edw. Hussey, Sir John Parsons and Robert Harley. *Ibid.*, ii, ff. 128–32.

[62] Cobbett, v, 778.

[63] Sir John Trenchard to Lord Capel, 2 December 1693. Dorset R.O., D.60X.36 (J. M. Lane Papers).

[64] (Dykevelt) Dispatch, 15/25 December 1693. *H.M.C. Denbigh*, iii, 219. Clarges, Musgrave and Granville are said to have spoken for king and kingdom in urging the vote which would almost certainly have been defeated, while Lowther, Trenchard, Comptroller Wharton, Ld Cornbury, Talmach and Russell led for the court side.

obstruction. Both the election of 1695 and the disclosure of the assassination plot served to make their task progressively easier. In 1694, although supplies were adequate, parliamentary approval of the tonnage and poundage bill had been conditional on royal acceptance of a triennial bill. In 1695, if 4·5 million pounds were eventually voted, the sum was half a million less than requested. There was an attempt to reduce the forces and even a motion, albeit with only a modicum of support, for a speedy peace.[65] Following the assassination plot even such half-hearted resistance subsided. After an attempt to reduce the land forces had been defeated 222–67,[66] parliament proceeded to vote considerable provisions for the war, past deficiencies and a recoinage.[67] Five million pounds were voted for war supply and bills passed to effect the liquidation of the five million pound debt.[68] Success bred success. The country party grew fearful that initial court victories might lead to a general excise[69] or, at the least, a cattle tax.[70] These rumours were spread so effectively that the government met comparatively little opposition when they raised less obnoxious taxes. While there were a few court reversals, usually they occurred only in a surprisingly full house.

Still, the king's success in votes of supply for war purposes did not extend to his other financial needs. Requests for additions to his civil list and for the aid of the court's favourites (and fervent supporters), the French Protestant refugees,[71] were usually ignored or provided for in such a way that they might as well have been included in the general votes of supply. In part, of course, this was because of the dangers inherent in making any king independent of parliament for more than his barest needs.[72] It must be said, however, that William sometimes proved to be his own worst enemy by appearing more a Dutch Stadt-

---

[65] Estates General Dispatch, 3/13 December 1695 in Feiling, *Tory Party*, p. 316.

[66] 4 November 1696. *H.C.J.*, xi, 576.

[67] See W. A. Shaw's extensive account. *Later Treasury Introduction*, pp. llxxiii–cxxxiv.

[68] This was largely provided for in the parliamentary deficiencies act. 8 and 9 William III, c. 20 and 21.

[69] R. Price to the duke of Beaufort, 19 November 1696. Bodl. Carte MSS., 130 f. 365. Vernon to Shrewsbury, 26 November. *Vernon Corr.*, i, 77–84.

[70] S. to s., 12 December. *Ibid.*, i, 117–22.

[71] 26 November 1695, 20 October 1696 and 18 February 1696/7. *H.C.J.*, xi, 339, 567 and 712.

[72] In this way, it should be noted, he was not treated very differently from Charles II.

holder than an English king. Despite warnings from his ministers,[73] William granted enormous tracts of Welsh lands to Bentinck, which caused strongly worded petitions to be aired in parliament. In a speech which Peter Shakerley thought 'left nothing unsaid',[74] Robert Price roundly condemned the grants as being suitable only for a prince of Wales as they were inalienable crown possessions.[75] While the king, with undisguised reluctance, withdrew the Welsh grants,[76] hopes for a more favourable consideration of his civil list during the next session were probably dashed when he gave Bentinck other large, if scattered, holdings in England.[77]

These grants served to make a mockery of William's subsequent pleadings for a larger civil list.[78] If that winter in a thinning house the court at first appeared to succeed in having a substantial supply voted to fulfil the king's request,[79] this highly abstruse bill was effectively destroyed in committee of ways and means. This seems due not only to the rallying of country party support, but the knowledge gained by their leaders in the commission of accounts.[80]

THE ASSASSINATION PLOT AND THE TRIUMPH OF JUNTO
FINANCE: THE FAILURE TO RENEW THE COMMISSION OF
ACCOUNTS

While the commission came to be relegated to more mundane tasks less dangerous to the government, it gained increased experience in ferreting out bribery and corruption. If the commissioners aimed fewer direct attacks at the court itself they nevertheless substantially hindered the

---

[73] Godolphin to Portland, 7 July 1695. N.U.L. PwA 474.

[74] Richard Edge to Roger Kenyon, 21 January 1695/6. *H.M.C. Kenyon*, p. 396.

[75] Price's speech was printed in pamphlet form as *Gloria Cambriae, or the Speech of a Bold Briton* and is included in *Somers Tracts* (1814), xi, 387–91.

[76] Cobbett, v, 986 and 986 n.–987 n.

[77] The subsequent grants were made in May 1696 and reported on 3 December. *H.C.J.*, xi, 608–9.

[78] In his speech, William said that without an adequate civil list, 'it will not be possible for me to subsist'. *H.L.J.*, xv, 599.

[79] 3 March 1696/7. *H.C.J.*, xi, 726.

[80] See W. A. Shaw, *Later Treasury Introduction*, pp. xx–xxiii. Price thought that '…if lesse land or money had been given the civil list might have been better payd.' To the duke of Beaufort, 18 February 1696/7. Bodl. Carte MSS. 130 f. 375.

court programme, often with the aid of other related committees which were usually led by themselves and directed by the commission's findings. Their relentless and time-consuming inquiries into bribery and corrupt practices were probably at the front of the king's mind when he dissolved the officers' parliament.

Abney and Houblon were not re-elected that session, Henry Boyle and Sir John Thompson taking their places. The other old commissioners were continued.

After the general election of 1695, the new commission continued much like its predecessor. It resumed its august function of inquiry into civil list and incomes expenditure,[81] and was shortly seeking out bribery and misappropriation. About the time of the election for new commissioners that February, it was rumoured that the king was employing much of a six million pound debt for unappropriated additions to the secret service.[82]

The election of the new commissioners is of considerable interest in itself, serving as it does to attest that the general election of 1695 had scarcely diminished the general desire for a strong body to serve as guardians of government expenditure. The four newly elected commissioners made it even more ardently country than formerly. Despite rumours that the enabling bill would encounter difficulties in the lords because the commissioners were 'all of one complexion',[83] the more outspoken country members, such as Peter Shakerley, noted delightedly that they had carried the entire commission.[84] Indeed, all of the commis-

---

[81] *H.M.C. Lords, 1695–7*, 156–89. See too W. A. Shaw, *Earlier Treasury Introduction*, p. clxxiv. Shaw considers this to be a retrogressive step.

[82] Dr N. Johnston to the earl of Huntingdon, 16 February 1695/6. *H.M.C. Hastings*, ii, 257.

[83] R. Price to the duke of Beaufort, 11 February 1695/6. Bodl. Carte MSS. 130 f. 357. The court's obstruction was unsuccessful, the bill receiving its third reading in the lords on 15 February. *H.L.J.*, xv, 669.

[84] None of Shakerley's list of the seven unsuccessful commissioners are included as supporting the opposition in any of the recorded divisions. The three former commissioners Shakerley listed were Sir Thomas Pope-Blount, Sir William Ashurst and Sir Edward Abney; the four new candidates were Sir William Ashurst, George Booth (a commissioner of the customs), William Norris and Robert Molesworth. All signed the voluntary association and voted for the royal board of trade. All but Ashurst are listed as voting for Fenwick's attainder in the commons. Perhaps he was absent on this occasion. To Roger Kenyon, 4 February 1695/6. *H.M.C. Kenyon*, p. 399. Richard Edge, writing to Kenyon the same day, also noted that none of the new commission had the court's support. *Ibid.*

sioners with one exception are listed as opposing the various court
proposals of that parliament. The exception was Foley, the Speaker, and
in this capacity he appears to have done much to aid the opposition if
only in promoting free and impartial proceedings. Perhaps they were
almost too violently against the court for the good of their cause: the
four new commissioners refused the voluntary association and, by showing considerable reluctance even when it became mandatory, endangered
the very life of the commission. Yet the commissioners were still far
from being a group of Jacobites. One of those who refused the voluntary
association had supported the Sacheverell clause while another had been
listed as being in opposition to James II in 1685.[85] Their apologies for
refusal seem sound[86] and confirm one's belief that the association was a
court and junto plan to confront a large segment of the opposition with
its own proscription order in the event of William's assassination.

Harley having employed considerable Machiavellian reasoning, they
all signed.[87] As the commission's enabling bill had received the royal
assent minutes before the disclosure of the assassination plot, it did not
meet the test of parliamentary sentiment that session. The following
February, however, it was not revived. Probably the king's campaign
abroad, the success of the association and the extremist nature of the
past commission accounted for this court success, although it was
clearly not as disastrous to country fortunes as if renewed under court
management, once thought a distinct possibility.[88] By a majority of
thirty-three, a commission dominated by the court and junto interest
had been thrown out and thus the commission of accounts was shortly
terminated.[89]

THE ASSASSINATION PLOT AND THE TRIUMPH OF JUNTO
FINANCE: THE FAILURE TO CREATE A PARLIAMENTARY
BOARD OF TRADE, ETC.

Probably because of overwork and lack of knowledge, power and

---

[85] All but three of the former commissioners signed the voluntary association, and one of these had never held a seat, while the other two were dead.
See Appendix B.

[86] See F. Gwyn to R. Harley, 11 and 27 May 1696. *H.M.C. Portland*, iii,
575–6.   [87] See R. Harley to W. Bromley, 28 April. *H.M.C. Portland*, iii, 575.

[88] Vernon to Shrewsbury, 8 December 1696. *Vernon Corr.*, i, 112.

[89] 15 February. *H.C.J.*, xi, 705. Manley and Archer were tellers for the
minority, and both refused the association.

jurisdiction, the commission of accounts seldom tackled the subject of trade—or rather the lack of it. Throughout the war even such ardent court apologists as Burnet all but admitted that trade was sadly neglected.[90] Convoys were so inadequate and infrequent that often merchantmen put to sea unprotected to face the French pirate ships said to '...cover the sea like locusts'.[91] Early in the reign, agitation began to find effectual outlets and a stream of pamphlets was emerging by 1693.[92] The body outwardly responsible for the losses, the lords of trade and plantations, was but a continuation of the privy council committee of previous reigns. With far more work to do than in the reign of Charles II, it met less often and was plagued by factiousness and incompetence. Some suggested that the king form a select and expert royal council of trade to deal with the problem as Charles had done in 1673.[93] Probably like Charles, who reverted to the privy council committee two years later, the king feared a diminution of his authority.[94] At the least, it appears William wished almost all naval expenditure to be put to the purposes of war while utterly ignoring merchant losses. Others implied that he preferred to see a decline in English trade to help advance that of the Dutch.[95] The sustained losses in the summer of

---

[90] Burnet, *Own Times*, iv, 37, 88–9, 209 and 294. The fact that a quarter of the patents issued between 1660–1700 were taken out during the years 1691–1693 bears witness to the necessity of finding substitutes for products unobtainable during the war years. J. Carswell, *The South Sea Bubble* (1960), p. 15.

[91] 'The French are come to a new way of fighting, they set out no Fleet, but their Privateers swarm and cover the sea like locusts, they hang on our trade like Horse Leeches.' John Cary, *An Essay on the State of England in Relation to its Trade* (Bristol, 1695).

[92] See for example, *A History of the Convention* (1690), p. 52. Plas Newyd MSS. Charles Davenport wrote a number of outspoken tracts on the subject of trade, and Cary wrote about three others.

[93] W. T. Root, 'The Lords of Trade and Plantations, 1675–1696'. *Amer. Hist. Rev.* (1917), xxiii, p. 37.

[94] Nottingham thought the earlier commission was '...then lookt upon at first to be only an honble way of giving money to Parlt men, and it was broke before it could doe anything considerable and there seemed no further need of their votes.' To Heneage Finch, 14 December 1695. Chatsworth, Finch-Halifax MSS., box 2.

[95] This constantly reiterated charge was reinforced by the courts, favour of prohibitions as opposed to duties. *A brief Account of some of the late Incroachments and Depredations of the Dutch upon the English; and of a few of those many Advantages which by Fraud and Violence they have made of the British Nations since the Revolution and of the Means enabling them thereunto* (December 20, 1695), *passim*.

1695 and the king's granting of privileges to the Scottish East India Company did little to change this image. Largely to ward off parliamentary initiative in the matter,[96] the king at last formed a royal board of trade consisting of the six leading ministers and eight others versed in trading problems.[97] To many, this solution was still unsatisfactory. Some, such as the Bristol merchants, complained because those selected did not represent the outports.[98] Others opposed the very principle of a royal board, believing that the king's influence would diminish its efficacy. Nottingham, for example, hoped '...the house does not intend such a constitution [of a board of trade] shall depend on the pleasure of some ministers, nor that they use it only to gratifie their friends and to amuse people with a seeming care of trade wch has bin so shamefully neglected and prostituted to our neighbors.'[99]

The alternative suggested was a board appointed by parliament.[100] When the matter was discussed in mid-December the court spoke against it at length as an unconstitutional infringement upon the royal prerogative. In what some believed the most fiery speech since 1641, Jack Howe faced this challenge head on, replying sharply that the realm might '...be without a king but not without a trade.'[101]

---

[96] 17/27 December 1695. Estates General Dispatch. Extensive quotations from several concerned parties are found at the end of R. M. Lees's article, 'Parliament and the Proposal for a Council of Trade, 1695–1696', *Eng. Hist. Rev.* (1939), liv, 38–66.

[97] The following officers were named to the board: the lord keeper, the president of the council, the lord privy seal, the two secretaries and the first lord of the admiralty. Others named were Viscounts Bridgewater and Stamford, W. Blathwayt, Poplar, Sir Philip Meadows, John Locke, Abraham Hill, John Methuen, Sir [Gilbert] Clark. Clark and Poplar were dropped in May and Abraham Hill and John Methuen took their places. 20/30 December 1695. *Ibid.*

[98] Bristol Corporation to John Cary, 28 December 1695 (Lees). See too, Professor W. E. Minchinton, 'Bristol—Metropolis of the West', *Trans. Royal Hist. Soc.* (1954) iv, 69–89.

[99] To Heneage Finch, 14 December. Chatsworth, Finch-Halifax MSS., box 2.

[100] *Ibid.* Nottingham compared the commission to the Old East India Company and thought that parliament, like it, should be able to name whoever it pleased as the former named 'even foreigners and jews'.

[101] To make his point perfectly clear, Howe added that while he knew of no other form of government than king lords and commons, and though the executive part was in the king, still the commons '...were fit to see what was fit to be done if he failed.' J. Hervey to Mr Mercier, 13 December 1695. *H.M.C. Downshire*, I, ii, 597–8.

What the court might expect from such a commission had already been indicated by the clause in the earlier supply bill requiring forty-three ships for the exclusive purpose of protecting coastal shipping.[102] In the early debates there was further talk along these lines[103] and the Bristol merchants spoke of increasing the number to eighty.[104] During the discussions in the commons' grand committee of trade, it soon appeared that the board might be a sister institution to the commission of accounts and surpass it in the efficacy of its inquiries, being empowered, as it was, to take evidence on oath, a right denied the earlier commission.[105] Probably the board would struggle to lower tariffs, end the war and enliven hatred of the Dutch, to say nothing of giving the opposition an extra tonic which might well cancel out the effects of the previous election. Two of Locke's friends thought that the court should stop at nothing to wreck this new abomination: if it could be done neither in the commons nor in the lords, then the king must reject it. Even if forced to accept the measure, then the court must ensure that any 'wiseman' who considered serving on the board was kept from doing so by blatant intimidation.[106]

The court supporters hoped that the bill might be defeated in the commons. The clause requiring the commissioners to be appointed by parliament had been approved by only one vote, and it might well be defeated on the first reading.[107] Wharton, moreover, had led in several court successes in weakening the bill. In order to reduce the enthusiasm of potential office seekers[108] and probably at the same time to diminish the danger of enlarging the opposition's patronage pie, it was provided that no member of parliament might serve on the board. To reduce tory enthusiasm the commissioners were to be required not only to recognize

---

[102] 5 William and Mary, c. i, s. 71.

[103] Estates General Dispatch, 3/13 January 1696 (Lees).

[104] Thomas Day and R. Yate, members for Bristol, to the Bristol Corporation, 31 December 1695 (Lees).

[105] 28 January 1695/6. *H.C.L.*, xi. 427.

[106] John Freke and Edward Clarke to John Locke, 19 December 1695. Bodl. Locke MSS., c. 8 f. 207. Citing precedents they noted that for parliamentary commissioners '…to execute a power inconsistent with the Fundamentals of our Constitution is dangerous tho an Act of Parliament should Authorize it.'

[107] The vote was 175 to 174. Ellis to Ld Lexington, 3 January 1695/6. *Lexington Papers*, p. 160. John Freke and Edward Clarke to John Locke, 2 January 1695/6. B. Rand, *The Correspondence of John Locke and Edward Clarke* (1927), pp. 429–30.

[108] Estates General Dispatch, 21/31 January 1695/6. (Lees).

William as king *de jure*, but abjure king James and '...every other person of the race of Stewarts.'[109]

On report from committee, the court failed in its attack upon the parliamentary commission without a division. By a vote of 209–188, the clause prohibiting members from serving on the board was also dropped.[110] The great battle was to be over the abjuration oath. Of the many who spoke for or against it,[111] the most outspoken was Harley's friend, Robert Price. When he quoted General Monk's axiom '...that they had more reason to repent of old oaths than contrive new ones,' Wharton accused him of implying a repentance of his oath to William. After replying that he was simply quoting Monk, he went to further extremes by speaking of the difficulty of swearing oaths to 'moot points.' When Montague charged that he implied William's title was a 'moot

---

[109] The speaker is said to have left this last phrase out of the printed votes. See p. 191 n.

[110] *H.C.J.*, xi, 440.

[111] Constituencies are added to the following lists. Abbreviations: T.G.F (t.g.f.); opposed (favoured) royal board of *trade*, devaluation of *guineas*, attainder of Sir John *Fenwick*. See appendix A. One the question of abjuration oath for commissioners the following spoke in favour: Ld Coningsby [t.g.f., Leominster], Chas. Montague [t.g.f., Westminster], Sir Philip Boteler [t.g., Hythe], Sir Walter Yonge [t.g.f., Honiton], [John Smith t.g.f., Andover], listed as Sir John Smith but this is probably a mistake as Sir John voted solidly country], [Sir Thomas Trevor] Attorney General [t.g., Plympton], [Sir John Hawles] Solicitor General [Wilton, t.g.f.], Maurice Ashley [Cooper], K.C., [Weymouth], Thomas Wharton, [t.g., Co. Bucks.]

The following spoke against the oath:
Sir Henry Gough [T.G.F., Tamworth], [William] Bromley of Warwickshire [T.G.F., Co. Warwick], Robert Price [T.G.F., Weobley], Sir Edward Seymour [T.G.F., Totnes], Sir W. Williams [T. [or T.G.F.] Beaumaris [or Co. Carnarvon]], [Heneage] Finch [T.G.F., Univ. Oxon.], Robert Harley [T.G.F., Radnor], Edward Harley [F., Worcester], Col. Granville [T.G.F., Plymouth]. See letter of Dr Nathaniel Johnston to the earl of Huntingdon, 4 February 1695/6. *H.M.C. Hastings*, ii, 253–4. Constituencies are added.

The following were noted to have voted against the oath:
Sir Thomas Stanley [t., Preston], Sir Rob. Bradshagh [T.G.F., Wigan], Cozen [Thomas] Preston [T., Lancaster], [Ambrose] Pudsey [T.f., Clitheroe], [Thomas] Brotherton [T.G.F., Newton], Leigh Banks [T.G.F., Newton], Peter Shakerley [T.G.F., Wigan]. 'All the Foley's,' [i.e., Paul Foley [speaker, Hereford], Philip Foley [T.G.F., Stafford], Thomas Foley [T.G.F., Stafford], Thomas Foley [T.f., Worcester], Thomas Foley [T.G.F., Weobley]]. See the letter of Peter Shakerley to Roger Kenyon, 1 February 1695/6. *H.M.C. Kenyon*, pp. 398–9.

point', Price retorted that points were moot only to those who did not understand the law. Only after a fierce debate, when it appeared that the majority of the house might be favourable to Price, did the court let the matter drop. If the disposition of the house had been otherwise, Price might well have been sent to the Tower.[112] There was a strong possibility too that the court was trying to muster strength to uphold the oath itself. If they carried it, some country members feared it might 'upon the rebound' be extended and made 'universal'.[113]

By a vote of 195–188, the oaths clause was thrown out. While some thought the slimness of the majority made it possible the bill might still be defeated, others had their doubts.[114] Unquestionably the vote fell like a thunderclap upon the court. One country observer wrote to the earl of Huntingdon: 'Your Lordship cannot conceive the influence this single vote has had on this city. Sir Thomas Littleton and Mr Montague, the Court managers, are become very contemptible, at Kensington neglected, despised in the House.'[115]

Unfortunately for the country party, the revelation of the assassination plot stopped the bill's progress, much to Harley's dismay[116] and the delight of such court supporters as the Dutch agent, L'Hermitage, who found it '...un des biens que la conspiration a produit.'[117] Delays had again worked in the court's behalf, for if the bill had not passed the commons and lords before the exposure of the assassination plot, it might well have accompanied the commission of accounts renewal bill. Even if it too was not continued the next session, it might, again like the commission, have been revived at the close of the reign. As it was, despite a few furtive attempts at renewal,[118] the concept of a parliamentary board of trade was truly dead and was never to be resuscitated.

---

[112] Dr Nathaniel Johnston to the earl of Huntingdon, 4 February 1695/6. *H.M.C. Hastings*, ii, 253–4. In a letter to the duke of Beaufort, Price noted another of Monk's remarks which compared oaths to extreme unction. 1 February 1695/6. Bodl. Carte MSS. 130 f. 357.

[113] Daniel Bret to the earl of Huntingdon, 3 February. *H.M.C. Hastings*, ii, 251–2.

[114] Estates General Dispatch, 4/14 February 1695/6 (Lees). Burnet, *Own Times*, iv, 295–6.

[115] From Daniel Bret, 3 February. *H.M.C. Hastings*, ii, 251–2.

[116] To John Methuen, 30 June 1696. *H.M.C. Portland*, iii, 577.

[117] Estates General Dispatch, 10/20 March 1696 (Lees).

[118] Godolphin and Rochester began agitation in the lords the next session for a parliamentary board, but little came of it. Vernon to Shrewsbury, 11 February 1696/7. Boughton, Shrewsbury papers, i, f. 67.

The successful exploitation of the assassination plot also aided the junto in defeating the country project of a land bank to the advantage of its own long-term borrowing institution, the Bank of England, and the war interest generally. So too, during the currency crisis of 1696, the timeliness of the plot allowed the court to force through a revaluation and recoinage programme effecting a hidden substantial increase in the session's vote of supply. How much of these questionable victories the junto planned rather than simply blundered into is a more difficult question and will be dealt with elsewhere.[119] Suffice it here to say that the cleverness of the junto leadership leads one to be cynical. Indeed, if the king once repented of his ministers' overenthusiastic monetary schemes[120] and was almost driven to self-imposed exile, he was saved in time and indebted to the junto for his salvation.

The superiority enjoyed by ministerial tories in the opening sessions of the officers' parliament was dependent upon the semblance of success—for William neither liked nor could afford outright losers. Their task was increasingly difficult, for owing to the development of the commission of accounts the opposition's leadership was becoming more professional, while Carmarthen's technique of crying 'quick victory' or 'wolf' to fool the country volunteers into allowing the court to go around their high hurdles was certainly widening the credibility gap. Still, success might have bred success and, as long as the country party did not think the administration disloyal or guilty of gross mismanagement, it might have continued; unlike the junto whigs, the country gentlemen had little desire to change men and not measures. But with the shipping disaster of the summer of 1693 and the aforementioned shocking display of Carmarthen's inability to control a considerable following, William was at last obliged to turn to the junto whigs in earnest.

In the spring of 1697, looking back over the financial years from the time of the junto ascendancy, king and junto must have been rather pleased. Unprecedented supplies were voted and the junto monetary schemes, if expensive, were on the whole successful. Such country projects as the land bank and the parliamentary board of trade were smashed forever, while the commission of accounts was not be be revived until the last days of the reign.

---

[119] See P. G. M. Dickson, *The Financial Revolution in England* (1967), chapter III.

[120] William to Shrewsbury, 4 June, 1696. *Shrewsbury Corr.*, p. 118.

Was such success a mixed blessing? It may be argued, for example, that the end of a commission of accounts which included at least some of the opposition was in a sense a blow to the prospects of keeping up the war. Aside from providing a steam valve for country discontent, it gave the country members a sense of trust in government finance. If, as Louis XIV believed, the side which put forth the largest financial outlay would eventually win, there can be little question that without a parliamentary commission of accounts confidence in government spending might well have been so shaken and supplies so substantially reduced that the war might well have taken quite a different course.

The general election of 1695 had not given the king any mandate for unbridled power: the first subsequent election for the commissioners of accounts and the attacks upon the Welsh grants had shown that clearly enough. The overwhelming successes had occurred largely because of the successful exploitation of the assassination plot, which helped the junto vaguely to identify opposition with treason. In keeping the ministerial tories from having any effectual part in the government, the junto ministers diminished the government's support and isolated its position. In denying the country party any first-hand knowledge of its spending, the court depended upon the continuation of the parallel between opposition and treason to maintain faith in the government. Time was already eroding that relationship and the end of the war would almost completely dissolve it.

FOUR

Free and Impartial Proceedings: The Attack Upon Rotten and Standing Parliaments.

The country party sought to ensure the free impartial parliamentary proceedings which the court tried so desperately to curtail. Many members saw their independence severely jeopardized as the court became increasingly efficient in employing patronage to augment its parliamentary following. Not only was crown office the shortest road to boundless wealth in the late seventeenth century, but as the government's size increased with the war, so did the road's width.

During the early years of the reign, the parliamentary distributor of the loaves and fishes was the commons' Speaker, and his enormous influence over affairs remained as formidable as in preceding reigns. The country party soon sought to prevent a court nominee from attaining the chair, and in electing country leaders on four occasions they deprived the placemen of their most natural leader. In the more ambitious aim of depriving them of their seats, they were less successful. But if initial proscription bills made little headway, it was not so with the subsequent and more modest plan of gradually excluding certain categories of revenue officers. Various provisos were to be tacked on to money bills and a clause was at least embodied in the act of settlement of 1701 excluding all placemen. If this clause had been carried into effect as it stood and (as some thought was indicated by the wording) at once, the English constitution might have developed on rather different lines.

A corollary to the attack on placemen was the struggle for more frequent and free elections. To many, 'standing Parliament' was but 'standing army' played in a minor key. While the bill of rights stated that parliaments ought to be held frequently, it was only after the court had frustrated repeated attempts that an ambiguously worded triennial act was passed guaranteeing triennial elections at the least. More frequent elections would mean that the court's practice of bribing and corrupting both electors and members must become more frequent, more expensive, more obvious and, as a result, considerably less effectual in securing the return of enough favourable candidates. Finally, measures were enacted attempting to free elections from the influence of court and allied factions.

THE SQUINT FROM THE CHAIR

In November 1964, the labour government decided to re-elect a conservative Speaker; because of tradition, his past impartiality and their desire to increase a narrow majority a little—for as Speaker one conservative would have but a casting vote. The conservatives agreed, in part, again because of tradition; but they also supposed that a Speaker of their mind, if no longer officially of their party, might be more likely than a government Speaker to ensure the impartial proceedings so essential to an opposition. But, saving such minor qualifications, today the Speaker's influence could probably be dismissed in a footnote. That the conservatives would not put forth another candidate when the Speaker died shows that a single vote was thought of more importance than the chair.

It would, however, be very difficult to over-estimate the Speaker's importance during William's reign. Even the statute of the convention parliament which gave him precedence over all but peers[1] provides only a faint indication of his power.

Certainly little aided the court more than a loose interpretation of past procedure, and a sympathetic Speaker might both smooth the passage of desired measures and check the country opposition. To the country party, it became increasingly clear that the Speaker should be a man of its own choosing, neither allied with the court nor violently opposed to it; the latter being all too often only opportunist members of whig or tory ministerial factions temporarily out of favour. If they

---

[1] 1. William and Mary, c. 21.

did not promote the whig or tory factionalism the convention parliament had shown to be unproductive of significant constitutional reform, places easily converted them into courtiers. What was wanted was someone who reflected broader country party sentiment; a man who did not have office because he did not wish office. This must be qualified, for not only was the Speakership an office, complete with a salary of five pounds a day and a number of perquisites including a crown gift of silver plate, but it was one of the most tempting offices. Easy access was afforded to the king's ear and purse—and also to the purses of vested interests wishing favourable legislation promoted in the commons. The country party wanted the Speakership to be an office of the commons rather than of the crown. While on any one issue the Speaker's influence was seldom noticed, the cumulative effects gave him a strength exceeding that of the mightiest peer. Indeed, his position is one of the most under-estimated by parliamentary historians.

In the contest for Speaker of the convention, Edward Harley noted that although Sir Edward Seymour, a Speaker in Charles II's reign, made 'considerable interest', Henry Powle carried it 'without the least opposition'.[2] Whig predominance, of course, was one of the chief reasons for Powle's success, but even at this time there was strong court influence.[3] A place is a good indication of royal favour, and if Powle had none when elected, he was not in want for long. In mid-February, he was sworn of the privy council and less than a month later, master of the rolls.[4] His control of proceedings did not go unnoticed and was described in one tract '...a capital blemish to the convention itself.'[5] That he was not nominated again after the 1690 election seems due both to the

---

[2] E. Harley to R. Harley, 22 January 1688/9. B.M. Add. MSS. 40,621 f. 5. Harley family papers. *H.C.J.*, x, 9.

[3] Powle was conducted to the chair by his two proposers, who were both fervent court whigs: Sir Vere Fane, later (1691) earl of Westmorland, and Charles (Paulet), styled earl of Wiltshire, later marquess of Winchester and 2nd Duke of Bolton. Both are listed as supporting the Sacheverell clause and were strong revolutionaries: Paulet had come over with William from Holland and was lord chamberlain to the queen; Fane was rumoured in 1693 to be captain of the band of gentlemen pensioners. G.E.C., *Peerage*.

[4] *A History of the Convention*, p. 25. Plas Newyd, Paget Collection.

[5] Walcott calls Powle a country whig (*English Politics*, p. 86 n.), basing his assumption on the debates. While perhaps he might be so termed during the first session of the officers' parliament, during the convention he appears as a whig holding office, not at all averse to the court in the sense that Foley and Harley were to be.

election results and the royal will, for Powle apparently exacerbated party conflicts.[6] Furthermore, his seat was controverted and the house was subsequently to affirm the findings of the committee of elections against him.[7]

Sir John Trevor was his successor. A cousin of Judge Jeffreys and elected Speaker with the crown's support in 1685, he was considered unscrupulous and his readiness to accept bribes came to prove his undoing.[8] With considerable justification opposition lampoonists asserted that Trevor's squint was the result of the oblique view he took from the chair; it being said that he acknowledged only court proponents.[9]

Only by following a number of the intricate parliamentary debates recorded in Narcissus Luttrell's copious abstract does one begin to realize the Speaker's subtle and insidious power. Trevor's bias was less tory than it was court. He was thought to show the gravest bias in financial matters and after reading the king's speeches during the officers' parliament one might well suppose that little else was of importance. On one occasion after a court success over estimates in committee, Lowther, wishing to capitalize on the victory, moved that the Speaker leave the chair so that the house might resolve itself into a committee of ways and means. The Speaker's order for the noes to go forth was considered unfair as it put them at a procedural disadvantage; owing to inertia, both physical and psychological, to stay was obviously easier than to go out. The Speaker's decision was disputed, and as a debate seemed imminent, Lowther was forced to withdraw his motion.[10] Similarly, the next session, the court attempted to bring a vote of supply before advice on the grounds that it was not a specific supply vote but a general one, and thus the equivalent of a vote of confidence in the

---

[6] The high-churchman, Charles Hatton, noted that he cleverly averted an almost indefinite postponement of the comprehension bill–(Hatton believed the bill destructive to the church of England by aiding the 'fanaticks'). To Visc. Hatton, 9 April 1689. *Correspondence of the Family of Hatton*, E. M. Thompson, ed. (Camden Soc., 1878), ii, 128–9.

[7] His seat was taken by Jack Howe, at the time a fervent court supporter.

[8] *H.C.J.*, x, 347. He was conducted to the chair by Lowther and Goodricke. Carmarthen's lieutenant, Goodricke, is listed as opposing exclusion, and both spoke for the court in debates. Both he and Lowther are listed on the three place lists for this parliament and neither are listed as supporting the partisan party measures of the convention.

[9] A. I. Dasent, *The Speakers of the House of Commons* (1911), pp. 229–30.

[10] 28 November 1691. Luttrell, Abstract MSS., i, f. 87. A motion for the house to resolve itself into a committee of supply passed in the negative. *H.C.J.*, x, 566.

government. Failing in this, the court tried to make the day for considering the question as early as possible. Paul Foley unwittingly helped by suggesting the subsequent Friday. Sir Christopher Musgrave, noticing Foley's slip, was quick to come to his assistance by proposing the following Tuesday. A dispute followed over which date should be put first, the court holding that Foley's should be, whether he still approved of it or not. In questions of supply the rule was that the day furthest off should be first put; but the Speaker waived this rule to the court's advantage on the ground that it was only a general vote of supply and did not therefore involve a charge upon the people. For the opposition, Sir Thomas Clarges argued that Trevor was wrong because any vote of supply was a charge upon the people. Still, it was only after Lord Castleton frightened the court by speaking against the effect of placemen in commons proceedings that the question was decided in favour of the country party without dissent.[11] A little over a month later there was a debate on the time of meeting for the committee of ways and means to deal with the land tax; the opposition first moved for Friday, the court for Wednesday. Luttrell notes that '...the Speaker irregularly of his own head without its being moved...' put the previous question, namely whether the question of Friday should be put, and then went on 'contrary to order' to have the yeas go out, '...whereas the noes ought who were agt. dispatch of businesse in this question'. On division, the court won, but Clarges noted two irregularities: firstly, that the Speaker had put the question himself without its being moved; secondly, that he had ordered the yeas to go forth. Nevertheless the order stood for Wednesday.[12]

Less than a fortnight later, the militia bill was referred to a private committee, although it was strictly a money bill and thus should have been referred to a committee of the whole house. Sir Christopher Musgrave protested and Luttrell thought him in the right, since to refer the matter to committee was indeed 'the sense of the house', but it was passed, 'unretractable'[13]—largely, it would appear, owing to the Speaker's authority.

---

[11] Luttrell, Abstract MSS., ii, ff. 32–4. *H.C.J.*, x, 700.

[12] 23 December 1692. Luttrell, Abstract MSS., ii, 221. The vote was 200 to 119. Col. Granville and [Paul] Foley were minority tellers while Sir John Guise and Clarke were tellers for the court majority. *H.C.J.* x, 767–8.

[13] 2 January 1692/3. Luttrell, Abstract MSS., ii, ff. 235–6. *H.C.J.*, x, 767. Luttrell noted that all who came were to have voices, which thus enlarged the committee.

In mid-January, the Speaker averted what could have been a very unpleasant situation when the opposition alleged that the court had tampered with the bill concerning royal mines. Sir Christopher Musgrave and others stated that one Mr Prinn '...took the bill home with him and made amendments to it' after it was reported, and that he would be 'kindly used if not expelled'. The Speaker came to the court's rescue claiming that the bill was but the duplicate of the original. Nevertheless the house is said to have 'resented it very much'.[14]

Subsequently, after a series of court victories, Sir Edward Seymour (then of the court) proposed in a rather thin house that the time for continuing tonnage and poundage should be enlarged, as it would allow easier borrowing for the waging of a vigorous war against France. He asked the house to resolve itself into a committee. When the Speaker stated his question and added a fixed date (a near one too, namely, 'tomorrow'), 'Sir Christopher Musgrave checkt him very severely [for this] as being contrary to the duty of the chair...' and declaimed against the lateness both in the day as well as the consequent thinness of the house. His words had their effect; only the proposer assented to the question, even though two placemen, Lowther and Hampden, supported it earlier.[15]

The Speaker used his influence even in the sacred domain of constitutional reform. During a complicated debate regarding the treason trials bill, the question arose whether or not to hold a free conference with the lords over amendments to the bill. The more determined of the opposition were in favour, as a free conference would assist the bill's passage. The Speaker interpreted the commons' privileges in such a way as to hinder inter-house agreement and was considered to have exceeded his authority in debating house privileges. Musgrave and Clarges[6] '...took him down to the orders of the house, for he ought not to debate any matter whatsoever'. Despite their arguments he persisted, as a member of the opposition excused him. Aided by the solicitor-general, Trevor produced further arguments against a conference.[16]

The next year, Sir William Whitlocke requested leave to bring in a similar measure. Sir Thomas Clarges seconded Whitlocke's motion,

---

[14] 16 January. Luttrell, Abstract MSS., ii, 269–70. *H.C.J.* 779. Prinn was possibly an assistant clerk of the commons.

[15] 23 February. Luttrell. Abstract MSS., ii, ff. 391–2.

[16] *Ibid.*, i, ff. 198–200. On this issue the commons narrowly agreed with the speaker against having a conference with the lords, the vote being 139–110. Gwyn and Bertie were minority tellers. *H.C.J.*, x, 615.

wishing to have it read at once, and asked the clerk to present a copy of the previous session's bill. The Speaker found it irregular to bring it in without leave, but Clarges, supported by Sir Joseph Tredenham, called his demand a 'new way and an innovation' as leave was needed only in money bills; moreover, the house had seen the bill before. This time the opposition succeeded, and it was soon ordered a second reading.[17]

Trevor helped to avoid censorship of crown policy. In the autumn of 1692, during the aforementioned great debate regarding admiralty affairs, the commons' committee chairman divided its advice on report, which Luttrell considered to be a 'blunder'; Trevor artfully exploiting this divided statement of advice by making the subtle distinction between positive resolutions on the one hand and motions on the other. According to the rules of procedure, to vote in favour of what was only a committee motion one had to go out to be counted; which, as noted, was a tactical disadvantage. To vote in favour of a positive resolution one simply remained. Not surprisingly, the chief reform, namely that the king '...constitute a Commission of the Admiralty of such Persons as are of Experience in Maritime affairs', Trevor found to be a mere motion. On the question being put, those in favour of the reform were of course obliged to go out, which brought defeat by twenty-three votes.[18]

In mid-March 1695, Paul Foley, reporting from the committee appointed to inspect the books of both the East India Company and the chamberlain of London, disclosed that Trevor had taken a bribe of a thousand guineas for assisting the passage of the orphans' bill. He absented himself from the house and was found guilty of a high crime and misdemeanour.[19] Many country members voted as they did, not merely because Trevor accepted bribes, but because they knew that he distributed them on behalf of the court.[20] The junto whigs probably agitated more strongly than anyone for his removal and his expulsion provided them with excellent propaganda for their pamphlets in the

---

[17] 11 November 1692. Luttrell, Abstract MSS., ii, ff. 10–11. *H.C.J.*, x, 698.

[18] 11 January 1692/3. The vote was 112 to 135. *H.C.J.*, x, 775. 'All the persons in office and generally the whig party were agt. this question wch was much wondered at.' Luttrell, Abstract MSS., ii, f. 263.

[19] *H.C.J.*, xi, 269–71. Trevor was alleged to have demanded twice that amount. *Ibid.*, pp. 269–70.

[20] Even Burnet admits that the speaker, with the king's approbation, bought off opposition members. *Own Times*, iv, 76.

following general election.[21] Nevertheless, the country party soon appeared by no means desirous of following these new court allies any further. The day after the vote of condemnation, it was proposed that a new Speaker be chosen at once. There were delays, however, occasioned by quibbles over the need for a mace, and in the early afternoon the clerk, who had temporarily taken the chair, moved to adjourn until the following morning.[22] On the king's behalf the next day, Goodwin Wharton declared that Trevor could no longer attend owing to indisposition and that they should select a new Speaker. When he then nominated Littleton on what many assumed to be the king's request, he was met with cries of 'no, no, no', with several members outspokenly objecting that it was the commons' right to nominate its own Speaker. After Goodricke seconded Littleton's nomination, disagreements ensued and Musgrave and Lord Digby proposed Foley. After a long debate the clerk put the question for Littleton and declared that the ayes had it. Upon division it was found that they did not, by thirty-three votes.[23]

Foley attempted to speak, probably genuinely to decline the nomination, but was shouted down; the question being put, he was elected without dissent.[24] The court had failed.

PLACEMEN II

The best answer to the problem of court influence was a direct one. The 'self-denying bill', introduced in December 1692, stipulated that in the future no office holder would be capable of election, while those members subsequently accepting office were to lose their seats.[25] Speaking for the court on the third reading, Sir John Lowther cleverly based his line of attack not upon the danger of diminishing the royal prerogative, but rather that of the commons. The bill's passage, he argued, would lead the king to appoint ministers exclusively from the lords.

---

[21] See p. 59–60 n.   [22] *H.C.J.*, xi, 271.

[23] *Ibid.*, ix, 272. The vote was 146 to 179. Col. Granville was majority teller and James Chadwicke for the court minority. It is difficult to tell whether the clerk's apparent bias clinched Littleton's rejection. Foley's local influence gained him the votes of all the Worcestershire and Herefordshire members. Feiling, *Tory Party*, p. 309.

[24] *H.C.J.*, vi, 272. Col. Granville and Henry Boyle conducted him to the chair, which was assumed after the usual formal protests.

[25] *H.M.C. Lords, 1692–3*, pp. 279–80. Those elected before 1 February 1692/3 were to be excepted during the continuation of that parliament.

His argument that peers would be reluctant to give up this right[26] probably led to the support shown for Boscowen's later amendment limiting the duration of the bill to a period of years, That the amendment failed 'clearly' on the second reading[27] seems indicative that many country gentlemen thought it mattered little who the ministers were or where they came from; the constitution was in need of permament rather than temporary reform. Sir Edward Seymour's arguments that the court would simply be reduced to 'more close connivances' and that the house might pass its own resolution forbidding members to hold office were evidently thought unworthy of an answer:[28] the discretion required for 'closer connivances' would probably at least reduce the numbers supporting the court; a self-denying ordinance would clearly be neither as effective nor as permanent as an act. Subsequently, the court argued that the bill would make the present parliament almost interminable, since the king would be most reluctant to dissolve such a well officered gathering, as he would have less influence over a new one. But the opposition was soon to provide against this option, much to the court's chagrin, with a bill limiting the length of parliaments. The chief argument for the bill was succinctly put by Paul Foley, who believed the measure '...the only way to prevent corruption in this house, 'tis no new thing to see a man encline one way and when he is once gott into a place to goe another way.'[29] Although passing the commons that day, and in the lords having a majority of two voices, it had four less proxies, thus failing by two votes.[30] Edward Harley and others blamed the loss on the court's influence, the episcopal bench coming in for special censure.[31] Certainly the court's narrow escape was but a Pyrrhic victory. Twenty lords had protested,[32] and the earl of Mulgrave's

---

[26] Luttrell, Abstract MSS., ii, ff. 217–19. Tollet wrote to Bishop King on 22 December 1692 that the lords would not oppose the bill as the commons were '...after some sort excluded from the ministry.' T.C.D. MSS. 122/251.

[27] *H.C.J.*, x, 760. Luttrell, Abstract MSS., ii, f. 219.　　[28] *Ibid.*, f. 218.

[29] Luttrell, Abstract MSS., ii, f. 218.

[30] *H.C.J.*, x, 761. *H.L.J.*, xv, 171–2.

[31] To Sir Edward Harley, 7 January 1692/3. *H.M.C. Portland*, iii, 511. In a manuscript pamphlet it was said that although the bill would probably not be too effectual, the court could not even stand the '...name of an impartial Parliamt.' 'A Speech which was Intended to have been spoken by Mr John Smith, A member of the house of Commons, on Saturday, the eight and twentieth day of January 1692/3 upon occasion of the Triennial Bill, and by Changing his Coat was unfortunately left at home in his Pocket'. (Hereafter cited as 'Smith's Intended Speech'). Chic. Univ. Lib., Misc. Eng. MSS.

[32] *H.L.J.*, xv, 172.

powerful speech advocating passage was published and widely circulated.[33]

In November, Harley was commissioned to draw up a 'Report of
Sums Issued for Secret Service, And Paid to Members of Parliament',
which was to make court influence seem as widespread as during the
reign of Charles II.[34] A number of pamphlets also appeared about this
time and helped to fan the flames.[35] A place bill similar to the previous
year's quickly passed the commons although the lords amended it to
allow placemen subsequently re-elected in a by-election after receiving
office to resume their seats.[36] Because of this proviso Macaulay and
others have considered the bill almost useless.[37] But if this was the case,
one is tempted to ask why the commons accepted the lords' amendment
and the king refused his assent.[38] One cause for both the bill's progress
and the verdict of the whig historians may be found in the very substantial changes being effected amongst the placeholders to the advantage of the junto, but certainly to most country members a more
moderate place bill was better than none at all. Indeed, a similar proviso
was included in the place act of 1705 and about one-quarter of the new
office holders were not returned.[39]

The king's use of his negative voice did not go unchallenged. Only
a few members dared dissent from a commons' committee resolution
condemning anyone who advised the veto as '...an enemy to their
Majesties and the kingdom' and the report received the commons un-
divided approval.[40] While the debate was dominated by such present
and future members of the commission of accounts as Clarges, Harley,
Hutchinson, Thompson and Bromley, two tory placemen (Sir John
Lowther and the younger Peregrine Bertie) evidently felt compelled to
speak for it, and only one (John Brewer) dared oppose it.[41]

---

[33] Cobbett, v, 751.   [34] *Ibid.*, p. 807.

[35] Such as the 'Hush Money Paper'. *Ibid.*, vol. v., app. ix.

[36] *H.M.C. Lords, 1693–5*, pp. 330–1.   [37] Macaulay, v, 2422.

[38] *H.M.C. Lords, 1693–5*, p. 331. *H.L.J.*, xv, 351. It should be noted that
the lords retreated from their clause concerning the Speaker although a protest was signed by Rochester and the Bishop of London on 5 January 1693/4.

[39] Betty Kemp, *King and Commons*, p. 149. In the parliament of 1715–22, 25
out of 107 were not re-elected; in the subsequent parliament, 16 out of 62.

[40] Cobbett, v, 829. 26 January 1693/4. *H.C.J.*, xi, 71.

[41]Cobbett, v. 829–30. John Brewer, M.P. New Romney, is listed on Samuel
Grascombe's place list as col. of a regt. of foot. Peregrine Bertie, jun., M.P.,
Boston, Lincs., was 2nd son of Robert, earl of Lindsey, and vice-chamberlain.
He is also included on an opposition list of December 1694. Lowther, a lord
of the treasury, needs no further introduction.

The next year, however, neither king nor lords needed openly to show their hand. The bill survived the second reading by only twenty-two votes[42] and whig attempts to resurrect the Sacheverell clause as an amendment were defeated on the third reading. After almost three months of what must have been deliberate delays to lower country attendance, it was lost 175–142.[43]

While the country party was for a time thwarted in its direct attack upon placemen, effective if indirect challenges played a large role in damping their influence throughout the reign. Attempts were made to reduce the number of crown offices and make them both less profitable and desirable, which would as a corollary increase the probability of a member maintaining his independence. During the war, efforts aimed at the reduction of offices could only be implemented negatively, spasmodically and rather ineffectively by preventing the creation of new ones.[44] Designs to lower crown salaries were, however, a different matter; in 1691 for example, the commons resolved to limit all but a few crown offices to only £500 a year.[45] For a member to accept a place came increasingly to mean being branded, usually by being included in opposition placelists, harassed in debate and, depending on one's outspokenness, vilified in lampoons.[46] Evidently most country gentlemen thought that if life, liberty and property were to be included among an Englishman's rights, place was not.

---

[42] The vote of 28 November 1694 was 138–116. *H.C.J.*, xi, 179.

[43] 20 February 1694/5. *H.C.J.*, xi, 238.

[44] An example is provided in the debate of December 1691 over the bill for registering servants. Sir Christopher Musgrave led in the argument against the bill, saying that it only intended to prevent kidnapping, its real function being but to create an office for Sir John Thompson to add another member to the court side. The court was ineffectual in arguing against the bill, losing by a wide margin (90–29) despite Thompson's help and a thin house. 16 December 1691, Luttrell, Abstract MSS., i, f. 144. *H.C.J.*, x, 589. Sir John Thompson had spoken on the country side but had more recently been silent. Several years after failing to gain this post he had regained enough confidence from the country members to become a commissioner of accounts and but two years after that won enough confidence from the king to be created Baron Haversham. After the war more positive steps were taken to reduce the number of offices. For Thompson's politics see appendix B.

[45] Cobbett, v, 681–2.

[46] Sir Christopher Musgrave said of the placemen, Sir Rowland Gwynne (M.P., Co. Radnor and Treas. of the King's chamber) that he '...hath a curious badg [badge] fixt upon his back which will shine over the world.' In a letter to Robert Harley, 18 April 1692. *H.M.C. Portland*, iii, 49.

THE TRIENNIAL ACT

The most effectual of the indirect attacks upon placemen was the act necessitating frequent periodic elections, which came to have a profound influence upon the court's plans. During the last session of the 1695 parliament Portland and the king were corresponding over the difficulty of effecting the royal programme, William believing that all the members were trying to '...court popular favour for the elections of the new parliament', while Portland said plainly that the cause of all the trouble was the triennial act.[47] The court was to proceed warily and not divide the house over constitutional issues which would expose '...all those that in any way depend on the king to the Animosity of the Country Gentleman...'.[48] For once, many placemen found their seats in greater jeopardy than their offices. Even those returned were to face such extensive 'garbelling' that some wondered if it had been worth the bother.[49]

Little wonder then that frequent elections were thought a necessary corollary to place bills. The first place bill, introduced in December 1692, was not retroactive, so placemen then sitting would retain their seats. For this reason George Tollet (clerk to the parliamentary commission of accounts) saw the bill as the prologue to the longest parliament in history, believing it would be '...perpetual, well near, for the king to preserve a party in the House will not dissolve it'. After a dissolution he believed the court party might also all but dissolve as '...few will speak in favour of the court within these walls (otherwise than of right they ought) when there is no prospect of imployments.'[50]

An answer was clearly required to the problem of interminable parliaments. While the bill of rights stated that 'Parliaments ought to be held frequently', it was left to the king to decide whether this meant frequent elections or simply frequent sessions.[51] In November 1689, a bill was brought into the lords designed to repeal the triennial act of 1664 (which had effected but triennial sessions) and revive the more robust measures of 1641. The matter was thought to require special

---

[47] William to Portland, 27 February/8 March 1697/8. Portland to William, 3/13 March 1697/8. P. Grimblot, ed., *Letters of William III and of their Ministers...1697–1700*, i, 212 and 226.

[48] Jo. Methuen to (Ld Galway), 8 January 1697/8. Blenheim, Sunderland Letter Book. Methuen says he was among those who defected.

[49] See below, chapter viii, pp. 283–4.

[50] To Bishop King, 22 December 1692. T.C.D. MSS. 1122/251.

[51] 1 William and Mary, sess, 2, c. 2.

treatment[52] and a new bill, vast in both scope and detail, ensuring compliance with parliament's wishes, was brought in designed to effect new parliaments every three years. Elections within a year following the dissolution were virtually guaranteed and a new parliament was to be neither dissolved nor prorogued without its own consent until fifty days after convening. Other clauses ensured the requisite elections and parliamentary meetings even if the government failed to issue the usual orders. Finally, the present parliament was to terminate by 29 August, 1691.[53] In this last aim only did the king quickly, if perversely, fulfil parliament's desires with a prorogation and subsequent dissolution.

The new parliament made no significant attempts to tackle the problem for several years; a delay which seems partially explicable from the proximity of the past election which made reform seem less necessary. In addition, the reformers were not united over the question of just how radical the bill should be. In January 1692, Shrewsbury proposed a bill for *annual* elections in the lords as a corollary to the aforementioned place bill.[54] After its second reading Robert Harley wrote sadly that the bill '…met with great difficulty there at the comtt [committee] and is much altered.' The alterations made the bill effect triennial parliaments with annual sessions and even then there was no compulsory clause annexed. Even though the bill passed the lords and was 'much altered', Harley still had fears for its future: '…when it comes down to the commons we shall see whither this be a long parliament or no.'[55]

In the commons the court tried to defeat the bill by employing arguments appealing to various sympathies. Attempting to arouse country sentiment and cause inter-house rivalry by exploiting the seat of the bill's origin, it was said that the peers took it upon themselves to limit the length of the present parliament. Tory feelings were appealed to by emphasizing the limitations the bill imposed upon the royal prerogative while the argument that passage of the bill was inexpedient in wartime was of course aimed especially at the whigs.

The last two arguments were quickly dispatched in a rebuttal. Sir Christopher Musgrave argued that the war was a very good reason to

---

[52] *H.M.C. Lords, 1689–90*, pp. 343–4.

[53] *Ibid.*, pp. 364–77. The proposed bill is about 10,000 words long. The cause and timing of the dissolution would have effected the date of an election.

[54] 12 January 1692/3 *H.L.J.*, xv, 181. For the lords' amendments and other actions see *H.M.C. Lords, 1692–3*, pp. 299–302.

[55] To Sir E. Harley, 17 January 1692/3. B.M. Portland Loan 29/187. The lords would have fixed 1 January 1693/4 as the date of dissolution.

proceed with rather than drop the bill to ensure the impartiality of members who were voting such considerable war supplies. Elections were said, moreover, to cause little disruption as prorogations kept parliaments from sitting continuously in any case. Then too, the bill was not a diminution of the prerogative, for the prerogative could not but be glorified by a measure which was an aid to the people. Harley, recalling the pensioners' parliament of Charles II, argued rather more realistically that prerogative was but too easily equated with arbitrary power.[56]

The greater part of the defence was applied to damp down the fires of jealousy caused by the bill's origin in the lords. The peers, it was reasoned, were perhaps atoning for their previous rejection of a similar bill;[57] with the exception of money bills, any bill might be sent between the two houses. The support of the moderate country leaders probably secured passage; Harley arguing that the bill was so essential that it should be passed despite its deplorable origins; Foley noting that the commons could change the termination date of the present parliament.[58]

The court's arguments answered, the opposition proceeded to the offensive. While some said that even a standing army was preferable to a standing parliament,[59] Harley took a more traditional approach, finding it to be but a revival of earlier acts which had been wrongly interpreted to require triennial sessions rather than triennial elections.[60] Notice was taken of the placemen who had spoken in favour of the bill[61]—and of some former country members who did not. In a descriptively entitled manuscript pamphlet serving to distinguish those placemen supporting the court's financial but not its constitutional programme, words are put in the mouth of the recently quiet but formerly outspoken country member, Jack Smith. In the speech (alleged to have been left at home because of changing his coat), Smith is made to say that although bribed by the court to keep quiet and '...allways to propagate money bills yet this [the question of frequent parliaments] is a

---

[56] Cobbett, v, 755–60.

[57] Probably the lords' rejection of the place bill is meant here. *H.L.J.*, xv, 172.

[58] Cobbett, v, 760–2. The termination date was lengthened by several months to 25 March 1694. Report of committee on 9 February 1692/3. *H.C.J.*, x, 809.

[59] Cobbett, v, 760–2.   [60] Luttrell, Abstract MSS., ii, 309.

[61] B. Bradbury to T. Wharton, 28 January 1692/3. Bodl. Carte MSS., 79 f. 475.

case that would make a cat speak.'[62] Although the court cat had Smith's tongue, the country party succeeded in diminishing the likelihood of such happenings in the future; the bill was ordered a second reading 210–132.[63]

While on that occasion the court only reiterated most of its former arguments, the opposition became more vicious, making outspoken attacks upon the ministry's corrupting influence which produced an increasingly rotten parliament. The bill was committed without a division.[64] Perhaps it was the lengthy debate[65] which caused Harley to be pessimistic and discount any country optimism as being rather facile. His fears that the court would make a vigorous attempt to obstruct, clog and delay the bill in committee[66] were shortly to prove well founded.

Although Foley did not succeed in adding a place clause,[67] the bill might have caused a far greater diminution of the royal prerogative than has generally been supposed; it was intended to require parliaments to last exactly three years, that is, not only no more than three years, but *no less* as well. As with the proviso of the act of settlement of 1701 regarding the time of commencement for the exclusion of all placemen from the commons,[68] the wording of the bill is ambiguous as it provided that no future parliament '...shall have any continuance longer than for three years *only at the furthest*.' That a difference is meant

---

[62] 'Smith's Intended Speech', Chic. Univ. Lib., Misc. Eng. MSS. John or Jack Smith sat for Ludgershall, Wilts. in 1679, 1681 and 1689, and Beeralston from December 1691. He was outspokenly against the court at first but then was sworn of the privy council in 1695 and became a lord of the treasury in the latter part of William's reign. He is not included in any of the placelists before 1695 but is clearly one of those thought bribed and waiting for an opportune time to accept a place.

[63] 28 January 1692/3, *H.C.J.*, x, 796. The majority tellers were Pelham and Harley.

[64] 2 February 1692/3. Cobbett v. 763–8. Misdated in Cobbett as 9 February. *Ibid.*, p. 763. *H.C.J.*, x, 802.

[65] R. Harley to Sir E. Harley, 2 February 1692/3, B.M. Portland loan, 29/187.

[66] In a letter of 4 [February] 1692/3, Robert Harley wrote to his father that '...the others think it [the triennial bill] sure wch is to me without grounds, and observed the art this day of putting it off from Monday to Friday.' (Harley dated the letter 4 January 1692/3 but internal evidence indicates that this is clearly a mistake).

[67] 28 January. Luttrell, Abstract MSS., ii, f. 310.

[68] See below, p. 176.

by the inclusion of the word 'only' would be indicated by the fact that it is not included in the clause requiring the king to call a new parliament 'one year at the furthest' following a dissolution,[69] which thus allows the king to hold a new parliament at any time up to a year. The same wording in regard to triennial determinations was employed in the triennial act of 1694[70] and its ambiguity is probably what permitted the king to flaunt it so blatantly in November 1701 when he dissolved a parliament which had sat for less than ten months. Certainly elucidation favourable to the court was thought necessary when, in the reign of George I, it phrased the septennial act to read that parliaments '...shall and may have continuance for seven Years, and no longer... unless... sooner dissolved...'[71] Sir John Lowther failed in the attempt to delete the three-year termination proviso by only seven votes, its supporters arguing that its omission would destroy the bill's efficacy. Harley wrote that despite the bill being '...very short...every clause admitted a debate of many Houers; after much struggle and several divisions it was carried by 11.'[72] Although only several words of amendment were added, and the termination date of the present parliament lengthened a year,[73] the court was able to continue its obstruction by postponing the committee's report.[74] Not without reason had the courtiers employed farfetched arguments and almost unprecedented obstruction in efforts to stop the bill,[75] for if effected as intended it would have been almost as significant a step towards the undermining of the executive power as the American practice of biennial congressional elections.

In lengthy speeches[76] on the third reading, the court roundly condemned annual sessions and parliaments of exactly three years' duration as an unjustified diminution of the royal prerogative, which they found

---

[69] *H.M.C. Lords, 1692–3*, pp. 301–2. Italics added. The unsuccessful bill of 1689, as has been noted, would have required sessions to last at least fifty days.

[70] 6 and 7 William and Mary, c. 2.

[71] 1 George I, c. 28.

[72] To Sir E. Harley, 7 February 1692/3, B.M. Portland loan 29/187. The clause for annual sessions was left in by a vote of 179–168.

[73] R. Harley to Sir E. Harley, 7 February 1692/3. B.M. Portland loan 29/187.

[74] Luttrell, Abstract MSS., ii, f. 336

[75] An example of them may be found in Sir John Lowther's objections to annual sessions when he stated that such a clause might allow the lords to keep the commons sitting until they agreed to a measure increasing the lords' prerogative. Luttrell, Abstract MSS., ii, f. 331.

[76] Rev. G(eorge) B(radbury) to Thomas Wharton, 9 February 1692/3. Bodl. Carte MSS, 79 f. 483.

especially foolhardy in wartime.[77] The country party made its defence
brief, Harley leading in the rebuttal with a fierce attack upon the grievance of standing parliaments.[78] The bill passing the commons by a vote
of 200–161 and the commons' amendments being approved by the
lords,[79] the grand question was, what was the king going to do with
it? Even earlier Harley had ventured doubts as to its future at Kensington,[80] and some thought that the king might well prorogue or dissolve
parliament to avoid passage.[81]

The king, probably not wishing to sour the session, was not to signify
his pleasure until what one observer called 'an artfull vote' of the lords
regarding the mutiny bill forced him to do so.[82] He rejected it. The real
gainers of the whole affair were the junto whigs, who by the bill's
success in the commons and lords were able to give the king a demon-
stration of the weakness of the ministerial tories and yet make them
appear responsible in the eyes of the country gentlemen for this refusal.[83]
These rather contradictory reasons partially account for the junto's rise
to power.[84] If Shrewsbury would have nothing to do with the ministry
unless the king passed the triennial bill, a price which William is said
to have found too high,[85] other whigs now took a different view. Indeed, one of the desired outcomes of the turning towards the junto
ministers in the summer of 1693 was to have the triennial bill 'laid
asleep'.[86] While this was of course not to be the case for long, the whig
defections were so extensive that Shrewsbury came to believe no party
remained which was in accord with his views.[87]

Some suggested countering the king's refusal by tacking the triennial

---

[77] Luttrell, Abstract MSS., ii, ff. 342–3.   [78] *Ibid.*, pp. 342–4.

[79] 9 February 1692/3, *H.C.J.*, x, 809. 10 February, *H.C.J.*, xv, 223.

[80] R. Harley to Sir E. Harley, 7 February B.M. Portland Loan 29/187.

[81] [Henry North to Sancroft], 27 February and 13 March. Bodl. Tanner
MSS., 25 ff. 8 and 10.

[82] C. Laty to James II, 8 March. *Cal. S.P. Dom.*, pp. 60–1. The lords
made it clear that the mutiny bill was not retroactive thus forcing the king to
signify his pleasure to the new mutiny bill and all preceding bills, including
the triennial bill.

[83] See the whig pamphlet: *An Enquiry; or a Discourse between a Yeoman of
Kent, and a Knight of the Shire, upon the Prorogation of the Parliament to the second
of May, 1693. (1693).*   [84] See Luttrell, *Brief Relation*, iii, 65.

[85] Sir Chas. Hatton to Visc. Hatton, 9 November 1693. *Hatton Corr.*, ii, 198.

[86] Sunderland Memoirs of June 1693, annotated by Portland, N.U.L.
PwA 1219.

[87] Shrewsbury to Mrs E. Villiers, 2nd December 1963, W. Coxe ed.,
Correspondence of Charles Talbot, Duke of Shrewsbury...(1821), p. 26.

bill to a money bill.[88] Such advice was soon to prove as useless as it was brazen, for a new bill was never to leave the commons. In mid-November 1693 a bill for biennial parliaments was moved although some believed that a triennial bill was first called for.[89] All went well enough until the third reading, when a debate occurred over substituting the word 'declare' for 'holden'. The country party, led by Harley and Musgrave, fought for this change, arguing that although it might appear to be but a quibble, the word 'declare' ensured annual sessions whereas 'holden' did not.[90] Apparently the country party was caught off guard: the clause was rejected by a vote of 129–89 and then, the court seemingly finding its strength and the country side not quite gathering sufficient forces in time, the bill thrown out 146–136.[91]

A triennial bill was read the first time by the lords three days after this defeat.[92] The bill's opponents appear to have been led by such high churchmen as Abingdon and Nottingham, who simply argued that the king had rejected it for sound reasons the previous year.[93] When the bill came down, there was also a considerable dispute over the words 'holden' and 'declare', the former being not only chosen, but elucidated to make it perfectly clear that no act, judgment or statute need pass at the meeting to make it constitute a session. It was this clog that caused the tory bishop of St David's to observe that the real obstruction had come from the court, for '...all those who were against the bill were for it and some others as the Lord [Monmouth] and all the bishops except one [himself?].'[94] The attempt to delete the clause in the commons failed again, this time by a vote of 222 to 131,[95] the bill itself being subsequently rejected 197–127.[96]

The court had exploited the distaste to do measures by halves. The failure to include the annual sessions clause had again ensured half-

---

[88] Some Electors of Members of Parliament, *A Letter to the Members of Parliament for the Country of...Concerning the Triennial Bill* (1693).

[89] Sir Chas. Littleton to Visc. Hatton 15 November 1693. *Hatton Corr.* See the letter of Sir E. Harley to Abigail Harley of 14 November 1693 praising Robert's speech. *H.M.C. Portland*, iii, 548–9. *H.C.J.*, xi, 3.

[90] 28 November 1693. Cobbett, v, 787. *H.C.J.*, xi, 13.

[91] *Ibid.*   [92] *H.L.J.*, xv, 311.

[93] (Dykvelt) Dispatch, 28 November/8 December 1693. *H.M.C. Denbigh*, p. 216.

[94] To Theophilus, seventh earl of Huntingdon, 9 December 1693. *H.M.C. Hastings*, ii, 234. 8 December 1692. *H.L.J.*, xv, 317.

[95] *H.C.J.*, xi, 40. Col. Granville and Sir Rowland Gwyn were minority tellers, Jack Smith and Bickerstaffe for the court majority.   [96] *Ibid.*

hearted support if not opposition from the more radical and idealistic country members. In addition, the bill faced conditions similar to the unsuccessful placebill of the same session. The court party was in a state of transition: many court-tories apparently voted as the king wished in the hope of staying in office; many would-be court-whigs in the hope of getting in. It was thought that the king made a signal example of Lord Mordaunt, who was deprived of his offices for having proposed the bill in the lords.[97]

Whip letters hurried country members to town for the opening of the next session, for then, as Paul Foley wrote to Robert Harley, '…will be the tryal of what you hint at.'[98] What Harley hinted at was quite clearly the triennial bill, the country party appearing determined upon passage. The opening of the session was six days later than expected and even then parliament was adjourned several more days.[99] It has been conjectured that the delays allowed time for the king and opposition leaders to strike a bargain over the triennial bill and it would appear that the king agreed to acquiesce at the time in order to gain their support for a bill of supply.[100]

But would the bill ever even pass the commons? Shortly after the opening, a list was circulated among opposition leaders of what appear to be supporters of the triennial bill.[101] Fifty, or between a quarter and a

---

[97] Chas. Hatton to Visc. Hatton, 6 February 1693/4. *Hatton Corr.*, ii, 200.

[98] 17 September 1694. B.M. Portland loan 29/187. The letter also urges Harley to make sure that 'our old Northerne Gentleman', i.e. Sir Christopher Musgrave, was in town for the opening of parliament.

[99] Ralph, in Cobbett, v, 860–1.

[100] Burnet called the supply bill the 'price or bargain' for the king's approval. *Own Times*, iv. 238. Ralph finds Burnet's suspicion confirmed by the fact '…that the first material order of the house, after adjournment, was for Mr Harley to prepare and bring in the said bill.' Cobbett, v, 860.

[101] The list appears to be written in the hand of Henry St John and is among Sir William Trumbull's papers in the Berkshire Record Office, Trumbull Add. MSS. 13/68. Although the list is not dated, Thomas Foley Jr., and the Hon. Philip Bertie were returned on 21 November and 6 December 1694. John Hungerford was expelled on 26 March 1695. Bertie is referred to vaguely, as the vice-chamberlain's brother, and as there were a number of Berties sitting, the author may have confused the name or thought him there when he was not. (See Browning, *Danby*, vol. iii, for the many examples which are given of this mistake.) Alternatively the list may have been written in expectation of a conflict with the lords. The statement that some members are not yet up, indicates that it was written at the beginning of the session, probably in late-November or early December. Indebtedness is expressed to Dr H. G. Horwitz for mentioning the existence of this list.

third, of the 171 members listed were placemen,[102] thus constituting about two-fifths of all the placemen. To account for this large minority, it should be remembered both that placemen were more likely to be in London when the list was compiled,[103] and that the court appears to have brought less pressure to bear upon placemen in matters of constitutional reform compared to matters of finance. The country gentlemen, of course, reversed the emphasis, bringing special condemnation upon those who betrayed what they believed to be ancient constitutional principles.

By comparing the number of placemen sitting in the last session who are also included in the placelist compiled before December 1692, the placemen in opposition may be constituted into the distinct groups of older and newer placemen in a two to one ratio. This proportion is almost in harmony with the tory-whig three to two ratio of the 69 members in opposition who both sat in the convention and opposed making William and Mary king and queen.[104] The consequent assumption that the newer placemen were far more amenable to court wishes and less independent would be reinforced by the overwhelming evidence that the king and his new junto ministers were by dismissals and appointments making the hardcore of the court party both harder and larger. As the efficacy of this plan became increasingly apparent, the repeated failures of the place and triennial bills of the previous sessions probably reinforced memories of the long parliament of Charles II. A sense of urgency prevailed in December 1694, for the longer the bill was put off, the more difficult it would be to secure passage. The displaced tory officeholders might retire to the country and more new whig placemen would find time to make a change of conscience seem more respectable. The present times were as auspicious as they would ever be. The weariness of long attendance, thought to have changed the minds of many who were formerly against the bill,[105] was compounded by the aforementioned leavening effect of a large number of half-hearted placemen.

---

[102] See chamber appendix A.

[103] Apparently he includes only those who were in London, thus omitting some from the distant North and West: '...many Northumberland, Cumberland, and other Northerne Friends are not yet downe; so for Shropshire, and the Western corner, who are friends likwise; and some in Dorsetshire [are] not yet downe.' *Ibid.*

[104] *Ibid.*

[105] Sir John Bland, M.P., Pontefract to Roger Kenyon, M.P., Clitheroe. 9 March. 1693/4. *H.M.C.* Kenyon, p. 289.

The need for support from at least some placemen would seem confirmed by the country party failure to maintain the clause terminating the parliament on 25 March 1695. The date was advanced a year, partly, it seems, because of the refusal of some placemen included on the opposition list to defect to the country side on this division.[106] In addition, some extremist junto whigs, led by Wharton, defied the king's wishes, and hoped to force him to call a new parliament which they hoped would be more whiggish. Montague, however, supported the later date as did many other junto whigs for fear, it seems, of incurring the royal displeasure.[107] Still, the opposition in mustering 147 votes had shown its strength and the court must have put aside any thoughts of killing the bill in parliament. There was certainly less need to do so. The committee's amendments were probably responsible for toning down the bill as it now only required triennial rather than annual sessions. The ambiguity in the phrasing requiring elections to be held exactly every three years was not clarified. The discussion and division had been smoothed over by the passage of time and the failure to be officially recorded, occurring, as it did, in committee.

The bill passed the lords unamended.[108] Would the king really approve the triennial bill, despite its more conservative nature? It seems most unlikely that Shrewsbury had accepted office the previous March without his promise that he would. But why then was William negotiating with opposition leaders for their approval of a money bill at the beginning of the session? Perhaps, of course, this was made a condition of Shrewsbury's acceptance or, alternatively, perhaps the triennial bill would have been passed regardless. Certainly this would be a more charitable interpretation than thinking that William had unfairly raised the price, but one is led to be cynical: when both the tonnage and poundage bill (the promised supply bill) and the triennial bill were before him, even his friends thought that he would renegue and pass only the money bill. In so doing he might rely on the effects of a

---

[106] Such as Samuel Travers, a teller for the court majority, the other was Jack Smith, now a model turncoat. Col. Granville and Henry Boyle were tellers for the country minority. Those supporting the clause had 147 votes but it is uncertain how many the court majority had as a misprint occurs in the commons journals. 13 December 1694. *H.C.J.*, xi, 187. Four lords protested against the bill as it continued the parliament longer than agreeable with the constitution. *H.L.J.*, xv, 447.

[107] Brandenburg dispatch, 11/21 and 14/24 December. Von Ranke, *History of England Principally in the Seventeenth Century*, vi, 256 and 258.

[108] *H.L.J.*, xv, 447.

remodelling, or quick prorogation and well-timed dissolution to secure a more malleable parliament. Circumstances beyond his control gave him little choice, for when the bills were before him, Mary was ill with the smallpox, lying on her death bed. To delay would be foolhardy and on the twenty-second of December, only six days before she died, the king assented.[109]

ELECTORAL REFORM

A period of intense electoral reform of a country nature following in the wake of the 1695 election reinforces the view that court and junto forces had scarcely been accorded a mandate. Attempts to expand their electoral influence appeared blocked, while conversely a number of new limitations were discussed, some made bills and several enacted. Admittedly, as Professor Plumb points out, they were not to have any considerable effect and corruption in the eighteenth century proceeded apace in spite of them.[110] To have really achieved its wishes, the country party would be obliged to tamper with the existing framework—let us say by increasing the number of county members, a fair enough demand considering the demography of 1700. But such a blow of the radical sword would indicate that the established electoral system was not sacrosanct and others might consequently be less inhibited in using the other side of the blade at a later date. Considering subsequent events, probably country policy was sound enough and had at least some effect for the remaining years of the reign.

Encouraging a famous candidate to stand for two or more constituencies constituted one of the more disreputable electioneering practices. This was done not, let it be hastily added, to assure the distinguished of at least one seat, but rather to keep a number of other seats temporarily vacant. Nor should the inevitability of a by-election be thought to have made the practice scarcely worth the bother. Enraged at Russell's return for three constituencies, one pamphleteer wrote that if the '...practice be suffered to pass without animadversion, a few popular men may engross half the elections of the kingdom, and at first sitting down, the parliament would be only a Rump...and before new writs could be issued out, and return'd, the great Business of the Nation

---

[109] Burnet, *Own Times*, iv, 246. Ralph in Cobbett, v. 862. *H.L.J.*, xv. 451.
[110] *The Growth of Political Stability in England*, esp. chapter III.

might be transacted by half a house.'[111] Behind this hyperbole, there is a grain of truth. If multiple elections never threatened to encompass half a house, often almost exactly half the house present might support a given court proposal and the other half oppose it. In such cases the absence of a few negative votes would prove decisive. If the grievance was not legislated against, the adverse publicity probably diminished the likelihood of the practice being developed, and aided in securing the passage of other similar bills.

Certainly such electoral tactics kept many country gentlemen from attributing any lofty motives to the effort of king and junto to effect the naturalization of French Protestants.[112] One opposition pamphleteer even argued that the presence of armed French Protestants in London was designed to increase the court's military power.[113] Although such assertions seem somewhat forced, the court might at least hope for increased electoral power.[114] Harley and Foley, for long unenthusiastic about such proposals, remained so despite repeated solicitations,[115] while the more extreme elements were articulate in their opposition. Robert Price had argued that the measure would '...bring few rich and all the poor of other countrys to make our own poorer.'[116] In the first session of the new parliament leave was not even given to bring the bill in[117] and the following year, while narrowly passing a first reading by ten votes, on the question of committal it was thrown out 168–127.[118]

---

[111] *A Letter to a Gentleman Elected a Knight of the Shire* (1695), p. 14. The complaint was reiterated in 1702 in *A Letter to a Gentleman elected to serve in the Present Parliament (1702)*.

[112] See especially the later letter of Somers to Sunderland, 5 September 1698. Blenheim, Sunderland Letter Book.

[113] There were said to be 'French Refugees in and about this city who are in full Union with their brethren in the Army; and who might well obey their countryman, the Duke of Lemster.' Ominously, he noted them to have bought considerable armaments. *A Supplement to his Majesties Speech* (1695), p. 20.

[114] See p. 186 regarding military influence in the 1698 election.

[115] E. Harley to Sir E. Harley, 20 January 1691/2. *H.M.C. Portland*, iii, 488, Anne, countess of Sunderland to Sir William Trumbull, 4 February 1695/6. *H.M.C. Downshire*, I, ii, 618.

[116] 24 February 1691/2. Luttrell, Abstract MSS., i, 352/3. R. Price to the duke of Beaufort, 1 March 1693/4. Bodl. Carte MSS. 130 f. 347. S. to s., *ibid.* 11 February 1696/7.

[117] 22 January 1695/6. *H.C.J.*, xi, 408.

[118] 22 February 1696/7. The vote was 130–120. Sir Henry Goff and William Bromley were minority tellers. *H.C.J.*, xi, 716. 2 March. Francis Gwyn and Bromley were majority tellers. *Ibid.*, p. 724.

There were a number of more positive measures enacted to aid country candidates. An act preventing electoral charges and expenses provided legal sanctions to keep the price of contest within the gentry's means.[119] If the act utterly failed to achieve its stated purpose, it did not appear so at the outset and initially there were occasions when bribery and treating were made less frequent, more difficult and less certain of permanent effect owing to the dangers of parliamentary nullifications.[120]

The measure known as the last determinations act prevented local changes in the established franchise, then generally thought to be made to the court's advantage.[121] The notorious practices of returning officers, especially the crown-appointed sheriffs, of adjourning polls on frivolous pretexts to secure the return of the desired candidate, also received legislative attention. By a clause in the same act, minors were forbidden to serve,[122] Musgrave having complained of this practice in his contest against the court interest in Westmorland where the young Richard Sanford was elected.[123] Indeed, the junto was only prevented from setting up the Russell heir, Wriothesley, Lord Tavistock, then not yet fifteen, by his mother's persistent refusals.[124] Although the act was to be subsequently ignored on numerous occasions, one might at least suppose that such parental objections became the rule rather than the exception.

The property qualifications bill was thought the most effectual method of diminishing the influence of the court and moneyed interest. Knights of the shire would be obliged to have landed incomes of at least five hundred pounds a year; burgesses and others, two hundred pounds. Jack Howe considered the measure but the first step to a good parliament; Vernon feared that a 'good parliament' meant a senate of patricians[125]—a group most unlikely to be disposed to a vigorous war policy.

---

[119] 7 and 8 William III, c. 4.   [120] See especially, pp. 309–10.

[121] 7 and 8 William., c. 7

[122] 7 and 8 William, c. 25, especially, s. 4 and 7.

[123] To Sir Daniel Fleming, 19 October 1695. *H.M.C. Le Fleming*, p. 338.

[124] He was born in November 1680 and was to succeed as second duke of Bedford. Somers and Shrewsbury urged his candidacy for Middlesex, saying that even if he did not attend they would have three extra votes, i.e. by keeping out 'two notorious tories' and bringing another whig in his train. Sir James Forbes to Lady Russell, 3 October 1695. *Letters of Lady Rachael Russell* (1853), ii, 129–30. She later all but changed her mind and decided that it might have been best to have let him stand after all. To Lady Roos, 8 December 1695. *Ibid.*, pp. 128–9.

[125] To Shrewsbury, 28 November 1696. *Vernon Corr.*, i, 84–8.

In the first session the bill passed both houses only to be refused the king's assent;[126] during the second session it was supposed that William would have again rejected the measure had it not been lost in the lords.[127] The earlier bill, Vernon noted, was 'driven on furiously by those who aim at making sure of the next parliament, now they despaire of this...'[128] The increase of government support following the announcement of the assassination plot sank this despair to new depths. Of the subsequent traumatic experiences, not the least disturbing was the fate of a censure motion branding those who had advised the royal veto of the earlier bill as enemies to king and kingdom.[129] The measure failing 217–70, its proponents could scarcely be said to be the country party, but only a beleagured tory rump, ironically identified with treason themselves.

---

[126] See *H.M.C. Lords, 1695–7*, pp. 199–201.

[127] *Ibid*. pp. 275–8. 23 January 1696/7. *H.L.J.*, xvi, 81. Fourteen lords protested.

[128] To Shrewsbury, 28 November 1696. *Vernon Corr.*, i, 86. The second bill was said to be less severe, allowing merchants to sit who had incomes of £5,000 *p.a.* and their next immediate heirs if they had £500 *p.a.* Henry Fleming to Sir D. Fleming 2 January 1696/7. *H.M.C. Le Fleming*, p. 345. A similar bill was enacted in 1710 but was to have little effect.

[129] 14 April 1697. *H.C.J.*, xi, 556. Bromley and Tredenham were minority tellers.

FIVE

Free and Impartial Proceedings: Tilting the Scales

Free and impartial judicial proceedings were thought at least as essential to English liberties as free and impartial proceedings in parliament. But while the glorious revolution was unquestionably a landmark in the history of the judiciary, it was not the watershed that it might appear in retrospect. Although the king could not safely oppose the national impulse in this regard and was forced to make pragmatic concessions, he scarcely relinquished complete control. In part, William simply wished to preserve the throne from forceful overthrow, but at the same time he might make his opponents more fearful of the court than formerly—and he could save the prerogative for better days.

The change in the ministry only aided him in his efforts, for the junto whigs defended the royal position here far more fiercely than in other constitutional matters. Still, both king and junto were well aware of the dangers inherent in supporting the same arbitrary practices which had helped secure James's downfall and their ascendancy. They were forced to fly false colours in opposing the reforms they theoretically ardently supported and became even more devious than Carmarthen and his henchmen had been. *Plus royalist que le roi*, albeit for different motives, they sought to brand their tory rivals as Jacobites and dominate the ministry. In instances, moreover, when court and junto thinking was not or could not be that of the courts, then they would attempt to conjure parliament into a court and attaint the accused. According to contemporaries, constitutional gains needed to be consolidated and codified.

It was not until the Act of Settlement was put into effect in 1714 that judges' salaries were ascertained and the crown obliged to make appointments during good behaviour rather than at the royal pleasure; it was not until 1760 that commissions ceased to expire with, or soon after, the death of the appointing sovereign.[1] Judicial independence existed, but at the crown's sufferance.

Nevertheless, one can see that it was only the years immediately following the revolution that there was any real danger. Few sovereigns had a higher view of the prerogative than the Dutch deliverer, and it is not at all certain that the judiciary was free from his designs. The fact that he made his new appointments during good behaviour proves little but his pragmatism; if there had been a change in the royal fortunes there might well have been a change in the royal policy. Nor would such a course of action have been unprecedented. As in the reign of Charles II, the practice of appointing judges during good behaviour might have been discontinued at any time, while a judge who already held a permanent appointment might be continued in his office and salary but not his duties.[2] To be a real judge, one must be a working judge. Even without resorting to such extremes, the king could hope for a fund of indebtedness, with dividends being placed on the court side of the judicial scales owing to the psychological state of the proud possessor of a judicial patent inscribed *quamdiu se bene gesserit* which, with a few strokes of the royal quill, might have been but *durante beneplacito Regis*.

The vigour with which William and his court party in the commons opposed any change attests to the benefits expected and received from

---

[1] 1 Geo. III, c. 23. The Regency Act of 1707 allowed judges to remain in office six months after the death of the sovereign unless sooner removed by the successor. 6 Anne, c. 41.

[2] When Charles II attempted to dismiss Archer J., in 1672, he refused to give up his office which he held *quamdiu se bene gesserit* without a *scire facias* showing evidence of misconduct and thus kept his profits but not his duties. A. Havinghurst, 'The Judiciary and Politics in the Reign of Charles II', *Law Quart. Rev.* (1950), lxvi, 76.

the existing relationship. A proviso in the bill of rights which would have effected judicial independence was deleted in committee.[3] In 1692 the king openly rejected a bill to that purpose.[4] Burnet finds that the bill would have been largely ineffectual in any case, as the judges' salaries were not to be ascertained. Macaulay, on the other hand, believes the bishop's memory muddled, relying instead upon an anonymous pamphlet (published a decade later) to deduce that by the bill's wording the judges' salaries would be derived from the royal revenue.[5] But although the king would unquestionably find such a clause distasteful, the implication that it would have received the king's acquiescence had it not included this proviso seems naïve at best. The royal revenue was largely mortgaged for war purposes as it was, and the measure eventually implemented was financed in just this way.[6] Then too, if the king had wished the bill well, why did he not instruct his placemen to try to delete the clause instead of allowing them to sit so quietly when it passed the commons?[7] Was he simply looking for an excuse? The argument that the bill's proponents did not really fear the misuse of the prerogative, as William made his appointments during good behaviour, needs little further discussion;[8] the presence of the bill attests to the presence of the fears. Indeed, it was during a debate over a similar measure the next session that a placeman took off the mask and plainly stated that '...it did entrench upon the king's prerogative and would render judges independent upon the Crown.'[9] On this occasion the court succeeded in throwing it out on question of committal. Perhaps, as some believed, the bill was too broad in scope,[10] but it is likely enough that the placemen did nothing to help; nor did the shift to the whigs change matters. Indeed, they did anything but promote the bill's revival and will be seen to have put as many clogs in the way as possible

---

[3] 2 and 7 February 1688/9. *H.C.J.*, x, 17 and 22. A new bill was to be formulated for this purpose. *Ibid.*

[4] Robert Harley to Sir E. Harley, 25 February 1691/2. B.M. Portland loan 29/186. 24 February. *H.L.J.*, xv, 92.

[5] Burnet, *Own Times*, iv, 154. Macaulay, v, 2139.

[6] Until it and other crown expenses were incorporated in the consolidated fund. 27 Geo. III, c. 13.

[7] Entry of 17 February 1691/2. Abstract MSS., i, ff. 328–9.

[8] Macaulay, v, 2139.

[9] 17 December 1692. Luttrell, Abstract MSS., ii, f. 200. *H.C.J.*, x, 746.

[10] George Tollet, clerk to the commission of public accounts, apologized for the loss by saying that it was large enough 'for 3 or 4 bills'. To Bishop King, 17 December 1692. T.C.D. MSS. 1122/248.

even when the measure came at last to be incorporated in the act of settlement of 1701.[11]

THE LANCASHIRE TRIALS

There were indications well before the queen's death of what the country might expect from the new ministers. Some of the first fruits of the new administration were the trials in Manchester of alleged Jacobites charged with being in active conspiracy the previous August. The guilt or innocence of the parties involved was not in itself an issue of national importance.[12] It would appear rather that, with a view to a general election, the court sought to exploit any convictions as an aid in branding any opposition as disloyal. One fervent court supporter wrote that if those in charge of the trials '...fairly convict a number, especially of the protestants, it will be in our power to choose (even in this county [Lancashire]) much better members of Parliament in case of a dissolution'.[13] The junto was determined to convict them fairly or unfairly, as became apparent by the disclosures of the double agent, John Taffe, and the obvious blatant perjuries of Lunt which led to the dismissal of the charges.[14]

Harley considered the whole affair '...a mystery of villanous perjury' fearing that if Lunt had succeeded, the practice would have been extended to '...all the counties of England.'[15] Although counter-charges against the government proceeded throughout much of the session in both houses, the country party failed to discredit the handling of the trials. By a narrow majority in a thin house, the court succeeded in allowing Lunt to read his statement in the commons.[16] Subsequently in

---

[11] See chapter VIII.

[12] T. C. Porteus has deduced from the Jacobite papers found in a wall at Standish, that many of the Lancashire gentry were guilty. See his *History of the Parish of Standish* (1927), chapter II and 'New Light on the Lancashire Plot, 1692–4'. *Trans. of the Lancs. and Cheshire Ant. Soc.* (1934), i. 1–64.

[13] Thomas Norris, M.P. Liverpool, to n. n., 6 August 1694. *Cal. S.P. Dom.*, p. 255.

[14] See *H.M.C. Lords 1693–5*, pp. 435–55 and *H.M.C. Kenyon*, pp. 292–372 *passim*.

[15] To Sir E. Harley, 13 November 1694. *H.M.C. Portland*, iii, 559.

[16] On 22 November the court succeeded in carrying the question that Lunt should attend the house the next day by a vote of 117–102. Sir Gilbert Clarke and Peter Shakerley were minority tellers. *H.C.J.*, xi, 175. Robert Price noted

early February the court won yet another narrow vote affirming that there were sufficient grounds for the trials even after the detection of false witnesses.[17] In the lords, the judges involved were exonerated of culpability, although a successful adjournment motion put a stop to a court proposal that there was at least a plot in Lancashire to take up arms against the government.[18] Certainly the court did not allow the principle employed in the trials to be in any ways diminished. A bill declaring wilful perjury or subornation of perjury in certain cases a felony was lost despite a considerable dissent.[19] So close were the divisions, however, that it would be less correct to say that the junto ministers succeeded than that they had merely escaped.

TRIALS FOR TREASON

The only major constitutional reform of the 1695 parliament was enacted shortly before the announcement of the assassination plot. Reflecting upon the Lancashire trials, the treason trials act required two lawful witnesses to the same overt act of treason; as it was to take effect the following March, the crown was given an added spur to end the costly war.

In five previous sessions the court succeeded in stopping similar bills, although usually only against vigorous country opposition. In 1692, Lowther argued on behalf of the court that the bill would only hurt good governments as bad ones would ignore it. By way of reply,

sarcastically that '...the courtiers are for justifying, and give credit to those base evidences...[as] the court would have the perjured evidence [of] Lunt.' To the duke of Beaufort, 22 November 1694. Bodl. Carte MSS. 130 f. 353. Speaking against the court were Sir John Mainwaring, Sir Robert Cotton, Shakerley, Sir Edward Chisnell, Sir Gilbert Clarke, Harcourt, Sir John Thompson and Sir Edward Seymour. *Ibid.*

[17] By a vote of 136 to 109, the country party failed to add the words making the prosecutions justified only before the falsity of the witnesses was discovered. Boyle and Harley were minority tellers. The resolution was passed 133-97. Shakerley and Col. Perry were minority tellers. *H.C.J.*, xi, 223-4.

[18] *H.M.C. Lords, 1693-5*, p. 452. 10 and 22 February 1694/5. See too, *H.L.J.*, xv, 498 and 503. Sandwich, Guildford, Rochester and Nottingham dissented in regard to the judges behaviour, claiming they employed gross partiality and unfairness.

[19] 11 December 1694-19 January 1694/5, *H.M.C. Lords, 1693-5*, pp. 410-12. 19 January 1694/5, *H.L.J.*, xv, 465-6. Eleven peers signed a dissent, noting the need for such a bill '...not only in former Times, but also very lately...'

Harley found that they must 'gett good lawes in a good reign' as they could not be had in bad.[20]

Court and country were not, however, the only divisions found in the debates. It is a step towards the development of the increasingly tory character of the opposition after 1693 that some tories, such as Nottingham, viewed the bill with favour even while in office; as a corollary, the junto whigs opposed it even before gaining predominance in the administration. Obviously, the junto had little to fear from the government courts and the bill's passage would quite clearly work to the detriment of the junto oligarchs' attempts to brand opponents as disloyal. Nottingham found that some of the bill's enemies had '...not stuck to say they were agt it, that they might the more easily be reveng'd of their enemies.'[21] Although one might suppose that the bill's opponents promoted the abjuration oaths and supported the association, the junto faction tended to hide its hand in opposition to such constitutional reform: in Montague's memoirs the bill is spoken of as his 'favorite',[22] and yet if he was the bill's friend it did not need enemies. With Somers and the Whartons he fought the bill with relentless vigour[23] although usually doing so through such indirect means as promoting institutional rivalries by opposing amendments made by the lords.

Foremost among the lords' amendments was the demand that trials of peers for high treason be brought before all the peers of the realm, rather than a select panel chosen by the lord steward. Twice this 'trick', as Nottingham termed the amendment, was effectively employed to gain support from those who thought '...not convenient barefaced to oppose.'[24] Certainly it was not thought of vital importance for the safety of the peerage, having been omitted in the bill sent down from the lords and tabled in the commons during the convention.[25] In 1691, Musgrave merely stated the obvious when he found that the fiercest opponents of agreement '...were most against the bill at first; and I hear not of any clause from those gentlemen to mend it.'[26] No one made

[20] 18 November 1692. Luttrell, Abstract MSS., ii, ff. 4–7.
[21] To Visc. Hatton, 22 December 1694. B.M. Add. MSS., 29,595 f. 68.
[22] *Memoirs of the Life of Charles Montague, Late Earl of Halifax* (sec. ed., 1716), p. 30.
[23] See especially the debates of 11 December 1691 and 28 November 1692. Luttrell, Abstract MSS., i, 131–2, ii, 93–6.
[24] To Visc. Hatton, 22 December 1694. B.M. Add. MSS. 29,595, f. 68.
[25] 6 March 1688/9. *H.L.J.*, xiv, 140. Admittedly, seventeen peers signed a protest.
[26] 11 December 1691. Cobbett, v, 675–81.

more of opposing the amendment than the bill's backfriend, Charles
Montague, who even attempted to refuse to serve as the commons'
manager in a conference with the lords, pretending to find the amendment too repulsive.[27] Despite both the complicated procedural points
raised by such gentlemen of the long robe,[28] and the questionable interpretations made by the court Speaker,[29] the commons, nevertheless,
substantially agreed to the lords' amendments. Indeed, Harley believed
that it was only the king's timely presence which had kept the lords
from passing the bill.[30]

In the next session, the bill did not even reach the lords. Court and
junto power had evidently overwhelmed the bill's proponents in committee and it emerged with no fixed date for commencement, being
simply deferred until the war was over. Luttrell found this practice
'...never seen in an act of parliament' and added that '...those for the
bill moved to disagree with the committee,' and give the bill a fixed date
of commencement, such as 25 April 1695. Montague served as one of
the tellers for the court and junto majority which defeated this proposal
145–125.[31] When the bill's opponents found their strength, Jack Smith
attempted to add a clause (totally foreign to the bill's original intention) making it high treason even to *say* that William and Mary were not
rightful sovereigns. The momentum of the day was swiftly checked; it
was brought to the notice of the house that the clause would make
words treason, and thus effect the repeal of an act, namely the treason
act of 25 Edward III. Leave was needed, therefore, to bring in the bill.[32]
Despite the support of Somers, Montague and the Whartons, the new
bill was to be successfully opposed on the question of committal by
Harley, Foley, and Sir Francis Winnington. The country success

---

[27] Montague asked that '...some of the gentlemen who were so zealous for
the clause might manage the same.' Luttrell, Abstract MSS., i, 269. It should
also be noted that Montague claims to have made the same speech in favour
of the clause guaranteeing council for the accused as that generally accredited
to Maurice Ashley, later third earl of Shaftesbury. See Montague, *Memoirs*,
p. 30. Also 'Life of the 3rd Earl of Shaftesbury, by his son,' P.R.O. 30/24/21
no. 225 (Shaftesbury Papers). See too *Gen. Dict. Hist. and Crit.*, ix, 179, in
Cobbett, v, 966.
[28] 21 January 1691/2. Luttrell, Abstract MSS., i, 253.
[29] See above, p. 98.
[30] To Sir E. Harley, 30 January 1691/2. *H.M.C. Portland*, iii, 488. For
a corrected draft of the bill see *H.M.C. Lords, 1690–91*, pp. 278–9.
[31] 1 December 1692. Luttrell, Abstract MSS., ii, 122–3. *H.C.J.*, x, 730.
[32] *Ibid.*, ff. 123–4.

occurred only in a very full house, the vote being 200 to 175.[33] As the likelihood of the country side mustering this many votes again was remote, it is not surprising to find the bill tabled for the rest of the session. During the 1693-4 session, although the bill survived numerous court attempts to defeat and delay it in the commons,[34] there was a new development when the bill reached the lords. When Burnet accused the bill's proponents of disloyalty, Halifax leapt to the bill's assistance and deftly countered the bishop's accusation, proclaiming that those who had voted the greatest supplies ever were more loyal to their country than 'some of the reverend bench' were to their Christianity. Nevertheless, Burnet's point was apparently telling: the bill was lost on the second reading, a result which some again attributed to the king's presence.[35]

The following session, the treason trials bill followed in the wake of the successful triennial bill. Its rapid passage in the commons was auspicious and its entry into the lords clamorous, being brought up by Henry Boyle and fifty friends.[36] Despite an uncomplicated committal,[37] Nottingham was correct in thinking that the 'old clause of tryalls of Peers'. would be added.[38] By seven votes the court also succeeded in changing the date of commencement from 1695 to 1698.[39] Although the lords subsequently withdrew this last amendment, they adhered to the former and the commons refused to relent. The bill was lost once again.[40]

The eventual passage in the new parliament should not be attributed to any diminution of court strength. 150 members opposed agreeing with the lords' amendment regarding the trial of peers—a number usually quite adequate to defeat the 'country volunteers'. There was simply an unusually full house; the country party mustering 192 votes to agree and thus virtually assuring success.[41] The court managers

[33] 14 December 1692. *Ibid.*, ff. 181-90.

[34] Note the court attempts of 14 November, 2 January and 9 February. *H.C.J.*, xi, 3, 45 and 88.

[35] R. Price to the duke of Beaufort, 1 March 1693/4. Bodl. Carte MSS. 130 f. 347. *H.M.C. Lords, 1693-5*, pp. 343-4. Luttrell, *Brief Relation*, iii, 276. Brandenburg Dispatch of 23 February/5 March. Von Ranke, vi, 241.

[36] Brandenburg Dispatch, 21/31 December 1694, *Ibid.*, p. 261.

[37] Brandenburg Dispatch, 26 January/5 February 1694/5. *Ibid.*, p. 269.

[38] To Visc. Hatton, 22 December 1694. B.M. Add. MSS. 29,595, f. 68.

[39] Chas. Hatton to Visc. Hatton, 10 January 1694/5. *Hatton Corr.*, ii, 210-211. *H.M.C. Lords, 1693-5*, pp. 416-20.

[40] *Ibid.*, *H.L.J.*, xv, 504.   [41] *H.C.J.*, xi, 396.

probably wished they could have delayed the bill for but a month, when they might have relied upon the reaction to the assassination plot to aid them in killing the measure, or at the least facilitate a defence of the royal veto upon the familiar enough grounds of national security.

THE ATTAINDER OF SIR JOHN FENWICK

As the treason trials act was not to come into force until 25 March, the court was able to proceed against most of those involved without the necessity of having two required witnesses to the same treasonable action. Sir John Fenwick was, however, not arrested until June and the junto was soon sulking over the adverse effects of the act following the disappearance of a required witness.[42] Ironically, his arrest almost proved their undoing: in a statement, he openly accused Godolphin, Marlborough, Shrewsbury and, most embarrassingly, Russell, of having correspondence with James II.[43] If it was likely that Fenwick was guilty, it soon became apparent that his charges might well have some foundation: to the junto's utter horror, Shrewsbury quickly offered his resignation, suggested that the other ministers do so as well and retreated into the country.[44]

It was now impossible to obtain Fenwick's speedy dispatch before parliament convened[45] and unlikely that the whole matter could be let fall. The problem was one of bringing the affair to parliament's attention in as favourable a light as possible.[46] If successful in this, might they not go further and show their strength by proceeding against Fenwick through means of legislative attainder?

---

[42] Somers to Trumbull (November 1696). *H.M.C. Downshire*, I, ii, 713.

[43] The king to Shrewsbury, 10 September 1696. *Shrewsbury Corr.*, p. 145. See Tindal's account in Cobbett, v, 998–1002.

[44] Shrewsbury to the king, 18/28 October, Portland to Shrewsbury 20/30 October. *Ibid.*, pp. 156–9. Shrewsbury to Wharton, 30 October. Bodl. Carte MSS. 233 f. 27 r.

[45] Somers to Trumbull (November 1696). *H.M.C. Downshire*, I, ii, 713. Alexander Johnson of Yorkshire told Trumbull that while one of Johnson's acquaintances was being examined before Vernon '...he heard Vernon bid him fear nothing, put but 1 witness agt him; and this Johnson sd., He wd make oath of; and was but 1 instance of a 100. He spoke also, as if Vernon knew or–etc. to Sr. Ja. Montgomery's escape etc.' Trumbull Diary, 17 October 1697. Berks R.O., Trumbull Add. MSS. 125, f. 32.

[46] Somers to Shrewsbury, 27 October/6 November. *Shrewsbury Corr.*, pp. 414–15. Wharton to Shrewsbury, s.d., *ibid.*, pp. 415–16.

The first obstacle disappeared in October when Godolphin was apparently tricked into resigning.[47] Certainly his departure from the ministry at first appeared doubly fortuitous. He had shown little enthusiasm towards the junto's monetary schemes and had outspokenly favoured peace. His going also made it easier to restrain their own more belligerent followers in the commons from demanding a full investigation with the apparent hope of having the head of a moderate tory accompany Fenwick's. While it seems most unlikely that the junto ever doubted that two heads were better than one, there was the danger of Russell's involvement, and his exoneration was of the first importance for the ministry's safety.

With the care of diamond cutters, the court approached its task. The day appointed for mentioning the disclosures, Secretary Vernon arose early to try to reach some understanding with the leaders of the opposition. Boyle he saw in his lodgings, and later Harley and Foley, apparently in the house.

Whether or not they aided in moving off the inquiry into Fenwick's allegations is difficult to say. Boyle and Harley sat silent although Foley '...framed fit questions at the very least.'[48] This is not surprising, for neither country nor tory factions found this suitable ground for a contest. To the country party, it was clearly a question of men rather than measures. To link Russell with treasonable activities would fly in the face of their chief contention that the junto was fanatically anti-French and blindly adherent to the king's war policy; to the tories, it was far more likely that an investigation would result in their further undoing if only through the power of junto votes. As feared, it was not the opposition, but some of the junto's own supporters who tried to upset the court's plans. Even after Montague '...threw out some words about the attainder' and succeeded in effecting a blanket repudiation of Fenwick's charges, there were still a few such protestations.[49]

Those who supported the court's attempts to secure an exoneration for the embarrassed ministers were not necessarily to support its efforts to secure Fenwick's attainder. In respect to any help from Harley and Boyle on this point, Vernon found that he might just as well have '...left them both alone.'[50] Wharton, Montague and Somers were well aware that Harley and many other country members who opposed attainder did so because of the constitutional principle involved, rather

---

[47] S. to s., s.d., *ibid.* See Kenyon, *Sunderland*, p. 285.
[48] Vernon to Shrewsbury, 6 November 1696. *Shrewsbury Corr.*, p. 426.
[49] *Ibid.*   [50] *Ibid.*

than any desire to subvert the government.[51] In the subsequent debates, Edward Harley believed it most unwise to deviate from the treason trials law. He argued it to be a foundation of liberty, finding it dangerous to place so much trust in the central government: 'If any will look into the history of England, they will find it hath often been the design of the crown to trump up plots upon the subject.'[52]

If only a hard core of the opposition remained to oppose the introduction of a bill of attainder, it was to pass by a very narrow margin.[53] Only the first part of Feiling's statement that the opposition was '...reinforced by moderate whigs and even by placemen' seems accurate.[54] As a matter of fact, the numbers voting on the court side had increased during the divisions. While Trevor, the attorney general, spoke against the bill, his name does not appear in a manuscript division list as having voted against it. Indeed, Pelham, the other notable court defector in the debates was followed by only nine others who had consistently voted for the court's financial proposals the previous session.[55] It is far more indicative of the general desire for places that even more changed sides to vote for attainder.[56] Such massive court defections as had

---

[51] Somers to Shrewsbury, 7/17 November 1696. Wharton to s., 10/20 November. *Shrewsbury Corr.*, 427–9. Montague, *Memoirs*, p. 45.

[52] Cobbett, v, 1149. For the extensively recorded debates see *ibid.*, pp. 998–1149.

[53] The motion for a bill of attainder was carried 179–61, the second reading, 196–104, committal 182–128, engrossing the bill, 125–88, and for passage but by 189–156. *H.C.J.*, xi, 577, 581, 588, 592 and 598.

[54] *Tory Party*, p. 324.

[55] The following voted against attainder but with the court on either the question of a royal board of *trade* [t.] or the devaluation of *guineas* [g.] or both [t.g.]: 1. William Howard [t.g., Carlisle], 2. Thomas Freke [g., Weymouth and Melcombe Regis], 3. William Monson [g., Lincoln], 4. Sir Richard Onslow [t.g., Surrey], 5. Thomas Pelham [t.g., Lewes], 6. Sir George Hungerford [t., Wilts.], 7. Francis Stonehouse [t., Great Bedwin], 8. George Hungerford [t., Calne], 9. Robert Monckton [t.g., Pontefract], 10. Tobias Jenkins [t., York]. Three others voted court on one of the divisions and country [T. or G.] on the other: 1. Lord Henry Cavendish [T.g., Derby], 2. Peregrine Bertie [t.G., Boston], 3. Henry Holmes [T.g., Yarmouth]. See chapter 3 and Appendix A for a discussion of the issues involved.

[56] The following voted for attainder but on the country side on either the question of a board of *trade* [T.] or the devaluation of *guineas* [G.] or both [T.G.]. 1. William Farrer [G., Bedford], 2. John Burrington [T.G., Oakhampton, Kent], 3. Sir William Bowes [G., Co. Durham], 4. Thomas Stephens [G., Co. Gloucester], 5. Chris. Lister [T., Clitheroe], 6. Amb. Pudsay [T., Clitheroe], 7. Sir William Ellis, [T.G., Grantham], 8. Samuel Fuller [T.G.,

occurred over the triennial bill could not occur now. The junto's court party purges had taken their toll. There was no prospect of a change in the ministry and neither peace nor an election was expected in the immediate future. Independent thinking was at an ebb.

Still, the opposition had developed from the meagre band who fought the bills of supply. Probably it was Burnet's 'sourer sort of whig' who had so augmented their numbers by the final division. The real threat to the junto's aspirations came less from placemen's consciences, than simply from a fuller muster of country supporters in both houses.[57] Perhaps it was to take advantage of this development that Fenwick's defence employed so many cavils and delays.[58] If the court could do little to counter this tendency, it did what it could both to lend an aura of impartiality to such *ex post facto* legislation[59] and to intimidate the members present. Vernon credited the success of the second reading to the effective employment of *argumentum ad hominem*; Boscawen roundly condemned those opposed to attainder as '...eluding justice and saving a notorious criminal.' When Colonel Granville tried to call him to account for this rather perverse attack, a timely call for candles was said to have '...putt him by his motion and the rest went on smoothly.'[60]

The bill's passage by thirty-three votes was not so smooth and might well have been even less so if the bill were thought to have had much

---

Great Yarmouth], 9. George England, [T.G., Great Yarmouth], 10. Charles Cox [T.G., Southwark], 11. Thomas Foley [T., Co. Worcester], 12. John Aislaby [T., Ripon], 13. Sir Rice Rudd [Co. Carmarthen].

Nine others voted country on but one of the divisions and court on the other [t. or g.]: 1. George Oxenden, [t.G., Univ. Cantab.], 2. James Kendall [t.G., West Lowe], 3. Thomas Erle [t.G., Wareham], 4. Sir Joseph Williamson [t.G., Rochester], 5. Sir Henry Belasyse [t.G., Morpeth], 6. Nicholas Hedger [t.G., Portsmouth], 7. Sir Thomas Barnardiston [t.G., Sudbury], 8. Jonathan Jenings [t.G., Ripon], 9. Sir Roger Puleston [t.G., Flint].

See appendix A for a discussion of the lists employed.

[57] Rochester was said to be leading the attempt in the lords to secure full attendance. Vernon to Shrewsbury, 14 November. *Vernon Corr.*, i, 62–3.

[58] S. to s., 13 November. Boughton, Shrewsbury Papers, i, f. 21. Robert Jennens to Thomas Coke, 19 November 1696. *H.M.C. Cowper*, ii, p. 367.

[59] Wharton noted that the decision to allow Fenwick's counsel to plead at the bar '... doth not seem to me (as it doth to some) to be done in favour to him; but rather there may appear all sorts of fair-dealing in the judgement, which (I fancy) the house will send up against him.' To Shrewsbury, 12 November. *Shrewsbury Corr.*, p. 431.

[60] Vernon to Shrewsbury, 13 November. Boughton, Shrewsbury papers, i, f. 21.

chance of passing the lords.[61] The court's first victory in this regard occurred when the opposition failed to add a clause disallowing the votes of the ecclesiastical bench, most of whom would almost certainly support the attainder.[62] If the court managers at first approached the greater undertaking with some temerity, they soon surpassed the king's greatest expectations in their mastery of the supreme arts of procedural finesse. Timely delays, the disallowing of proxies, the allowing of depositions by absent witnesses and the declaring of at least one favourable witness incompetent all served to herald the bill's seedy progress to a narrow seven-vote passage in the face of a fierce protest signed by fifty-three peers.[63]

If, as Somers put it, 'What we aimed at, we had,'[64] one might well ask if their quest was well advised, and their victory not Pyrrhic? Fenwick's subsequent execution at best showed the king wanting in magnanimity and underlined the trickery employed to gain his end.[65] If Godolphin's resignation and the driving out of such moderates as Trumbull[66] gave the junto even greater domination, Shrewsbury's retreat and Sunderland's opposition to attainder served to isolate their position. As with the tories in the summer of 1693, the junto's monopoly of power was probably a mixed blessing. For the country opposition to direct a blow at measures might henceforth also mean directing one at men; for it was king and junto alone who who were now responsible. The gains made by the war interest from the Lancashire trials, the proscriptions following the association and now this legal lynching had only been made possible in the first place by the war. Yet while the war would soon come to a close, the memories of their ruthlessness would not.

[61] Brandenburg Dispatch, 20/30 November. B.M. Add. MSS. 30,000 A. f. 250 v. The vote was 189–156. *H.C.J.*, xi, 598.

[62] Geo. Tollet to Wm. King, 21 November 1696. T.C.D. MSS. 1122/513. Twelve bishops voted for attainder, nine voted against and five were excused from attending. That even nine should have voted against the proposal was thought by Vernon to be surprising. To Shrewsbury, January 1696/7. *Vernon Corr.*, i, 134.

[63] *H.L.J.*, xvi, pp. 19–49. *H.M.C. Lords, 1695/7*, pp. 274–95.

[64] To Shrewsbury, 20 January 1696–7. *Shrewsbury Corr.*, p. 464.

[65] Price to Beaufort, 10 December 1696 and 28 January 1696/7. Bodl. Carte MSS. 130 ff. 367 and 371.

[66] Trumbull wrote that while he had told the king of the plot before it had occurred, the junto treated him '…as if I had been in it.' Trumbull Diary, 18 October 1696. Berks. R.O., Trumbull Add. MSS. 125 f. 4. Subsequently, he states that he was excluded from Shrewsbury's office after the latter's departure from the ministry. Entry of 8 July 1697. *Ibid.*

SIX

Disbandment

The War of the League of Augsburg characterized as it was by seemingly interminable sieges, soon came to be regarded as the second hundred years war. Agitation for peace had for long been building up and reached a fever pitch during the currency crisis of the summer of 1696. Shrewsbury urged the king to put an end to the war, doubting '...that a town more or less is very material to your majesty's interest.' He believed that a good peace '...everybody would desire and many are so weary as to be content with a bad one.'[1] In the autumn, the ever-present problem of diminishing funds reared its head once again.[2] Despite the junto's monetary successes in the ensuing session it was a question if the war could go on. Shrewsbury believed that '...many continue still willing to support the war in the best manner they are able, but most begin to conclude it will be difficult if not impossible.'[3] William realized the growing urgency of the situation,[4] and through

---

[1] To William, 23 June/3 July and 21/31 July 1696. *Shrewsbury Corr.*, pp. 126 and 128.

[2] William Norris wrote to Thomas Norris (high sheriff of Lancs.), that he did not believe there was enough money to carry on a war. 6 October. *Norris Papers*, ix, 34.

[3] To Portland, 23 June 1697 N.U.L. PwA 1388.

[4] Scandalous prints sent from abroad mocked the English gentleman's position, depicting the taxation which burdened him as gross weights upon his outstretched body. A jest was also made of England's position as an outsider at the peace conference during the summer. One print pictures the Englishman looking through a keyhole, while a second shows him oppressed

Portland's famous private negotiations, peace was at last concluded.

To court and country the peace meant quite different things. The king appears to have considered it little more than a cease fire.[5] To the country as a whole, however, it meant far more. Francis Gwyn wrote that 'The News of the Peace is very welcome [,] in the country they fancy that when it is setled they shall pay noe more Taxes, but I doubt they will be deceived in their expectation upon that point.'[6] If the guns were not fired from the Tower, there were bonfires and fireworks which made some think hell would hold few wonders; indeed, the nation apparently believed that the war burden was at an end.[7] Sunderland thought permanency assured, believing the peace '...cost the French too much not to be a lasting one.'[8] To Henry Guy, the Jacobites' fury was also an auspicious omen.[9]

The Jacobites' distaste provided a sharp contrast to the delight of the ministerial tories. Harley was told that the government might now be strengthened by '...using abilities of some who only for the notion or suspicion of being Tories were clamoured at.'[10] There were signs that Sunderland was looking to Harley for support and, although not mentioning names, Guy noted that '...several heere have changed their stile since the Newes of the Peace.'[11] By October, the junto was becoming increasingly fearful. Orford wrote that '...one party of people expects and prepares to be ill treated.' It was thought that if the junto proved incapable or unwilling, the ministerial tories were prepared 'to bid for the king'.[12] As Feiling points out, some ministerial tories were believed to be interested in office, but their enthusiasm waned sharply

---

with great weights. Upon the Englishman's head is the inscription '..."a free born Englishman", betwixt his legs "liberty" and "property" and upon his breast, belly, arms, thighs, legs and shoes, "capitation", "excise", "aids", "assessments" and all other of the impositions of the late parliaments'. Dr Nathaniel Johnston to the earl of Huntingdon, 12 May. *H.M.C Hastings*, ii, 291.

[5] To Portland, 14 September., Portland to Shrewsbury, s.d., Grimblot, *Letters*, i, 122–3.

[6] To William, second Marquis of Halifax, 9 August. Althorpe, Halifax MSS., box 4.

[7] W. Snowe to Robert Harley, 14 September. *H.M.C. Portland*, iii, 587.

[8] To Portland, 17 September. N.U.L. PwA 1272. See too, his letter to Burnet, 21 September [1697]. Bodl. Add. MSS. A191 f. 23.

[9] To Portland, 17 September. N.U.L. PwA 517.

[10] Robert Southwell to R. Harley, 27 September. B.M. Portland loan 29/156/13.

[11] Guy to R. Harley, 23 September. B.M. Portland loan 29/188.

[12] To Shrewsbury, 21/31 October. *Shrewsbury Corr.*, p. 502.

as they discovered the king's desire to keep a large standing force in peacetime and the nation's opposition to such a proposal. At first even Harley appears to have had some thoughts of aiding the king in opposing immoderate opposition,[13] but as he writes to his father of the growing uproar against the standing army,[14] one senses that he was about ready to put all but the most modest plans aside. The junto seems to have realized the problem as well and shuddered at the thought of defending the king's more immoderate desires.

During the war the size of the military establishment was a matter left largely to the consciences of the independent members. If the moderate country leaders usually tried to 'hold the line' this was not done out of fear of the army, but rather to ensure that England would bear but its fair share of the war's expenses. With the end of the war came the end to such moderation. If some ministerial tories and perhaps even Harley had at first been willing to compromise over the question of forces reduction, this was before they realized the vast distance which separated the two camps. If the more extreme libertarians hoped to have no standing army at all, the enormity of the king's demands was thought far more outrageous and aided in freezing country sentiment. The court hoped for as many as 40,000 troops, almost all of whom were to be foreign, with only the English being disbanded.[15] To say that such a force merely indicated the king's fears of the French would be very charitable and might even be correct. Nevertheless, most Englishmen were not willing to be the subjects in an experiment involving a horde of foreign mercenaries; for the very map of Europe was warning enough against putting one's faith in princes.

Little wonder then that when such whigs as Sir John Trenchard wrote at length abhorring the very concept of a standing army, they had enormous influence. Trenchard argued for a renewal of the militia, believing that '...the constitution must either break the Army, or the Army will destroy the Constitution.' He called for a return to a 'Gothic balance' making the militia consist of the same parts as the government: the king was to be the general, the lords the great commanders and the freeholders the body of the army. The Dutch guards were especially censured. Trenchard cited many past examples where troops of royal mercenaries were so enlarged as to result in tyranny. Any standing army, moreover, might prove a danger. If Charles I had had an additional 5,000 men he believed no revolution would have occurred. If James II

[13] Feiling, *Tory Party*, p. 322. [14] 23 November. *H.M.C. Portland*, iii, 593.
[15] See below, p. 138.

had been content with arbitrary power without popery, he too would
have succeeded. It was by enlarging his forces that Charles II was
enabled to stifle objections to his use of the suspending power. Nor,
Trenchard argued, would parliamentary control of the purse serve as
a real deterrent, it being '...as certain that an army will raise Money as
that Money will raise an Army.' If the exchequer was shut up '...there
will be near 3 million a year ready cut and dry'd for them.' While some
might say that they must have an army whatever the consequences as
it was better to be a slave to a protestant prince than a popish one, he
believed with the whig, Samuel Johnson, that '...putting an epithet upon
Tyranny is false Heraldry; for Protestant and popish are both alike; and
if I must be a slave, it is very indifferent to me who is my Master...'
Being ruled by an army was the worst that a conquest could impose.
Still, owing to the strength of the navy and England's admirable defensive position such an event was thought most unlikely. Trenchard
reiterated that a militia was the nation's proper defence and suggested
that it might be reduced by half to 60,000 men, while the money saved
might be employed to keep a third of them in constant exercise. It was
the militia that secured the invulnerability of the plantations, the Channel
Islands, Poland, Switzerland and the Grissons. 'If the court would give
their hearty assistance in promoting this design...we should quickly see
the young Nobility and Gentry...show a generous emulation in out-
vieing one another in military exercises and place a noble Ambition in
making themselves serviceable to their country...' To buttress his
argument he relied upon the writings of Machiavelli, Bacon and Harring-
ton. Bacon observed that a militia was best for defence, for they would
try to preserve their estates, while a mercenary army was best for
offensive invasion, for they hoped to gain foreign estates.

Noting the revolutionary temper of the army, he believed that one of
the best ways to restore King James was paradoxically to maintain a
standing army to keep him out. Over half the Roman emperors were
deposed by their own army, while in England under Cromwell they
twice expelled parliament and under Monk destroyed it and restored
Charles, who disbanded them. Reminding the reader of their recent
support of William of Orange, he compared the soldiery to ravenous
fish who do best in a storm.[16]

---

[16] *An Argument shewing that a Standing Army Is Inconsistent with a Free Government and Absolutely Destructive to the Constitution of the English Monarchy* (1697).
Walter Moyle was co-author. In a subsequent debate the court stated that the
militia numbered 120,000 men but that it was ill-prepared. See below, p. 142.

The chief government defence was put forth by Somers in another widely circulated pamphlet. He argued that while under former kings an army was a great danger, under William it was not. The proponents of the blue water school had overstated their case. The victories at La Hogue and Calais were largely, he argued, owing to good fortune.[17] Admittedly, there were many different court arguments put forth in various pamphlets which Miss Lois G. Schwoerer points out.[18] Nevertheless, the court must have found the very variety of the arguments a mixed blessing, for they probably served to confirm many country gentlemen's belief that the court would stop at nothing to effect its ends. Still, most of the arguments in Trenchard's pamphlet found their mark. Sir John Lowther had fears for its influence noting that it was soon '...in every hand.'[19] Vernon thought that whatever the author says '...to guild the pill, he is thought to be no friend of the government.'[20] But if the old whig Trenchard was not a friend, then who could be? If indeed the opposition came, as the court's friends generally asserted, from those who were '...not well inclined to the government though from very different principles and designs,'[21] one wonders just why the court was supporting the need for such force. Nottingham wrote of the standing army:

> I can't see the necessity of its being so great as is projected for halfe the number, if faithfull to the late King, had prevented the revolution: or if it must be so great, why so many, if any, foreigners: after 50 millions [i.e., the votes amounting to about 50 million pounds for war expenses], an association in England and Scotland and an abjuration in Ireland such subject[s] might be trusted, for if those things be not a Security to the Governmt 'tis hard tht they have bin prest wth so much vehemence.[22]

---

[17] *A Letter Ballancing the Necessity of Keeping A Land-force in Times of Peace; With the Dangers that may follow on it* (1697).

[18] 'The Literature of the Standing Army Controversy, 1697–99.' *Hunt. Lib. Quart.* (1965), xxviii, 187–212. See too, her 'Role of William III of England in the Standing Army Controversy–1697–1699' *Journ. Brit. Stud.* (1966), v, 74–95. Both articles do much to fill in the literary background of the controversy and the latter helps explain William's actions in a sympathetic manner.

[19] To 'My Lord', 30 November 1697. Cumb. R.O. Lowther Letterbook.

[20] R. Yard to Ambassador Williamson, 26 November *Cal. S.P. Dom.*, p. 487.

[21] J. Ellis to Ambassador Williamson, 30 November. *Cal. S.P. Dom.*, p. 494.

[22] To William, second marquis of Halifax, 22 November. Althorpe, Halifax MSS., box 7.

Certainly maintaining a belief in a threat from within could not hold much ground, or if it did, Nottingham was quite correct in finding the court and junto hoist with their own petard owing to the very success of the association. The problem of foreign troops provided an even graver problem which the king's subsequent insistence upon the maintenance of his Dutch guards was to accentuate. Over the greater request the king could expect little support. Even one of the court's friends was so incensed as to write that: 'The Court Whigs have a mind to keep an army of 30,000 men to enslave the nation, but I hope those two rogues, Seymour and Musgrove [Musgrave] who never did a good thing, will oppose the motion and save the nation.'[23] Then too, as William himself admitted, it was not England alone which was disarming, but in fact all the confederate powers.[24]

While the admirals might reinforce Somers's arguments as to the dangers inherent in relying on the navy, it was to little avail. Why did the court have so little faith in the blue water school or the militia proposals? Was this due to the king's foreign aims and ambitions which were not the same as those of most English gentlemen? So many country gentlemen thought, and so they continued to think as the session approached.

The king's main design was to reduce the numbers in each regiment and not to break them up, thus postponing the complete disbandment of any regiment at all.[25] Many believed that while some members would have 30,000 men, the minimum desired was 20,000.[26] That even this latter belief was rather naïve was not obvious at the time. Had not the junto forces won a considerable victory the previous session? Were not the same members still sitting? Had not the court presented fierce defences in the pamphlet battle? Was not France keeping up a large military establishment? Was there any reason to believe that the peace had so drastically altered the members' attitudes?

The members' attitudes, however, were being shaped by other forces. Aside from the traditional fears of a standing army, the triennial act would effectively force the members to go to the country before they sat again. To keep this session from being their last, some members who might otherwise have supported the king in his designs now had

---

[23] Ellis to Williamson, 23 November, *Cal. S.P. Dom.*, p. 484.
[24] To Heinsius, 17/27 December. Grimblot, *Letters*, i, 142–3.
[25] William to Galway, 8/18 October. *Ibid.*, i, 129. R. Yard to Williamson, 19 November. *Cal. S.P. Dom.*, pp. 478–9.
[26] William to Heinsius 19/29 November. Grimblot, *Letters*, i, 137.

a view to the electorate—an electorate which wished for an end to the heavy taxes. In the West Country, where very strong opposition to a standing army was expected, Seymour's fervent mustering of forces for heavy attendance met with considerable success; an extremely large number of members arrived before the opening of the session.[27] The king's reaction to such inauspicious portents was to delay the opening the better to concert the court's plans.[28] Probably they could never be good enough, although this was not immediately apparent. On the day of the opening, Vernon found '...a pretty near Ballance in the house at present, by this days Question whither the vote of the supply should be postponed to the consideration of the speech it was carried but by 156 against 153.' Still, court defections were noted.[29] Only gradually did the court come to realize the extent of the opposition to the standing army proposals. Even in late November, it was still thought difficult to tell what the outcome would be.[30] On 9 December, moreover, £60,000 was voted to provide for the military expenses.[31] Probably this was simply designed to keep down a military revolt, for on the day the disbandment issue was discussed 30,000 men were said to be quartered within a day's march of London.[32] When they came down to actually naming the number, the temper of the parliament was clearly seen. Harley noted that the ministry would not agree, while the king's suggestion of 36,000 men was clearly out of the question.[33] Any earlier thoughts Harley may have had of a generous compromise were evidently put aside. With Jack Howe rapidly seconding his proposal, he moved that all troops raised since 29 September 1680 be disbanded. This crushing reduction would leave William with scarcely 7,000 men.[34]

Against government arguments emphasizing the state of emergency, the opposition, led by Harley, countered that such a state might well be

---

[27] R. Yard to Ambassador Williamson, 19 November. *Cal. S.P. Dom.*, pp. 478–9.
[28] William to Heinsius, 16/26 November and 26 November/6 December. Grimblot, *Letters*, i, 137 and 139.
[29] To Shrewsbury, 7 December. Boughton, Shrewsbury Papers, i, f. 161. Gwyn and Hammond were minority tellers. *H.C.J.*, xii, 3.
[30] William to Heinsius, 19/29 November. Grimbolt, *Letters*, i, 137.
[31] Newsletter to Williamson, 10 December. *Cal. S.P. Dom.*, p. 508.
[32] Edward Harley, 'Harley Family Memoirs'. *H.M.C. Portland*, v, 646.
[33] 'Account of Robert Harley's Conduct'. B.M. Portland loan 29/165/3 f. 4. See below.
[34] James Sloane to Sir J. Williamson, 10 December. *Cal. S.P. Dom.*, p. 507.

almost eternal, existing as it did as long as Louis, James or the Pretender were alive. All the country gentlemen were said to have given in to Harley's motion, which was carried by a three to one majority. To government observers, what was so frightening about the debate in committee was not this unanimity of the usual opposition, but the large number of government defectors.[35] Probably it was the country gentlemen, however, who were so enthused as to shout down government attempts at a diverting motion favouring a land force as necessary for public safety.[36] So great was the feeling that the court did not think it wise to suggest 6,500 men, believing it best to leave even that paltry number to connivance.[37] In the eventual division at the end of the day, the attempt to recommit the bill was defeated 185–148.[38] Robert Price thought that if the vote had been over the disbandment question itself, the court would not have had a hundred votes. Indeed, to avoid such an unpleasant discovery was the very reason they had averted such a division. When the question to disband was proposed, it was noted to have been carried by a great cry.[39]

James Sloane (one of the minority tellers), thought that the defeat arose from the court's uncertainty. When they actually came to provide a number there were no less than four estimates given: 16,000; 14,000; 12,000 and 10,000. To no small degree, the court's vagueness might again be attributed to the king's original greediness, it being believed that he wished to keep up from 30,000 to 40,000 men who would be entirely foreign, only the English troops being disbanded.[40] The court had hopes that the vote was only temporary and that it was not occasioned simply by the hatred of a standing army. Various other causes were suggested. Some attributed it to the country gentlemen's anger against Montague.[41] His subsequent proposal, however, for granting William his civil list request of £700,000 was carried by a large majority, 225–86. Seymour and Musgrave were completely unsuccessful in keeping the commons from going into the civil list at all, and subsequently in an attempt to make them go into particulars

---

[35] Norris, Sir William St Quinten, Sir William Strickland and Sir Herbert Crofts being the most notable amongst them. *Ibid.*

[36] *Ibid.* R. Yard's newsletter to s., s.d. *Ibid.*   [37] *Ibid.*

[38] James Sloane to Williamson, 14 December. *Cal. S.P. Dom.*, pp. 511–12. *H.C.J.*, xii, 5.

[39] To the duke of Beaufort, 11 December. Bodl. Carte MSS. 130 f. 385.

[40] James Sloane to Williamson, 14 December. *Cal. S.P. Dom.*, 511–12.

[41] R. Yard to Williamson, 14 December. *Ibid.*, p. 513. J. S. Champneys to s., 17 December. *Ibid.*, p. 517.

which would have slowed down the proceedings almost indefinitely. Subsequently, an opposition attempt to recommit the bill failed as well.[42] The country party would not support the more extremist tory position. They did not oppose the king, but only wished to prevent him from becoming absolute. Upon this point they remained adamant.

The court retained fond hopes that the country party might fear the men rather than the measure. If it was not Montague's continuance in the ministry which caused the fears of the standing army, some thought it might well be the 'evil genius' Sunderland.[43] After Sunderland gave up his post as lord chamberlain, however, the commons' resolve was not appreciably to diminish. On 8 January, after concerting their plans the previous night at the Rose Club, the junto moved that the committee of supply be instructed to consider the sum necessary for guards, garrisons and other expenses. By this move, they hoped to add to the vote of the previous month by instructing a sum to be voted of £500,000 which they expected would maintain very nearly 15,000 men. When the whole matter was revived, so were the old objections. Once again, it was argued that a navy was adequate for England's defence. A standing army was not needed for security and was dangerous to individual liberties. With protestations from naval officers, the country side argued that the court managers were trying to lead the commons by the nose. Montague rejoined that it was more apparent that managers from the French court were doing so. Perhaps such treasonous aspersions might have proved conclusive in the wake of the assassination plot, but they did not do so in the wake of the peace.[44] It soon appeared that the opposition was well acquainted with the junto's plan. By putting a tactical question which kept the court from slipping its measures through, the court again suffered a defeat, by 188–164.[45]

Still, it was the country leaders themselves which gave the court some cause for hope. They intimated that they would not tie the court down to the number of troops maintained in 1680, but would allow for numbers in Tangiers and Holland as well as for a regiment of horse and dragoons. 'If they really mean as their leaders Intimate,' wrote Vernon, 'I don't perceive they are very wide from one another in their reckning both intending it shall be a summ rather than any Express

[42] R. Yard to Williamson, 21 December. *Ibid.*, pp. 521–3.
[43] Leeds to Viscount Lonsdale, 1 January 1697/8. *H.M.C. Lonsdale*, p. 108.
[44] Brandenburg dispatch, 11/21 January. B.M. Add. MSS. 30,000 B. f. 9 r.
[45] Vernon to Shrewsbury, 8 January. Boughton, Shrewsbury Papers, i, f. 177. *H.C.J.*, xii, 37.

number.' He thought that much of the agitation over the disbandment issue was simply a tory manoeuvre to discredit the whig management. The king under their plan, would be as well provided for as previously and '...in one respect better since if it went as the Tories would have it no Enquiry should be made whither the Dutch Guards were kept up or not.' Methuen and Molesworth defended Harley's plan and broke with the junto, arguing that the earlier vote did not preclude the house from providing for the safety of the kingdom.[46] In Methuen's subsequent apology to the king he said that he acted as he did only after noting the failure to speak against foreign troops during the debate. He was simply desirous of promoting unanimity and had been thinking of his majesty's long-term interest. The junto leaders, he found to his sorrow, demanded a more limited view and he wrote that he '...suffered much with Mr Montague and our managers for my Dissenting from them.'[47]

The junto leaders were right. It was soon clear that the country party and its leaders had little place for moderation, being noted by Vernon to '...maintain their ground against them and let things go no otherwise than they will have it.' In committee, Harley began very early by proposing £300,000, believing this to be 'very fair' as exceeding Charles's establishment of 1680 by £15,000. Pelham, on behalf of the court, thought this too strict and moved for £400,000, a sum Montague was thought willing to close with, seeing no reason to expect more. 'In all probability,' Vernon believed, the court might have gained Pelham's sum if Sir Christopher Musgrave had not begun '...preaching up unanimity and of what consequence it was that all should concur in a matter of that moment...' Sadly he noted that others concurred but only '...being sensible they could do no better.'[48]

William concealed his displeasure at the vote for pragmatic reasons. He knew that as it stood, it would probably allow him to maintain only 10,000 men, but he was also determined to make the money go as far as possible. Despite his belief that the vote would contribute to French cavilling[49] which was promulgated in whip letters urging court supporters to attend to stop the country movement,[50] the tide of disband-

---

[46] Vernon to Shrewsbury, 8 January. Boughton, Shrewsbury Papers, i, f. 177.

[47] To Galway, 11 January. Blenheim, Sunderland letter book.

[48] To Shrewsbury, 9 January. Boughton, Shrewsbury Papers, i, 178.

[49] To Heinsius, 11/21 and 21/31 January. Grimblot, *Letters*, i, 147 and 149.

[50] See, for example, the letter of Portland to Viscount Lonsdale, 17/27 January, 28 April and 1 May 1698. *H.M.C. Londsale*, pp. 108–9.

ment continued. Vernon even doubted the advisability of the court's trying to increase the number,[51] believing that no ministerial faction would dare brave popular sentiment on this issue. He was quite correct. After a resolution to continue officers who were disbanded on half pay, Methuen sadly observed that '...the house began to resume their heat and inserted that it should extend only to such Officers as were natural born Subjects of England to exclude those naturalized and likewise the debate ran that no Forreiger [foreigner] should be in the Troops continued here.'[52] While a vote for continuing many officers on half pay caused William considerable delight as it provided for the needs inherent in rapid mobilization, the amendment caused him particular worry for it obviously meant an end to his Dutch guards. Apart from the general distrust of foreign soldiers they were evidently expensive as well: William believed that if he were to be forced to readmit them to the Netherlands it would mean sacrificing '...six Scotch regiments and a few Swiss regiments besides.'[53]

Certainly William's relations with the confederate powers were not facilitated by the commons' refusal in March to vote the foreign princes any part of the sum due to them '...a down right negative being put upon so small a proportion as the 6th part.' It was not, Vernon thought, due to any failure on the part of the court spokesman but rather that the whole opposition '...kept almost their whole strength together.' He noted that in private or party business such as the Duncombe issue, the junto's forces did well enough, but in such public matters as the disbandment question, it was a different matter: '...this mustering up in private business, and being scattered in publick concerns gives no very good idea of a party.'[54] Although Vernon does not state the reason, it seems implied clearly enough: many members deemed it expedient to abstain, fearing the loss of court patronage if they voted against such proposals and the rancour of the opposition and the electorate if they voted in favour. Indeed, in discussions amongst court and junto leaders it was decided not to attempt to increase the number of marines from 3,000 to 6,000 men, it being feared that even this would ruin the little good will that remained.[55]

It was not that the court's opponents had no concern for national

---

[51] To Shrewsbury, 15 January 1697/8. *Vernon Corr.*, i, 465–6.
[52] To [Galway], 18 January. Blenheim, Sunderland letter book.
[53] To Portland, 21/31 January. Grimblot, *Letters*, i, 150–1.
[54] To Shrewsbury, 8 March. Boughton, Shrewsbury Papers, i, f. 75.
[55] S. to s., 8 February. *Ibid.*, ii, 1–5.

defence, for they obviously did. If the king was provided with but £350,000 for the maintenance of all guards and garrisons in mid-January, the security provided by the fleet and the militia was evidently thought to be enough.[56] In December it was made exceedingly apparent that a large naval force was to be maintained. The house did not even balk at a projected naval establishment of 10,000 men.[57] In the same month Sir Richard Onslow moved for a bill to be brought in to make the militia more useful.[58] When the commons had asked the king for the numbers of the militia, he was obliged to reply that there were 120,000 men.[59] Clearly then, it was not simply the expense involved. Indeed, some thought that an efficient militia would be more costly than a large standing army.[60] While the court might argue that it was inadvisable to depend upon the militia as the men lacked training and were unreliable,[61] whose fault was that? Why could the king not follow the advice in Trenchard's pamphlet and make the militia more useful? Or was it that he would not? The country party wanted a decentralized force over which it might have more control. Without court help, however, little could come of any militia plans, and it was no secret that William had no sympathy for such designs. In allowing the militia to decline, William was but following the policy of his predecessors who thereby exhibited the need for a strong standing army—a standing army which would now at best be used for foreign wars which the country party did not want.

The king added to his problems by stoking the fires of xenophobia: in early June as the matter of supply was still dragging on, some did not scruple to say that the money would have been voted and the session over if the king had not again spoken of going to Holland.[62] One suspects that the country gentlemen were asking themselves if William was really an English king or a Dutch stadtholder with English possessions —or simply a would-be tyrant. Still, the attack was neither generally against the court nor even against King William, but was simply a

---

[56] Brandenburg dispatch, 11/21 January. B.M. Add. MSS. 30,000 B. f. 9.
[57] *H.C.J.*, xii, 13.
[58] Vernon to Ambassador Williamson, 17 December 1697. *Cal. S.P. Dom.*, p. 516.
[59] Brandenburg dispatch, 11/21 January 1697/8. B.M. Add. MSS. 30,000 B. f. 9.
[60] J. Ellis to Williamson, 17 December 1697. *Cal. S.P. Dom.*, p. 516.
[61] T. Hopkins to s., 17 December. *Ibid.*, pp. 516–17.
[62] Brandenburg dispatch, 7/17 June 1698. B.M. Add. MSS. B. f. 132 r.

matter of country policy. Those who had sought other reasons were ignoring the most important one; it was fear of endangering constitutional liberties which was decisive in determining most members' votes. In writing to Heinsius it is clear that William thought this to be the case: 'People here only busy themselves about a fanciful liberty.'[63] He wrote to Portland that '…they think only of saving and supporting themselves; they do not trouble themselves about what is passing in other countries any more than as if there were none in existence.'[64] The French envoy thought so too. Indeed, Tallard provides the greatest evidence that the country gentlemen were at least not disloyal. Correcting the earlier false impressions of the French court, he reluctantly wrote to Louis that those opposed to the king's will were not opposed to his government. They were not even obstructionists, but simply wished to keep him from becoming absolute.[65]

Late in the summer of 1698, the Brandenburg envoy stated that there were over 33,000 troops in the British Isles about half of whom were stationed in England. The king had maintained a far larger military establishment than authorized.[66] Perhaps William thought that as parliament had neither fixed a date nor made full financial provisions for cashiering the troops, his delays might be excused. Then too, mention had been made neither of the number of troops to be maintained in Scotland and Ireland nor the nationality of the troops which remained in England. Perhaps the king had taken advantage of these loopholes, thinking that as the French continued their mobilization and the health of the Spanish king declined, the commons' anger would appreciably

---

[63] 11/21 January 1697/8. Grimblot, *Letters*, i, 147–8.

[64] 8/18 February. *Ibid.*, i, 176.

[65] Abbé Renaudot's 'Memorandum on the Affairs of England', 3/13 February 1697/8. It was at first thought that either England had no fears from France in respect to King James or that it did not fear his restoration as William did. This interpretation was corrected by Tallard who wrote: 'Mais Sire, il faut remarquer que ces gens qui sont contre ses volontés, ne sont point contre son Gouvernment, ne voulant point de desordre et ne desirant que d'émpecher qu'il ne devienne le maître.' 30 March/8 April 1698. P.R.O. 31/3/180f. 52. Trans. in Grimblot, *Letters*, i, 355.

[66] Bonet noted there to be 16,615 men in England, 5,000 in Scotland and 12,000 in Ireland, totalling 33,615 in all, not counting those stationed abroad. Brandenburg dispatch, 4/14 October. B.M. Add. MSS. 30,000 B. ff. 191v–191r. The account presented to the commons in December showed 14,834 men stationed in England, including 3,681 horse, 1,179 dragoons and 9,974 foot. There were 15,488 men in Ireland. *H.C.J.*, xii, 356–8.

cool.[67] He was mistaken. At the beginning of October, members up early for the new parliament were said to deplore William's breach of honour, considering it an infringement upon their liberties. Under special censure was his maintenance of a large force in Ireland, which was thought to be first upon the opposition's agenda of attack.[68] The commons' concern was heightened by fear. In April 1698 the mutiny act expired and was not to be renewed until war appeared imminent several years later. The commons' action was motivated by a desire to ensure that the king would have less control over the armed forces. An undisciplined army, however, unlike an undisciplined militia, was a two-edged sword, and at a time when parliament was striving to cashier troops, the blade was far nearer to the commons than the king. More swords must be beaten into ploughshares. By late November another virulent anti-standing army pamphlet emanated from Trenchard's pen. Robert Price applauded it for its efficacy, roundly condemning the turncoat junto-whig attitude as 'miraculous': 'Surly patriots grow servil flatters, old comonwealts men declare for prerogative and Admirals against the fleet.'[69] Any hopes the court may have gained from its victory in electing Littleton Speaker were soon dashed. After the king's speech was taken into consideration, the commons quickly came to some resolutions calling for the established force not to exceed 7,000 troops in England and 12,000 in Ireland, consisting in both cases of natural-born subjects.[70] On Saturday, 17 December, the resolutions were effected in a bill after a debate in which the court spokesmen were thought not even to have been listened to. Vernon believed that if William had let it be known that he would be satisfied with 10,000 men, he would have been granted them. But the king thought that no less than twice that number would be adequate and the court managers were again at a loss, fearing William's criticisms for not obtaining what they believed to be the impossible, and a vicious attack from the country members for furthering the means of arbitrary government. As a result

---

[67] Vernon believed country hostility was lessening for the reasons mentioned above. To Shrewsbury (20 Aug. 1698, is the date suggested by D. H. Somerville), *Vernon Corr.*, ii, 179–81.

[68] Brandenburg dispatch, 4/14 October. B.M. Add. MSS. 30,000 B. f. 229 r.

[69] John Trenchard, *A Short History of Standing Armies in England* (1698). R. Price to Granville, 26 November. Bodl. Carte MSS. 130 f. 394.

[70] *H.C.J.*, xii, 359–60. It would seem that about 5,000 troops were provided for in Scotland. Brandenburg dispatch 4/14 October. B.M. Add. MSS. 30,000 B. f. 197 r.

when Sir Charles Sedley proposed the aforesaid number of 10,000 men, it was scarcely seconded.[71]

Shortly after the matter was settled, Jack Howe made his maiden appearance in his capacity as knight of the shire for Gloucestershire. Always ready with salt and vinegar for his enemies' wounds, he charged into the commons saying that he had just come from the provinces where everyone was asking whether there was peace or war. It was impossible to tell, as there were so many soldiers occupying all the best rooms at the inns and the people were still plagued with taxes. When told of the vote to disband the troops to 7,000 men, he was said to have rejoiced loudly, pretending not to have known of it.[72] Howe's action was largely, of course, mere exhibitionism, for the king had been given a severe enough blow. If the number of troops to be allowed was to be much the same as the present establishment, the location was quite different: Ireland or Scotland was not London, as the French envoy noted ecstatically. In addition, the demand that all troops must be natural-born Englishmen was an even greater slight to the king than at first might appear. Not only did it cast aspersions upon the Dutch nature of the monarch but it would deprive him of the leadership of Galway and Schomberg.[73]

On 14 December William wrote to Heinsius of his apprehension of the parliamentary proceedings; on the sixteenth that things were going so badly that he would not even discuss them; on the twentieth he expected to see him 'earlier than he expected'.[74] Once again the king was contemplating forsaking the crown and returning to the Netherlands. William wrote a resignation speech which he told Heinsius would astonish parliament.[75] It would certainly have done that—but what would the effect have been? Why was he dissuaded from giving it? In part, because of his ministers' advice as to the possible unforeseen results of such a course of action. Still, one wonders why he told so many. Somers, privy to the king's plan stated:

He has spoken of it to my Lord Marlborough (which one would

---

[71] Vernon to Shrewsbury, 17 December. *Vernon Corr.*, ii, 235–7.

[72] Brandenburg dispatch, 20/30 December. B.M. Add. MSS. 30,000 B. f. 284 v.–285 r.

[73] French dispatch, 23 December 1698/2 January 1699. Grimblot, *Letters*, ii, 225.

[74] *Ibid.*, pp. 212–13, 214 and 219.

[75] 6/16 December. *Ibid.*, p. 233. Debate of 6 January misdated 1 January in Cobbett, v, 1192–3.

wonder at, almost as much as the thing itself), Mr Montague, and to my lord Orford and, I believe, to diverse others.[76]

Part of William's design was perhaps to make sure that the ministry would do its best out of fear of what the commons would do to them after the king left.[77]

The ministers did appear to do their best, but probably their best was still not thought good enough. On 23 December, the court was able to change the articles regarding troops from 'subjects born in England' to 'subjects of England' which would allow for both Scotch and Irish to serve as well as preserve the command of Lord Galway.[78] In an attempt to confuse the entire issue, Montague argued that the current wording of the bill would effectually disband the militia, noting too that provision was not being made to disband the army. Harley found that most of Montague's objections were frivolous and might be ironed out in committee. The one matter not open to subsequent dispute was the number of troops, which was to remain at but 7,000 men. Although Montague (evidently putting the mask aside) asserted that this too might be open for discussion, there was no conclusive decision.[79] The debate had lasted but two hours and the court had not dared a division. If the bill had been made somewhat less effectual, still there had been no strong challenge. Harley believed that the court had been trying to spoil the bill,[80] but as it stood it was still quite healthy. If there was to be any augmentation to the number Vernon thought '…it will be something very inconsiderable which will give little satisfaction at Kensington.'[81] Some supposed that the king would be satisfied with 10,000 men.[82] but Somers knew he would not. Not even that number could be carried '…unless the country gentlemen would enter into the debate, which they would never do, unless it might be said to them, that it

---

[76] To Shrewsbury, 29 December. *Shrewsbury Corr.*, pp. 572–4.

[77] Somers wrote: 'I think, also, there is an extreme difficulty upon all our friends, who will, in the conclusion, fall under censure, however they act in this matter.' To Shrewsbury, s.d. *Ibid.*

[78] French dispatch, 23 December 1698/2 January 1699. Grimblot, *Letters*, ii, 215.

[79] Vernon to Shrewsbury, 24 December 1698. *Vernon Corr.*, ii, 239–41.

[80] To Sir E. Harley, 24 December. *H.M.C. Portland*, iii, 600.

[81] To Shrewsbury, 23 December. Boughton, Shrewsbury Papers, ii, f. 123.

[82] The placeman, James Lowther, wrote to his father that '…it's thought the House will come up to allow of ten thousand, with which the Co[t] [court] will be pretty well satisfied.' 24 December. Cumb. R.O., Lonsdale MSS.

would be an acceptable service to the king, and that he would make the best of that number.' It was of course not to be, for William believed that to say that would be '...but to deceive us.'[83]

Probably the king was once again stalling for time, hoping that the house would thin. The house committee which was to meet on the twenty-third was put off until the next day, a fact which effectually precluded it from meeting until after the Christmas recess.[84] Even then it was not to meet immediately, but rather at a later period during the next week. The French envoy noted that in the interim the court had had it rumoured about that the commons would get what it wanted even faster than expected. Troops would be disbanded before the date set and ships were on their way to take the Dutch Guards home.[85] Was the court sincere or was it simply trying to ensure that the country gentlemen would take a very long Christmas vacation? The court made serious efforts over the holidays to make converts in their now more modest design to maintain at least 10,000 troops.[86] Nevertheless, the day the king was supposed to give his resignation speech, the attempt to instruct the committee to reconsider the number of forces scarcely got off the ground. Harley was joined by Lord Hartington, Pelham and Sir Richard Onslow in opposing the instruction, while Montague and Blathwayt presented the court's case, deploring the military inadequacies. Still, the commons' mood had not changed and with but a few words regarding the size of the establishment of Charles II, Harley effectually silenced the court. Despite a long debate, there was no division.[87] Vernon believed that a division would be worse than pointless, fearing that it would give further occasion for disunity. In committee it was decided that they were to be first paid and, by 26 March 1699, disbanded.[88] In committee of the whole house on 11 January, in order to minimize any danger of military tumult over the actual disbandment, Harley advocated voting £300,000 to cashier the troops, and this was unanimously approved and agreed to the next day. Foley, however,

---

[83] Somers to Shrewsbury, 29 December. *Shrewsbury Corr.*, pp. 572–4.

[84] Vernon to Shrewsbury, 23 December. Boughton, Shrewsbury Papers, ii, f. 123.

[85] French dispatch, 21/31 January 1698/9. Grimblot, *Letters*, ii, 244–5.

[86] French dispatch, 4/14 January. *Ibid.*, p. 230. Edward Harley believed that the court was gaining help from the dissenting ministers. To Sir E. Harley, 3 January 1698/9. B.M. Portland loan 29/189.

[87] James Lowther to [Sir John Lowther], 7 January. Cumb. R.O., Lonsdale MSS.

[88] To Shrewsbury, 5 January. *Vernon Corr.*, ii, 246–8.

urged that it would be better not to vote an outright supply but simply a fund of credit,[89] evidently to ensure that it would be employed for the desired end. The militia was of course to be maintained. Nothing had been said about the marines. Vernon interpreted the omission as meaning that the current establishment would neither be taken away nor doubled as the court had hoped.[90] On 16 January the bill was reported and ordered engrossed. The king continued to go through the motions of preparing to disband the troops, making it appear that he believed the passage of the bill inevitable.[91]

Surprise was the court's weapon. On the third reading it soon became apparent that they were going to brave debate and probably a division which Robert Price noted to be '...contrary to all expectations.'[92] Also against all expectations, thought Secretary Vernon, was the fact that at least some of the country gentlemen spoke against the bill. He noted happily '...many country gentlemen coming in voluntarily and without any concert to declare their dislike of so small a number.'[93] Perhaps too much has been made of this. Apart from the fact that it was quite possible that persuasion had been employed by the junto unknown to Vernon (they did not confide in him to any considerable extent), it is a question as to what degree the defectors were truly country gentlemen or simply court tools trying to make a court proposal appear popular. Of the seven so-called country gentlemen he names, four sat in the previous parliament. While two of these had consistently voted country, two had consistently voted court.[94] In any case it would appear that

---

[89] Vernon to Shrewsbury, 12 January. *Ibid.*, pp. 250–1.

[90] Vernon to Shrewsbury, 5 January. *Ibid.*, pp. 247–8.

[91] French dispatch, 14/24 January. Grimblot, *Letters*, ii, 238–9.

[92] To the duke of Beaufort, 19 January. Bodl. Carte MSS. 130 f. 397. James Lowther to [Sir John Lowther], 17 January. Cumb. R.O., Lonsdale MSS.

[93] To Shrewsbury, 17/27 January. *Vernon Corr.*, ii, 251–2. Chas. Hatton to Visc. Hatton, 19 January. *Hatton Corr.*, ii, 238–9. Tallard believed that the attempt to make the bill appear popular and expand the forces rather than allow it to pass as a simple compromise is what secured its fate. To Louis, 21/31 January. Grimblot, *Letters*, ii, 244–5.

[94] Vernon to Shrewsbury, 17/27 January. *Vernon Corr.*, ii, 251–2. He names Sir William Blacket [Newcastle, voted country in two divisions the previous parliament], Sir John Philips [Pembroke, voted country in two divisions], Richard Norton [Co. Hants., voted court in two divisions], Sir John Mainwaring [Co. Chester, voted court in three divisions], Col. Henry Cornwall [Co. Hereford], [Steven?] Harvey [Reigate?], Sir James Houlton [Hindon]. Chas. Hatton to Visc. Hatton, 19 January. *Hatton Corr.*, ii, 238–9. See Appendix A.

the court was once again too greedy in its demands. While some simply
wanted to increase the number to 10,000 men, others wished to vote a
sum without setting any number by the act.[95] It was probably this
which sealed the bill's fate. The country leaders, taken by surprise, sat
silent until eight or so had spoken and finally revived the traditional
arguments in the lengthy debate.[96] If the courtiers' rhetoric and appearance of popularity won anyone over, they should not have renewed
their talk of the precariousness of the king's title and the danger of a
fifth-column movement. Sir John Packington had apparently been
waiting for this. After declaring that he saw nothing precarious about
the king's title, a king who had been declared rightful and lawful, he
noted that the only person who did question it was Bishop Burnet. If
further security was wanted, then they might have it by hanging the
bishop, as the burning of his book had not had the desired effect. One
might suppose that some of the laughter which followed was a bit
forced.[97]

The court apparently was still indulging itself in gross delusions as
to what the commons would permit. It sought to retain not only the
Dutch Guards and D'Auverquerque's regiment but Portland's besides.
The French envoy, a usually pessimistic observer, believed that the
court might have succeeded in its plans if Portland's regiment had not
been included, which the commons would never allow. It appeared
that the court did not seek a compromise, but almost a complete rever-
sion of sentiment. The only concession that it would allow was to replace the Dutch soldiers with English when they died.[98]

The opposition could be just as tenacious as the court: notice had
been sent out to the city to give members warning of the intended division. After the three-hour debate it finally came and the country members appeared in force, supporting the existing bill, 221–154.[99]

Robert Price believed there to have been little popular support for
the maintenance of a standing army, noting that at least 120 court
officers were in the minority of whom at least 40 were military men.
Having flushed the court supporters, Price and his friends were determined to bring them down: 'Wee met severall of us,' he wrote, 'and
have within a very few, fixed the names of those who voted pro and

---

[95] To the duke of Beaufort, 19 January. Bodl. Carte MSS. 130 f. 397.
[96] Vernon to Shrewsbury, 17 January. *Vernon Corr.*, ii, 251–2.
[97] Chas. Hatton to Visc. Hatton. 19 January. *Hatton Corr.*, ii, 238–9.
[98] French dispatch, 21/31 January. Grimblot, *Letters*, ii, 244–5.
[99] French dispatch, 19/29 January. *Ibid.*, pp. 238–9.

con;...'[100] If those who supported the proposal believed they had the
wishes of the country behind them, inclusion in a black list would see
how earnest they were. The list was quickly circulated and it soon
appeared which was the better side to be associated with. Sir George
Fletcher, who had previously voted court and was said to have done so
again, had written to his less favourably disposed neighbour, Sir Daniel
Fleming, of his delight at the disbanding bill's progress.[101] Another so
listed denied all knowledge of the debate, deplored a friend's inclusion
as well and even brought the matter to the attention of the house.
Colonel Chivers, caught red-handed in sending out a copy of the list
was also alleged to have incorrectly recorded the vote. He was not,
however, censured for doing so and only a general resolution was made
regarding parliamentary privileges.[102] Subsequently a vote demanding
that he be sent for in custody was defeated 134–99.[103] Indeed, any considerable change of heart over the matter would appear to be put out
of court by one of 'the immortal seven', the duke of Devonshire.
Following the hearty promotion of the bill by his two sons and the
king's reprimand for their actions, the duke threatened to resign the
office of lord steward. He said that he took the attack as one upon himself for he believed their reasons were sensible, as the king was forbidden to maintain a large establishment.[104]

When the bill was brought up to the lords, Robert Price had a few
doubts as to the likelihood of its passage. It was, in effect, a tack to a
money bill, but Price expected that the credit clause for disbandment
would probably be a sufficient guarantee of passage.[105] The court again
employed delaying tactics, evidently in the hope that the commons
would pass the money bill in the interim. The first reading was adjourned
until the following Thursday, although a motion of the earl of Essex to
adjourn for two weeks was let fall if only because the commons would
almost certainly have adjourned for a similar period. The lords, Vernon

---

[100] To the duke of Beaufort, 19 January. Bodl. Carte MSS. 130 f. 397 (out
of order).
[101] 21 January 1698. *H.M.C. Le Fleming*, p. 353. For the list see Browning,
Danby, iii, 213–17.
[102] Henry Blake to Walter White, 11 February 1698/9. Lord Lansdowne,
'Wiltshire Politicians, *c.* 1700'. *Wilts. Arch. and Nat. Hist. Mag.* (1932–4),
xlv, 73–4. The vote was 134–99. Norris and Harcourt were majority tellers.
15 April 1699. *H.C.J.*, xii, 645.
[103] *H.C.J.*, xii, 643.
[104] French dispatch, 22 April/2 May. Grimblot, *Letters*, ii, 320–2.
[105] To the duke of Beaufort, 19 January. Bodl. Carte MSS. 130 f. 397.

thought, had best not tamper with the bill. Even to force a conference would be but to waste time and kindle commons resentment.[106] Godolphin thought so too. He believed that there were such '...divisions and distractions that to reject it would be worse and make it harder to have even that much again.'[107] Extremists in the commons were delightedly preparing for such an occasion. One wrote: 'A bill if Rejected is preparing and I heard Sir Bart. Showre [Shower] say the other day, he would assent most heartily in it.'[108] Not surprisingly then, further attempts to delay were quashed in the lords. While there were debates over the insufficiency of the number, it was generally agreed that for reasons either of policy or of expediency the bill must pass. The third reading was almost perfunctory, only token opposition being registered.[109]

The next day, 1 February, William passed the bill and made a speech, criticizing the authors of the measure. Vernon hoped this would have a good effect.[110] The commons moved to thank the king for his speech and subsequently to take it into consideration. In both instances, Harley seconded the motion. Secretary Vernon became increasingly anxious as he knew there was little the court could do, for the concurrence of the country gentlemen was essential '...they having still the lead.' The fact that they had the lead did not mean that the extremists amongst them would have their way. The disbandment controversy was by no means over and Vernon had only suggested a rapid passage in the lords so that the subject of the nation's security might be re-opened under more auspicious circumstances.[111]

Certainly the king would appear to have been forced to some sort of fresh action. The death of the electoral prince of Bavaria had effectually put an end to the first partition treaty and again raised the problem of the Spanish succession. Perhaps the commons would have done well to delay disbanding until they fathomed the French designs. If the commons had been truly privy to the negotiations and the treaty, then they might have done so. As it was, they were to see the subsequent court attempts to expand the forces in a very strange light. When the

---

[106] To Shrewsbury, 21 January. *Vernon Corr.*, ii, 254-5.
[107] Lord Coningsby to Viscount Lonsdale, 21 January. *H.M.C. Lonsdale*, p. 111.
[108] Sir Geo. Fletcher to Sir Daniel Fleming, 21 January. *H.M.C. Le Fleming*, p. 353.
[109] To Shrewsbury, 31 January. *Vernon Corr.*, ii, 257.
[110] To s., 2 February. *Ibid.*, p. 258.   [111] To s., 31 January. *Ibid.*, ii, 257.

king's speech was taken into consideration in early February, it was thought that '...the courtiers had promised the King to retrieve his Dutch guards.' When the debate opened, however, '...the Gentlemen were impatient to be imposed on [to have] a disbanding vote one day and to set up an army by a vote the next.' A subsequent court attempt to put off consideration of the king's speech was effectually blocked. Harley promised a bill to make the militia efficient, which Vernon believed to be a service under the circumstances, '...as if it were a good deliverance from a debate that was perhaps apprehended on all sides.'[112] Some had their doubts as to the efficacy of the militia proposals.[113] It would seem probable that the king had little use for this design; a design which would jeopardize his plans for an offensive continental war and but serve to buttress the arguments of the proponents of the blue water school. The slowness with which the bill progressed would indicate a lack of court initiative on a proposal for which it had little use.[114]

In contrast to the commons' action, the lords resolved that the king be allowed to maintain his Dutch guards unless another expedient was found.[115] A considerable protest to the resolution was signed by the dissenting peers, who noted the irregularity of the action.[116] In the commons, the lords' resolution was not even given the privilege of being attacked; it was simply ignored.[117] On 18 March the king employed a more direct approach. He sent Lord Ranelagh to the commons with a request specifically designed to maintain his Dutch guards. Subtlety was employed, for it was said that the unauthorized troops would be disbanded presently, as would the Dutch guards unless, as the king hoped, the commons gave him permission to maintain them. Perhaps if the king had made his request during the initial debates it might have been complied with, but now it was thought too late. Vernon wondered, indeed, what it was that even prompted the king to make the request; a request which the opposition roundly condemned as entailing the repeal of a most recent bill. Compared to what else was

---

[112] French dispatch, 9/19 February 1698/9. Grimblot, *Letters*, ii, 270–1.
[113] Robert Price to the duke of Beaufort, 9 February. Bodl. Carte MSS. 130 f. 399.
[114] For the introduction of the matter see *H.C.J.*, xii. 484 and 491.
[115] R. Price to the duke of Beaufort, 3 February. Bodl. Carte MSS. 130 f. 399.
[116] French dispatch, 9/19 and 16/26 February 1699. Grimblot, *Letters*, ii, 272 and 288.
[117] French dispatch, 16/26 February. *Ibid.*, p. 288.

said, this blunt statement might almost be considered a eulogy. Harley opposed even taking the matter into consideration, saying that the mere delivery of the message gave him irrepressible disquiet. Tongue in cheek, he absolved the ministers from responsibility in tendering it—at least those who were members. Ireton spoke along the same lines, vindicating the ministers in such a way that Vernon believed he might have better left them alone. Jack Howe, always one to spell out subtleties for the more obtuse, said plainly that mere impracticality was not a clear enough reason. The request was in itself inherently repugnant, for it preferred strangers and simultaneously brought suspicion upon the reliability of the native English to guard the king. Such a policy, he added, with caustic innuendos, was responsible for the alienation of King James from his army. The request was not even formally considered, it being carried simply to give reasons for refusal.[118] The king expected the reasons to be impertinent. On 20 March when the reasons emerged from committee his fears were fulfilled. An attempt to recommit the measure was defeated 175–156 and so too were court chances to alter substantially the fervency of the commons' resolutions. Still, the court in committee was to salvage a number of amendments toning down the measure. More blame was placed upon the ministers for making the request, while the request itself was now said only to be disrespectful of the constitution, rather than actually doing violence to it. The court also succeeded in modifying the charge that the king had renegued upon his original declaration by keeping a standing force in peacetime without parliamentary consent.[119] Having succeeded so far and quite obviously relying upon diminishing country attendance, the court attempted to amend the crucial paragraph out of existence—the scotched snake was well on the way to recovery. There was an attempt to delete the clause referring to the phrase the king had used in his original declaration promising to send back all the foreign forces he had brought over with him. If the court had succeeded in this, it was thought probable that there would have been yet another motion to allow the king to maintain his Dutch guards. After a great debate, the amendment was thrown out, if only by six votes. The fact that the court had almost succeeded was not because the country members had any considerable change of heart. It would appear rather that it was due to continued court attendance and the opposition's expectation that the

---

[118] Vernon to Shrewsbury, 18 March 1698/9. *Vernon Corr.*, ii, 269–70.
[119] 18 March. *H.C.J.*, xii, 604.

matter of the guards itself would not be revived.[120] What would have
happened if the court had succeeded is difficult to say. Perhaps there
would have been a remustering of country forces and the matter would
have been brought up yet again. But the court did not succeed,
although the battles were not yet over.

One other method of maintaining the guards and increasing the
number of marines would be to augment the naval establishment of the
previous year which had allowed for 10,000 seamen and 3,000 marines.
Here was an easy way for the court to effect its end; by employing
semantics it might exploit the country party's disposition for a very
large naval force. In committee, 15,000 men were voted for the navy
and the court kept the word 'seamen' from even being allowed in the
question.[121] Robert Price supposed that the court would succeed in its
designs, unless the bill was not agreed to on report.[122] Perhaps with a
view to mustering forces to scuttle this latest court plan, some of the
opposition now attempted delaying tactics. If Harley and Musgrave were
willing to proceed in 'lumping' the ordinary revenue of the navy, a
gesture which Vernon believed to be benevolent, others were not so
compliant. Seymour, for example, wished to employ the old obstructionist tactic of inquiring into particulars and Jack Howe seeing '...a
more Waspish thing proposed, hee closed with it.' Although the moderate country position prevailed, Secretary Vernon expected the committee's report would result in one of the 'tuggingest days' of the session.[123]
On that day, if the court succeeded by only four votes in maintaining
the 15,000 men for the sea service, the country leaders were effectively
to preclude any exploitation of the tricky wording. Some of the court
support fell off, and it was carried 187–178 that they be seamen in 'the
antient usage of the Navy'. 'We apprehended,' wrote Robert Price, 'the
court had a mind to Keep up the Dutch footguards on the nav [navy]
establishment as marine Regiments and there [thereby] to elude our
disbanding bill wch they are def [defeated] in to our great satisfaction
and there [their] confnd [confoundment?] att Kensington.'[124] Vernon

---

[120] The majority tellers were Col. Granville and Francis Gwyne. *Ibid*. James
Lowther to [Sir John Lowther], 25 March 1699. Cumb. R.O., Lonsdale MSS.
[121] Robert Price to the duke of Beaufort. [9?] February 1698/9. Bodl. Carte
MSS. 130 f. 399 (out of order).
[122] To s., 18 February. *Ibid*., f. 396 (out of order).
[123] Vernon to Shrewsbury, 16 February. Boughton, Shrewbury Papers,
ii, f. 145.
[124] To the duke of Beaufort, 18 February. Bodl. Carte MSS. 130 f. 396.
Harcourt and Winnington were majority tellers. *H.C.J.*, xii, 518.

noted sadly that it was probably all too true, for while there would be
'...more Seamen this year than wee know how to employ,' the garrisons
would be undermanned. As the '...point of the marines was not to bee
maintained' he saw '...little expectation of gratifying the King'.[125]

Such expectations as remained were dispelled in late April. The
commons called for the presentation of the list of officers of the regiments that were to be cashiered, and it was ordered to lie on the table.
The possibility of providing half pay for officers was briefly considered
but nothing had been done by the time the house adjourned. In part
this might be accounted for by the king dining away from London with
Orford, thus raising tory resentment.[126] More widely, however, it was
thought that national feelings were aroused by his preferment of his
young Dutch favourite, Albemarle, over Ormond. For a time the court
even had fears that a vote might be passed against strangers being in
any military post 'as late as it is in the session'.[127]

About the same time, the marines were showing that to disband
them was not without its dangers. Coningsby, one of the most ardent
proponents of disbandment, was assaulted by one of the cashiered
officers. The latter was, however, soon ordered to be taken into custody
by the serjeant-at-arms and prosecuted.[128] Probably by acting in this
way, the marines did their cause more harm than good. Subsequent
disorders in July[129] probably but tended to confirm the country gentlemen in their belief that a standing army was a menace.

The menace had been minimized: the standing army was reduced to a
shadow of its former self. It had not been easy. The court had shown
the utmost in tenacity. There had been, as one member wrote, not less
than '...six set battles besides the many Avenues which were all
defended.'[130] As the king admitted, it was a true country victory in
which French money played no part.[131] The country party maintained

[125] To Shrewsbury, 18 February. Boughton, Shrewsbury Papers, ii, f. 146.
[126] French dispatch, 22 April/2 May 1699. Grimblot, *Letters*, p. 314.
[127] Vernon to Shrewsbury, 15 April. Boughton, Shrewsbury Papers, ii,
f. 171.   [128] 9 April. *H.C.J.*, xiii. 319.
[129] See the letters of Vernon to Shrewsbury, 6 and 13 July. Boughton,
Shrewsbury Papers, ii, f. 207, *Vernon Corr.*, ii, 319–20.
[130] Sir G. Fletcher to Sir D. Fleming, 30 May. West. R.O., Le Fleming
Papers. It is of course a question as to which side(s) of the barricades Fletcher
was on. See above, p. 150.
[131] William wrote: 'If France has advanced any money for this purpose,
it has turned it to very bad use. I can assure you that nothing is more superfluous...' To Heinsius, 13/23 January. Grimblot, *Letters*, ii, 238.

its ground on this issue in the next session as well. It was to be dominant for a time even in matters of supply. One placeman wrote:

> The House tells them [the army?] they must have fewer Horse and more Foot, for that they will not allow quartering in the Country, and they must take care to keep within the compass of £300,000 for if they exceed [that sum] they will not make it good. Mr Harley now manages the whole business of supply and the House has hitherto entirely approv'd of his scheme.[132]

As the session progressed, there was of course the usual decline of country initiative,[133] but the disbandment issue was in fact closed and the court was not successfully to re-open the matter until the end of the next parliament.

---

[132] James Lowther to Sir John Lowther, 23 January 1699/1700. Cumb. R.O., Lowther Corr.

[133] See for example the letter of John Coke to Thomas Coke in which he notes that '...the court seems to have gained the majority, and that the country party may once carry a question they save the courtiers the pains of moving for a bill of supply.' N.d., February 1699/1700. *H.M.C. Cowper*, ii, 396. But note too, that Harley's aforementioned proposals were maintained in mid-March. Vernon to Shrewsbury, 14 March. Boughton, Shrewsbury Papers, iii, f. 45.

SEVEN

Irish Forfeitures

As the xenophobic Englishman's wish that Ireland be sunk into the sea seemed unlikely of fulfilment, the next best plan was for it to become an unenfranchised 'West England'. By the accession of James II, between two-thirds and four-fifths of the cultivable Irish land was held by Protestants.[1] Following the revolution and general subjugation of the country, the lands forfeited by the Irish Catholic rebels came to be thought of as a new lake of spoils which might serve to relieve the English tax burden. To the tax-payers' chagrin, however, this source rapidly began to evaporate. Not only were many of the Irish allowed to retain their lands, but even much of that which was confiscated William gave away. Precedent clearly lay with the king and, indeed, some of the grants were thought justified. Nevertheless, William's predilection for bestowing vast tracts of land upon his foreign favourites during the expensive war rekindled the flames of country resentment smouldering since the affair of the Welsh grants. Even the usual court apologists were to admit the general extravagance.

Unlike the disbandment controversy, however, the matter was not of vital concern to the country. Certainly the nation was not jeopardized, and whig and tory as well as individual interests were seen in the ensuing dispute which was both financial and complex. Nevertheless,

---

[1] N. Lawrence, *The Interest of Ireland* (1682), p. 50, and E. Curtis, *A History of Ireland* (6th ed., 1964), p. 263. Curtis estimates that by 1700 the Irish catholics held less than one-eighth of the freehold land. *Ibid.*, p. 276.

whenever a straightforward country situation arose, as when the issue became embroiled in an inter-house dispute, so too did the earlier unanimity. Still, in some ways the matter was a constitutional one; many saw it as a crusade to prevent the Dutch king from alienating English property. As with the disbandment controversy, the king in the end was to give way. The essence of the conflict was to be incorporated in one of the restricting clauses of the act of settlement, forbidding the giving of crown property to foreigners.

While there had been talk of the Irish forfeitures for years, little was effectively done until the waning of the court's power following the peace. It was not until then that the times were auspicious.[2] The first action was to vote leave to bring in a bill to vacate all grants made in Ireland since 13 February 1688–9 and to appropriate them to the use of the public. This was probably the most that could be redeemed, although few seem to have known it at the time. In rapid succession other measures were proposed extending the bill first to England and then progressively dating it to 1660: '...they have so loaded the cart, by taking in all the Grants since the year 1660,' wrote one observer, 'that they will not be able to get it along; which those Gentlemen were sensible of, who opposed looking back so far, but there was so great a majority against them, that they could not stand their ground...'[3] This was largely true. By looking back so far, quite obviously a number of the old tories and their friends found their financial interests jeopardized and would aid in sinking the bill. Those principally aimed at, the greatest beneficiaries, the junto and the Dutch favourites, saw that by including others they might save themselves. The court had argued that the measure was not for the public benefit, but simply an indirect attack upon certain persons whom the king had gratified.[4] That the bill failed seems due both to lack of interest, and to the likelihood that many were simply awaiting a new parliament. Country attendance had been declining and the court had won a number of tactical victories. There was an attempt, for example, to require all holders of beneficial grants (i.e., grants of which the commons approved) made since 1666 and then 1660, to pay one quarter of the value to confirm them. Some opposition

---

[2] Sir John Banks to Heneage Finch, 8 February 1697/8. Chatsworth, Finch-Halifax MSS., box 5.

[3] R. Yard to the earl of Manchester, 28 January. C. Cole ed., *Memoirs of Affairs of State* (1735), p. 10.

[4] Brandenburg dispatch, 21/31 January. B.M. Add. MSS. 30,000 B. ff. 17 v.–18 r.

leaders believed that the proponents of this measure were simply trying to safeguard their shaky grants. Nottingham wrote:

> I fancy some of the late grantees are apprehensive tht the next Parlt may not be so favourable to them as this has bin and therefore are content to pay a fixe for an argument agt a resumption and tht such a resumption may still be more dificult they desire to be linked with others who are now to be opprest that those may enjoy more securely their ill gotten favours.[5]

In the end, the grantees were not to get this opportunity. Nothing was heard of the bill after 19 May when the first (of what promised to be numerous) heart-rending petition arrived requesting exemption.[6] The court had also succeeded in instructing the committee to preserve one-third of the grants for the use of the crown.[7] It would have been most unwise for the country party to let the bill proceed as it was. Attendance was diminishing, and the bill would probably provide less tax relief with each passing day.

The opposition learned a grim lesson from trying to bite off more than it could chew. The country concept of what was just had to be reconciled with what was possible. The opposition had profited from its mistakes and at the cost of some delay proceeded to effect the necessary machinery to achieve its aims. On 18 April 1699 a clause was offered to be added to the land tax bill which would call for an account to be taken of the forfeited Irish estates. This was twice read, a clause added to name commissioners and the next day a commission of seven elected. While none were to be members,[8] the result of the ballot proved unfavourable to the government. Four of the seven were associated with the opposition, and they included Sir John Trenchard, the most prestigious of the pamphleteers opposing the maintenance of a standing army. When the bill reached the lords there were complaints that the commission should have been established by a separate act. After an angry debate, the bill passed, albeit by but a few votes. Still, if Secretary Vernon appears correct in noting that the tack angered the lords and almost resulted in the rejection of the money bill,[9] it seems that a separate bill would have

---

[5] To William, second marquis of Halifax, 21 May 1698. Althorpe, Halifax MSS., box 7.
[6] French dispatch, 11/12 April. Grimblot, *Letters*, i, 406–7.
[7] *H.C.J.*, xii, 132.   [8] *Ibid.*, pp. 652–3.
[9] Vernon wrote to Amb. Williamson that while the lords passed the land tax bill '...they were so offended at the tacking [of] the clause for the Irish

secured acquiescence by neither the peers nor the king. Evidently the peers' anger cooled considerably for there was only a token protest signed in the upper house against the procedure of tacking.[10] The clause caused considerable worry to the court and utter horror in Ireland, especially to the *de facto* leader of the Irish country party, Bishop King. He thought that the commission would break all of Ireland's legal securities and '...take away all the ready money in Ireland and we shall not recover in twenty years.'[11] Still, even he subsequently came to believe the size of William's grants scandalous.[12] Scarcely anyone defended the grants and the opposition eagerly awaited the forfeitures report.[13] Robert Price wrote: 'It is thought wee are to meet with some great men amongst them.'[14] He was correct: the grants of Portland and Albemarle exceeding as they did 240,000 acres, were generally 'found prodigous great'.[15]

On report from committee there was dissent: three of the seven commissioners refused to approve certain parts of the report wherein they argued that the commission surpassed its authorized function. This charge was aimed at several controversial articles wherein it was argued that the king went beyond the articles of Limerick in pardoning rebels who did not deserve pardons; that if a searching enquiry was made it would have been found that more estates might have been confiscated; that the work was thwarted by men in high stations; that the estate given to the countess of Orkney was not authorized as the land formed part of the crown property of James II. While the first charge might be answered by asserting the king's right to pardon whomever he wished and the second by noting that it was a matter open to con-

---

commission that they came within 5 or 6 of rejecting it.' 28 April 1699. *Cal. S.P. Dom.*, p. 150.

[10] Only nine signed the protest. *H.L.J.*, xvi, 453.

[11] To Sir Robert Southwell, 15 June. T.C.D. MSS. 1489 (Bishop King's letterbook).

[12] Bishop King wrote: ''Tis a scandalous thing that a million in forfeitures should be given away and not any thing that I can hear of to any publick or charitable use.' For the sake of Ireland, however, he would '...rather have them stand as they are than be disposed of by an English Parlement.' To the bishop of Killaloo, 24 October. *Ibid.*

[13] Chas. Davenant to Thomas Coke, 6 September. *H.M.C. Portland*, iii, 609.

[14] R. Price to the duke of Beaufort, 6 December. Bodl. Carte MSS. 130 f. 403.

[15] Sir John Vanbrugh to Manchester, 25 December. William (Montague), duke of Manchester, *Court and Society from Elizabeth to Anne* (1864), ii, 54.

jecture, the authorities in Ireland had not made the commission's task an easy one.[16] The last charge showed that the four commissioners had gone out of their way to attack the king for his action in giving away the private estate of James II to the countess of Orkney. They were not empowered by their original commission to report on these lands which were part of the hereditary royal domain and thus not included amongst the estates forfeited after the Irish war. The earl of Drogheda, Sir Francis Brewster and Sir Robert Leving were the three dissenting commissioners, the last being so outspoken as to assert that the commission's report had spoken in dishonour of the king. The four who signed the report argued that if the other three had found any objections then they should not sign it at all. The country majority in the house agreed with the majority of the commissioners. Leving was quickly rewarded with a room in the Tower for being '...the author of groundless and scandalous reports on the four commissioners,'[17] One placeman wrote sadly: 'The House looks upon it that these things were started to obstruct the going on with the bill.'[18] Following the second reading, it was further determined that in the grants the ministry had laid heavy taxes upon the people and '...highly failed in the performance of their trust and duty.' While Vernon's proposal had not even occasioned a division, when there was a vote the junto whigs either 'sat supine' or even voted against the court.[19] There was probably little they could do in any case but they certainly showed slight concern over what happened to the estates of the foreign favourites.

There were great hopes as to what the forfeitures might bring. The majority report estimated their value at just under £1,700,000, which when added to the £337,940 grant of James II amounted to over £1,000,000. Robert Harley confidently hoped for 1.6 million pounds and even a placeman thought that the forfeitures would yield this figure[20] which would serve to confirm the king's fears. Nevertheless,

---

[16] *H.M.C. Lords, 1699–1702*, p. 40.
[17] Cobbett, v, 1206–16. He and Brewster received but £500 from parliament; the others, £1,000. *H.C.J.*, xiii, 273.
[18] James Lowther to Sir John Lowther, 16 January 1699/1700. Cumb. R.O., Lonsdale MSS.
[19] 'I do not see,' wrote Vernon, 'how they can ever rise again.' To Shrewsbury, 18 January. *Vernon Corr.*, ii, 413.
[20] *H.M.C. Lords 1699–1702*, pp. 44–54. R. Harley to Sir Edward Harley, 26 September. *H.M.C. Cowper*, ii, 292. James Lowther to Sir J. Lowther, 16 January. Cumb. R.O., Lonsdale MSS.

a court tract entitled *Jus Regium, or the king's Right to Grant Forfeitures*, estimated the net value of the estates to be but £500,000 in all.[21]

In the event, this last estimate was to prove far more accurate for the sale was to yield only about £725,000.[22] The commissioners had at first hoped that they would gain £300,000 *per annum* but in the event only £80,000 *per annum* was expected, and quite half of this was to be devoured by the commission's expenses. Of course, this was not known at the time. It was popularly believed that the sale would go far towards maintaining a peacetime army. Indeed, a rare sense of determination overhung the proceedings as the committee's recommendations were embodied in a resumption bill.[23]

Soon after the commissioners' report was first read it was resolved that '...a bill be brought in to apply all the forfeited Estates and Interests in Ireland, and all the grants thereof, since the 13th day of February 1688[/89] to the use of the Publick.'[24] Harley, one of those named to draw up the bill, certainly found the pace gruelling, writing '...this week has been very difficult. I think I have not exceeded four hours sleep. I bless God I am well and now the Irish bill is agreed and to be presented to-morrow.'[25] On 18 January, the commons rejected a motion made on the king's behalf by Secretary Vernon, and against his ministers' best advice, that one-third of the forfeitures should be reserved for his disposal. While this was incorporated in the unsuccessful bill of the previous session, a placeman now wrote that the house '... would not harken to a motion for giving the king any part of them.'[26] Indeed, the commons were proceeding slowly and with care, apparently only so as not to be swamped.[27]

On 6 February another bill was ordered '...to resume the Grants of all lands and revenues of the Crown, and all pensions granted by the Crown since 6 February 1684, and for applying the same to the use of the public.'[28] Perhaps this more revolutionary move was designed to secure court acquiescence for the more moderate proposals or to ensure

---

21 Cited in the introduction to *H.M.C. Lords 1699–1702*, pp. iv–v
22 G. N. Clark, *The Later Stuarts* (2nd ed., 1955), p. 316.
23 *H.M.C. Lords, 1699–1702*, pp. 206–12.
24 15 December 1699. *H.C.J.*, xiii, 66.
25 To Sir E. Harley, 11 January, 1699/1700. *H.M.C. Portland*, iii, 614.
26 T. Lowther to Sir J. Lowther. 19 January. Cumb. R.O., Lonsdale MSS. Macaulay finds that the nation was in a mood to accept the statement without enquiring more closely. vol. vi, p. 2964. Estates General dispatch, 19/29 January. B.M. Add. MSS. 17,677, f. 131 r.
27 *Ibid.*, ff. 131 v.–133 r.   28 13 February. *H.C.J.*, xiii, 208.

that the estates of the countess of Orkney would not go untouched. Certainly each house kept the fire directed at the Irish grants, with a commons' resolution finding them the cause of the nation's debts and taxes. William's reply that he had but rewarded those who served well was met with a cold reception.[29] Even if Ginkell (created earl of Athlone) and Rouvigny (created earl of Galway) played a considerable part in the war and may be said to have earned their grants, they had received but a small part of the total and were, alas, still foreigners.

To consider claims against the resumption, a commission was formed and its creation caused considerable debate and disagreement amongst the opposition. Harley, Musgrave and Seymour took what appeared to be a moderate position in comparison to the violent anti-court view expressed by Sir Bartholomew Shower and Jack Howe. Harley and his friends preferred having a commission of thirteen who might be members of the commons, and at the same time wished to exclude the four former members; that is, the four who had signed the report, the other three evidently not even being considered, one being in the Tower. Harley and Musgrave argued that in fairness, the tribunal '... which is to determine of men's Estates without either Jury or appeal ought to bee composed of the ablest discretest men they can find and of such a number as may be equall to a Jury.' Shower and Howe on the other hand, wished to exclude members and to include the four former commissioners. They made no secret of the fact that this plan was not aimed at impartiality, believing that the four former members and one 'good man' to create a majority, was all that was necessary to conduct the whole affair.[30] Secretary Vernon thought that the breach between the opposition leaders might be widened if the court and junto forces were to side with the moderates. He was not listened to: at a whig party meeting, probably at the Rose Club, it was resolved to appeal to popular sentiment and cause the court all the trouble possible. The moderates' stand was opposed and it was agreed to exclude members. Although no resolution was taken in regard to the four previous commissioners, Vernon believed that only evil could come from the obstructionism and pandering to the desires of the extreme opposition: 'I am afraid this will only put us on the Defensive again and unite others to give us all the mortification they can.'[31]

---

[29] Cobbett, v, 1216.
[30] Vernon to Shrewsbury, 16 March 1699/1700. Boughton, Shrewsbury Papers, ii, f. 46. [31] To s., 21 March. *Ibid.*, f. 48.

Not surprisingly the extremist position prevailed. No member was to be a commissioner, '...the party against employing members was very strong therefore it was not much opposed.' Still, there were to be thirteen commissioners.[32] Few were so naïve as to believe that the commission would be apolitical. One prospective commissioner knew that the office was not without its drawbacks. The very nature of the work would make him obnoxious to either court or country: '...this whole business is I believe not very gratefull to the court and 'twill be I fear impossible to act so as not to be obnoxious to the Kg [king] or People.'[33]

In the balloting, Vernon feared that the four old commissioners, with their secretary, would be elected, noting that Lord Hartington and Jack Howe had so concerted their lists. Musgrave, Harley and Seymour are said to have left out these five and included the moderates, Sir Cyril Wyche and Sir John Werden.[34] In the event, the four old members and their secretary were elected. Indeed, Seymour himself challenged Werden's election, arguing that he held an office, albeit for life. Perhaps not very much should be made of this, as Vernon questioned the value of the discovery, thinking that Speaker Littleton would probably have given his casting vote to 'his old friend Rawlins', whom Vernon evidently believed to be no friend to impartiality. Vernon thought that '...Hee and Cary of Bristol will make a Majority for the five old ones.'[35]

Despite the progress of the bill, by late March it became obvious that direct petitions to the commons were to be allowed. Lord Hartington was said to have 'broke the ice' and Howe was strongly in favour of exceptions. 'One may see,' wrote Vernon, 'all hee [Howe] aims at is to load the administration with faults and to affect a shew of Justice and good nature in all other particulars.'[36] In the event very few grants were saved. Such as Howe did exempt caused Musgrave to call him a proselyte, adding ominously that those who pretended to govern the

---

[32] S. to s., 26 March 1700. *Ibid.*, f. 50.

[33] William Bridges to Francis Brydges, 10 February 1699/1700. Herefs. R.O., Unsorted Brydges Collection. When he first learned of the opportunity open to him, he left his decision 'to the advice of his friends', believing the large salary of £2,000 for two years to be the only really viable reason. Even then, while the sum was more than he could earn in legal practice, he thought that he would have to start his practice anew at the end of his tenure. *Ibid.*

[34] S. to s., 28 March. *Ibid.*, f. 51.

[35] S. to s., 30 March. *Ibid.*, f. 52.

[36] To Shrewsbury, 21 March. Boughton, Shrewsbury Papers, iii, f. 48.

house would soon find that they did not.[37] Subsequently, only a few riders gave any relief and there was almost a clause inserted which would have precluded such amendments altogether.[38] Still, Harley believed that the bill was running into severe difficulties: 'The Irish Bill has taken up four days report and 9 or 10 hours every day; the worst has been that many of those who were for the bill before are now against it wch hath obliged [us] to greater labour.'[39] Vernon thought that many leading men wished the bill to miscarry but expressed themselves with caution. Some tories would be pacified if the bill failed and the whigs were discarded, while some whigs might try to gain royal favour by accepting the rejection of the bill and carrying out the rest of the royal programme. Lady Orkney and the king attempted to draw off the bill's proponents by offering Somers's dismissal. The king went so far as to stipulate that only £200,000 of forfeitures were essential to secure his fall.[40] Perhaps, some ministerial tories believed, they could get him out without paying such a ransom. In any case, the king had failed to reckon with Robert Harley who in sniffing the air for country sentiment decided to utterly ignore all the king's overtures.[41] Despite Harley's worries for the success of the bill, those who had most to lose, the Irish, saw little likelihood of it being rejected in the commons and even less that the king would do so.[42]

Indeed, as the bill proceeded in the lords, commons' unanimity was maintained as was their confidence in appealing to opinion from out of doors. The reports of the Irish commissioners were at last ordered printed together with the votes regarding the grants, the king's answer and the subsequent commons' resolution. So too was the king's resolution of April 1690 and his speech of January 1690/91 promising not to dispose of forfeitures without parliamentary consent.[43]

---

[37] S. to s., 23 March. *Ibid.*, ii. 454–5. Vernon thought that the riders were making the bill increasingly insignificant. To Shrewsbury, 30 March 1700. *Ibid.*, f. 52.   [38] S. to s., 2 April. *Ibid.*, iii, 1–4.

[39] [To Sir Edward Harley], 23 March 1699/1700. B.M. Portland loan 29/189.

[40] Vernon to Shrewsbury, 4 April 1700. *Vernon Corr.*, iii, 4–6. Vernon thought that it created an ill impression.

[41] S. to s., 20 and 29 February 1699/1700. *Ibid.*, ii, 435 and 444. See also 'Account of Robert Harley's Conduct,' B.M. Portland loan 29/165/97 ff. 6–7.

[42] To Sir E. Harley, 23 March 1699/1700. B.M. Portland loan 29/189. Ezekiel Burridge to Bp King, 23 March 1699/1700. T.C.D. MSS. 1122/676.

[43] Vernon to Shrewsbury, 9 and 13 April 1700. *Vernon Corr.*, iii, 9. Somerville finds that the letter was written on 9 April and answered on 13

Despite or perhaps because of the commons' unanimity, the bill was encountering difficulty in the lords. While it was committed 70–23, there had been outspoken opposition coming from many quarters. Some genuinely wished for the bill's defeat to teach the commons a lesson. There had been a number of largely irrelevant clauses tacked to the bill and if the lords did not stop the practice now, perhaps they never could. Others, however, who claimed to oppose the bill for this reason, did so under false colours, really wishing to destroy a bill which included a year's supply. Thus when various amendments were threatened, Vernon expressed his doubts about the advisability of such a course of action. The bill, he believed, would be even worse if made over and the commons' displeasure might even result in impeachments. Rochester was the bill's chief proponent, but despite his strong reasons for passage[44] on 6 April there were amendments. Harley put the blame upon the thin house.[45] Nevertheless, the vote which threw out one of the commons' leading tacks, namely that barring excise officers from being members of parliament, was carried 56–33, thus showing considerable strength. So great was the fear caused by the peers' action in this regard, that some believed the court would be forced to have a short prorogation and another session immediately.[46] Some members were driven almost wild by the lords' action over the place clause, while Robert Harley prayed to God to '...dissipate this black cloud.' As the commons steadfastly adhered to the original bill, the lords only insisted by a majority of thirteen, which gave some hope that they would relent. 'It takes up all our thoughts' Harley wrote to his father.[47]

Tempers were growing thin. About London it was being said the

April. 'The Dates in the *Vernon Corr.*' *Eng. Hist. Rev.* (1933), lxii, 629. Earlier there was a very long debate over whether or not the commissioners' report should be printed. The court naturally opposed this move. Secretary Vernon noted that the 'great men' kept silent and eventually even the parts regarding the grants and forfeitures which the more fervent opposition members most wanted printed were let fall, the leaders and temper of the house being against it. James Lowther to Sir John Lowther, 13 January 1699/1700. Cumb. R.O., Lonsdale MSS. Vernon to Shrewsbury, 13 January. *Vernon Corr.*, ii, 405–7.

[44] S. to s. 4 April 1700. *Vernon Corr.*, iii, 4–6.

[45] To Sir E. Harley, 6 April. *H.M.C. Portland*, iii, 617.

[46] W. Fleming to Sir Daniel Fleming, 9 April. *H.M.C. Le Fleming*, pp. 354–5. James Lowther to Sir John Lowther, 6 April. Cumb. R.O., Lonsdale MSS. Vernon expected the commons to be in '...a higher ferment when they meet again on Monday than over I yet saw them.' To Shrewsbury, 6 April. Boughton, Shrewsbury Papers, iii, f. 55.

[47] 6 April. *H.M.C. Portland*, iii, 617.

only real opponents to the amendments were bishops, beggars and bastards.[48] During the first three days of the next week one placeman found '...there was hardly any mention made of anything but the bill... and of the dangerous consequences in case it should miscarry.'[49] It almost did. The continued agitation by Lonsdale, Pembroke, Wharton and Archbishop Tenison against the bill had been countered with undisguised reluctance by Somers, who urged the lords to think long and well before failing what was also a great money bill. Nevertheless, the proposal to adhere was just carried 43–37. The news hit the commons like a cannon-ball. Preparations were made for a civil war. The lobby was cleared and it was ordered that no one should be allowed to leave.[50] Harley, seldom one to exaggerate, said it was time '...to think of Engd [England] and since that was the last time probably they were to sit there, to shew they were not quite insensible.'[51] What he meant by insensible is not easy to say. Perhaps it was a request for moderation but it seems more likely that he aimed at stripping the crown of its remaining military power. Motions and resolutions rolled on at a red hot pace. The army was to be disbanded, foreigners were to be evicted from the privy council and impeachment proceedings were to be rapidly begun. Perhaps fearing to be caught in a no-man's land between court and country camps, even Jack Howe appeared genuinely frightened. He requested the forgiving of past trespasses, and called for the unity which he himself had done so much to dispel. He asked all to join hands for liberty and England.[52] It would appear that his England had little place for the junto and no place for the Dutch. Younger members spoke of banishing Portland and Albemarle,[53] which was only one step from banishing the king himself.

Despite the orders for no one to leave the commons, 'Harry B.' (Boyle or Blake) was said to have 'snuck out' and '...frighted the Principle Secry out of his witts.' The tales of the banishment of the Dutch,

---

[48] That is, by prelates, greedy courtiers and the illegitimate sons of Charles II. Vernon to Shrewsbury, 9 April (date suggested by Somerville). *Vernon Corr.*, iii, 9–17.

[49] James Lowther to Sir John Lowther, 6 April. Cumb. R.O., Lonsdale MSS.

[50] Vernon to Shrewsbury, 11 April. *Vernon Corr.*, iii, 19–25.

[51] N.n. to the earl of Torrington, 11 April. B.M. Add. MSS. 28,053 ff. 402-3 (Finch MSS.).

[52] Vernon to Shrewsbury, 11 April. *Vernon Corr.*, iii, 19-25

[53] N.n. to the earl of Torrington, 11 April. B.M. Add. MSS. 28,053 ff. 402–3.

especially of the young Albemarle, were said to have completely turned
the king's head, for 'Directions were quickly had by water' and pressure
was brought to bear on the lords to recede from the amendments.
While none but Jersey was said to have changed his mind, several
others including Archbishop Tenison apparently left, while Marlborough and Burnet rushed in, the latter crying 'stuff, stuff' to Lord
Anglesey's insistence upon the lords' rights.[54] While the vote was
40–37 there were three proxies against. With the vote even, the question
was not to pass. But what was the question? If it was adhering to the
bill, the bill failed, but if it was adhering to the amendments, then it
passed. After putting this question it was decided by five votes that it
applied to the amendments. Quite clearly the vote had applied to the
bill but the court's new disposition made it just as clear that the king
wanted the bill to pass.[55] In such close issues a forced interpretation
was perhaps not out of line, for the king could always create a few more
peers in any case. The commons was so united on this matter that
further opposition would only strengthen the court's opponents.

The country party was again victorious. The Irish forfeitures controversy had set another strong precedent for the commons' custom of
tacking, and as a direct corollary, its legislative supremacy. Harley considered the success a triumph of the godly.[56] Xenophobic feelings had
been assuaged and once again grants to foreign-born favourites had been
resumed. The court had succeeded neither in letting the proceedings
dissipate amidst whig-tory factionalism nor by promising to let junto
blood by dismissing Somers. Through the impeachment proceedings
this last step was to be achieved without cost. Nevertheless, it was only
the conflict with the lords which had made the issue seem so heated and
the commons so united. The earlier unanimity seen in the disbandment
controversy and wavering throughout this question of the forfeitures
was to become largely a thing of the past as the opposition's attack
came to be aimed at men as well as measures. Only in regard to constitutional reform was the general country party strength precariously
maintained.

---

[54] Burnet when challenged for his strong words pleaded that he had acted
out of zeal for the royal cause and '...so got off with that fumbling excuse as
foreigne to the matter as his sermons are usually to his texts.' *Ibid*. Wharton
went to Newmarket and Sunderland took Orford's advice. Kenyon, *Sunderland*, p. 315.

[55] Vernon to Shrewsbury, 11 April. *Vernon Corr.*, iii, 19–25.

[56] To Sir E. Harley, 16 April. *H.M.C. Portland*, iii, 618.

EIGHT

The Act of Settlement

THE SETTLEMENT

The death of Anne's son, the duke of Gloucester, in July 1700, made it advisable to make further provisions for the succession. His demise was a blow to the ministerial tories, who were building upon the continuance of the Stuarts,[1] and caused considerable consternation among court moderates, although some tried to make the most they could of the situation. The junto was said to be striving for a commonwealth in which five lords and ten commoners chosen by parliament would execute the royal power. The great financial interests were thought certain to be fervent supporters of this plan as it would provide the best possible way to safeguard investments.[2] There was also talk that William intended to marry again, and a rumour widely circulated (some say deliberately by the king) that he would permit the pretender's accession. Probably such talk was but a ruse designed to gain the acquiescence of Anne and the duchess of Marlborough to his plans for a Hanoverian succession.[3] Harley, in extended correspondence with many, would appear to have concurred and certainly aided in the

---

[1] See esp. the letter of the earl of Chesterfield to Thomas Coke, 3 August 1700. *H.M.C. Cowper*, ii, 402.

[2] The matter is discussed in an unaddressed and unsigned letter (apparently written in August) which gives the pros and cons of the policy and its possible sources of support. *H.M.C. Portland*, iv, 3.

[3] Coxe, *Walpole*, i, 10. Coxe cites *Cunningham*, i, 185 and Somerville, *History of King William*, p. 547.

169

development of the practical details.[4] The price for the support of the ministerial tories was a new parliament.[5] They had argued that it was too important a matter to be begun in the fag end of an old one. Probably they were really aiming to increase their power by exploiting electoral feeling, which was even less favourably disposed to a war than in 1698. The king mentioned the problem of the succession in his speech and Harley led in the new plan, rapidly stepping between whig and tory extremists.[6] On 20 February, after Colonel Granville's report from the committee of advice to the crown, Harley, from the chair, admitted that while it was not in order for him to speak, he had heard some comments about the prince of Wales and intended to cut the problem off at the roots.[7]

The house of Hanover appears to have been immediately grateful to the faction which it believed most supported its claims, probably the whig junto.[8] Harley argued, however, that at the time the whigs tried to hinder the nomination by setting up an examination of the pretended prince of Wales.[9] Admittedly, Seymour, Musgrave and some of their friends appear to have been far from enthusiastic in making preparations for a Hanoverian succession; when it came to the point of recognizing the Electress Sophia by name in the bill in her full electoral dignity, they made a show of leaving to demonstrate that they had nothing to do with the affair.[10] Still, they had not openly opposed her succession and all the questions dealing with it went 'pretty unanimously'.[11]

---

[4] See the coded correspondence from Henry Guy to Harley between August and December. *H.M.C. Portland*, iii, 625–41, *passim*. See too, Sir C. Musgrave to Harley, 7 and 28 November and 5 December. *Ibid.*, iv, 7–9. See below.

[5] See p. 204.

[6] 'Account of Robert Harley's Conduct', B.M. Portland loan 29/165/97 f. 11.

[7] Estates General dispatch, 21 February/4 March. B.M. Add. MSS. 17,677 WW., f. 169. Brandenburg dispatch, 21 February/4 March. B.M. Add. MSS. 30,000 E., ff. 48v.–49r. Granville's report was made on 20 February 1700/1. *H.C.J.*, xiii, 349. Harley's remarks, of course, are not included in the Journals.

[8] Princess Sophia to Mr Stephney, n.d. (summer 1701). Philip (Yorke), earl of Hardwicke, *Miscellaneous State Papers*, ii, 443.

[9] 'Account of Robert Harley's Conduct', B.M. Portland loan 29/165/97, f. 11.

[10] Estates General dispatch, 15/26 April 1701. B.M. Add. MSS. 17,677 WW. f. 220. *H.C.J.*, xiii, 487.

[11] James Lowther to Sir John Lowther, 11 March 1700/1. Cumb. R.O., Lonsdale MSS.

Perhaps (as Harley insists) the success of the plan was the result of its coming between both parties.[12]

NEW LIMITATIONS

Such obstruction as there was had occurred indirectly through the placing of new limitations upon the prerogative. These limitations were eight in number and form the third paragraph of the act of settlement. They embody the basic country grievances aired throughout the reign and it is not surprising to find that they were resolved upon before, rather than after, the settlement was enlarged. Harley states that he told the king it would be an easy matter to prevent the limitations from coming into effect during his lifetime.[13] Perhaps it was, but by the phrasing of the bill it is doubtful, and at the least there appears to have been faulty drafting. By the wording, of the eight clauses only four unquestionably came into effect upon the Hanoverian succession, another two might well be interpreted as coming into effect on William's death, while two others could be said to come into effect at once.[14]

The clauses which came into effect unquestionably only upon the Hanoverian succession are the second, fourth, fifth and seventh. In the event of a future successor who was not born in England, the nation was not obliged to go to war to defend any foreign territory without the consent of parliament. The scope of the privy council was enlarged and advice was to be signed by those who gave it. Foreigners were to be members of neither the privy council nor parliament. They were to hold neither civil nor military positions nor be granted any crown property either directly or indirectly. The seventh clause required judges' commissions to be made during good behaviour rather than the royal pleasure and their salaries to be ascertained. A provision that a judge could be removed upon the address of both houses has generally been interpreted as meaning that the power of their removal was transferred from the crown to parliament. While this is true enough on the surface, less follows from it than might be supposed. If the power had been shifted to the commons alone, then there might have been an effect somewhat similar to the review of executive appointments subsequently practised

---

[12] 'Account of Robert Harley's conduct', B.M. Portland loan 29/165/3 f. 11.   [13] *Ibid.*, f. 9.

[14] For the statute see appendix C. Contemporaries were puzzled by the timing of at least one of the clauses. See below, p. 176.

by the American Congress. It was, indeed, originally planned to have the judges removed upon an address of either house, but the court was successful in having this amended.[15] Probably the opposition acquiesced, seeing as much likelihood of the lords acting in concert with the crown as with themselves, since the two houses had been increasingly at logger-heads during the previous few years. Once again, however, the court showed its colours and attempted to delete the entire clause. In this they were unsuccessful,[16] and from the time of the king's approval, the most perilous period of the judiciary's independence came to a close.

Two clauses which may be interpreted as coming into effect upon William's death required all future sovereigns to be Anglicans and pro-hibited their departure from the British Isles. The sixth and eighth clauses might both be said to come into effect at once. The eighth provided that a royal pardon was not pleadable to an impeachment by the commons in parliament. Although it seems unlikely that the imme-diate implementation would have had much effect even upon the course of the ensuing impeachments, if the sixth clause excluding all crown office holders from parliament had taken effect either then or even within the next hundred years, the nation's history might well have followed a rather different course. The problem of placemen again requires a separate discussion.

PLACEMEN III

Before the election of 1698 it was said that if a list of placemen was to be published '...the people of England would refuse to give their votes for them in the next Election of Parliament, and in their stead will elect members of a contrary temper'.[17] But such a list was in fact printed,[18]

[15] 10 May. *H.C.J.*, xiii, 525. [16] *Ibid.*
[17] *A Letter to a Victorious Prince...* (1698), p. 17.
[18] *A Letter to a Country Gentleman...To Which is Annexed, A List of Names...* (1698). Samuel Grascombe's list annexed to his pamphlet of 1694 predates this, but it is in manuscript and probably was not published. Bodl. Rawl. MSS. D. 864 ff. 1–6. See too, the following pamphlets discouraging electors from returning office-holders: James Toland, *The Danger of Mercenary Parlia-ments* (1695?); *Some Cautions Offered to the Consideration of Those who are to Chuse Members to Serve in the Ensuing Parliament* (1695); *A Letter to a Country Gentle-man, setting forth the cause of the Decay and Ruin of Trade. To which is annexed a list of the Names of some Gentlemen who were Members of the last Parliament, and now are, (or lately were) in Public Employments* (1698); James Drake, *Some Necessary Considerations Relating to all future Elections of Members to Serve in Parliament...*

and while the court party was substantially reduced, a large number
remained. It was far easier to identify placemen than to be rid of them.
The first reason for this failing was the existence of impenetrable
government electoral strongholds (such as almost all the cinque ports)
or those held by court-aligned factions. Perhaps this accounts for Sir
John Verney's defeat in Wharton's Buckinghamshire despite his bold
electoral poster proclaiming:

NO PENSIONER

NO PLACEMAN

NO JUDAS[19]

The usual government majority of the active peers did what they could
to influence elections, as did government employees despite subsequent
commons' measures forbidding such interference.[20] Some placemen
were returned from constituencies where, although it might be believed
that returning placemen was a bad practice in general, it would be
continued until reforms were made forbidding it; to set an example in
this regard might well reduce government benevolence for their
borough, city or shire.

While the war had inhibited parliamentary attempts to alleviate the
problem, the peace allowed these aims to be reasserted. With the end of
the war putting an end to war finance, considerable reductions of office
became the order of the day. In 1698, one placeman noted that parliament '...had three hundred displaced officers upon their hands un-
provided, and when the malt tax expires they will have as many more
that will be discharged.'[21] Nor did the country party appear willing to
allow the court to replenish its reserves by effecting a union with Scotland. Jack Howe called the proposal but a court trick '...to bring 30 or
40 Scotchmen into the House to supply the places of so many Revenue
Officers that were to be dismust [dismissed]'.[22] On the first reading of a

[19] Margaret Verney, *Verney Letters*, i, 155.   [20] See pp. 214–15.

[21] James Lowther to Sir John Lowther, 7 March 1698/9. Cumb. R.O.,
Lowther Corr.

[22] Vernon to Shrewsbury, 5 March. Boughton, Shrewsbury Papers, iii,
f. 41. If what occurred when the union was effected in 1707 is anything to go
by, it would appear that Howe for once did not exaggerate. Walcot notes
that of the forty-five members selected by the Scottish parliament to go to
Westminster, twenty-eight were members of the Scottish court party and
thirteen were of the court aligned *Squadrone Volante*, leaving but four independent members, only two of whom had opposed the union. (Walcott,
English Politics, pp. 127–8). With the convention parliament still sitting in
Scotland in 1700, the court was unlikely to have done worse.

preliminary bill, Harley wrote delightedly that '...the sham union bill with Scotland was flung out without a division,'[23] Secretary Vernon believed that if the house had divided, there would have been a two to one majority against it.[24] Another placeman wrote that '...there was no great debate upon it, the chief friends if found were some of the court and most of the northern gentlemen.'[25] Obviously there were other reasons for the bill's defeat, such as its origin in the lords, the lack of authority in Scotland (as exemplified by the continuation of the convention parliament for over a decade) and the immediate impracticability of the measure. Still, the threat of increased court influence seemed the most telling.[26]

Concrete results emerged to deplete the court's ranks as legislation was enforced against various categories of office-holders following the election of 1698. Edward Harley noted the constraint upon courtiers as they came to fear for their seats.[27] One wrote that '...both the Commission, and the customs are threated openly in the House, as if Men of Experience were turn'd out to fill it up with such as have little other pretence but being Parlt. men.' He found that '...all young men that have places meet with the greatest discouragment that hardly any venture to speak.'[28] In William's last parliament he believed the placemen were under a '...very great disadvantage' and that those who were already incapacitated from sitting had '...little reason to be sorry'.[29]

If the country party had its way, they would not have been there at all. The more open method of exclusion having been tried and found wanting, they were proceeded against by a series of clauses tacked to money bills. It was a backhanded way to be sure, but even as Secretary

---

[23] R. Harley to Sir E. Harley, 5 March 1699/1700. *H.M.C. Portland*, iii, 616. *H.C.J.*, xiii, 267.

[24] Vernon to Shrewsbury, 5 March. Boughton, Shrewsbury Papers, iii, f. 41.

[25] James Lowther to Sir John Lowther, 5 March 1699/1700. Cumb. R.O., Lowther Corr. The northern members were predominantly court supporters. See p. 360. See too, the letter of the same date of William Fleming to Sir Daniel Fleming complaining of the loss and fearing that the Scots would greatly resent the ill words put forth in the debate. *H.M.C. Le Fleming*, p. 354.

[26] Vernon to Shrewsbury, 5 March. Boughton, Shrewsbury Papers, iii, f. 41.

[27] To Sir Edward Harley, 11 February 1698/9. *H.M.C. Portland*, iii, 602.

[28] James Lowther to Sir John Lowther, 6 January 1699/1700. Cumb. R.O., Lowther Corr.

[29] S. to s., 6 January 1701/2. *Ibid.*

Vernon came to admit, it appeared the only way to get the measure past the lords and to secure the King's approval.[30]

The most obnoxious placemen were attacked first. The frequent complaints against the numerous revenue officers who sat in the commons resulted in the initial part of the remedy being effected in the spring of 1694, when the committee of supply provided against members being concerned in duties granted by parliament (excepting the commissioners of the treasury and officers and commissioners for managing the customs and excise).[31] The exclusion was incorporated as a clause in the act for duties on salt and beer, ale and other liquors,[32] but caused little concern at the time. For a number of reasons, undoubtedly including a deficiency of country party strength, the clause went unexecuted until after the 1698 election and created considerable surprise and comment when it came to be enforced.[33] Several revenue officers holding new positions were expelled that session in what the French envoy thought was an unmitigated attempt to lower the court vote[34] and Robert Price candidly admitted to being outright 'garbelling'.[35]

A bill which passed the commons to limit the number of placemen was committed in the lords on 20 April 1699, but was not heard of again.[36] This direct method failing, Edward Harley succeeded in his proposal to extend exclusion to the commissioners of the excise by once again simply tacking the clause to a money bill.[37] Secretary Vernon thought that the act would come into effect at once and expected that as most placemen would rather give up membership in parliament than their offices, there would be a further reduction of the court party. He thought that the exclusion would affect nine members '…if they shall choose rather to stick to their Employments.'[38]

The earl of Shaftesbury believed '…the time is now coming tht Parliaments will be no more under the influence of courts as formerly, so

---

[30] Vernon to Shrewsbury, March 1699/1700. *Vernon Corr.*, iii, 452–3.

[31] 3 March 1693/4. *H.C.J.*, xi, 116.

[32] 5 and 6 William and Mary, c. 7, s. 59.

[33] French dispatch, 10/20 February 1698/9. Grimblot, *Letters*, ii, 277.

[34] *Ibid.*, p. 278.

[35] To the duke of Beaufort, 18 February. Bodl. Carte MSS. 130, f. 396 (bound out of order). [36] *H.L.J.*, xvi, 444.

[37] *H.C.J.*, xiii, 287. 11 and 12 William III, c. 2., s. 150. Robert Harley in a letter to his father, was of course delighted with this country success. 19 March 1699/1700. *H.M.C. Portland*, iii, 617.

[38] Vernon to Shrewsbury, 14 March. Boughton, Shrewsbury Papers, iii, f. 45.

that, be it what Parlemt it will, their councils will be the same...' The exclusion of excisemen would be completed and '...extend itself to the thorough purgation of Parlemt, and reducing it solely and wholly to the country bottom.'[39] Vernon's supposition that the customs officers would soon be expelled was correct.[40] When in late March 1701 the house voted to incapacitate them, one placeman unhappily supposed '...it will be done by a clause to the Land Tax. Other Offrs. must expect to follow in a little time.'[41]

Steps to effect the final solution had begun earlier that month when the commons added the aforementioned clause to the act of settlement to exclude all placemen. Although there was no voiced opposition to the measure when proposed, some paid it a back-handed tribute, saying that the court would be better off, as many who spoke against it were but out-of-place whigs and tories hoping to be appeased by place or pension.[42] Nevertheless, in May, the court made a surprise attempt to delete the measure. Speaker Harley responded with alacrity, ordering the serjeant-at-arms to summon all the members in the area and despite the lateness in the session, the court did not dare a division.[43]

While it has generally been supposed that the provision would not take effect until the Hanoverian succession, at the opening of the next session one worried placeman believed that '...by the wording of the Act it is a doubt whether it ought not to take place immediately.'[44] Luttrell wondered too.[45] No more is heard of the matter, however, as the opposition probably believed itself too weak to carry the proposal,

---

[39] Shaftesbury to Furley, 15 November 1700. *Shaftesbury Corr.*, p. 108.

[40] 2 March 1699/1700. *Vernon Corr.*, iii, 453.

[41] To Sir John Lowther, 25 March 1701. Cumb. R.O., Lowther Corr. 12 and 13 William III, c. 10.

[42] Brandenburg dispatch, 14/25 March 1700/1. B.M. Add. MSS. 30,000 E. f. 79.

[43] 10 May. *H.C.J.*, xiii, 524–5.

[44] James Lowther to Sir John Lowther, 3 February 1701/2. Cumb. R.O., Lowther Corr.

[45] In his entry of 25 December 1701, Luttrell wrote: 'In the act past last session for limitation of the crown...is a clause, That no person who has an office or place of profit under the king, or receives a pension from the crown, shall be capable of serving as a member of the house of commons; and the words (that after the said limitation shall take effect) not being inserted, as they are in the preceding and following clauses, 'tis said several members will, on Tuesday next, insist and a division be thereon, that no member shall sit in the house who receives any profit from the crown.' Luttrell, *Brief Relation*, v, 125. Indebtedness for this reference is owed to Dr. W. A. Speck.

although the placemen were given signal tokens of the country gentle-men's contempt.[46] Still, if nothing was done at the time, it must be remembered that nothing was done or said about the first clause excluding the new revenue officers until auspicious times arrived, several years and two parliaments after passage. If one might suppose for the purposes of conjecture that William lived on and on and the ministerial power of the junto again rose and abruptly declined, it seems more than likely that this clause of complete proscription would be said to have become effective on the date of enactment.

No matter when the new limitations came into effect, there can be little doubt that the nature of William's policy, especially its foreign nature, was what was thought to have necessitated them. But although the resolutions were in many ways then an indirect vote of censure, their effect was upon the future. While it was said in debate that they might make the crown unacceptable to the Hanoverian successors, such arguments apparently carried little weight, perhaps because crowns were usually found quite acceptable no matter what the limitations. The defence for the restrictions was expanded in subsequent pamphlets[47] and the fact that some of them were later mitigated by no means proves that even as they stood effective government would have been impossible. The rigid separation between executive, legislative and judicial powers which would have been effected by the act as it stood was, of course, to be embodied in the American constitution with the concomitant diminution of foreign designs and development of an isolationist policy. Admittedly then, the restrictions might have made an expansionist imperialist war policy unlikely, but then this was scarcely what the country party wanted.

---

[46] The placeman, James Lowther, noted that a house committee '...left a distinguishing mark upon offices by charging them at 5s. in the pound which is a hardship never known before, but by this you may see how they are regarded in the house.' To Sir James Lowther, 12 February 1701/2. Cumb. R.O., Lowther Corr.

[47] See esp. James Drake, *A History of the Last Parliament* (1702).

NINE

Ministerial Responsibility: On Men and Measures

The impeachments of the war ministers lay at the heart of the opposition's final strategic move to safeguard the peace or, at the least, to maintain parliamentary and individual liberties in the event of war. The impeachments rested upon the old whig principle that the king could do no wrong. As many came to believe that wrongs had been committed, it was the responsible ministers who were to be held accountable. Opposed to this view was the old tory belief now held by the junto whigs, that the king could do wrong; a plea made repeatedly but ineffectually throughout the proceedings. The principle employed in bringing charges against only some of the ministers, that is, the junto ministers, was that of responsibility of office coupled with common fame.[1] William's policy of a mixed ministry, then, required a modification of the theory of collective cabinet responsibility. This modification was said to be designed to censor those thought most culpable of concurring in a censored act, but in practice it was aimed at those thought most likely to pursue an undesirable policy in the future. The difference between theory and practice was necessitated by the consciences of the country members who demanded sound charges before voting against the accused. To allay such scruples, opposition leaders were forced to

---

[1] Clayton Roberts, 'The Growth of Ministerial Responsibility to Parliament in Later Stuart England.' *Journ. Mod. Hist.*, (1956), xviii, 222–3.

approach their prey in a circuitous way: during one such attack on the
junto, Secretary Vernon was to write that '...these heats don't arise
from the subject matter but are resolutions form'd to take away any
occasion for excluding those they have so great an aversion to from
ever coming into power again.'[2] Moderate country opinion was divided
over the matter, for many believed it possible that the king was right
and that a war would be necessary. While some even came to believe
that the junto would be the best war leaders, this view seldom seemed
truly representative of general country sentiment. If a war was necessary
then a largely tory ministry might direct it, as, indeed, was to be the
case throughout much of Anne's reign.

Not surprisingly, the very method of impeachments to implement
policy caused considerable dissent within the country party. Only in
part was this due to the confidence gained in the king by his eventual
compliance with parliamentary demands over disbandment. The chief
reason, of course, was that the attack was now aimed far more at men
rather than measures. In his later life, Harley made it a point to deny
having initiated the impeachment proceedings,[3] probably forseeing
that as a result of the conflicts rival ministerial factions might bid for
the king's favour, leading to a growth of the royal prerogative. Still,
Harley's denial was written after the event under a very different climate
of opinion. The apparent inconsistency with country principles of
attacking men rather than measures made the impeachments difficult to
defend at any time. If, however, Harley did not initiate the proceedings
he certainly took an active part once they had begun. It seems unlikely,
moreover, that he really forsook his country principles in doing so.
Forcing the junto from office and subsequently keeping them out might
be defended as being necessitated by the situation: to attack measures
it is sometimes necessary to attack men. In a later letter to William
Heysterman in Amsterdam, Harley seems sincere in wishing that England had learned through experience '...not to hate *only* the person who
exercises Arbitrary Power but to hate Arbitrary Power itself.'[4] In his
condemnation of those who had made the past war a commercial enter-
prise, sacrificed constitutional liberties and, most important, were
likely to do so again, he would appear not to have promoted but only

---

[2] To Shrewsbury, 20 October 1700. Boughton, Shrewsbury Papers iii,
no. 131.
[3] Edward Harley, Harley Family Memoirs. *H.M.C. Portland*, v, 646.
'Account of Robert Harley's Conduct'. B.M. Portland loan 29/165/97 f. 14.
[4] 13/24 January 1701/2. B.M. Portland loan 29/146/7. Italics added.

reflected opposition. His election as Speaker in three consecutive parliaments seems proof enough of this. Harley prided himself on running
with the pack. If the country party changed its course he would be
among the first to scent the new game. At first, it should be reiterated,
there was little country support for the policy of an aggressive war and
concomitant heavy taxation—especially if it involved England in a considerable continental campaign.

PEACE AND THE MINISTRY

Following the peace in 1697, however, the junto's strength at first had
hold good if only defensively. They seem to have enlarged their monopoly
of power during the session although concurrently, of course, increasing the power of the opposition leadership. In early December, Secretary Trumbull resigned. In part it was because he had felt shamefully
neglected; he had not been included among the lords justices of the
previous summer and to his replacement, James Vernon, he said that
he had been treated more as a footman than a secretary.[5] Some believed
that Trumbull simply feared the junto forcing him from office.[6] While
such ministerial tories as Nottingham at first thought that Trumbull
would be unlikely to engage in 'opposition to the great men',[7] it soon
became clear that he would not be their friend. Such was the case too,
with Sunderland, who was wary of being the victim of a junto-led attack
in the commons thinking that few were likely to defend him.[8] Despite
the king's abhorrence of a further diminution of the non-party elements
in his ministry, Sunderland succeeded in giving up his gold key of
office.[9] He told Vernon '…there was no rack like to what he suffered
by being ground as he had been, between lord Monmouth and lord
Wharton.' Vernon believed Sunderland '…wholly turned from any
thing that may be called a Whig.'[10]

---

[5] Vernon to Shrewsbury, 2 December. *Vernon Corr.*, i, 432–2. See too the
entries of 26 November–1 December in his memoirs. Berks. R.O., Trumbull
Add. MSS. 125 ff. 17–21.
[6] R. Yard's newsletter to Ld Ambassador Williamson, 3 December. *Cal.
S.P. Dom.*, p. 498.
[7] To Visc. Hatton, 26 November. B.M. Add. MSS. 29,595 f. 128.
[8] J. Sloane to Sir J. Williamson, 24 December. *Cal. S.P. Dom.*, pp. 528–9.
[9] R. Kenyon, *Sunderland*, p. 300. Trumbull Memoirs, 29 December. Berks.
R.O., Trumbull Add. MSS. 125 f. 22.
[10] To Shrewsbury, 27 December 1697 6 January 1697/8. *Vernon Corr.*, i, 450.

The king saw the danger of the government's position but he was almost helpless. Pressure on Shrewsbury to accept the key proved unavailing despite Vernon's flattering assertion that 'If the Nation were to bee polled you would have 1000 to one voting for it...'[11] Shrewsbury thought a return to office would imply he censured Sunderland's conduct,[12] and argued that the junto should reaccept Sunderland, who would always provide a good sacrifice when the going became rough,[13] —a barrel for the whale to play with. The junto chose to ignore this advice, evidently believing themselves strong enough as they were. While Vernon thought they might preserve their own interest, he doubted that they could further the king's national designs.[14]

As the proceedings in public affairs developed during the ensuing session, Vernon's prognosis proved accurate. There was said to be considerable confusion owing to the great manager's departure[15]— a confusion promoted by the defections of his friends, Trumbull, Methuen, Pelham and Duncombe.[16]

The defections amongst the junto's allies were soon felt in a scandal involving forgeries of exchequer bills. Originally, the ministerial tories had hopes of generally discrediting Montague and the exchequer. Very quickly, however, Montague succeeded in not only avoiding personal involvement but turning the tables and directing an attack against a moderate tory member, Charles Duncombe. Harley appears to have generally co-operated, probably trying to show impartiality in his opposition to corruption. It was he who suggested proceeding by a bill of attainder rather than by an impeachment, thinking that Duncombe would find it all too easy to hamper impeachment proceedings

---

[11] 28 December 1697. Boughton, Shrewsbury Papers, i, f. 172.

[12] Shrewsbury to Portland, 30 December. N.U.L., PwA 1395.

[13] '...I think he [Sunderland] will be so ill esteemed by the Country gentlemen, that when he begins to play tricks, you always have it in your hands to be ridd of him,...whatever may be advised contrary to their [the country gentlemen's] likeing, they are most inclined to lay the blame on him...' To Lord n.n., 22 January 1697/8. B.M. Add. MSS. 15,895 f. 17 v.

[14] To Shrewsbury, 29 December 1697. *Vernon Corr.*, i, 451–2. S. to s., 8 March 1697/8. Boughton, Shrewsbury Papers, i, f. 75.

[15] Jo. Methuen to [Ld Galway], 22 January and 3 February 1697/8. Blenheim, Sunderland letter book.

[16] *Ibid.* Sunderland denied responsibility. Sunderland to Shrewsbury, 15/25 January. *Shrewsbury Corr.*, 526–7. Vernon to Shrewsbury, 22 February. *Vernon Corr.*, ii, 18–20.

through his friends in the lords.[17] Certainly the prospect of confiscating a large proportion of Duncombe's estate, which Montague believed would provide a 'Golden Sacrifice showering down Treasure enough to have amply provided for some of the emergent Occasions of the state,'[18] would have served to mollify many members' moral qualms over the principle of legislative confiscation. Still, some of Harley's friends did not share his view; Seymour, Musgrave and Howe led in the opposition.[19] Indeed, observers noted much the same spirit of faction as had characterized the Fenwick proceedings of the previous session.[20] Such observations would seem confirmed by Secretary Vernon's belief that Duncombe was stalling for time awaiting help from a new parliament 'when it shall be a little more Toryish'. Vernon thought that any saving Duncombe ('the covetous Wretch') made through failing to make a bargain with the treasury was probably being eaten up by legal fees.[21] It would seem, however, that some feared the junto would make party capital out of this whole affair. Then too, as may be inferred from the diminishing attendance,[22] the issue was probably not considered important by many members. Indeed, the bill was carried in the commons on 26 February only by a vote of 138–103.[23] When it reached the lords, although the court avoided the trap of an enlarged interhouse dispute[24] it was lost by one vote. This would seem due less to indignation at legislative confiscation, as Feiling asserts,[25] but rather to general indifference and mistaken complacency.[26]

---

[17] Vernon to Shrewsbury, 22 January and [1] February. *Vernon Corr.*, i, 475 and 486. D. H. Somerville notes that the second letter is misdated 8 February. 'The dates in the *Vernon Correspondence*', *Eng. Hist. Rev.* (1933), xlviii, 627.   [18] Montague, *Memoirs*, p. 51.
[19] Brandenburg dispatch, 15/25 February 1697/8. B.M. Add. MSS. 30,000 B. f. 41 r.
[20] Brandenburg dispatch, 1/11 March. B.M. Add. MSS. 30,000 B. f. 58 r.
[21] To Shrewsbury, 24 February. Boughton, Shrewsbury Papers, i, f. 197.
[22] To Shrewsbury, 19 February. *Ibid.*, f. 195.
[23] *H.C.J.*, xiii, 133. Gwyn and Poultney were minority tellers. The bill was committed on 14 February after a call for candles was carried 161–107. Perry and Gery were minority tellers. *Ibid.*, p. 101.
[24] Vernon to Shrewsbury, 17 and 18 March. Boughton, Shrewsbury Papers, i, ff. 84–7. Brandenburg dispatch, 15/25 March 1697/8. B.M. Add. MSS. 30,000 f. 70 r.   [25] *Tory Party*, p. 328.
[26] Robert Price wrote that '...severall persons went out of the house not thinkeing there was any danger of loosing it, being not much debated.' To the duke of Beaufort, 15 March. Bodl. Carte MSS. 130 f. 392. *H.L.J.*, xvi, 235.

As spring passed into summer, the commons dispelled any sense of complacency the court might have had regarding supply. Pressure was put upon the king to disband most of the troops. Musgrave, indeed, led an address to that purpose.[27] William's fears of the commons' spirit confirmed in this respect, he also had doubts as to its willingness to vote adequate supplies.[28] As the Spanish king's health improved and the danger of a renewal of war seemed even more remote, these fears increased.[29] As, too, the triennial act made dissolution seem imminent the court leaders were said to be growing increasingly fearful of the electorate: it was seldom that they were outspoken.[30] How desperate the king's straits were may be seen in a fascinating letter from Louis to his envoy; it was suggested that despite the resources of the United Provinces, William would be well advised to unite with him, as he appeared incapable of waging war because of his inability to find a party to do his bidding.[31] Although the remarks might be considered as one of the sun king's not infrequent delusions of grandeur, they at least indicate that William was at the end of his tether. Perhaps the commons' subsequent unanimous passage of the civil list request showed their awareness of this fact. The French envoy thought that the court's success was at least in part attributable to wholesale bribery and poor attendance.[32] Still, whatever the cause, the vote left the king quite pleased. Secretary Vernon thought that he had never seen him in a better humour.[33] Probably he became even more cheerful when the two million pound supply bill finally secured passage, despite Godolphin's sobering belief that its success was determined almost solely by the lateness of the session and subsequent diminishing country attendance.[34]

At the close of the session one of the more embarrassing questions for the junto was that of trade with the East Indies. The old company's monopoly had been extended in 1693, but the parliamentary decision the following year underlined the basic country policy favouring independent trading in the East. This attitude was not to change, for the

---

[27] William anticipated the address in a letter to Portland, 22 April/2 May 1698. Vernon to Shrewsbury, 2 June. Grimbolt, *Letters*, ii, 27.

[28] To Shrewsbury, 28 May. *Ibid.*

[29] William to Heinsius, 22 April/2 May. *Ibid.*, i, 439.

[30] Brandenburg dispatch, 15/25 April. B.M. Add. MSS. 30,000 B. f. 87 r.

[31] To Tallard, 2/12 June. Grimbolt, *Letters*, ii, 30.

[32] French dispatch, 2/12 June. Grimbolt, *Letters*, ii, 27.

[33] To Shrewsbury, 28 May. *Ibid.*, p. 27 n.

[34] French dispatch, 2 June. *Ibid.*, p. 27.

general country desire that '...all trade be free, open and not in joynt stocks,'[35] was still thought to have been upheld by the house. This general distaste of monopolistic practices court and junto plainly flaunted. The junto openly supported the offer of the projected New East India Company to lend the government two million pounds, almost three times the sum offered by the old company. Their bias was seen, however, in the fact that when the old company did come up to the sum they rejected it, arguing that the bid had come too late.[36] Aside from wishing to enlarge support by offering a new outlet for investment, the junto was thought to have had general court concurrence in wishing to punish the old company for bad faith and found a new one to provide funds for emergencies.[37] Although it was one thing to break up the old company, it was something quite different from establishing a new one. Some were thought to have favoured the old company's destruction only in order to confuse matters and the bill proceeded most slowly through parliament. The matter was of prime urgency to the king and it was thought by some that unless the bill passed the previous session might be considered almost utterly wasted.[38] The court was reduced to such straits that whip letters emanated from Lambeth Palace urging such as Bishop Burnet to the house. Tenison believed that unless the bill passed '...the government will sink...'[39] With debates lasting occasionally up to seven hours,[40] the friends of the old company wasted few words in their vituperative condemnation of the court and junto cause. Rochester went so far as to declare the new company's proponents to be '...rogues and men who deserve to be hanged.'[41] While in the end the court was to prevail by its numbers, the battle had been so fierce that Montague admitted he '...repented heartily, it was ever attempted.'[42]

If the junto had almost failed the king in attempting to keep up a standing army and provide supply they had at least survived and main-

---

[35] Sir John Banks to Heneage Finch, 3 May. Chatsworth, Finch-Halifax MSS.   [36] Montague, *Memoirs*, p. 52.

[37] Brandenburg dispatch, 24 June/4 July. B.M. Add. MSS. 30,000 B. f. 148 v.

[38] French dispatch, 2/12 July. Grimblot, *Letters*, ii, 61.

[39] Tenison to Burnet, 17 June. Bodl. Add. MSS. A 191 f. 67.

[40] Sir John Banks to Heneage Finch, 2 July. Chatsworth, Finch-Halifax MSS., box 5.

[41] French dispatch, 2/12 July. Grimblot, *Letters*, ii, 61.

[42] To Shrewsbury, 16/26 July. *Shrewsbury Corr.*, pp. 543–4.

tained their unity. Still, their situation was becoming more precarious, for their allies were decreasing and they would not come to terms with such middlemen as Sunderland. Montague had at first said that if Duncombe was disgraced, the junto would find an accommodation easier with his master.[43] Although Duncombe had not been attainted, he had certainly been disgraced. Indeed, one of the major reasons for the failure to attaint him in the lords was said to be mistaken junto complacency because of Montague's earlier success in overwhelmingly defeating a censure motion against his receipt of an Irish grant.[44] Apparently then, the junto had changed their minds and were said to think themselves strong enough as they were.[45] By late April, the king wrote that they spoke no more of Sunderland 'than as if he were dead'. Nor were they content to stop there. The demand was reiterated that Wharton be made lord chamberlain.[46] The 'church' was said by Vernon to be unanimously opposed to such an appointment,[47] as was William who found himself as little inclined to make him lord chamberlain as he was to make him secretary of state.[48] Still, it was not until June that the moderate tory, Marlborough, was admitted to the ministry.

The king had long thought the session marked by private animosities and party quarrels which showed very little public spirit.[49] He had been forced to have parliament drag on and on, apparently relying on diminishing country attendance to permit the passage of court proposals.[50] Montague knew that his successes were largely defensive, fearing that the old parliament would be defeated by the triennial act and that a new one would be even less amenable. Ominously, so did the French envoy, who believed that the phoenix to arise from the ashes would not be propitious for junto fortunes.[51]

---

[43] Vernon to Shrewsbury, 25 January 1697/8. *Vernon Corr.*, i, 477–8.

[44] The motion was defeated 206–97. In a subsequent vote he was complimented as having deserved the grant. R. Price to the duke of Beaufort, 19 February. Bodl. Carte MSS. 130 f. 379 (out of order). It was thought that if the attack on Montague had succeeded one on Somers would have followed. Vernon to Shrewsbury, 17 February. *Vernon Corr.*, ii, 14–18.

[45] S. to s., 20 January. *Ibid.*, i, 472–5.

[46] To Portland, 22 April/2 May 1698. Grimblot, *Letters*, i, 437.

[47] To Shrewsbury, 4 April. Boughton, Shrewsbury Papers, ii, f. 5.

[48] To Portland, 22 April. Grimblot, *Letters*, i, 437.

[49] To Portland, 3/13 February 1697/8. *Ibid.*, pp. 157–8.

[50] William Fleming thought that the session would be extended 'Some months' [i.e., until September, at least] if the East India bill did not pass. To Sir D. Fleming, 2 July 1698. West. R.O., D/Ry 5279 (Le Fleming papers).

[51] French dispatch, 9/19 May 1698. Grimblot, *Letters*, i, 496.

THE ELECTION OF 1698 AND THE NEW MANDATE

It was generally believed that a dissolution would shortly follow the prorogation, the triennial act putting another purposeful session out of the question. The king would probably not wait until the last minute, for it was inadvisable to have the nation unsettled all summer. In addition, by having the election at the time of the harvest, the generally anti-court influence of the agrarian interest might be dampened, as many farmers would be too busy with their crops to vote.[52]

Other portents were less auspicious. The undisguised delight of William and Portland at the prospect of leaving England for Holland was both noted and deplored, causing even many of the court supporters to grumble.[53] Country complaints were also expected owing to military influence in elections. It had been argued that the troops victimized constituents who opposed the court, resulting in charges that elections were not free. To quiet such opposition, William ordered the officers to move the troops back from electoral areas three days before elections took place[54] but evidently the order was only half-heartedly made, or at least only half-heartedly complied with, for there were still to be complaints.[55] Such signs are indicative of the broader aspects of a campaign strongly marked by a court-country cleavage. Its outline was sketched during the disbandment controversy, although the court appears not to have known this at the time. In opposition pamphlets the blame for the taxes and the ruin of trade was put squarely upon the court; to one a list of placemen was appended. Electors were advised to choose wealthy gentlemen who were eminent in their shires.[56]

---

[52] Sir J. Verney to Sir Roger Hill, 17 July 1698. Lady Verney, ed., *Verney Letters of the Eighteenth Century* (1930), i, 155.

[53] French dispatch, 5/15 July and 1/10 August. P.R.O. 31/3/181 ff. 133 and 150.

[54] Brandenburg dispatch, 15/25 July. B.M. Add. MSS. 30,000 B. f. 171 r.

[55] This complaint was to be introduced ineffectively by Colt in the controverted election at Westminster. French dispatch, 19/29 December 1698. Grimblot, *Letters*, ii, 218. Jack Howe made a general complaint and Major Holmes was said to have seconded it, specifically accusing Lord Cutts of meddling in the Isle of Wight elections. James Sloane to Ambassador Williamson, 18 December. *Cal. S.P. Dom.*, p. 511.

[56] *A letter to a Country Gentleman, setting forth the Cause of the Decay and Ruin of Trade. To which is annexed, A list of the Names of some Gentlemen who were members of the last Parliament, and now are (or lately were), in Public Employments.* 16 July 1698. Cobbett, vol. v, app. XVI, clxiii-clxxiv.

Even before the general election, the straws in the wind pointed to a country victory. In late March, with the expectation of Goodwin Wharton's death causing a by-election at Cockermouth, the duke of Somerset's agents prepared to nominate someone less dominated by the junto:

> For the most substantiall Burges are true Churchmen, and (to our observation) have (of late) made their remarks touchinge the behaviour of Whiggish members in generall, and have declared their aversion to have such members serve in parliamt.[57]

As it was, of course, Goodwin Wharton lived on, although in the general election he was not to be returned for Cockermouth despite his talk of avoiding party labels.[58] In the county Sir Daniel Fleming appears to have remained neutral, not daring to support Sir Christopher Musgrave in the face of the Lowthers. Still, Sir Christopher at least had his support in case of a vacancy[59] and was returned for Oxford University.

Goodwin Wharton had been forced to retreat to his native Buckinghamshire, but even there the junto encountered difficulties. Earlier in the parliament Wharton was thought to be gaining considerable successes in by-elections by unfair practices. Sir John Verney wrote, for example, that '...ordinary people are cautious if not fearfull of disobliging men in power.'[60] Such caution was evidently dispelled and perhaps even turned to a desire for vengeance when it came to appear that they would soon be out of power. Indeed, Vernon thought Wharton's losses at Malmesbury in keeping with his losses elsewhere, subsequently finding him 'run down in all places'.[61]

In Surrey too, it appeared that the country gentlemen were not to be intimidated. It was said that they grew angry at an allegedly unfair return of Foot Onslow at Guildford, and as a result Sir Richard Onslow was almost turned out of his seat as knight of the shire. As it was, John

---

[57] [Mr Ewart] to [Chas. Heron], 31 March 1698. Cockermouth Castle, Leconfield Estate Documents.

[58] Tho. Alkinson to John Rolfe, 21 July. *Ibid.*

[59] Sir Daniel Fleming to Sir Christ. Musgrave, 27 April and 3 May 1698. West. R.O., DRy/5254. *H.M.C. Le Fleming*, p. 351.

[60] Sir John Verney to Roger Hill, 9 January 1696/7. Margaret Verney, *Verney Letters*, i, 54.

[61] To Shrewsbury, 9 and 16 August 1698. *Vernon Corr.*, ii, 147–9 and 152. For a thorough coverage of the junto campaign see Dr E. L. Ellis, 'The Whig junto from its inception to 1714' (D.Phil. Oxon., 1961), i, ff. 356–400.

Weston succeeded in capturing at least one of the seats.[62] In Stafford-shire too, the gentry became offended by the government manipulations and successfully set up Edward Bagot, a fervent government oppo-nent.[63] The whole tone of the election had changed from that of 1695. Instead of fear of being identified with Jacobitism, it was thought in-advisable to have the support of the dissenters; the placeman, James Lowther, now thought this to be the kiss of death.[64]

The enthusiasm of the election was widely noted. In some counties it was said that a dozen stood for knight of the shire and in Gloucester-shire, where there were half a dozen standing, Jack Howe was noted by one court supporter to have won by a great margin '…though he hath not a foot of land in the county. The Truth is people are so galled with taxes that they kick and whine at every one.' [65]

It was only natural that the country party should find some problems. One country supporter, Thomas Mansell, was persuaded to stand only because of fear of creditors coupled with the belief that not to stand would be a clear '…demonstration of being an enemy to the present government which is Protestant.'[66] Occasionally, too, there were out-right setbacks. In Worcestershire, Thomas Foley was not returned again despite pleas that he had broken from his relations and voted consistently with the court in all matters of importance, especially votes of supply. Nevertheless, the court had doubts as to Foley's reliability as might be inferred from Harley's urgings that Shrewsbury either support Foley or not take part in the elections.[67] In the event, Shrews-bury supported the junto favourite, John Walsh, to the delight of Somers and Vernon.[68] The court was less pleased about Sir John Packington's victory for the other seat, and, indeed, with a bit of shuffling

---

[62] Vernon to Shrewsbury, 6 August 1698. *Vernon Corr.*, ii, 145–7.

[63] N.n. to Sir John Lowther, 16 July. Cumb. R.O., Lonsdale Misc. Un-sorted Corr.

[64] Dr Lancaster wrote to James's father and denied making any such allegations. 16 July. *Ibid.*

[65] Sir Miles Cooke to Sir Jos. Williamson, 9 July and 19 August. *Cal. S.P. Dom.*, pp. 376–7.

[66] [Sir] Edward Mansell to his son, Thomas, 20 July. N.L.W., Penrice and Margam MSS. L. 348. Thomas was returned for Cardiff. He voted against the court on all recorded issues the previous parliament, and was not to vote in favour of the standing army.

[67] Vernon to Shrewsbury, 30 June. *Vernon Corr.*, ii, 118.

[68] Somers to Shrewsbury, 5/15 July and 16/26 August. *Shrewsbury Corr.*, pp. 541–2 and 553.

all the Foleys were returned by mid-January.[69] Even Thomas Foley's initial defeat was in part due to his compromises with the court and his alienation from the electorate over purely local interests.[70] In Hereford, Paul Foley at first found some reluctance on the part of his supporters to give him their pledges and but gradually did they all come over.[71] In Somerset, a general improvement of the country position was expected but did not materialize. In Warwickshire, which was solidly country the previous parliament, most of the members were noted by Francis Gwyn not to have taken the trouble to stand again.[72] Gwyn himself was not returned until a by-election at Seymour's pocket borough of Totnes in January. In Rutland, Nottingham also had fears of the court candidate's succeeding by default, although in the event they proved groundless.[73] A new country man, Richard Halford, was returned for one seat while Lord Burleigh succeeded in coming in again for the other. To the court's chagrin, Sir Andrew St John, the sitting member, was displaced.[74]

In London and Middlesex, the court maintained its domination only by great efforts.[75] Still, Sir John Fleet maintained his seat and Warwick Lake succeeded in Middlesex. Montague and Vernon were, moreover, forced to fight a very determined contest to secure their seats and subsequently an even more ferocious one to maintain them in the committee of elections.

William had not openly supported any ministerial faction before he left and Somers wondered if he would do so even when he returned.[76]

---

[69] There was some thought of challenging the elder Thomas Foley's election at Droitwich in January on grounds of bribery, but the matter was quickly dropped as the evidence was too weak. R. Harley to Sir E. Harley, 10 January 1698/9. B.M. Portland loan 29/189.

[70] Sir T. Littleton to Visc. Hatton, 6 July 1698. B.M. Add. MSS. 29,579 f. 34 r.

[71] To Sir E. Harley, 1 August. B.M. Portland loan 29/75/2. Foley questioned the general country optimism regarding the composition of the next parliament.

[72] To William, second marquis of Halifax, 9 July. Althorpe, Halifax MSS., box 4.   [73] To s., 4 June. *Ibid.*, box 7.

[74] G. Dolben to Sir Justinian Isham, 19 July. Nottingham to s., s.d. Northants. R.O., Isham MSS., box xiv., nos. 1586 and 1588.

[75] Brandenburg dispatch, 28 June/8 July. B.M. Add. MSS. 30,000 B. f. 154 v.

[76] To Shrewsbury, n.d. [early winter 1698]. Philip (Yorke), earl of Hardwicke, *Miscellaneous State Papers* (1778), ii, 435 (transcribed from the originals by Somers).

Possibly the king's neutrality was a blessing in disguise: an overt ex-
pression of favouritism at that time, with the country sentiment running
as high as it was, could have had paradoxically adverse effects. Still, the
depth of country sentiment was not immediately apparent. In early
August some, such as Foley, thought that the election would bring
little change. Others such as Viscount Weymouth believed that '...those
not in search of place do not trouble to go and incur expenses of long
sessions.'[77] Weymouth's surmise was generally to be proved wrong,
and the wish for new members was fulfilled. Francis Gwyn believed that
there would be almost 200,[78] while the Brandenburg envoy thought
there were 177.[79] Harley drew up two cross-reference lists, with a
special mark by the 186 members who had not sat in the previous parliament.[80] Nottingham, while regretting the absences of Gwyn and
Dyke, also noted the phenomenon and believed that the parliament
was '...much better than the last.'[81] Some court supporters such as
the Brandenburg envoy were at first optimistic, believing that as the
largest part were not overly rich it might be easy to enlist them by
bribes or places.[82] Others who at first concurred were soon less certain.
Ambassador Williamson was told by another court supporter that
while he at first

> ...had some consolation from the consideration that the loaves and
> fishes were on our side, and upon that consideration did not much
> doubt a majority. But (upon second thoughts) I cannot be very
> confident in that matter, when I also consider that (without a
> miracle) 4 or 5 basket fulls of preferment will be hardly able to feed
> above 500 persons and most of them sharp enough of all conscience.

Although he hoped that they would have until the end of November
'to consider of the matter',[83] evidently it was not long enough. It was
from their express beliefs that Lord Lonsdale drew the conclusion that

[77] To Col. J[ames] G[rahme], 22 July 1698. *H.M.C. Bagot*, p. 334.

[78] To William, second marquis of Halifax, 10 August. Althorpe, Halifax
MSS., box 4.

[79] Brandenburg dispatch, 26 August/5 September. B.M. Add. MSS. 30,000
B. f. 205 r.

[80] B.M. Portland loan, 29/164/86–7.

[81] To William, second marquis of Halifax, 27 August. Althorpe, Halifax
MSS., box 7.

[82] Bonet wrote: '... la plus grande partie d'entr'eux ne sont pas gens fort
opuleus...' Brandenburg dispatch, 26 August/5 September. B.M. Add. MSS.
30,000 B. f. 205 r.

[83] From Sir Miles Cooke, 19 August. *Cal. S.P. Dom.*, p. 376.

the country was '...tired out with taxes to a degree beyond what was discerned 'till it appeared upon the occasions of the late Elections.'[84] Nevertheless, even the junto realized that the new members were not Jacobites. Somers noted that some of the extremist leaders had been left out.[85] Montague admitted them to be '...such as will neither hurt England, or this government, but, I believe, they must be handled very nicely.'[86]

The new members were then numerous, and generally tired out with taxes, loyal and not too rich—mere gentry in effect. As the session wore on, Matthew Prior in a letter to Portland distinguished them from the tories, believing that they '...compose that body which they call the Country party...[which] despite the fact that most of them have been and still are whigs are the ones who obstruct the king's business.' Unlike the new members, Prior notes that the tories vote against their principles (which one may suppose to mean support of the royal prerogative) and follow their 'peevish chiefs' who '...are against the court right or wrong because they are not of it.'[87] Still, the two groups were generally united if only negatively, although positively at least one clear dichotomy was seen in the contest for the Speakership.

Paul Foley found the position of Speaker difficult. He had tried to maintain his country principles and yet avoid complete opposition, for a purely destructive policy seemed not only irresponsible but likely to change only men and not measures. On one occasion, indeed, apparently in the service of moderation, he is said to have tampered with the printed votes to the court's advantage.[88] Vernon noted that in the Fenwick affair Foley played his part and 'framed fit questions' at the

---

84 To William III, 28 August. Cumb. R.O., Unsorted seventeenth-century manuscripts.

85 Somers to Shrewsbury, 16/26 August. *Shrewsbury Corr.*, p. 554.

86 To s., 11/21 August. *Ibid.*, p. 551.

87 8/18 March 1698/9. *H.M.C. Bath*, iii, 324.

88 An example is seen regarding the oath for the members of the proposed parliamentary board of trade. Daniel Bret thought that the oath which would have involved recognizing William as rightful and lawful king, also declared '...that no other person of the race of Stewarts (for so I am informed upon good grounds it was put, though the speaker hath been pleased to disguise it in the printed votes) hath any title [save that enacted during the Convention Parliament].' Thus Foley had made the rejected oath appear far less radical than, in fact, it was. To the earl of Huntingdon, 3 February 1695/6. *H.M.C. Hastings*, ii, 252.

very least.[89] While such moderation appears to have incurred the wrath of opposition extremists,[90] the French envoy, Tallard, writing to Louis XIV at the close of the next session, expressed his belief that Foley was one of the court's four leading opponents.[91] Tallard may have remembered the altercation a year earlier between Foley and Jack Smith, a model turncoat and leading placeman. During a debate concerning the witnesses in the Duncombe affair, Foley moved that unless candles were produced, the house should adjourn. Smith tried to avert the adjournment by saying, somewhat inconsistently, that he had something to offer in way of compromise. Foley, it is said, repeated the word 'compromise' 'in an exposing way', and Smith bade the Speaker learn more manners. The motion for candles failed, and the house was adjourned. But after the adjournment, Smith continued his attack on the Speaker, saying that if he did not treat him better he would pull him by the nose. Friends of both Foley and Smith threatened to bring the matter before the house and the quarrel went no further, as it was considered a discredit to both parties.[92]

There were other occasions when Foley showed reluctance to serve the court and yet showed moderation in his opposition. Vernon wrote that in a matter of supply the court unexpectedly found that the 'Speaker hath put a rub in their way'. 'Before they were aware', he referred the revenue account to a select committee, which had other accounts before them, and not to the committee of supply.[93] Led by Montague and Sir Thomas Littleton, the court subsequently proposed a resolution authorizing a special oath to be taken by the commissioners of the board of trade. Crucial as this proposal was, the court lost.[94]

It is true that even Foley could not have found the Speakership without its rewards. It would certainly seem, however, that he received these less directly than his predecessors[95] and that they were partially

---

[89] Vernon to Shrewsbury, 6 November 1696. Coxe, *Shrewsbury Corr.*, i, 425–6.   [90] Foley to R. Harley, 30 October 1699. B.M. Portland loan 29/75/2.
    [91] 29 March/8 April 1698. Grimblot, *Letters*, i, 352.
    [92] 24 January 1697/8 (Account of Proceedings in the House of Commons), *Cal. S.P. Dom.* 1698, p. 43. 22 January 1697/8, *H.C.J.*, xii, 59.
    [93] To Shrewsbury, 18 December 1697. Boughton, Shrewsbury Papers, i, f. 167.   [94] See above, pp. 96–7 and 191 n.
    [95] When he received the compliments of Lord Galway, conveyed by Methuen, Foley owned his respects, but had 'at his heart a great resentment'. Galway is said to have overlooked one of Foley's relatives suggested for ecclesiastical preferment. Methuen to [Galway], 21 April 1698. Blenheim, Sunderland letterbook.

offset by new dangers. For failing to promote the interests of the Hereford leather trade in parliament, Foley was on one occasion confronted
by the trade's representatives in the house—the grimly titled 'leather
mob', who threatened to pull his house down.[96] It is seldom easy to be
a moderate.

Foley was for long considered the opposition's most hopeful candidate. In 1698 a placeman, James Lowther, wrote that although '...
they talk little of Mr Foley...I believe they will think it convenient to
stick to him at last, or they will make little of it on t'other side.'[97] Only
a fortnight before the session opened, Sir John Banks wrote of a
'seeming current' for Foley.[98] Yet Foley did not stand for the Speakership. His reasons seem to have been various. The office of Speaker was a
thankless one and his health was not at all good.[99] More important
still, there were a large number of candidates among the opposition. At
first it was 'whispered' that Foley 'would mend his manners and be by
the court'.[100] At one time, the court had seemed likely to nominate
Foley, because it was probable that if they did not, the chair would be
won by Seymour.[101] But later, the court was fairly united, and did
not therefore need to nominate 'heavy Paul Foley as a moderate
man'.[102]

Sir Edward Seymour was known to have been interested in the chair
since October,[103] but among the opposition the prospect of his

---

[96] This was a serious threat, as Foley's house at Stoke Edith was one of the
finest constructed in the late seventeenth century. Sir J. D. Colt to Sir Wm.
Trumbull, 22 May 1697. *H.M.C. Downshire*, I, ii, 743.

[97] To Sir John Lowther, 5 November 1698. Cumb. R.O., Lowther Corr.

[98] To Heneage Finch, 22 November. Chatsworth, Finch-Halifax MSS., box
5.

[99] See Foley's letter to Robert Harley of 30 October 1699. B.M. Portland
loan 29/75/2. He complained of what might be diagnosed as chronic bron-
chitis ('such a cough in my lungs as does near strangle me') and mentions
that a similar condition kept him at Hampstead much of the previous winter.

[100] Sir Miles Cooke to Sir Joseph Williamson at the Hague, 27 September
1698. *Cal. S.P. Dom.*, p. 393.

[101] Robert Price to Beaufort, 26 November 1698. Bodl. Carte MSS. 130
f. 394.

[102] Bonet noted earlier (in his Brandenburg dispatch of 8/18 November)
that if the current was too strong for Seymour, the court would support Foley
who had at least kept the commons involved in non-volatile matters ('medi-
ocres sujets'). B.M. Add. MSS. 30,000 B. f. 251 v.

[103] E. Harley to Sir E. Harley, 29 October 1698. *H.M.C. Portland*, iii,
599.

candidacy caused considerable alarm. Nottingham wanted Seymour to step down, believing that '...if one of our friends does not, the third will certainly carry it which in itself would be very ill and the consequences much worse for it will break all confidence among our acquaintances...[and hinder] all measures that should be taken'.[104] Robert Price was even more sceptical about the extent of Seymour's support, remarking that '...the country sets up Sir Edward Seymour, or at least he sets up himself.' Price thought that Seymour was setting one country candidate against another to the disadvantage of the party. Although Granville was thought at first to have had the 'most friends', Seymour induced his supporters to defect and 'sett up Harley and Harcourt to divide the Granville interest'. Nor was this Seymour's last attempt at manipulation, for he was twice seen dining with Montague, apparently to attract court support in order to '...come between court and country.' Price believed that Seymour might be stopped by those who had observed with whom he dined, for the knowledge was 'very carefully divulged'.[105]

A further attack on Seymour was found in a pamphlet on the choice of a Speaker.[106] While criticizing the court candidate. Sir Thomas Littleton, for being a placeman, it made an oblique reference to someone else—Seymour, it was thought—as an even worse choice. He was described as:

> ...an old Prostitute of the exploded Pension'd Parliament in Charles the Second's Reign, who has from that time bin tricking in the House in so shameful a manner, that the Several Periods of his Life may be mark'd out by the bargains he has made there, when the court has come up to his price.'[107]

There still appeared to be a chance for the country party when Granville, as a result of vigorous canvassing, seemed to be enlisting even some court supporters. Moreover, by September 1698, it was believed that Littleton was finding his place in the treasury counting heavily

---

[104] Nottingham to Halifax, 12 November. Althorpe, Halifax MSS., box 7.

[105] To Beaufort, 26 November. Bodl. Carte MSS. 130, f. 394.

[106] The pamphlet was entitled: *Considerations Upon the Choice of a Speaker of the House of Commons In the Approaching Session* (1698). Vernon believed that the country pamphlet against a standing army 'is supposed from the same club'. Vernon to Shrewsbury, 29 November. *Vernon Corr.*, ii, 217

[107] Considerations Upon the Choice of a Speaker...(1698), p. 8.

against him and was consequently beginning to abandon hopes of the Speakership.[108] By late November, the court had doubts of both his loyalty and his powers. He was, after all, the younger son of a poor baronet and his early life had been somewhat unpromising.[109] Some courtiers feared that his intention was rather to forsake his post as a lord of the treasury in order to be elected Speaker in this and following parliaments. It was thought that he would find the office of Speaker a profitable one[110] and evidently the king also had suspicions about him, for Vernon found himself accused by the junto of having turned the king's head. With Littleton's experience as chairman of the committee of ways and means during the previous parliament, he would certainly be formidable in opposition. On Littleton's behalf, Vernon denied the junto's accusations, believing that Littleton was assured of 284 votes in the election for the Speakership despite last-minute caballing by Seymour and Granville for yet another opposition candidate, Sir Christopher Musgrave. As with Seymour, it was probably feared that if Musgrave were elected Speaker he would probably become a courtier, although nothing was said at the time.[111]

In the end, the court appears to have thought that Littleton would find a place more secure than the Speakership; on 6 December 1698, the commons convened and elected him by a majority of over a hundred votes.[112] The division was preceded by a debate lasting almost two hours in which Sir Edward Seymour led the opposition in the attack. No other candidate was proposed, but the opposition, with the aid of selected arguments from the printed pamphlet,[113] made an unsuccessful attempt to prevent Littleton's election. In one placeman's eyes, the reasons for the opposition's defeat appear quite obvious. 'The others

---

[108] Sir Miles Cooke to Amb. Williamson at the Hague, 27 September 1698. *Cal. S.P. Dom.*, p. 393.

[109] Before his older brother's death, Littleton was apprenticed to a city merchant. G.E.C., *Baronets*.

[110] Brandenburg dispatch of 29 November/9 December. B.M. Add. MSS. 30,000 B. ff. 264 v.–265 r.

[111] Vernon to Shrewsbury, 29 November. *Vernon Corr.*, ii, 217–19.

[112] *H.C.J.*, xii, 347. The teller for the yeas was Ld Coningsby (242), the noes, Norris (135). He was proposed by Ld Hartington (Vernon believes by Ld Spencer as well) and supported by Montague, Pelham, Smith and Sir Richard Onslow in the debate. Vernon to Shrewsbury, 6 December. *Vernon Corr.*, ii, 226–7.

[113] *Ibid.* The other speakers against Littleton were said to be Byerly, Norris, Hammond and Sir John Rolles.

were not agreed who to set up in case they had carried their question.'[114]
The opposition's problem was not a lack of strength, but rather an
excess. Like many composite bodies that are united only under stress,
it soon split again into component parts once the difficulties no longer
seemed so menacing. The attempts of Seymour, Musgrave and Harcourt were regarded by many as bids for power by tories temporarily
out of favour with the court who were quite ready to be bought off.
Granville had a better reputation for honesty, but his support was probably too limited. The many new members, who would have voted
unanimously for a moderate country candidate like Harley or Foley,
were no doubt confused and quite probably disappointed by the
quarrels of their leaders. The court, on the other hand, to which such
wrangling had hitherto been largely confined, continued its alliance
with the junto and thus faced the election with a large, orderly and as
yet relatively undisturbed cadre of supporters.

There were limits, of course, to what even the Speaker could do to
serve the court. The junto knew what the king did not: for although the
country party did not set '…an avowed enemy at the head of the House
of Commons, yet they would be at liberty in other things…'[115]

They were indeed and any court optimism was soon to be dispelled.[116]
Still, liberty was not license. A sense of fairness was seen in the country
members' attitude in controverted elections. When Sir Henry Dutton
Colt challenged Montague's election at London on very shaky grounds
he was unsuccessful;[117] only Colonel Granville opposed agreeing with
the committee's resolution affirming the legality of the election. Nevertheless, the resolution finding the petition vexatious was nowhere near
so unanimous.[118] If the junto's opponents did not come off too badly
when they had a bad case, when they had a good one there was no stopping them. As a number of electoral petitions went successively against

---

[114] James Lowther to Sir J. Lowther, 6 December. Cumb. R.O., Lowther
Corr.

[115] Somers to Shrewsbury, 15 December. Coxe, *Shrewsbury Corr.*, pp. 569–
571.

[116] Ellis believed that Littleton's election was '…a promising beginning for
the king's affairs.' In February, however, he wrote that the government had '…
never carried a vote upon a division since the first concerning the Speaker.'
6 December 1698 and 3 February 1698/9. *Cal. S.P. Dom.*, p. 424, and *Cal.
S.P. Dom., 1699*, p. 41.

[117] French dispatch, 19/29 December 1698. Grimblot, *Letters*, ii, 218.

[118] Vernon to Shrewsbury, 23 December. Boughton, Shrewsbury Papers,
ii, f. 23.

the junto, Vernon believed that it was the continuation of the disbandment controversy which so served to unite the country side and divide
the court: 'We are a dispersed routed party, our oppressors bear hard
upon us, and we see no means to help ourselves.'[119]

MINISTERIAL APPEASEMENT

The king no more wanted the junto ministry to go than he had wanted
the war to end.[120] Since he viewed the peace as but little more than an
armed truce it seems clear from the very nature of his policy that he
must have opposed their complete removal. The junto, however,
appears to have been far from willing to accept even a relegated role
and wished to expand their domination of the ministry, demanding,
for example, that Wharton be given a secretarial position.[121] The general
failure of court and junto in the election made the retention of the war
ministry all the more difficult. Parliament's attack upon the standing
army, the Irish forfeitures and an all but successful vote against Orford
were left as the high-water marks of an appalling session. William saw
the attacks upon the ministry as being really aimed at himself and his
policies. He saw clearly enough the general difficulty of his situation[122]
—and the problem would become worse before it got better. By late
April the French envoy was able to note with delight that in the interior
of England it was act of parliament alone which regulated matters beyond a certain date. When commissioners were appointed by such acts
to put some matter into execution they were given wide interpretative
powers and considerable autonomy from the crown.[123] This fact in
itself was probably enough to force the king to make some readjust-
ment in his ministerial balance, appointing some ministers more in

---

[119] To Shrewsbury, 31 January and 2 February. *Vernon Corr.*, ii, 256–60.
S. to s., 27 January and 1 February. Boughton, Shrewsbury Papers, iii, ff. 25
and 27. The placeman, James Lowther, considered the turning out of Hedges
and Sir Th. Felton, '...the hardest measure ever.' To Sir John Lowther, 3
February 1699/1700. Cumb. R.O., Lonsdale MSS.
[120] It was said '...that the king would shortly call into place all the great
ones who are of the Church of Engld...I cannot say that it is very agreeable to
the king's inclination...' Capt. E. Cork to Bp. King, 20 April 1699. T.C.D.
MSS. 1122/603.   [121] Feiling, *Tory Party*, p. 329.
[122] Somers to Shrewsbury, 30 March/9 April 1699. *Shrewsbury Corr.*, pp.
581–3.
[123] French dispatch, 22 April/2 May 1699. Grimblot, *Letters*, ii, 316.

keeping with the sentiment of the new parliament. But even when it came to making the changes it was only the 'Whig grandees' whom he was said to be consulting: '...no unfortunate Tory can be admitted into his presence,' wrote Colonel Granville, 'when these great misteries are unfolded.'[124]

Truly significant changes, such as the return of Sunderland, the junto would not abide and Sunderland was unwilling to force his way back to court.[125] Still, there were considerable tory advances which began in May and proceeded until almost the opening of the session: Jersey became secretary of the southern department; Pembroke, president of the council; Lonsdale, keeper of the privy seal. Secretary Vernon was increasingly thought of more as a moderate tory than a moderate whig despite his denials.[126] Portland, Orford and Montague resigned, but while the treasury position was filled by Tankerville the tory victory in the admiralty board was less convincing. If Rooke was now included, so too was Littleton, while the board was led by Bridgewater. If an appearance of popular support was given to this new ministry by Shrewsbury's acceptance of the office of lord chamberlain, it would appear that he accepted it only under the king's incessant urgings; he was a sick man and thought only of retiring.[127] The moderates' support of the ministry was constantly diminishing. Offers extended, for example, to the country supporter, Sir William Blackett, of a position in the treasury, were half-heartedly met and evidently declined.[128]

THE IMPEACHMENT PROCEEDINGS OF 1699–1700

The first problem in bringing impeachment proceedings against the junto was to have a just cause, as the honest country gentlemen would

---

[124] To William, second marquis of Halifax, 9 May. Althorpe, Halifax MSS., box 4.

[125] J. P. Kenyon, *Sunderland*, p. 307.

[126] Vernon wrote that '...no man has ever had so little conversation with the Torys as myself.' To Shrewsbury, 13 May 1699. Boughton, Shrewsbury Papers, ii, f. 83. Still, Vernon realized that when Harley sat next to him in the commons, saying that he did so 'to blast your reputation' with the junto, he was at the least thought of as a moderate. To s., 1 December 1698. *Vernon Corr.*, ii, 220.

[127] D. H. Somerville, *King of Hearts*, p. 141.

[128] Chas. Montague to Sir Wm. Blackett, bart. of Wallington, 11 May 1699. North. R.O., Blackett (Matfen) MSS.

not proceed without one. An opportunity was found in a commission of 1695 authorizing Captain Kidd to capture pirate vessels. The money had been raised by Somers, Russell, Sidney and Shrewsbury, the king having authorized that they should receive the revenue accruing from the venture.[129] Kidd's ship the *Adventure* soon began to behave very suspiciously, and after the conclusion of the peace was said to be destroying Old East India Company shipping throughout the Indian Ocean.[130] Somers feared that the old company, no friends of the junto owing to the latter's support of their new rival, would '...make the most malicious use of it they can.'[131]

He was correct. The old company's cause was given support by the country leader, Robert Harley, who with Seymour moved for the impeachment of Somers. This direct attack failed, but a subsequent more modest resolution, condemning the issuance of the letters patent as dishonourable, unlawful and destructive of trade, at least caused a division, although the motion was defeated 189–133. The court took great heart in the outcome; Shower, Harcourt and Edward Harley were said to be the only lawyers favouring the proposal.[132] Somers had believed that the investigation would show '...there can be no crime, though perhaps we may appear somewhat ridiculous.'[133] Indeed, it seems that Robert Harley was wavering in his leadership of the proceedings, allowing Jack Howe to take direction—a good sign of a lost cause. One court supporter thought that the country gentlemen were coming to look upon Howe '...more as a discontented courtier than a patriot; and as in this vote they left him, so abundance of 'em now [say] they are ashamed of him, as he declares he is of them, swearing there never was before such a crew of rogues as this parliament. He had great hopes of 'em last session, he says, but now he gives 'em over.' Nevertheless, it was said that only Somers' popularity and the justness of his cause '...made a great many vote 'em innocent who [would] have been heartily glad [if] they could

---

[129] Feiling, *Tory Party*, p. 336. Feiling notes that it was 'secretly' authorized for them to gain the revenue. One assumes that he means it was secret only to those not involved in the project.

[130] See the East India Company's depositions presented to the council of trade and plantations, 4 August 1698 and following. *Cal. S.P. America and the West Indies, 1697–8*, pp. 363 and following.

[131] To Shrewsbury, 15 December 1698. *Shrewsbury Corr.*, p. 570.

[132] Vernon to Shrewsbury, 28 November 1699. *Vernon Corr.*, ii, 368–9. John Freke (franked by Edw. Clarke) to John Locke, 7 December. Bodl. MSS. Locke C. 8 f. 230.

[133] Somers to Shrewsbury (15 December 1698). *Shrewsbury Corr.*, p. 570.

have found 'em guilty.' If some thought that the size of the majority precluded it from being attributed solely to court influence,[134] Robert Price thought that the loss was due to more familiar causes: 'We had 60 or 70 [more members],' he wrote, '[but] some sneaked [out] and others had not the patence and soe went out.'[135] The volunteer concept of the country party, the danger of attacking powerful men and the questionable nature of the charges had all aided in securing an acquittal. In mid-February, a question upon the state of the nation served as another thinly veiled attack upon the lord chancellor. On division, the attack failed 232–182; if by a few less votes the court could take heart that it had occurred in a fuller house.[136] The session was not over. In late March a further attack caused Secretary Vernon to doubt the continuance of the breach in the opposition's leadership which he had noted earlier. Howe appeared very forward to second Seymour's motion for an inquiry into the government's changes of the justices of the peace, the deputy lieutenants, the charters and other matters, some still relating to the Kidd affair.[137] The first grievance concerning the justices was quite obviously an attack upon the attempted junto monopolization of local offices. It was carried, moreover, that 'the good men' who had been turned out were to be restored and those of small estates removed. The subsequent junto attempt to limit the change to those '…who are well affected to his Majesty and his Government' was countered with the argument that the phrase obviated the very intent of the motion, it being said '…that the pretence of people being disaffected was made use of by Ministers to oppress whom they would.' This line of reasoning was apparently telling. Despite the fact that the debate had lasted until eight o'clock, the court's amendment was defeated 120–112.[138]

In April, the Irish forfeitures controversy fanned the flames of hostility amongst the country members. In committee on the sixth, there was another attack upon Somers and a motion followed to exclude

---

[134] Sir John Vanbrugh to Manchester, 25 December 1699. *Court and Society*, ii, 53–4.

[135] To the duke of Beaufort, 6 December. Bodl. Carte MSS. 130 f. 403. Indeed, the division had not occurred until 'about 9 o'clock'. *Ibid.*

[136] James Lowther to Sir John Lowther, 13 February 1699/1700 Cumb. R.O., Lonsdale MSS.

[137] Vernon to Shrewsbury, 21 March 1699/1700. Boughton, Shrewsbury Papers, ii, f. 48.

[138] S. to s., 26 March 1700. *Ibid.*, f. 50. Vernon recorded the vote as 119–113, the Journals have 120–112. *H.C.J.*, xii, 301.

foreigners from the privy council. The speeches against Portland and Albemarle were probably but opening gambits for no questions were put. One placeman noted, however, that the attack became far more candid, '...their business being as they openly declared to break the Ministry.'[139] On 10 April when the Irish forfeitures bill had so narrowly passed the lords, the commons upon hearing that 'the Lords had struck their Flagg, slackened there [their] fire and called for the List of the Privy Councill.'[140] Somers was primarily aimed at, and held responsible for the king's ill reception of their petitions regarding the Irish forfeitures and the lords' recusancy over passage. A moderate motion for Somers's impeachment which might have carried was turned into one calling for his removal from the king's council forever. This more hostilely worded motion was lost, 167–106.[141] Despite the apparent victory, Secretary Vernon thought Somers should take little encouragement from the vote, believing that many did not vote against him simply because they believed that if left alone he would retire on his own. The subsequent court failure to secure a timely adjournment, though by but 11 votes, confirmed him in this belief. The moderate nature of the house was the greatest feature of the day. The only effective action taken (and this he noted had only occurred after considerable debate) was in a resolution calling for the removal of all foreigners from the council. Some thought the measure largely ineffectual, as only Schomberg, Portland and Galway would be affected. While there was talk of another motion which would allow only native-born subjects to serve in the troops, the country leaders, believing that they had done enough, finally permitted an adjournment.[142] The next day, with no speech from the throne, the king prorogued parliament.

FURTHER MINISTERIAL APPEASEMENT

In William's mind, the moderate changes which were made in the ministry had little effect on a session which he considered to be the worst ever.[143] To some the problem lay in the fact that the junto thought

---

[139] James Lowther to Sir John Lowther, 6 April. Cumb. R.O., Lonsdale MSS.

[140] N.n. to the earl of Torrington, 11 April. B.M. Add. MSS. 28,053 ff. 402–3.

[141] James Lowther to Sir Lowther, 6 April. Cumb. R.O., Lonsdale MSS.

[142] Vernon to Shrewsbury, 11 April. *Vernon Corr.*, iii, 19–25.

[143] To Heinsius, 12/23 April. Grimblot, *Letters*, ii, 398.

themselves still far from out. The problem of declining ministerial influence had continued unabated. Vernon sarcastically remarked that Somers and Montague '...are still called the Ministers tho there are none that I see who take upon them any management.'[144] Harley mockingly compared them to Don Quixote and Drawcansir.[145] Sunderland also found their pretended domination ridiculous and wrote to Portland '...they [the junto] thought themselves so much masters as to need no help of any kind and were as glad to be rid of Lord Shrewsbury as of me.' They wished '...that all the credit might be in three or four hands which I believe every body sees is not sufficient to carry on the business...' While he thought the personnel of the ministry to be of little matter in good times, the political situation had deteriorated so much in the past six months that it was now an explosive question.[146]

William's power was declining with that of his ministry. The bishop of Derry found that the king was becoming '...only a sort of sheriff to execute their [parliament's] orders.'[147] The army in Ireland was more parliament's than the king's: '...if he [the king] had occasion for them they obey the parlement of England, not him. And some doe call themselves the parlement Army.'[148] The situation was so bad that William found it necessary to have the royal robes in preparation in case the Irish forfeitures bill failed in the lords. Even though it passed, Vernon believed that the court had made a tactical error in not proroguing parliament immediately after its success; if the commons had known that Albemarle had voted to maintain the lords' amendments, the session might well have had a far worse outcome.[149] Evidently the king came to think so too. The opposition, in refusing to grant William £200,000 out of the forfeitures as a return for Somers's dismissal, was to have it without even paying the price. On 27 April the seals were sent for. Vernon states that one reason for dismissal was his support of a bill unfavourable to the court,[150] but this was probably only an official excuse. Basically it seems that the king had simply decided that he had nothing to lose in experimenting. If it was the junto which had incurred

---

[144] To Shrewsbury, 5 March 1699/1700. Boughton, Shrewsbury Papers, iii, f. 41.
[145] To [Sir William Trumbull], 31 October 1699. *H.M.C. Downshire*, I, ii, 794.
[146] To Portland, 20 March 1699/1700. N.U.L. PwA 1279.
[147] [To Sir Robt. Southwell], 19 November 1700. T.C.D. MSS. 1489.
[148] To Sir Robert Southwell, 4 February 1699/1700. *Ibid.*
[149] To Shrewsbury, 11 April 1700. *Vernon Corr.*, iii, 23–4.
[150] To Shrewsbury, 11 May 1700. *Vernon Corr.*, iii, 43–4.

parliament's displeasure, might they not be displaced without a change in basic policy? It was nature and not the king which abhorred a vacuum. The appointment of the comparative nonentity, Sir Nathan Wright, did not fool Sir Christopher Musgrave, who asked if it was '...not ominous to chuse a Lord Keeper from the Gravel Pits?'[151] Probably many saw that William was simply biding his time until he found it opportune to return to the junto. The moderates whom Matthew Prior was to refer to as being sought to 'support the Crown, rather than oblige their party,'[152] were still in fact expected to support the basic junto policy. Probably it was for this reason that Harley could not be reconciled with a place. 'Some think,' Vernon wrote to Shrewsbury, 'he would not meddle with any Employment whatsoever...' It was thought certain that he would not do so under any sort of junto management.[153] Apparently he did not find the court sufficiently changed in regard to measures to alter his opinion, despite Somers's dismissal.[154] William faced little serious challenge from the junto leaders in the immediate future. They must have sympathized with the king's predicament and their sinecures were not as secure as they might seem.[155] In addition, their hands were to be full with the impeachment proceedings[156] and they would be weakened in the event of an election.

DISSOLUTION AND ELECTION

Despite all that the old parliament had done against the court interest, the king would probably rather have retained it than call a new one. In the by-elections the country mood had been maintained. In May 1699, Francis Gwyn wrote that they had '...noe sort of oposition in the two Neighbouring Countys of Devon and Somerset for the filling of the Vacancies of Kts of the shire, and the Country is very well pleased.'[157]

---

[151] To R. Harley, 30 May. *H.M.C. Portland*, iii, 620.

[152] To Manchester, n.d. December. *Court and Society*, ii, 83–4.

[153] 5 March 1699/1700. Boughton, Shrewsbury Papers, iii, f. 41.

[154] 'Account of Robert Harley's Conduct', B.M. Portland loan 29/165/3 f. 6.

[155] 'And though he [Montague] has a place that can't be well taken away; yet it is liable to be curtailed by lessening the fees, which when it shall be urged, will carry a great shew of reason with it and regard to the subject.' Vernon to Shrewsbury, 11 July 1700. *Vernon Corr.*, iii, 111.   [156] *Ibid.*

[157] To William, second marquis of Halifax, 31 May 1699. Althorpe, Halifax MSS., box 4.

Still, the country gentlemen would not condone opportunism. One indication of the depth of genuine country sentiment was the fate of the status seeker, Richard Alan, *né* Anguish; upon inheriting the estate of his uncle, Richard assumed his name as well, and by the end of that very month hoped to be returned at the Dunwich by-election on the church interest. The rather realistic high-churchman, Humphrey Prideaux, sadly noted it all to be of little avail, for if he refused to stand on the 'fanatic interest', the gentry were not '...very forward to give any reguard to him.'[158] Despite a baronetcy, it would appear that the establishment could not be joined in a fortnight.

A surer sign of the times was Charles Duncombe's successful election as sheriff of London. Davenant wrote that those who campaigned on his behalf had done so '...as a just rebuke to those invaders of property who had so unreasonably persecuted him last parliament.' On the same day he noted that in a poll for a bridgemaster '...the old Whigs (who are now turned Tories) lost it by 1300; which I hope is a symptom that the revolters from their old principle of liberty begin to lose ground, as 'tis hoped they will do throughout the whole kingdom.'[159]

The king was faced with the problem of choosing the lesser of two evils. Without a new parliament the tory ministers would be unwilling to settle such matters as the succession. If he continued the present parliament it was thought he would gain but little. The triennial act would make the next session the last and it was thought that the junto in order to court popular favour would sit still—or worse. The effects of the triennial act on the last session of the previous parliament, a parliament originally far more favourably disposed, were well remembered. A new parliament would obviously not have this disadvantage, but then it might well have others. The tory leaders thought that they could form a coalition which they might influence, showing how well they could manage. Still, there were fears either that they might be mistaken or that their programme might not be the king's programme. Although Vernon hoped that such a desperate course of action would not be embarked upon he feared that '...as one [parliament] is broke, another should be called.' Even if the tories proved incapable or unwilling, he doubted that parliament would 'let the nation sink'.[160]

---

[158] To Ellis, 29 December. *Prideaux-Ellis Corr.*, p. 193. Alan (Anguish) was created a baronet on 14 December 1699.

[159] To Thomas Coke, 1 July. *H.M.C. Cowper*, ii, 388.

[160] To Shrewsbury, 18 July and 8 August 1700. *Vernon Corr.*, iii, 113–14 and 125–6.

It was not until December, however, that expectation of a new parliament was clearly in the air. One junto friend wrote to Somers that he was appalled at the preparations already made by the tory leaders:

> ...there have been Circular letters written to all the Members of one side to let 'em know there would certainly bee a New Parlmt; I do not know how they come to bee so well informed of the Councills, but they haveing made preparations every where upon this, it wou'd be convenient for those who are not admitted into these secrets to be a little more upon their Guard too.[161]

By mid-December, ministerial changes made the prospect of an election appear imminent. 'Everybody believes it,' wrote one observer, 'and those only that know it are modest upon the subject.'[162] If the king faced it with apprehension, the junto expressed utter horror. The ministerial tories expected a great success. Sir William Russell only reflected the common belief when he wrote that '...the wigg party decline booth at Court and the Country [and] the churchmen [are] like to be chosen every where.'[163] On 19 December, parliament was dissolved.

Although Harley had a few butterflies in his stomach when the date of the new parliament was announced[164] he had for long scented in the air '...a spirit which will maintain the antient government of England in Church and State and will not neglect the opportunities which are like to be presented...'[165] Advantage was taken of the opportunities. Viscount Weymouth thought that the election would 'support a sinking trade not to say nation'.[166] The rabid whig, Shaftesbury, believed that even the king had second thoughts about the timing, believing it was 'enough to ruine us all'.[167]

---

[161] From Wm. Walsh, 4 December. Reigate Corp. R.O., B/19 (Somers Papers).

[162] Ld Burlington to Abp. Sharp, 12 December. Gloucs. R.O., Lloyd Baker MSS., box 4/B32.

[163] To Sir Cyril Wyche, 17 December. Irish P.R.O., Wyche Corr., Ser.1/198. Lady Gardiner wrote to Sir John Verney: '...'tis believed most of the old members will be chos again as was not for the Cort party.' 27 November 1701. Lady Verney, *Verney Letters*, p. 164.

[164] He thought the date of 6 February inauspicious while Guy argued that it was the late prince of Gloucester's birthday. 26 December 1700. *H.M.C. Portland*, iii, 640–1.

[165] To Viscount Weymouth, 5 November. *H.M.C. Portland*, iii, 634.

[166] To Robert Harley, 24 September. *H.M.C. Portland*, iii, 629–30.

[167] To B. Furley, 11 January 1700/1. T. Forster, *Original Letters of John Locke, Algernon Sidney and Lord Shaftesbury* (1830), pp. 113–16. Hereafter cited as Forster, *Shaftesbury Corr.*

Much of their ruin occurred in the North. In Westmorland, for example, Wharton's hopes that Major Lowther could come in for the county[168] were soon abandoned. Musgrave, despite his professed reluctance to stand, was the unanimous choice and despite Carlisle's opposition[169] he succeeded in bringing in the suspected Jacobite, Henry Grahme;[170] the latter even being accorded a progress through the county on his way to London.[171] In Cumberland too, there were court and junto losses. Seats were contested there despite court attempts led by peers to prevent it[172]—attempts which were subsequently to result in severe condemnations of aristocratic influence in elections.

In Oxfordshire the court lost every seat but one. At Oxford University, court attempts to return a member were notably unsuccessful. At first, there were doubts amongst the country side that both Finch and Sir Christopher could be elected.[173] As it was known that Musgrave would probably be returned for Westmorland and perhaps Surrey as well,[174] the court hoped to exploit the university's pride by proposing candidates who would definitely sit if chosen. At the least it was thought that Sir Christopher would be forced to sign a declaration saying that if elected he would sit for the university.[175] As it was, Musgrave was returned for both the university and Westmorland. He sat for the latter constituency, allowing a tory extremist, William Bromley of Bagington, to come in for Oxford in the by-election. Harcourt was returned for Abingdon, unopposed.[176]

There were other impressive opposition victories. Richard and Jack Howe encountered little resistance in Wiltshire and Gloucestershire.[177] In Fowey, Cornwall, Colonel Granville was unanimously elected. Although the other seat was fiercely contested, the sheriff secured the

---

[168] J. Lowther to Sir J. Lowther, 12 Sept. 1700. Cumb. R.O., Lowther Corr.

[169] Carlisle in a letter to Gilford Lawson said that if Musgrave attempted to exclude Fleming, then he would try to exclude Sir Christopher. 7 December. West. R.O., Unsorted Le Fleming MSS. (Appleby).

[170] Henry Fleming to Sir Daniel Fleming, 5 December. *Ibid.*

[171] Edw. Wilson to s., recd. 29 January 1700/1. *Ibid.*

[172] L. Simpson to Jos. Rolfe at Cockermouth, 1 September 1700. Cockermouth Castle, Leconfield Estate Documents.

[173] Simon Harcourt to R. Harley, 14 December. *H.M.C. Portland*, iv, 9.

[174] L.W. Finch to [H. Finch, M.P., Univ. Oxon], 18 December. Chatsworth, Finch-Halifax MSS.

[175] Simon Harcourt to Robert Harley, 21 December. *H.M.C. Portland*, iv, 9–10.   [176] *Ibid.*

[177] Visc. Weymouth to Col. Grahme, 3 January 1700/1. Levens, Bagot MSS.

return of John Williams by employing highly questionable polling pro-
cedures against the court candidate Thomas Vivian.[178] Indeed, it would
appear the court was aware that even such successes as it achieved might
prove ephemeral; Matthew Prior suspecting strong opposition in his
attempt to come in for Cambridge University, feared the election would
be controverted even if he succeeded.[179] In the event, he was not even
returned.

It was all the junto could do to make even minimal gains. In the
contest for Worcestershire, William Walsh found that he made little
headway in increasing their influence, believing that even his own past
supporters '...were more upon the reserve.' While he was in the event
returned, he witnessed the development of a concerted opposition.[180]
Blathwayt's and Alexander Popham's unanimous return at Bath was a
victory of two moderates that probably gave the junto little cause for
jubilation.[181]

The usual cause for such court successes as there were was simply
poor preparations by their opponents. Attempts to bring in Lord
Chandos in Herefordshire were spoiled by lack of planning, and it was
thought that the country gentlemen resented his late entry.[182] Such
reluctance and subsequent tardy preparation also put an end to plans
to return two country members for Stafford. Thomas Foley, although
himself successful, sadly noted that his uncle's refusal to stand even
though a seat was offered him allowed the court candidate to gain
electoral pledges simply by default. He thought that if a country candidate had presented himself earlier they would almost certainly have
won the other seat as well.[183]

---

[178] Tho. Vivian to Will. Blathwayt, 13 January. Gloucs. R.O. DpA/D.1799/
C.5 (Dyrham Park Archives, Blathwayt Family Papers). The election was
upheld although the practices employed were condemned. *H.C.J.*, xiii, 512–
513. Williams was re-elected in December 1701.

[179] Math. Prior to Manchester, n.d., December 1700. *Court and Society*, pp.
84–5.

[180] Wm. Walsh to Somers, 4 December. Reigate Corp. R.O., B/18.

[181] Benj. Barber, Thomas Gibbes and Walter Hicks, J.J., to [Wm. Blath-
wayt], 8 January 1700/1. Gloucs. R.O., DpA/D.1799/x 9. Neither Popham
nor Blathwayt were blacklisted by the junto but Blathwayt probably supported
Harley for the speakership in 1700/1 and Popham is listed by Walcott as a
follower of Seymour and Lord Powlett. Walcott, *English Politics*, p. 181. See
appendix A.

[182] T. Bateman to Robt. Harley, 29 December 1700. B.M. Portland loan
29/189.

[183] To Robt. Harley, 16 December. *H.M.C. Portland*, iii, 638.

In Derbyshire, Thomas Coke's defeat may at least in part be accounted for by the action of government postal authorities on behalf of two of the junto's candidates, lords Hartington and Roos. It was said that a letter in support of Coke from Lady Halifax was delayed by over a fortnight until most of her interest was made against him.[184] Admittedly, Coke's loss was not entirely of court-country significance, involving as it did, his own questionable electoral tactics and voting record regarding county land taxation.[185] Still, the court-country division predominated and Coke thought himself on the side of the angels as did his friends.[186]

The junto was well aware of the change in national sentiment. Occasionally, for example, they masked candidates as independents when many believed them to be fervent junto supporters. In Buckinghamshire for example, where Fleetwood Dormer's candidacy for the county aided in dividing the country gentlemen. Dormer claimed to be standing as an independent, although some had positive beliefs that he had the junto's support. Although only returned for Chipping Wycombe, his candidacy for the county was thought to have divided the country interest, aiding in the return of Colonel Wharton.[187]

The king's unwillingness to put forward a candidate for the Speakership displayed the extent of the court's defeat. William certainly could not have found this a very pleasant decision. Matters might have been even worse during the previous parliament without Littleton's presence—or temporary absence; one of the more useful parts of Littleton's body was his poor bladder, which could be called upon to effect a prorogation at just the right moment. A young placeman believed that the ministry was

---

[184] Sir Gilbert Clarke to Thomas Coke, 3 February 1700/1. *H.M.C. Cowper*, ii, 417. Another indication of the court's determination to defeat Coke may be found in the actions of the duke of Newcastle who suddenly and unexpectedly turned his interest against him. Lady Mary Coke to Thomas Coke, 14 January. *Ibid.*, p. 415.

[185] Thomas Wright to Coke, 17 December 1700. *Ibid.*, p. 412.

[186] Capt. Henry Tate to T. Coke, 17 December. *Ibid.*, ii, 412. His friends were, indeed, to do all they could to secure a seat for him in the event of a by-election. See the letter to Coke from Capt. John Beresford, 25 February 1700/1. *Ibid.*, p. 401. P. Legh to s., s.d. *Ibid.* Coke to Stanhope, 27 February (draft). *Ibid.*

[187] Sir John Verney to Ld Cheyne, 10 November 1700. *Verney Letters*, i, 159–60. Dormer to Verney, 5 December. *Ibid.*, p. 162. Verney to the earl of Lichfield, ed. 12 December. *Ibid.*, pp. 162–3.

given a day's grace from 'the malice of 170 men' during a period of un-
relenting attack, by the stone troubles of the Speaker.[188] Again, on 10
April 1700, at the height of the controversy with the Lords over Irish
forfeitures, the day when the commons' doors were locked, and the
spirit of '41 hovered briefly over St Stephen's Chapel, the late arrival of
the Speaker gave the court a precious morning to secure acquiescence,
or at least the promise of abstention, from those too enthusiastic peers
who hindered the passage of the bill. Although parliament was to
convene at eight o'clock, the members did not gather until noon, '...the
Speaker having an excuse always good in his bladder.' Quite naturally
this vital attack of bladder trouble was believed to have occurred at the
instigation of the court.[189]

On occasion, Littleton was also able to prevent minor yet controversial matters from coming before the commons.[190] Although it is not
certain how important the court found Littleton's services, the opposition did not want him to be re-elected. On 10 February, the day for the
election of the new Speaker, Littleton's absence was taken to indicate
submission to the king's wishes, for the king and most of the courtiers
were to agree—albeit temporarily—to the election of Harley as Speaker.[191]
While opposition was expected to come from Sir Rowland Gwynne
and Sir Richard Onslow,[192] in the end only Onslow was proposed.
Gwynne was the more consistent courtier, always voting with the
court, which may have been why the junto proposed Onslow as a compromise. Although Onslow usually supported the court, in the disbandment controversy he and Lord Hartington (one of his proposers)
spoke for and voted with the opposition.[193] This may have been a reason

[188] William Fleming to Daniel Fleming, 20 February 1699/1700. *H.M.C.*
Le Fleming, p. 354. West. R.O., DRy/5470 (Le Fleming Papers).

[189] N.n. to Torrington, 11 April 1700. B.M. Add. MSS. 28,053 ff. 402–3.

[190] He is said, for instance, to have stopped a bill being brought before the
house to relieve the impositions on foreign books, advising that it be left
until 'quieter times'. Dr Geo. Hickes to Dr Austen, 22 May. Bodl. Ballard
MSS., xii, f. 146.

[191] For what might be the list of Harley's supporters see Appendix A.
Brandenburg dispatch, 11/22 Feburary. B.M. Add. MSS. 30,000 f. 34. It was
generally known even earlier. See the letter of Wm. Clayton to Rd. Norris,
Mayor of Liverpool, 6 February 1700/1. *Norris Papers*, ix, 55.

[192] *Ibid.*

[193] Vernon to Shrewsbury, 5 January 1698/9. *Vernon Corr.*, ii, 246–8.
Vernon believed their defections to be one of the more severe setbacks for
the court. He spoke for Littleton in the 1698 debate for speaker. S. to s., 29
November 1698. *Ibid.*, ii, 226–7. See too *H.M.C. Onslow*, pp. 458 and following.

for his gaining few court supporters. It was the king's view that if those who opposed him over disbandment were his friends then he did not need enemies.[194] Onslow's candidacy was as puzzling as Seymour's had been previously, especially as the fathers of Spencer and Hartington, his two proposers, were apparently supporting Harley.[195] Some believed that Spencer and Hartington were ordered to propose Onslow to mask the allegiance of their fathers[196] who were themselves anxious to avoid alienation from the junto. Littleton being pointedly absent, the court really had no candidate.

On this occasion, the country party was united. Foley was dead, and the ministerial tories found Harley acceptable. It has been asserted that Marlborough assisted Harley to become Speaker.[197] If this is true, it may help to explain why Littleton stood down, since Marlborough had considerable interest in Woodstock, Littleton's constituency.[198] Godolphin, who may have been supporting Harley since 1698,[199] informed him that Seymour was also offering him his interest.[200]

Harley was an excellent candidate. Apart from his experience in parliamentary commissions, his outstanding knowledge of precedents[201] and his family tradition in opposition, he was a man of rare courage. During the disbandment controversy, for example, a military pressure group was brought into play apparently by court sympathizers who had soldiers clamouring for pay outside the doors of the commons.[202] Harley, whose outspoken support of disbandment was well known, heard they were about to fall on him; but instead of slipping out by the

---

[194] See the king's letters to Heinsius of 14/24 December and 16/26 December in Grimblot, *Letters*, ii, 212–14.

[195] Estates General dispatch, 11/22 February 1700/1. B.M. Add. MSS. 17,677 WW. f. 151. L'Hermitage was surprised and attributed it to maxims peculiar to England (one of the maxims would appear to be limited liability). There is no mention of Onslow's nomination in the Journals. *H.C.J.*, x, 325.

[196] Brandenburg dispatch, 11/22 February. B.M. Add. MSS. 30,000 E. f. 34 v.

[197] Coxe, *Marlborough*, p. 83.

[198] For William's last parliament, Walcott calls Woodstock a pocket borough of Marlborough's (*English Politics*, p. 22). While this is more than somewhat confusing, it would appear possible that at the least, Marlborough's acquiescence was obtained.

[199] Harley wrote to Godolphin of the seven years he had enjoyed his protection. 21 July 1705. *H.M.C. Bath*, i. 73.

[200] Godolphin to Harley [January (?) 1700/1]. *H.M.C. Portland*, iv, 14–15.

[201] See Oldmixon, *History of England*, p. 459.

[202] 10 February 1700/1. *H.C.J.*, xiii, 325.

back way, walked through them all and, like Foley before him, heard threats to pull his house down.[203] With justice then, he thought of himself as proudly recalcitrant: '...I was never to be frightened into a complyance, but I might be Provok'd into an opposition.'[204] He combined courage with the rarer (and more vote-catching gift) of being able to turn old enemies into friends.[205]

It was generally agreed that if Harley antagonized the court at all, it was not through malice. Indeed, his clear knowledge of the court was partly due to his conferences with the king almost every session.[206] Vernon observed that Harley could have made matters much more uncomfortable for the court the previous year than he did.[207] Although he was not an avowed enemy to the court and was privy to many of its secrets, his sympathies remained country. He never received a place in William's reign, and his own memoirs and those of his brother tell how he refused the office of auditor of receipts, and that of secretary of state, though the latter was offered to him twice at least.[208] Moreover, it was rumoured that he was so far above temptation as to refuse a barony.[209] Harley refused to court popularity by standing for a city or shire, although it was expected of him by Seymour, Jack Howe and others.[210]

---

[203] R. Harley to Sir E. Harley, 29 February 1699/1700. *H.M.C. Portland*, iii, 615.

[204] R. Harley to James Bridges, 5 October 1700. G. Davies and Marion Tinling, eds., 'Correspondence of James Bridges and Robert Harley', *Hunt. Lib. Quart.* (San Marino, Calif., 1938), i, 459.

[205] Although Harley duelled some years before with the Lewis brothers, Thomas Lewis offered his support in the Weobley election of 1698. Abigail Harley to M. Harley, 7 October 1693. *H.M.C. Portland*, iii, 543. Thomas Lewis to R. Harley, 1 August 1698. B.M. Portland loan 29/149/10. In a letter of 17 December 1700, Henry Ashburton offered Harley his support for the speakership despite past differences. *H.M.C. Portland*, iv, 9.

[206] 'Account of Robert Harley's Conduct'. B.M. Portland loan 29/163/3 ff. 3–4.

[207] Vernon to Shrewsbury, 27 February 1699/1700 and 30 May 1700. *Vernon Corr.*, ii, 444 and iii, 67.

[208] 'Account of Robert Harley's Conduct'. B.M. Portland loan 29/163/3 f. 2. 'Harley Family Memoirs'. *H.M.C. Portland*, v, 646.

[209] Robert Price to R. Harley, 12 December 1700. *H.M.C. Portland*, iii, 637–8. 'The Town designs you to be our speaker and others make you a Baron and to tell you all their surmises will make a volume.' *Ibid.*

[210] In a letter of 8 November, Seymour in a vivid analogy, offered to hold Harley's head while Jack Howe brought him to the basin. *H.M.C. Portland*, iv, 8. Perhaps Harley looked ahead to the shift of electoral sentiment which was to occur within the year, when Howe and Seymour would be far too busy

He was proposed by Seymour and Sir John Leveson Gower, who led him to the chair after his victory over Onslow.[211] The defeated candidate, although deprived of the votes of the court party, had much of its sympathy. One placeman noticed that the court spoke for neither candidate, only voting for Harley in the division.[212]

That the active participation of the placemen in the contest for the Speakership might have resulted in a wicked backlash became apparent as the court received a number of very sobering blows in the committee of elections. The country party leaders thought they might have gained an even greater success if it had not been for the money spent by court-allied interests in securing the return of favourable candidates. Shortly before the election, Harley wrote to Sir Richard Middleton of these 'pernicious designs': 'I need not mention to you the faction at London are very likely to get in such who may give up the old English government.'[213] As the election progressed, Viscount Weymouth wrote that while the returns from the West Country would appear to be going far better than previously, '...the Banke [of England] and new E. [East] I. [India] Company are not sparing of their money.'[214] The bribery was thought unprecedented both in scope and scale; forty and fifty pounds being reported as the price paid for many votes.[215]

Such hopes as the junto had to take advantage of these not insignificant ill-gotten electoral gains were soon dashed. At first one placeman thought that the committee of elections would not do anything very

---

themselves to give him much help. Indeed, Howe was to lose Gloucestershire by over a thousand votes. Harley's maintenance of a safe borough seat may well have been a decisive reason for the narrow defeat of the court and junto candidate, again Sir Thomas Littleton, the next December. Simply standing for knight of the shire was an arduous task. Visc. Weymouth wrote to Col. Grahme on 15 November 1700, that he believed there was '...not a more slavish employment that to solicite for the knightship of a shire.' Levens, Bagot MSS.

[211] *H.C.J.*, xiii, 325. The vote was 249–129. Leveson-Gower, member for Newcastle-upon-Tyne, was an arch-enemy of the junto and played a leading role in the impeachment trials. The majority teller was Sir Robert Davers, of Bury St. Edmunds, who had a solid country-tory voting record.

[212] James Lowther to Sir John Lowther, 11 February 1700/01. Cumb. R.O., Lowther Corr. The letter is largely in shorthand, but is at length decipherable by the use of Lowther's key. See too appendix A.

[213] 3 October. N.L.W., Chirk Castle MSS. E. 6138.

[214] To Col. J. Grahme, 3 January 1700/1. Levens, Bagot MSS.

[215] To Robert Harley, 14 January 1701. *H.M.C.Portland*, iv, 13.

significant, noting its delay in choosing a chairman and believing that few petitions could be heard that session.[216] He might have taken heart too in the fact that Sir Rowland Gwynne, the court candidate, was elected chairman, although 'Coll. Granville was likewise proposed but it did not come to a division'.[217]

In spite of such auspicious opening moves, the worst fears of the court were soon realized. Robert Walcott has discussed at some length the very successful action taken against the New East India Company candidates. Their open employment of hard, cold cash to buy votes was considered despicable by the gentry.[218] Perhaps if the East India interest had employed such more traditional means as the buying up of land holdings, the hearings of the controverted elections might have had a different outcome, or at least the ferocity with which their candidates were attacked might have been tempered. Still, the new company's alliance with the junto and war interest was generally thought to have made some sort of attack inevitable.[219] It was the extent of the success of the country petitions which made the placeman, James Lowther, think it so extraordinary. 'I dare state,' he wrote to his father, 'things were never anything like what they are now in all the time you satt in Parlt. I never heard that so many petitions about Elections have successively gone every one [the other way?] before [:] they have plainly by that very thing carried the question against the 3 Lords.'[220] Still, the court seems to have shown considerable reluctance in allowing the debates to be printed.[221]

Sir Edward Seymour had led the purge and was voted the thanks of the house despite his own somewhat questionable electoral practices. James Buckley of Totnes presented the commons with three letters;

---

[216] James Lowther to Sir John Lowther, 18 February 1700/1. Cumb. R.O., Lonsdale MSS.

[217] Trumbull's diary, 12 February. Berks. R.O., Trumbull Add. MSS. 130. This is not mentioned in the Journals.

[218] 'The East India Interest in the General Election of 1700–1701', *Eng. Hist. Rev.* (1956), lxi, 223–39.

[219] John Locke wrote: '...I believe it may be suspected that this Parliamt will not be friends to the New Company and so perhaps may shake it.' To Peter King, 24 January 1700/1. Bodl. Locke MSS. 40 f. 96.

[220] The phrase which appears to be 'the other way' is in shorthand. 19 April 1701. Cumb. R.O., Lonsdale MSS. John Travers writing to [Rd. Norris], Mayor of Liverpool, also noted the 'sad run' on the new company's members.

[221] Peter Shakerly to the mayor and others of Chester, 13 February 1700/1. Chester City Arch. M/L./4/568 (Mayor's letters).

two from Thomas Coleson and one from Sir Edward Seymour. Both promised favours to the corporation for a favourable return, Seymour specifically offering to provide an organ. Buckley's petition was unsuccessful. An earlier commons resolution, moreover, had provided against frivolous and vexations petitions and his petition was adjudged to be one of these. The Brandenburg envoy thought his bad fortune simply due to being less strong than his prey.[222]

The committee of elections was nevertheless not quite a committee of affections. The act for preventing expenses at an election was just that, an act; both court and country were well aware of the dangers of flaunting it.[223] Seymour was the exception which proves the rule. The honesty of the country gentlemen could be relied upon to keep the committee from ever becoming grossly unfair. Country candidates expected little mercy from it especially if they offered cash in part payment for votes. When, for example, Viscount Weymouth's electoral agents made this mistake in soliciting votes for his son, he reluctantly had him step down in order to avoid the vengeance of the parliamentary committee.[224] When Seymour directed a petition against the duke of Bolton's brother, Lord William Paulet, the sitting member for Winchester, on what was thought to be a completely frivolous pretext, he was voted duly elected. It must be noted, however, that the petition was not voted frivolous, as some thought it should have been.[225]

Court opponents sometimes took advantage of the court's plight by simply causing a petition to be made even when they knew that it could not be successful. On such occasions it was not designed for the petition ever to reach the committee. Such was thought to be the case of the petition against the members for Carlisle: Sir Christopher Musgrave delayed its presentation '...rather to make a noise and to talk of at Carlisle.'[226]

There was also an attempt to reduce the power of the peerage in

---

[222] *H.C.J.*, xiii, 553. 20/31 May 1701. B.M. Add. MSS. 30,000 E. 202 r.–203 r. See too, the Estates General dispatch, s.d. B.M. Add. MSS. 17,677 WW. f. 265.

[223] The placeman, James Lowther, wrote to his father: 'Every body is advis'd for fear of being supris'd with [the] act for preventing expenses at Elections to forbear all things that may be interpreted to come within the reach of that law.' 17 December 1700. Cumb. R.O., Lonsdale MSS.

[224] Weymouth to Harley, 3 December. *H.M.C. Portland*, iii, 636.

[225] James Lowther to Sir John Lowther, 10 May. Cumb. R.O., Lonsdale MSS.

[226] S. to s., 11 February 1700/1. *Ibid.*

elections. In 1699 a resolution had been passed forbidding the lords to vote.[227] Sir Christopher Musgrave wished to carry the prohibition a step further and had requested that the lords should not meddle in the elections. It was not that those opposed to the court did not benefit from many peers' support, but rather that they benefited less or received their support more quietly and as a matter of course. What was being aimed at by Musgrave, was less the influence of peers as a whole than that of those who were favourably disposed to the court. Indeed, one placeman thought that but for the influence of some peers Musgrave might himself not have found a seat in the 1695 election: 'I don't wonder that the other side takes exception at Peers meddling in elections when they espouse the opposite party.'[228] Still, probably a trend could be seen, for it seemed advisable to prohibit their future influence, as it became apparent that the majority of the active peers favoured the court. Soon after the new parliament met, the commons passed a unanimous resolution to the effect that for peers to concern themselves in elections was an infringement of the liberties and privileges of the commons of England.[229] Sir Christopher Musgrave took immediate advantage of the occasion, taking notice that one peer, who was believed to have been Carlisle, had written circular letters to the gentlemen of Cumberland urging them to delay the election of a knight of the shire until he came down. At that time he was also said to have called the justices together for that purpose.[230] There was little effective action taken.[231] Perhaps a general reduction of the peers' activity in future elections was aimed at. Perhaps the agitation was designed simply to keep up the commons' anger against the lords to aid in the impeachment proceedings and the maintenance of a peace policy.

---

[227] A candidate could also require voters to take a freeholder's oath. 7 and 8 William III, c. 25 and 27. The disqualification of peers was to be reiterated and expanded in 1701. *H.C.J.*, xiii, 64,333 and 648.

[228] James Lowther to Sir J. Lowther, 14 September 1700. Cumb. R.O., Lonsdale MSS.

[229] 15 February 1700/1. *H.C.J.*, xiii, 333. James Lowthe rto Sir John Lowther, 15 February. Cumb. R.O., Lonsdale MSS.

[230] *Ibid.*

[231] As has been noted, the specific attempt to reverse the election of Lord Paulet at Winchester owing to the meddling of the peerage was unsuccessful.

TEN

Ministerial Responsibility: Chimera of Peace

Only for a matter of months following the country successes over the Speakership and the controverted elections was there anything which may be called a tory ministry and a peace policy. Still, even this must be qualified, as the first minister, the king, did not really appear to want peace and almost all the placemen were inclined to the junto.[1] Even before the election, the junto was becoming increasingly jingoistic: 'The Whigs at present,' wrote Charles Davenant, 'are all for "To your tents, O Israel" and are very full of a war.'[2] In this design they met with increasing success, by employing almost every means at their disposal. What made the court so bold as to challenge such a country measure as the place clause in the act of settlement was quite probably the change in popular sentiment regarding a war. In mid-April 1701, one observer wrote that, while the peace party[3] in parliament was in the majority, the whigs and the preponderance of political opinion favoured

---

[1] In May 1701 Harley wrote that '...all the courtiers were Whigs...' 'Account of Robert Harley's Conduct', B.M. Portland loan 29/165/97 f. 14. For a fuller quotation see in text below, p. 231.

[2] To Thomas Coke, 10 December 1700. *H.M.C. Cowper*, ii, 410.

[3] The peace party is said to consist of '...those who are pleased to call themselves the church party, every one of those who are known and suspected [of being Jacobites?], and the greatest part of the dissenters, viz. the Harley, Foleys, Winningtons, Joliffs etc.' Ezekiel Burridge to Bp. King, 17 April 1701. T.C.D. MSS. 1122/78.

a war.[4] This change in sentiment will be seen to have been considerably exaggerated by the junto who exploited the concept to the full by bringing pressure to bear on the commons from out of doors.[5]

At first the commons' temper seemed opposed to war. The house met the French occupation of 'the barrier' in early February with an apparently mild reply. Largely owing to the multitude of electoral petitions, the initial resolution was not taken until the fourteenth. While William's opening speech was not considered until the next morning, there was an immediate motion for an address to support the king, the Protestant religion 'and the peace of Europe'. A more powerful wording imploring the king to 'maintain the balance of Europe' (used in the lords' address) was not employed, and even the phrase calling for the maintenance of the peace of Europe was upheld only 181–163.[6] Seymour, Musgrave and Howe had opposed it, arguing that those who proposed to maintain the peace had as their real motive relighting the war. England, they proposed, was to avoid becoming involved in a war such as the last and should employ her influence to promote peace. The court did not argue directly for war but simply held that to maintain the peace it was necessary at least to obtain the appearance of power, thus encouraging the allies and discouraging the French. This reasoning upon defensive lines is what appears to have won the day.[7] On 20 February there was a further resolution asking the king to open negotiations with the Dutch and others in order to maintain the peace, while also promising to support the Estates General according to the treaty of 1677/8. Only Howe appears to have strongly opposed the address and he was hissed for his efforts. Indeed, another fervent junto opponent, Robert Monckton, was said to have made the comment that to recognize the duke of Anjou would be tantamount to recognizing the Pretender. The great cause of England and her allies must be maintained at all costs and he indicated his willingness to eat only roots if necessary.[8] Perhaps the prolonged applause which followed was, however, occasioned largely out of relief that the day's vote scarcely

---

[4] *Ibid.*   [5] See below, pp. 219–22.   [6] *H.C.J.*, xiii, 332.
[7] Estates General dispatch, 18 February/1 March 1700/1. B.M. Add. MSS. 17, 677 WW. f. 162. Brandenburg dispatch, s.d. B.M. Add. MSS. 30,000 E. f. 43.
[8] Brandenburg dispatch, 21 February/4 March. *Ibid.*, f. 48 v. L'Hermitage also noted the promise, although he states that the diet was to be restricted to crusts rather than roots, Estates General dispatch, s.d. 17,677 WW. 168 v. Monckton was a member for Aldborough.

entailed the eating of roots. The treaty of 1677/8 had obliged England to supply Holland with but ten thousand men and then only if she were directly attacked.

The motion was at least a step forward; forward towards a war, and the rare unanimity was delightedly noted by junto supporters.[9] Despite Holland's recognition of the duke of Anjou, the country sentiment of the previous summer, which would have inclined parliament to do so likewise, was not maintained. To the extreme whig, the earl of Shaftesbury, the address was not enough. It would have gone further, he thought, had it not been for the damper placed on the proceedings by the tory ministers. The paradox of ministers stopping actions which the king favoured struck him as being little less than miraculous: 'If we fall on his ministry,' he wrote to one of his friends, 'you say it is meant against himself; and if we let his ministry alone, they do the work of France and force us to peace. I writt to you in my last [letter] that the king has given up his friends and now he has his cause.'[10] He had scarcely done that. William was simply marking time.

William probably found time passing slowly for much of the next two months. A debate in early March regarding the number of troops necessary to preserve the peace could have provided the court with little cause for optimism. Once again England's main line of defence was to be the fleet. The admirals' speeches condemning the practice of relying upon the winds were said not even to have been listened to, and roughly the same sum was voted for military defence as the previous year.[11] A month later the court's attempt to maintain that the Treaty of Ryswick was not sufficient for the maintenance of the peace was effectively countered by the argument that such a declaration was tantamount to declaring war.[12] To assure unanimity, a more modest question was proposed, namely whether to consider the Anglo-Dutch treaty of 1677/8.[13] Nevertheless, pressure was being applied to the new ministry.

---

[9] Wm. Clayton to R. Norris, Mayor of Liverpool, 22 February. Liv. Pub. Lib. MSS. 920/Nor.1/86 (Norris Papers).

[10] To B. Furley, 6 May 1701. Forster, *Shaftesbury Corr.*, pp. 133–6.

[11] Estates General dispatch, 11/12 March 1700/1. B.M. Add. MSS. 17,677 WW. f. 187.

[12] French dispatch, 22 March/3 April 1701. P.R.O. 31/3/188 f. 368 r.

[13] Estates General dispatch, 4/15 April. B.M. Add. MSS. 17,677 WW. f. 217.

INFLUENCE FROM OUT OF DOORS

One of the clearest indications that king and junto were working hand in hand in the spring of 1701, was the appeal of the war interest to opinion from out of doors. In early May the commons was presented with a jingoistic petition signed by the freeholders and grand jury at Maidstone quarter sessions. Whig management was thought almost undoubtedly to have been behind the affair owing to the junto's continued control of the lord lieutenants and justices. There can be no doubt either of the king's sympathy with the contents, which implored the commons to turn their 'loyal addresses...into bills of supply, and that his most sacred majesty...may be enabled powerfully to assist his allies before it is too late.'[14] The king took immediate advantage of the opportunity. That same day he sent parliament a message regarding the dangers of the Dutch, accompanied by two letters; one from the Estates General stating their fear of imminent invasion, the other a covering note from Stanhope telling of French exclusion of the English from a Franco-Dutch conference. They were ordered to be taken into consideration the next day and then it was unanimously resolved to support the allies and immediately fulfil the Anglo-Dutch treaty of 1677/8. An address followed, asking for an estimate of the expenses.[15] At first Musgrave was noted to have been in outspoken opposition to the precipitous resolution. He, Seymour and Sir Bartholomew Shower only reluctantly concurred, led as they were by Jack Howe (thought by some to have again turned his coat) who finally said that he believed war imminent.[16] The Dutch agent found some rightly arguing that help need not be sent unless Holland itself was attacked. All, he noted delightedly, finally went along nevertheless as if the spirit of Kent motivated them.[17]

The court had employed agents to effect its wishes and it was decided that these agents must pay the price. The 'peace party' was said to have decided to make an example of the Kentish worthies in order to discourage London and other constituencies from making similar

---

[14] Defoe, *History of the Kentish Petition* (1701), pp. 3–4.
[15] *H.C.J.*, xiii, 518–20 and 523.
[16] French dispatch, 12/23 May 1701. P.R.O. 31/3/188 ff. 424–7. Shaftesbury to B. Furley, 9 May. Forster, *Shaftesbury Corr.*, p. 137. Brandenburg dispatch, 13/24 May 1701. B.M. Add. MSS. 30,000 E. f. 285.
[17] Estates General dispatch, 9/20 May. B.M. Add. MSS. 17,677 ff. 251 v.– 252 r.

petitions. The petition itself was condemned as '…scandalous, insolent and seditious; tending to destroy the constitution of parliaments and subvert the established government of this realm.' The five petitioners were by subsequent resolutions found guilty of promoting the resolution and ordered into the custody of the serjeant-at-arms.[18] The court supporters defended the subjects' right of petitioning but did not venture a division, evidently believing there to be a question of the commons' institutional integrity.[19] The commons' action had had some effect: future petitions were usually directed to the king, rather than the house.[20] On the whole, however, the commons' action was probably ill advised. It was not harsh enough to incite real fear and made the commons' majority appear not merely as bullies but, what was far worse, ineffectual bullies who became the butt of cynical jests.[21] Secretary Vernon noted, however, that while the petitioners '…make our topping men uneasy', the means being employed to suppress the petitioners '…may blow them up higher'.[22] Defoe's *Legion Letter* added fuel to the flames and promoted the division that Vernon had so feared. The chief complaints expressed against the house in the Kentish petition were reiterated and another series added. It was declared that 'Englishmen are no more to be slaves to parliaments than to kings.'[23] Special mention was made in the *Legion Letter* of Jack Howe, and he appears to have become increasingly touchy about personal accusations. Howe accused one of Wharton's friends, Sir William Strickland, of misrepresenting his views in an effort to set the people against him and his friends, who were in fact the most zealous defenders of English liberties.

---

[18] *Ibid.*, 250 v. and 251 r. *H.C.J.*, xiii, 513.

[19] Brandenburg dispatch, 9/20 May. B.M. Add MSS. 30,000 E. 178 v.–179 r.

[20] James Lowther wrote: 'There are a great many Petitions of this nature going on, but they talk of directing them to the king and not to the House.' To Sir John Lowther, 13 May. Cumb. R.O., Lonsdale MSS.

[21] In a letter of [Sir] C[harles] T[urner] to Robert Walpole of 15 May it is stated that the reason he does not comment on the proceedings was '…for fear of keeping the Kentish Petitioners company.' Sir Edward Mansell wrote to his son, Thomas: 'We in the country do not overmuch approve of what the house of commons dos but desire not to come under the Serjeant at Arms Clutches.' Walcott (*English Politics* p. 68) calls Mansell a follower of Harley, but he is not black-listed by the junto nor is he listed as supporting Harley for the speakership. See appendix A. Camb. Univ. Lib., Cholmondeley MSS. 142. 23 June. N.L.W., Penrice and Margam MSS. L. 430.

[22] To Shrewsbury, 15 May. *Vernon Corr.*, iii, 145–6.

[23] *Legion Letter*, printed in Cobbett, v, 1255.

Strickland replied that if he was truly one of these zealous defenders then he and his friends had nothing to fear from the English people. Further insults ensued and Harley as speaker was forced to intervene and calm the disputants.[24]

Although no one had signed the letter, an offer was made to do so later if asked. For the time being it was ominously stated that '...our name is Legion and we are many.'[25] Some thought that the anonymity was well advised, being really but a cover for cowardice. In one tract it was asserted that if '...these men put their names to their letter, the House would have exerted themselves with the courage suitable to the majesty of parliaments, and we might have seen the whole strength of Legion, exalted in two or three pillories.'[26] A committee was appointed to draw up an address to the king to voice the commons' antipathy to the seditious nature of the petition, but despite considerable bluster, there was little effective action taken. Although the committee was to sit daily, and was empowered to send for persons, papers and records, in the end no report was made and the whole matter was let drop.[27]

To what degree was the threat of an imminent war well founded? Almost unquestionably king and junto overestimated its inevitability. Viscount Weymouth believed it was '...plaine the French would avoide warr could they keep what they have gotten without it.'[28] In late May, the French envoy stated that the crown was grossly exaggerating Holland's plight in preparation for new efforts to gain men and money for war,[29] and thought that part of the difficulty was because of French reluctance to deal with the English envoy, a reluctance which had finally been overcome. It was the Dutch and King William who continued to embarrass negotiations by pleading the cause of the emperor. If they continued to do so, he hoped that at the least the English peace party might argue that war was necessary in neither the English nor the Dutch interest.[30] Still, he noted with sadness the currency of the belief that France was sending vast sums for bribery. There was said to be no more telling remark than that France was bribing a member to

---

[24] Estates General dispatch, 20/31 May 1701. B.M. Add. MSS. 17, 677 WW. f. 264.
[25] *Legion Letter*, Cobbett, v, 1253.
[26] James Drake, *The History of the Last Parliament* (1702), pp. 144–5.
[27] Cobbett, v, 1257–8.
[28] To Col. Grahme, 7 May 1701. Levens. Bagot MSS.
[29] French dispatch, 29 May/9 June. P.R.O. 31/3/188 f. 446.
[30] 5/16 June. *Ibid.*, f. 453.

betray his country.[31] The effect of the agitation out of doors, moreover, had had its effect; Jack Howe, for example, was said to be thinking of retiring to the country, believing himself unsafe in the capital.[32] Once again the opposition to the war was being silenced by accusations of disloyalty.

It would be difficult to overestimate the effect of the agitation. The junto's opponents were largely thwarted in their attempts to exploit the frustration of the lower clergy when it met in convocation, and even failed to renew the commission of accounts. Most important, the impeachments of the junto ministers were notably unsuccessful, while large supplies were voted to implement a war. The royal prerogative waxed unchecked.

CONVOCATION

The question of convocation was also the subject of much speculation. The clergy were fighting for a way of life in much the same way as the gentry.[33] As a class, their influence had reached new depths in William's reign as secularism appeared all but triumphant, especially as the crown-appointed bishops were notoriously unrepresentative of the sentiments of the lower clergy. For some time they had little means of expressing their grievances. They had not met since 1689[34] and William appeared at least as anxious as his predecessors to avoid the voicing of clerical opinion. The political ramifications of another chamber in which opposition to royal policies would echo were obvious. Following the peace, however, agitation had become more outspoken. Almost all the clergy thought that some good might come of it[35] and it was a condition of the new ministry that convocation should meet again.[36] During

[31] 7/18 July. *Ibid.*, 189 f. 485.

[32] 19/30 May. *Ibid.*, 188 f. 434 v.

[33] Even Bishop King, usually one of William's supporters, hoped for good to come from its meeting. He feared that those of the court 'mean religion no good'. If the court had the clergy 'alone and without the guards, tho' they layd them aside to oblige the court,' they would suffer as in the previous two reigns. To the Bp. of Clougher, 20 January 1701/2. T.C.D. MSS. 1489.

[34] The refusal to approve the comprehension bill had resulted in its prorogation.

[35] See White Kennett, 'Life and Reign of William III' in *A Complete History of England*, vol. III, pt. iv (1791), esp. pp. 800–50.

[36] See Feiling, *Tory Party*, p. 341. Burnet, *Own Times*, iv, 519.

William's last two parliaments it fulfilled the junto's worst fears. The lower house at Canterbury, in an attempt to safeguard its continuance, asserted its independence of both the king and the bishops, and brought censure resolutions against that leading Socinian, Bishop Burnet.

The sentiments of the lower house were echoed by many in the commons. A bill for fixing bishops to their sees and hindering their removal worked hand in hand with the lower house's policy of reducing the king's influence upon the bishops.[37] The court's opposition to the bill is seen in April 1701 when the bill was committed by a majority of but seven votes.[38] Reports from committee were continuously and indefinitely postponed owing once again to diminishing country attendance and influence from out-of-doors.

THE SPANISH SUCCESSION AND THE IMPEACHMENT PROCEEDINGS

After 1 November 1700, the stock-jobbers who had for decades considered the poor health of the heirless king of Spain in their daily speculations were to do so no longer. King Charles was dead and with a view to this event Louis and William had concluded two successive treaties partitioning the vast Habsburg empire. The first, made in the autumn of 1698, was negated by the death of the electoral prince of Bavaria. The second treaty was completed in February 1699/1700. It gave the Emperor Leopold's second son (the Archduke Charles) Spain, Spanish America, the Spanish Netherlands and various island possessions. The duke of Lorraine was to have Milan and France while also gaining Lorraine, Naples and Sicily, Guipuscoa and the Tuscan ports. The Spanish king, however, made a will on his death bed, leaving the entire empire to Louis' grandson, Philip of Anjou, on condition that the crowns of France and Spain were never united. Within a few weeks, Louis had accepted the will and repudiated the treaty. In defending his action he argued that all the conditions of the treaty were not fulfilled[39] and that the will of the king of Spain was not known before the signing

---

[37] The Brandenburg envoy thought that the move was specifically directed against Burnet, who wished to be translated from Salisbury (£2,000 *p.a.*) to Winchester (£8,000 *p.a.*). 11/12 March 1701. B.M. Add. MSS. 30,000 E. f. 57 r.

[38] The vote was 96–89. *H.C.J.*, xiii, 501.

[39] The dowry of Maria Theresa had not been paid. This seems a minor point.

of the treaty. Austria had not accepted the treaty either, and as a Franco-Austrian conflict appeared imminent, England would probably be forced to go to war in any case. The breaking of the treaty, moreover, appeared to give France less power, not more, as the Dauphin lost the lands formally granted him.[40] If then the will made possible the unification of the two crowns, the partition treaty involved immediate French advances endangering English trading interests in the Mediterranean. Generally national sentiment appears to have favoured the Spanish king's will,[41] a fact that William acknowledged and which caused him considerable worry.[42] At the time some thought that William might have had the will he wanted if he had but employed effective diplomacy at the Spanish court.[43] While on the one hand Louis was distrusted,[44] on the other an immediate war involving the emperor and the allied interests had apparently been avoided.

M. A. Thomson has shown that the country position regarding the succession was by no means unreasonable, especially when the factors surrounding the treaty are taken into consideration. Despite the fact that parliament was sitting when the second treaty was signed, William did not consult it with regard to any of the negotiations, an omission probably caused more by fear of parliamentary objections than by the need for security.[45]

Questionable French military actions in the autumn of 1700 had aided the king in calming the storm of parliamentary protest building up since the disclosure of the treaties earlier the previous summer. Still, a late opening was not thought to be enough, and to counter parliament's reluctance to go to war, king and junto again appeared willing to stop at nothing. Aside from frequent messages to the commons which

---

[40] R. Lodge, 'The Spanish Succession', *History* (1938), xii, 333–38.

[41] R. Harley to Ld. Weymouth, 5 November 1700. *H.M.C. Portland*, iii, 634. Davenant to Harley, 19 September. *Ibid.*, iv, 5. Feiling, *Tory Party*, p. 354.

[42] To Heinsius, 16 November 1700. Hardwicke, *Miscellaneous State Papers*, p. 394.

[43] In Ireland, Bishop King found the Irish pacifists saying that the will was made as it was '...for want of 2 or 300000 of pistols, if some had dextrously been distributed amongst the Grandees and Courtiers of Spain, they might have had what they pleased for the king.' To Sir R. Southwell, 4 February 1700/1. T.C.D. MSS. 1489.

[44] Lord Powlett wrote to Robert Harley that while he believed the French refusal of the treaty to be most just, yet he still wondered if France was truly pacifistic. 3 December 1700. *H.M.C. Portland*, iii, 636.

[45] M. A. Thomson, 'Parliament and Foreign Policy, 1689–1714'. *History* (1953), xxxviii, 334–43.

obliged prompt replies—replies which were published— the court directed a considerable barrage of pamphlets against the pacifist opposition with a view to bringing pressure to bear from out of doors. This pressure came in the form of petitions and representations with thinly disguised threats of force. Overt actions of London mobs caused some members to leave the city in fear of their lives. Concomitant with the king's desire for a return to war was of course a return to a junto ministry, which he saw as the best way to gain all the requisite war supplies; to many others, however, the junto's reappearance seemed synonymous with a policy that would not only bring the country to a vigorous war but keep it to it, while diminishing constitutional liberties. The attack upon the partition treaties then provided one of the few effectual and respectable methods of attacking the junto's return to power and a vast continental military involvement. In some ways attacking court and junto for the partition treaties was a paradox: the earl of Shaftesbury was correct in noting it '...founded on a supposition of these men having acted for the interest of France.' Thus it was, that the war spirit was diverted '...only by stratagem and arts...The cause against France is still more and more advanced, tho' we are untowardly diverted in our means of prosecuting it.'[46] Still, the court employed such methods itself. In arguing against French acceptance of the Spanish king's will, it claimed that French perfidy was seen in rejecting the overly advantageous partition treaty.[47] Both sides wished to have it both ways.

The initiative for the proceedings was taken in the lords, where the treaties were first brought under observation.[48] Secretary Vernon was increasingly called upon to supply the necessary correspondence and not surprisingly his co-operation caused the junto to regard him as a Judas.[49] The first matter seized upon was the questionable method of their creation: Somers had put the seal to a blank commission and the commons had been told nothing of the entire proceedings. As might be expected, in the lords the court succeeded in bringing the inquiry to

---

[46] Shaftesbury to B. Furley, 15 April 1701. Forster, *Shaftesbury Corr.*, p. 130.

[47] S. to s., 18 March 1700/1. *Ibid.*, p. 176.

[48] *H.L.J.*, xvi, 596. Brandenburg dispatch, 14/25 February. B.M. Add. MSS. 30,000 E. f. 41.

[49] Somers's friends '...roare at Mr Secretary as a Man put in at First by the Man behind the curtain etc.' N.n. (in Dublin) to [Nottingham], 14 May 1700. Leics. R.O., Finch MSS., box V/22.

a swift and happy ending. Still, twenty-seven peers signed a strong protest and in doing so they lent vital support for impeachment proceedings to be begun in the commons.

There the attack was led by Jack Howe, who roundly condemned the court's secrecy and became so vicious when a defence was attempted that the Brandenburg envoy dared not even relate Howe's terrible words to his autocratic master.[50] A boldness reminiscent of the standing army issue remained a part of the opposition's strategy: when the house was considering one of the king's addresses and some members called for a reading of the partition treaty, Secretary Vernon rose to say he was astonished to hear the house thank the king for his graciousness in such a way. He was quickly silenced, one member saying that it was not at all astonishing Vernon did not want it read, considering the part the secretary had in it. An address followed openly condemning both the treaty and the secrecy involved in its creation. A court attempt to mention the war effort in the address was also rejected, if but by six votes. Indeed, it was only by a timely suggestion that the commons put off further questioning until the French replied to some English inquiries that the address was kept from going further.[51]

It was not until April, however, that the impeachment proceedings began in earnest. On the first, Vernon handed over the necessary correspondence, and for one of the involved parties there was little delay; without a division Portland was at once impeached. Subsequently, though with tears in his eyes, Vernon turned over an additional twenty-eight letters sent to Portland, Stanhope and Methuen in the autumn of 1698. In the subsequent investigation, particular emphasis was placed upon a letter from Vernon to Portland in which it was stated that William would not enter into negotiations without the concurrence of the ministers. It was believed then that they had definitely acquiesced, and the proceedings against Somers, Orford and Halifax reached new heights. The junto had also made a very considerable tactical error. Young Lord Hartington, during Musgrave's questioning of Vernon, accused Musgrave of being disaffected to the state and challenged him to come out of doors, evidently for a duel. Musgrave was old enough to have been Hartington's grandfather. If Harley in his capacity as Speaker forced a reconciliation, the damage to the junto cause was

---

[50] Brandenburg dispatch, 18 February/1 March 1700/1. B.M. Add. MSS. 30,000 E. 44 v.

[51] French dispatch, 22 March/2 April. P.R.O. 31/3/189 ff. 368–9 r. The vote was 193–187. *H.C.J.*, xiii, 419.

done:[52] In Hartington's challenge to the elder statesman one suspects many members saw the junto less as victims than as bullies.

Any doubts as to Harley's eventual concurrence with the impeachments vanish when one inspects his attitude as Speaker. At the least he was neutral, and he probably reflected the spirit of the house. The junto's defence suffered a sharp and immediate setback as soon as Somers entered the commons to defend himself against the charges. Harley demanded to know why he had dared enter the house bare-headed and who it was that had informed him of the impeachment proceedings.[53]

The advantage Somers gained by his subsequent excellent defence and the unconvincing arguments of opposition leaders against him was quickly cut away by an untimely retort of one of his supporters to the very weak case put against him. Even more important was the action of the Speaker. Harley deliberately omitted to ask whether Somers had given advice on the treaties, and put the question in such a way as to have it assumed that he had. Considering that the two sides were very nearly balanced, this omission was probably telling.[54] He, Orford, and Halifax were declared guilty by votes of 198–188, 193–148 and 186–136.[55] The diminution of the supporting vote was in part due to the decrease in popularity of the accused and the fact that some court supporters evidently found little reason to stay once the basic issue was decided. Unquestionably the attack was aimed almost solely at the junto. Jersey, one of the other principals involved in the partition treaty, was exonerated largely by Seymour's efforts. In his defence, Seymour had argued that he was devoid of both motive and malice. Others thought the real reason was simply that the opposition leaders wished to avoid attacking anyone they did not consider dangerous, and feared the loss of badly needed support. The following day when the commons proceeded to addresses calling for the removal of Somers, Orford and Halifax, Portland's name was also added. Various observers noted that an enthusiastic new member, anxious to make his mark, had secured his insertion believing that it had simply been omitted in committee.[56]

---

[52] French dispatch, 14/25 April 1701. P.R.O. 31/3/188 f. 391, Estates General dispatch, 15/26 April. B.M. Add. MSS. 17,677 WW. f. 219.

[53] *Ibid.*, f. 229 v.

[54] Brandenburg dispatch, 15/26 April. B.M. Add. MSS. 30,000 E. ff. 143 r.–144 r.

[55] *H.C.J.*, xiii, 489–90.

[56] Estates General dispatch, 18/29 April. B.M. Add. MSS. 17,677 WW. f. 233 r. Brandenburg dispatch, 25 April/6 May. B.M. Add MSS. 30,000 f. 156 r.

There was considerable doubt, however, that the opposition leadership concurred in this, and it would appear that at least the more cunning amongst them wished that Portland's name had never been mentioned. The king either would or could not let him fall prey to country vengeance; but vengeance simply upon the whig ministers might well have been a different matter. Harley remarked:

> Those who had the secret of the King and the Earl of Sunderland, were for breaking with the Whigs and consequently for Prosecuting three of the Lords. Mr How and some others for particular reasons engaged agt the Earl of Portland, and the Discontented of both partys joyned to turn the prosecution of all of them into Impeachmts which occasioned the Ld. Sunderland saying 'O Silly, Silly, Had they left alone Lord Portland and the Civil List, they might have hanged the other three in a Garret.'[57]

The junto did not wish to be a royal sacrifice. Edward Harley noted that they had shifted the preponderance of blame to the Dutch elements of the court and almost succeeded in avoiding the latter's attempt to incriminate them. The country party would have been most reluctant to allow Portland's name to have been purposely deleted in any case. If the country members were willing to allow such allegedly pacifist ministers as Jersey to go untouched despite the junto's repeated and eloquent attempts to include him,[58] there were limits to their sophistication. To be rid merely of the ministerial whigs without taking a blow at the real promoter of the design, the king, or at least his former 'second self', the earl of Portland, would be all too clear an attack upon men rather than measures. Jack Howe then reflected country spirit if not policy, and the junto appears to have exploited it, forcing the king to muster support for their cause. In the event, Portland's name was to be quietly deleted when the impeachments were brought before the lords. Perhaps if the other impeachments were successful, Portland's might well have been revived at a later date. Still, there can be no doubt that this development diminished the general country enthusiasm for the attack.

In the lords, by a majority of only thirteen, it was decided to present the king with a positive address, suggesting that in effect he ignore the commons' address until the lords were legally proceeded against.

---

[57] 'Account of Robert Harley's Conduct', B.M. Portland loan, 29/165/97 f. 13.

[58] Brandenburg dispatch, 25 April/6 May. B.M. Add. MSS. 30,000 E. 156 r.

Twenty-five peers signed a fierce protest, arguing that such an action would cause an inter-house dispute, deeming the motion most improper. If there is some doubt as to the constitutional propriety of the commons' action, there can be no question either that the court had employed heavy-handed tactics: by a subsequent resolution the dissent was expunged from the Journals. At the least this serves to condemn the means employed by the court to obtain its ends. Probably this was a tactical error in any case, for a subsequent resolution against the action was signed by twenty-two peers.[59] This protest in turn allowed the commons to make an inquiry into the expunging in June, which helped to keep the fires hot.[60]

As the impeachment proceedings dragged on, the lords tried to force the commons to hurry and bring a judgment against the peers, making clear their belief that the commons was simply employing the impeachments to stall for time.[61] Indeed, the impeachments did serve as a circuitous means of delaying supply, and some threatened that without William's acquiescence there would be no supply at all. In May, one of the opposition leaders is reported as saying that even if the Dutch were far more pressed and the French at the doors of London, the commons were resolved to give the king neither a penny nor a man until he explained his position in regard to the four lords.[62] Strong words, perhaps, for so late in the session, but the commons' apparent determination in refusing to be browbeaten gave them credence.

The lords continued their agitation to precipitate a conclusion. Somers, in an attempt to exploit his popularity, succeeded in having the lords resolve that the commons should proceed against him first as it was he whom the charges were first brought against. Although the lords did not hold to this, in a subsequent message they did demand that action be taken by a fixed date, which they prescribed to be within the week.[63] Inter-house conferences tended to explode as the lords

---

[59] Estates General dispatch, 18/29 April. B.M. Add MSS. 17,677 WW. f. 233. Brandenburg dispatch, s.d., B.M. Add. MSS. 30,000 E. ff. 146 v. and 147. r. *H.M.C. Lords, 1699–1702*, iv, 295. *H.L.J.*, xvi, 654–5.

[60] Maurice Annesley to Sir Cyril Wyche, 19 June. Irish P.R.O., Wyche Corr. Ser. 1/232.

[61] Estates General dispatch, 15/26 April. B.M. Add. MSS. 17,677 WW. f. 231.

[62] French dispatch, 15/26 May. P.R.O. 31/3/188 f. 428.

[63] Estates General dispatch, 6/17 June. B.M. Add. MSS. 17,677 WW. 282 v.–282 r.

reiterated the complaint that all involved were not being prosecuted. Aside from Vernon and Jersey, Sir Joseph Williamson, Pembroke and Marlborough were also said to be culpable. The lords made little secret in conferences, either, of their wholehearted support of the accused. On one occasion, Lord Haversham said that they were the best servants of the state. This caused Sir Christopher Musgrave to break up the conference, and the commons to bring charges against Haversham for his offensive remarks. The lords in turn brought counter charges against Sir Bartholomew Shower, reiterated much of Haversham's speech and expressed their abhorrence of the commons' addressing the king before the impeachments were terminated.[64] Attempts to support such attitudes in the commons met with severe treatment. In June, Sir William St Quintin declared that he did not oppose the articles against Halifax because he believed them to be to Halifax's advantage. Ominously Harley ordered the clerk to take down this back-handed tribute, causing Sir William quickly to beg the pardon of the house and to make the feeble claim that he had spoken neither with malice nor with a desire to bring discredit upon the commons.[65]

When the lords sent the commons yet another message as to the manner of proceeding at the trial, the commons answered by prohibiting members to appear without leave. The lords' forwardness in this action was speedily condemned and it was indicated that the commons would not budge until satisfaction was given for Haversham's remarks. Seymour proceeded to defend the commons' right to take its time, urging that it should not be hurried by the peers' vivacity. There were more pressing matters to engage them. Nevertheless the lords proceeded, although it was carried to do so but by 57–36, a somewhat smaller majority. Their message to this effect was never received by the commons, who had promptly adjourned in order to avoid accepting it.[66] In the subsequent 'trial', Somers was acquitted 56–31. Not surprisingly, loud hosannahs arose in the streets of London and only a feeble protest in

---

[64] Brandenburg dispatch, 17/28 June. *Ibid.*, f. 266 v. Estates General dispatch, 13/24 and 17/28 June. B.M. Add. MSS. 17,677 WW. 292 r.–293 r. and 295 v.–296 v. *H.L.J.*, xvi, pp. 742–3 and 746 and 759–61. *H.M.C. Lords, 1699–1702*, iv, 298 and 388–9.

[65] 9 June. *H.C.J.*, xiii, 606.

[66] French dispatch, 22 May/2 June. P.R.O. 31/3/188 f. 436 v. Seymour claimed that the proceedings against him in Charles II's reign took even longer. Court antiquarians quickly showed that he was mistaken. Estates General dispatch, 23 May/3 June. B.M. Add. MSS. 17,677 WW. f. 267. Brandenburg dispatch, 17/28 June B.M. Add. MSS. 30,000 E. f. 276.

the lords.[67] Still, the issue was scarcely over and was a leading question in men's minds throughout the summer.

QUESTIONS OF FINANCE

One of the most visible effects of the Kentish petition occurred over the king's civil list request. In early May, Jack Howe had proposed to reduce the 700,000 pounds voted the previous Saturday by one-seventh and proceeded to explain why the reduced sum would be adequate: the king had asked for merely £680,000. £50,000 had been allocated for Mary of Modena, which need no longer be paid, and £30,000 for the duke of Gloucester, by now deceased. Despite considerable oratorical force the court was unsuccessful in defending the original sum which was reduced by a vote of 163 to 116.[68] When the committee's action was reported to parliament, there was a debate lasting four hours, in which the French envoy found the parties embarrassingly mixed. Seymour was said to be strongly in favour of deprivation and would apply the sum to acquit the public debts.[69] On division it was carried to do so 214–169.[70] Harley was later to put the real blame for the reduction upon the junto: 'Those who were under the influence of what was called the Junto though they had places at court voted for taking this away from the King.' In his capacity as Speaker, Harley claims to have done what he could to bring the matter within a very few votes '…notwithstanding all the Whig Courtiers (and all the courtiers were Whigs) which were very numerous [who] appeared against it.'[71] At first, then, it would seem that out of place whigs had united with out of place tories to leaven the more recalcitrant parts of the country opposition. Under royal and popular pressure, however, most were to give way and even ways and means were to be shortly settled upon.

---

[67] Estates General dispatch, 20 June/1 July. B.M. Add. MSS. 17,677, f. 229. *H.C.J.*, xiii, 634–5. *H.L.J.*, xvi, 754–6. *H.M.C. Lords, 1699–1702*, xiv, 299–300. Brandenburg dispatch 24 June/5 July. B.M. Add. MSS. 30,000 E., f. 293 r.

[68] *H.C.J.*, xiii, 511. Estates General dispatch, 2/13 and 6/17 May 1701. B.M. Add. MSS. 17,677 WW. 244 v.–245 r. and 246. Brandenburg dispatch, 2/13 May. B.M. Add. MSS. 30,000 ff. 171 r.–172 r.

[69] French dispatch, 8/19 May. P.R.O. 31/3/188 f. 420.

[70] *H.C.J.*, xiii, 513.

[71] 'Account of Robert Harley's Conduct', B.M. Portland loan 29/165/97 f. 14.

The change of heart was sudden. On 9 May there was a unanimous resolution to assist the king in support of the allies in maintaining the peace of Europe. Seymour apologized for his past conduct and went on to say that he would always sacrifice three-quarters of his wealth to protect the fourth. Holland was now deemed indispensable to the English interest even to the point of going to war. Despite much smoke, Seymour had not burnt his bridges, finding the matter so important that it must be weighed carefully. Jack Howe spoke upon similar lines. While stating his abhorrence of French politics, religion and ideals he still urged caution.

But the French envoy noted Howe and his friends rushing to stop the execution of the resolution reducing the civil list. In little more than a week following the original reduction, the sum deducted was not only voted to be added again, but was almost doubled. This action was generally attributed to the ministerial tories trying to re-ingratiate themselves with the king.[72] Certainly Seymour had made an abrupt about face which the French envoy believed indicated that he had once again made engagements with the court and would shortly be repaid,[73] but perhaps Seymour was simply reflecting enlightened country opinion. Still, the court was only able to prevent the re-establishment of a commission of accounts in the lords. This probably did the opposition extremists far more good than harm and aided country party unity and popularity. Hammond, for example, was delighted; they were able to put the blame of losing the bill on the government majority, which he thought might set both the army interest and the soldiers' creditors against them.[74] Indeed, the lords' rejection of the enabling bill was to play a significant role in the next election, one pamphlet being specifically designed to curry favour with country sentiment in general and the army interest in particular.[75] The war interest answered with another

---

[72] Shaftesbury to Furley, 23 May 1701. Forster, *Shaftesbury Corr.*, p. 141.

[73] French dispatch, 19/30 May. P.R.O. 31/3/189 f. 434 v.

[74] To Thomas Coke, 19 July 1701. *H.M.C. Cowper*, ii, 432–3.

[75] The title of the pamphlet explains the contents and appeal: *England's Great Concern In the Perpetual Settlement of a Commission of Accounts: With Clauses and Powers Fixing National Benefit Thereby in the Several Branches Following, viz. The Exact Quota of the Faithful Collecting and Disposing thereof, The Securing to all Persons in the Army and Navy Their Full Pay at Fixed Times, The Providing for those that are Maim'd and for the Indigent Widows and Orphans of those that Die in the Nation's Service, The due Payment of all Souldiers and Seamen's Debts to their Creditors, without Suit or Charge at Law. The Making Good the Deficient Funds, Clearing the Nation's Debts and Raising the Publick Credit, And*

justifying the lords' rejection on the grounds that part of the bill relating
to the accounts was ineffectual, noting also that the commons would
allow no conferences. It tried to safeguard the government from army
vengeance by arguing that parts of the bill relevant to their interest
were not amended.[76] W. A. Shaw's semi-modern defence of the lords'
action[77] does not obviate the most telling point: the lords had once
again tampered with what many commoners believed to be a money bill
and alterations would not be tolerated in such matters. As court and
country were to be so closely balanced in the ensuing election, probably
the lords' action was a serious mistake for the court side.

Nevertheless, Godolphin wrote that many who had recently come
from the country had found people genuinely upset at parliamentary
proceedings which were thought to have degenerated into petty squab-
bles to the neglect of the national interest. He believed there should be
some vote providing for the better preservation of the nation's security,
to prevent a change of ministry and the dissolution of the present
parliament.[78] If in mid-June it was still thought that the commons would
be unlikely to pass any bill until satisfaction was given regarding the
impeached lords, and there were remarks that the lower house intended
to become sole governors of England,[79] the bills of supply finally passed.
Despite delays, there were no major divisions.[80] No one appears

the Ordering of Taxes so as Maybe Most Favourable to the Value of Land, and
Advancement of Trade, With a Discovery of Some Notable Frauds Committed in
Collecting the Supplies.

[76] *Some Remarks on the Bill for Taking, Examining, and Stating the Publick Ac-
counts of the Kingdom; And on the Proceedings Thereon in both Houses, The Last
Session* (1702). Shaw believes this might have been written by Sir John
Thompson, now Lord Haversham.

[77] *Later Treasury Introduction*, p. clxxvi. This defence can only be termed
'semi-modern' because no less than three thousand words are quoted from
the aforementioned pamphlet in summarizing the history of the commission
without either mentioning the opposition's pamphlet or the obvious junto
bias of that quoted. He praises the various excerpts as 'an illuminating account',
'an illuminating passage', and of another that it is given '*almost* authorita-
tively' (my italics). See *ibid.*, pp. clxv–clxxv.

[78] Godolphin to 'my Lord', 'Whitsun' (15 May 1701). Northants R.O.
MSS. 4053 (Finch-Hatton Corr.).

[79] Maurice Annesley to Sir Cyril Wyche, 19 June 1701. Irish P.R.O.,
Wyche Corr., ser. 1/232. See too, the letter of Wm. Clayton to Richd. Norris,
mayor of Liverpool, of 19 June 1701 stating his outrage at the delay. Liv.
Pub. Lib. 920 Nor. Ser. 2/218.

[80] If any of the minor amendments serve as indications of strength, both
sides mustered under a hundred votes apiece. *H.C.J.*, xiii, 634.

to have dared directly challenge the money bills.[81] While a commons address was also carried calling for the reduction of French power, Musgrave succeeded in avoiding a more strongly worded motion, but appears not to have ventured a division owing to fear of implementing Godolphin's terrible prophecy.[82] The Brandenburg envoy noted that all those not made blind by their prejudgements believed that the king had benefited from their conflicts and was never more absolute.[83]

When the Kentish petitioners were released they soon made a triumphant public appearance in the city and subsequently as guests of honour at a banquet in the Guildhall. The junto made little disguise of their support for the petitioners. Defoe claims that they were given a rousing welcome on their return to Kent.[84] Some of the junto peers were said to have treated them especially well and were thought to have paid the bill for the propaganda display.[85] Addresses of support for the king's policy followed in which a hearty war policy was commended, a new parliament called for and the old parliament condemned. Nevertheless, petitions, letters, skilful debate, dinners and hearty welcomes were one thing; an overwhelming change in electoral sentiment something quite different. The Kentish petitioners were said, for example, to have received an ill reception from some country gentlemen at assizes while the grand jury did not vote them thanks, as was claimed in some of the junto's propaganda pamphlets.[86] Secretary Vernon, well aware of this fact, expressed his hope that the enemies of the present parliament did not take '...improper methods to be rid of it.' Addresses urging dissolution were well advised only if done '...by national impulse without coercion.' If coercion was employed, it might have a detrimental effect.[87] Although the degree of coercion remains a question,

---

[81] French dispatch, 16/27 June, P.R.O. 31/3/188 ff. 466 v.–467 r.

[82] Brandenburg dispatch, 20 June/1 July. B.M. Add. MSS. 30,000 E. f. 284 r.   [83] 8/19 July. *Ibid.*, f. 303.

[84] '...the people shouting all the while a Colepepper, a Colepepper, and the poor strewing the way with greens and flowers.' *Kentish Petition*, p. 16. Bonet, Brandenburg dispatch, 8/19 July. B.M. Add. MSS. 30,000 E. ff. 302 r.– 303 r. Estates General dispatch, 8/19 July. B.M. Add. MSS. 17,677 WW. f. 313.

[85] It was said that such 'particular subscribers' as Lord Hartington and the duke of Bolton treated the petitioners especially well. Robert Jenning to T. Coke, 6 July. *H.M.C. Cowper*, ii, 431–2.

[86] William Morley to Thomas Coke, 21 August (misdated). *Ibid.*, ii, 403.

[87] To Shrewsbury, 14 July (corrected by Somerville from 19 July in 'Dates in the *Vernon Corr.*' *Eng. Hist. Rev.* (1933), xlii, 629). *Vernon Corr.*, iii, 148–51.

the addresses clearly did not have unanimous support. One from Buckinghamshire had been supported by thirteen and opposed by eight. In Hampshire there were only three opposed and they were classed as mere gentry, being said to be '...men of very small estates'.[88] Although a mere country gentleman was of comparatively little significance as an individual, collectively it was a different matter especially if they united with the freeholders. War taxation, which generally fell hardest upon the lesser landholders, had a pronounced effect upon the development of jingoism. During a lull in the junto's attempts to procure a new parliament in the summer, Secretary Vernon was genuinely relieved, fearing that an election might have an unfavourable result.[89]

---

[88] S. to s., 7 August. *Ibid.*, pp. 154–5.   [89] To s., 21 July. *Ibid.*, p. 153.

ELEVEN

Ministerial Responsibility: Reappraisal of Policy

THE SNAP DISSOLUTION

William's popularity towards the close of the session was thought phenomenal. 'The Duke of Monmouth,' wrote one observer, 'was never more universally the darling of the common people than the king is now of the comonaltie and the whole citty.'[1] In appearances the ministerial tories were not to be outdone; a parliamentary address of support was thought to have been sponsored by Rochester, Goldolphin, Seymour and Musgrave. The last moreover was not only seen inquiring after the king's health, but kissed his hand, which caused considerable comment considering Musgrave's large following.[2] Many were cynical about such actions, believing them done purely to assuage public rancour, disarm the junto whigs and, most important, to forestall a dissolution.[3]

At the conclusion of the session, Harley's speech to the king listed the recent achievements of the commons; among them were the establishment of the Protestant succession and a peacetime subsidy of unprecedented size. An observer explained how Harley's speech was 'very

---

[1] Maurice Annesley to Sir Cyril Wyche, 14 June 1701. Irish P.R.O., Wyche Corr., ser. 1/280.

[2] French dispatch, 16/27 June. P.R.O. 31/3/188 f. 466. Bonet adds Nottingham, Abingdon and Harcourt. Brandenburg dispatch, 20 June/1 July. B.M. Add. MSS. 30,000 f. 269.

[3] Brandenburg dispatch, 17/28 June. *Ibid.*

kindly returned by the king', and that there was an era of good feeling existing between king and commons '…to the mortification of those who wished for and bespoke a dissolution.'[4] The royal speech approving the commons' proceedings greatly upset such extreme whigs as Shaftesbury who declaimed against the '…sham vote against the exorbitant power of France…' who thought it designed simply 'to blind the people'.[5]

Would the parliament be continued? Many had their doubts and almost all had hopes or fears. By late July the general belief amongst the peace party was that war was by now unavoidable. Unfortunately as many county members saw it, although war might be designed for their preservation it would also contribute to their ruin. Following the prorogation Sir Edward Seymour had his coach prepared to leave London at the break of dawn to go down into the country to disperse unfavourable rumours and enlarge his interests.[6]

The events of the early autumn provided ample justification for such wise preparations. James II died on 6 September. Louis XIV acting against the preponderance of his court's opinion immediately recognized his son, James III, as rightful king of England.[7] Almost undoubtedly this splendid gesture was based far more upon religious and personal rather than political considerations. There was little doubt in anyone's mind that in so doing Louis XIV had broken the Treaty of Ryswick. Shrewsbury had written at the time of the signing that whether the name of King James was mentioned or not the treaty '…might yet be so strong and so particular, that he [Louis] should have no excuse to renew the one, or assist the other, without plainly forfeiting his word, and breaking his engagements; which no reasonable man will be persuaded ought to be done, upon a motive of honour and conscience.'[8] Shrewsbury's wishes had been carried out; William had made

---

[4] Maurice Annesley to Sir Cyril Wyche, 24 June. P.R.O. of Ireland, Wyche Corr., ser. 1/234. See too, the letter to Annesley from H. Shaw to same effect, also of 24 June. *Ibid.*, no. 235. Harley's draft speech of 23 June. B.M. Portland loan 29/161/11. *H.L.J.*, xvi, 769–70.

[5] Shaftesbury to Furley, 20 June 1701. Forster, *Shaftesbury Corr.*, p. 103.

[6] Estates General dispatch, 17/28 June. B.M. Add. MSS. 17,677 WW. f. 295.

[7] Manchester believed that the dauphin and Madame de Maintenon had prevailed against the ministers urgings. To Vernon. 13/24 September 1701. C. Cole, ed., *Historical and Political Memoirs*…(1735), p. 422. Hereafter cited as Cole, *Affairs of State*.

[8] To the king, 20/30 July 1697. Coxe, *Shrewsbury Corr.*, pp. 169–70.

it quite clear that nothing was to serve as a pretext for the recognition of the Pretender.[9] Nor had the effect been overestimated.[10] Many juries sent addresses to the government abhorring the French king's recognition, while Harley was to write later that it '...gave a handle for stirring up a ferment in the Nation...'[11] Another observer wrote that it '...has so opened the eyes of every body, that no one dares hardly speak against a war.'[12]

Another blow to pacifist fortunes occurred a little less than a month later. Poussin, the French envoy, and Navarra, the Spanish consul, were seen dining with Hammond, Tredenham and Davenant. Davenant claimed that Poussin had come in and sat down with them (apparently uninvited). Hammond, moreover, was uneasy in the presence of their new dining companion and left as soon as he was finished eating.[13] Thus Tredenham alone was blamed for tempting them into the compromising situation.[14] Be that as it may, the incident caused understandable alarm among their friends.[15] It was suspected that in the event of an election the junto would exploit to the full the common enough assumption that birds of a feather flock together.[16]

As late as mid-October Hammond still maintained hopes that there would not be a dissolution, and even if there was he believed '...that party will not benefit, and if they don't, it knocks 'em down forever.' Nevertheless, even he thought that a war was now inevitable although he doubted that it would be very difficult to defeat a France which had

---

[9] Equivalent terms were ordered to effect the unmentionable. Marshall Boufflers to Louis, 25 June/5 July 1697. Grimblot, *Letters*, i, 29. Manchester found the recognition of the Pretender against the fourth article of the treaty '...if words can mean anything.' The subsequent prohibition of English commerce was said to be against the fifth article. To Vernon, 17/28 September 1701. Cole, *Affairs of State*, p. 424.

[10] Henry Norris (B.N.C., Oxon.) to Rd. Norris, Mayor of Liverpool. 20 September 1701. Liv. Pub. Lib. MSS. 920/Nor. i/137.

[11] 'Account of Robert Harley's Conduct'. B.M. Portland loan, 29/165/97 f. 15.

[12] Robert Jennens to Thomas Coke, 4 October. *H.M.C. Cowper*, ii, 436.

[13] Vernon to Rochester, 30 September. S. W. Singer, ed., *The Correspondence of Henry Hyde, Earl of Clarendon and of his brother, Laurence Hyde, Earl of Rochester*...(1838), ii, 397. Hereafter cited as Singer, *Hyde Corr.*

[14] Robert Jennens to T. Coke, 4 October. *H.M.C. Cowper*, ii, 436.

[15] Vernon to Rochester, 30 September. Singer, *Hyde Corr.*, ii, 397. Weymouth to Harley, 7 October. *H.M.C. Portland*, iv, 24.

[16] Davenant came to wish Harley a happier Christmas than he could ever expect. 26 December. *H.M.C. Portland*, iv, 30.

such extensive territories to defend.[17] It should not be thought that the great change of sentiment regarding a war was simply due to fear of the electorate. Members were changing their minds on their own accounts. Some thought that England would now bear only her fair share of the war's expenses, which was a smaller part than she would have been obliged to under the second treaty of partition. Imperilled foreign holdings had largely been renationalized or transferred and were not as subject to the earlier dangers. Holland's position appeared far more dangerous and even the more reactionary country members came to believe that '...the subsistence of Holland out of the French power is absolutely necessary to the preservation of this kingdom.' It was thought too, that the war would be far more remote and fought largely in 'ships and money' which would minimize the danger of a standing army. While the sincerity of such reasoning is certainly open to question, the facts would appear to speak for themselves. England was unquestionably in a far better position to wage a war than the previous year when opinion from out of doors almost forced her to it.[18]

The king was quite slow in making up his mind over the matter. The attacks upon the ministry had done their bit. Fears that the whigs could not serve him made him inclined to try the tories once again, for they had given him great promises. But Sunderland once again had the king's ear, arguing that the whigs were really the only possible choice and a new parliament was essential. William should not be deceived by the tories' compliance with his principal requests the previous session as they were motivated simply by fear of a dissolution. He reminded the king of their earlier pacifism and thought that even if they were forced into a war, money would be slow in coming and, for the nation, painful in its extraction. He thought that the king was mistaken in '...believing himself more cunning than a whole party, by whom he was beset and who weedles him every day; and of which, in his whole reign, he never yet could gain any one man.' He reminded the king of the dangers of trying to change the ministry in the middle of the session; it should be changed then or not at all. In weighing his decision, William must not expect whig support for the present ministry owing to patriotism, for such leadership would lead to both the nation's downfall and their own. An indemnity bill, although a good idea, was thought an impossibility, for both partisan groups would find it unacceptable, each believing

---

[17] To Thomas Coke, 11 October. *H.M.C. Cowper*, ii, 437.
[18] J. Brydges to T. Coke, 8 November 1701. *Ibid.*, pp. 437–8.

that they had extensive enough support to proscribe their opponents. It was to Somers that the king should return, for advice at the least. While he had credit enough with his party to direct a vigorous war policy, the tory ministers could not lead the opposition '...any further than they can persuade the king to be undone.'[19] Subsequent correspondence between Sunderland, Somers and the king leaves little doubt that William wished the tories to go, if only Somers could prove that the junto was capable of managing.[20]

When the king made up his mind to dissolve the parliament is not certain but he clearly did all he could to minimize the fortunes of the ministerial tories: Rochester he kept in Ireland, Marlborough in Holland, telling them both nothing of the possibility of a dissolution. He made excuses for postponing sailing back to England until electoral opinion was believed most auspicious.[21] As late as 8 November many still thought it quite possible that the old parliament might sit again.[22] A currency situation in France as serious as the earlier recoinage crisis in England was accompanied by an appearance of the English fleet off Brest in mid-September; both served to make it thought that the French would be little inclined to start a war.[23] Still it was the war party which the king was said to be listening to. Most of the tory ministry had not even seen the king, 'the other party' being said to have been exclusively at his ear.[24] It was this exclusive company which provided the clue to the dissolution, which became almost a certainty as the caballing became secretive: one of Harley's friends had an unexpected nocturnal encounter with '...Ld. Somers in the Covered Passage at H. [Hampton] C. [Court] wrapt up in his cloak...' Harley in turn told this to Godolphin, who remained sceptical to the end as to the possibility of a dissolution.

The end came on the morning of 11 November. Godolphin was summoned by William and told that parliament was to be immediately dissolved. He kissed the king's hand and surrendered his place in the

---

[19] To the king, 11 September. *Miscellaneous State Papers*, ii, 443–4.

[20] Sunderland to Somers, 15 September; Somers to Sunderland, 20 September; Sunderland to Somers, 1 October; Somers to Sunderland, 3 October; William to Somers, 30 September/10 October. *Ibid.*, pp. 447–52.

[21] See Coxe, *Memoirs of John, Duke of Marlborough* (1818–19), i, 102–3.

[22] A. Hammond to T. Coke, 8 November. *H.M.C. Cowper*, ii, 438–9. James Lowther to Sir John Lowther, 8 November. Cumb. R.O., Lonsdale MSS.

[23] Manchester to Vernon, 10/21 September and 17/28 September. Cole, *Affairs of State*, pp. 422–3.

[24] J. Brydges to T. Coke, 8 November. *H.M.C. Cowper*, ii, 437–8.

treasury.[25] The dissolution surprised many others. Viscount Weymouth was apprehensive, writing that some had heard of the dissolution earlier 'than the rest of the world' and noted that '...one side are very active, I wish the other be so too.'[26] One rabid court opponent stormed that it was designed '...to set up the old ministers, and to debase the House of Commons which may inflame this kingdom.'[27] The junto was at least apprehensive and tried to avoid responsibility for the dissolution: 'It is whispered here,' wrote one of their opponents, 'that the advice for the dissolution was given in Holland, but that is a sham to excuse some here.'[28]

It remains a question as to who got the best of the voluminous pamphlet battle[29] which centred on the conduct of the previous parliament. The junto's attack began the previous May with Defoe's defence of the Kentish petitioners. This was probably their best case and they appear to have made the most of it, emphasizing the arbitrary nature of the commons' proceedings.[30] Even in this, however, the commons had its defenders: if power had eventually to rest somewhere, then better the house of commons than the many-headed multitude.[31] It was, moreover, a very thorny question indeed as to whether the Kentish petitioners were acting as a result of a change in electoral sentiment or simply at the junto's urgings.[32] Nevertheless, it was the junto whigs who dared become specific in their appeal to the electorate, publishing a black list of those variously supposed to have supported either the commitment

---

[25] 'Account of Robert Harley's Conduct', B.M. Portland loan 29/165/97 f. 16.

[26] Robert Jennens to Thomas Coke and Chesterfield to Coke, 13 November, 11 November. *H.M.C. Cowper*, ii, 439.

[27] To Harley, 14 November. *H.M.C. Portland*, iv, 26.

[28] R. Jennens to T. Coke, 11 November. *H.M.C. Cowper*, ii, 439.

[29] Davenant wrote to T. Coke that he was sending him '...forty of one sort of papers, and eighteen of the other.' 6 October. *H.M.C. Cowper*, ii, 436–7.

[30] See for example, *Jura Populi Anglicani or the Subjects Right of Petitioning Set Forth...*(1702). In Cobbett, vol. V, app. xiii.

[31] [James Drake], *An Account of Some Late Designs to Create a Misunderstanding between King and People* (1702), *passim*.

[32] Vernon mentions the two most outspoken pamphlets: *Vindication of the Right of the Commons as to Impeachments* and *Vindication of the Proceedings of the Commons in the Last Session*. The first he thought to be written by Sir Humphrey Mackworth, the second by Harley. To Shrewsbury, 1 September 1701. *Vernon Corr.*, iii, 155–7.

of the Kentish petitioners or the impeachment proceedings[33] The junto's assault upon the impeachment proceedings, and consequent defence of the partition treaties,[34] however, were less well made and elicited even more violent counter attacks.[35] Their attack upon the very mixed nature of what they chose to call 'the tory party' was even less wise, containing as it did such old whigs as Harleys, Foleys and St Johns. On this charge they were met head on. The junto whigs were said to be truly inconsistent, having no right whatsoever to the traditional usage of the word 'whig' and even less to that of 'country'.[36] Was it not they who had opposed constitutional reform, favoured a standing army, done so much to increase William's prerogative and aid Dutch interest? They were not the great losers from the failure of country party financial schemes, William's exorbitant grants and crippling taxation.

In their more general attacks the junto whigs did even less well, being answered point for point on practically all major issues.[37] On the succession question there could be no doubt that the tories had done their bit the previous parliament.[38] Implications that there were designs for a Jacobite restoration[39] were parried with the assertion that it was the junto whigs who intended to sidestep the succession, and this in an

---

[33] A copy of the list is printed in [James Drake], *Some Necessary Considerations Relating to all future Elections of Members to Serve in Parliament*...(1702), pp. 23–8. See Appendix A.

[34] See J.D., H.W., T.S., R.L., etc., *A Letter from Some Electors to One of their Representatives in Parliament. Shewing the Electors Sentiments, Touching the Matters in Dispute between the Lords and Commons the Last Session of Parliament, in Relation to the Impeachments. And giving Some Advice to their Member, How to demean himself in Parliament for the Future* (1701). *The Late King of Spain's Will, and The Treaty for the Partition of the Kingdom of Spain, Recited and Consider'd, Paragraph by Paragraph: With Animadversions upon Both, tending to Prove, That it is in the Interest of all Europe, to Adhere inviolably to the Partition of the Spanish Monarchy, and more particularly conducing to the Welfare of England* (1701).

[35] See James Drake, *The History of the Last Parliament* (1702).

[36] *Honest Advice to the Electors of Great Britain. In the Present Choice of their Representatives* (1702). *The Mouse grown a Rat: or the Story of the City and Country Mouse Newly Transpos'd In a discourse Betwixt Bays, Johnson and Smith*. See too, Feiling, *Tory Party*, pp. 354–5.

[37] *The Whigs Thirty two Queries and as Many of the Tories in Answer to them* (1702).

[38] [Charles Davenant], *A True Picture of a Modern Whig in Two Parts* (1702).

[39] *An Argument, Shewing, That the Prince of Wales, Tho' a Protestant, has no just Pretensions to the Crown of England: With some Remarks on the late Pretended Discovery of a Design to Steal him Away* (1701).

unpatriotic manner: it was thought that upon William's death an immediate Hanoverian succession was planned, thus excluding Anne.[40] Harley, moreover, claims to have remained truer to the settlement than the king. In his unpublished memoirs he states that William, after some thought, decided against it and cared little what happened after his death, in England or anywhere else.[41]

Robert Walcott has discussed at some length the membership of William's last parliament.[42] Because of his concentration upon division and small family groupings, however, it would perhaps be worth while to attempt a study of that part of the election which was fought on court-country lines. In some ways of course to speak in court-country terms during this election might seem a paradox, for the tories, because of their domination of the ministry, might seem to dominate the court party. In fact they did not. It must be reiterated that the first minister was the king, that the king wanted a vigorous war, and in this desire he must be considered a supporter of the junto whigs. Almost all of the placemen might be similarly described.[43] In addition, many of the ministerial tories were largely country in their outlook. Such influence as they had may then be said not to have been employed in favour of candidates who supported a vigorous war. They had in fact been almost forced upon the king, who had grave suspicions as to whether or not they either could or would enthusiastically support a war policy. In the event of any considerable junto success in the ensuing elections, all but the most pliable would almost certainly lose their places as they had in 1694.

Godolphin was pleased with the court's losses in the West.[44] Earlier William Walsh, member for Worcestershire, wrote to Somers urging the dissolution of the old parliament and spoke glowingly of their electoral prospects:

...wee may very well reckon upon two of our ['our' is crossed out]

---

[40] Noted by Dartmouth in Burnet, *Own Times*, iv, 553.

[41] During a conference with the king in November 1701, Harley was told: '*Mr Speaker, your Project of the Succession has done me no good.*' Harley's italics. B.M. Portland loan 29/165/97 f. 15. William is reported as saying that he '...was entirely unconcerned what become of the world when he was out of it, and would not have been displeased that it had perished with him.' Dartmouth's note to Burnet, *Own Times*, iv, 566.

[42] *English Politics*, pp. 34–69.   [43] See Harley's comment above, p. 231.

[44] To Harley, 4 December 1701. *H.M.C. Portland*, iv, 28.

the same side for the county, one for the city, one for Evesham and one for Wych; we shall have a very fair game if well manag'd for one for Bewdley another for the city, and if they can keep Mr Rudge in at Evesham it will be better than Mr Parkins, and then of our nine members there will bee only one at Wych tht is absolutely agt us.[45]

Probably what Walsh based his hopes on was the success of a Worcestershire address the previous summer calling for a dissolution. Although all signed it, many did so only to avoid treasonous incriminations. Thomas Foley was said to have found '...great fault in the wording' and Harley spoke '...very highly against the Insolence of it, and assures his friends of the ridiculousness of 'em expecting this parlmt will be dissolved this year.'[46] Although this latter expectation was not ridiculous, Walsh's hopes for Worcestershire certainly were. If the elections throughout the nation had approached this disappointment the junto would almost certainly have lost their heads. For the king, Somers and Walsh (who incidentally lost his seat), the returns from that county must have been a sobering experience. Instead of only one court opponent being returned, there were six.[47] And where the junto's friends took a more realistic approach to the elections, their fears were usually fulfilled. In Oxfordshire, where eight of the nine members had been blacklisted and little change was expected,[48] none was forthcoming. In the country party stronghold of Wales, there was again little change. In Derbyshire, Thomas Coke, smarting from his defeat the previous election, was taking no chances. The talk of the court allowing the seats to be split, with Coke being allowed to come in with Lord Hartington, made his supporters '...suspect a snake in the grass.'[49] The proposal that the other country candidate, John Curzon, should stand down to

---

[45] 26 October 1701. Reigate Corp. R.O., B. 20 (Somers Papers).

[46] *Ibid.*

[47] The three blacklisted members were Sir John Packington (County), Salway Winnington (Bewdley), Samuel Swift (Worcester). The other country members were: William Bromley of Holt Castle (County, not to be confused with his famous namesake of Bagington who was member for Univ. Oxon. See R. Walcott, *English Politics*, p. 231); Edward Foley (Wych); Hugh Parker (said by Walcott to be a follower of Rochester. *Ibid.*, p. 212). The three favourably disposed to the court were: Thomas Wylde (Worcester); Sir James Rushout (Evesham) and Charles Cocks (Wych, a placeman and follower of Somers).

[48] Henry Norris to Sir R. Norris, 19 December 1701. Liv. Pub. Lib. MSS. 920 Nor/i/145.

[49] John Coke to Thomas Coke, 4 December. *H.M.C. Cowper*, ii, 441–2.

avoid a contest was treated with contempt; one of his friends thought it would alter the double interest and cause future electoral indifference.[50] In this analysis, Secretary Vernon would seem to have reluctantly concurred, noting sadly that there was a bias among the freeholders against being represented by two lords.[51] They succeeded in avoiding being represented even by one, both Coke and Curzon being returned. Lord Hartington was defeated and forced to make a retreat, a humiliating one in his father's estimation,[52] to Walpole's borough of Castle Rising in a by-election. Lord Roos cannily anticipated the shift of sentiment, standing instead for Leicestershire, where he was returned with Lord Sherrard. Although this was largely a court-country contest with two blacklisted members being deposed, both successful candidates modified their attachment to the court.[53] In the Northamptonshire contest, the country party would again appear to have improved its position. John Parker, earlier listed as having supported the standing army, was not returned. Nottingham deplored the insults hurled at 'great patriots', and was pleased with the success of Thomas Cartwright and Sir Justinian Isham.[54]

Godolphin feared country losses in the North.[55] The court brought ecclesiastical intervention to bear in Yorkshire. Archbishop Sharp was asked by the young William Lowther, then standing for Pontefract, to dissuade Lowther's own father from opposing him and supporting his cousin Robin Lowther '...whom most people knows not to be soe well inclined for the good of the present Government as he ought.'[56] The letter apparently had its effect, for his father promised the archbishop to desist in his support both for Robin and Sir John Bland, another government opponent. In the event the seats were split, one going to William Lowther, the other to Bland. In the election for knight of the shire, the archbishop was again solicited to direct the votes but it is a question as to whether or not he did so. Lord Irwin, although given overwhelming junto support,[57] was objected to on the grounds of having no

---

[50] Lord Scarsdale to Thomas Coke, 27 December. *Ibid.*, p. 444.

[51] To Shrewsbury, 17 October. *Vernon Corr.*, iii, 157–9.

[52] A. Hammond to T. Coke, 19 December. *H.M.C. Cowper*, ii, 443–4.

[53] J. Coke to s., 20 November. *Ibid.*, ii, 440.

[54] To Visc. Hatton, 27 November. B.M. Add. MSS. 29,595 f. 204.

[55] To Harley, 4 December. *H.M.C. Portland*, iv, 28.

[56] 18 November. Gloucs. R.O., Lloyd Baker MSS., box 4/U/11 (Sharp Papers).

[57] Sir Chas. Hotham to Visc. Irwin, 23 September. *H.M.C. F. L. Wood*, p. 84.

religion.[58] Perhaps the archbishop overlooked this fact or did not intervene. In any case Irwin's campaign was given considerable aid by the withdrawal of his most obvious opponent, Sir John Kaye. Lord Irwin was told that Sir William Lowther had overtaken Kaye '…as he went home and discorsing upon this subject he told him if he voted as he was inform'd he did last Sessions that he must expect none of his interest if he stood againe…'[59] Under considerable pressure from the Irwin interest, Kaye finally stood down, which caused great satisfaction on the court side owing to the fear of an inevitable election petition which would factionalize the committee.[60] Irwin was returned along with another court supporter, Lord Fairfax. In Westmorland the court had mixed success in its attempt to displace Henry Grahme and Sir Christopher Musgrave. There, Sir Richard Sanford argued that the king dissolved the last parliament because he did not love them, while Daniel Flemming tried to whip up enthusiasm amongst the freeholders by asking them all to shout: 'A Sanford and a Dalston'. To his chagrin, however, almost all cried, 'A Grahme and a Musgrave'. In the event the seats were split; Grahme and Sanford both being returned, with Musgrave standing at the bottom of the poll.[61] One reason for the defeat was his threat to turn some junto supporters out of the commission of the peace. Thomas Pulleine, one of the affected justices, said that he intended to do all he could to displace Musgrave from his seat in Westmorland: 'I will doe one good turne for another, he's come down post and I hope he will be sent back wth a flye in his eare.'[62] Indeed, Musgrave was forced to make a retreat to Seymour's pocket borough of Totnes. Godolphin's fears of Northern losses were well founded, for there the court achieved what amounted to virtual domination: only about 16 of the 66 members of the six northern counties may be considered to have opposed the court in the ensuing parliament. A week after the new parliament convened, the placeman, James Lowther, wrote: 'We had a meeting of the North Country Members of our side today, 34 of us dined together 5 of Cumb. 4 of North. 2 of West. 6 of Lancash. 1 of Durham and 16 of Yorkshire

---

[58] N. Drake to s., 22 November. Gloucs. R.O., Lloyd Baker MSS., box 4/C/13.

[59] Thomas Pulleine to Lord Irwin, 20 August. Leeds Pub. Lib. TN/9 (Temple and Newsom MSS.).

[60] Lowther to s., 17 November *Ibid.*

[61] Henry Grahme to Sir Rd. Sanford, n.d. November. *H.M.C. Bagot*, p. 336.

[62] To Ld Irwin, 17 November. Leeds Pub. Lib. TN/9.

and we have as many more out of those Counties as will make up 50 in all.'[63]

In London and Westminster, the two blacklisted tories were also displaced; despite Sir John Leveson Gower's popularity, he was successively opposed by the junto whigs who set up Sir Henry Dutton Colt.[64] Where the court took considerable time and effort they usually succeeded. Such was the case in Wiltshire where Sir George Hungerford and Richard Howe lost their seats as knights of the shire. 'Ash and Ashey is the word...,' wrote one of the court's friends, 'I wish you deliverance from Squire Hungerford's opposition...'[65] Shaftesbury rejoiced over the court gains there and in Dorset '...two counties long in the hands of the inveterate of the adverse party.'[66] Dramatic court successes occurred against a few other extremist leaders. One pamphlet appeared to be drawn up for the exclusive purpose of defeating Jack Howe in Gloucestershire.[67] With many candidates standing some of his friends hoped he would be able to come in between them.[68] They were mistaken, for Howe was said to have lost by over a thousand votes.[69] Against the 'Poussineers', the court had considerable success. If they could not evict Tredenham from his pocket borough of St Mawes, they found considerable consolation forcing out Davenant and Hammond who did not enjoy similar immunities.[70]

There can be little doubt that the king gave his whole-hearted support to the junto in the election,[71] and yet when the returns came in the court had few delusions of having made anything more than moderate gains.[72] In many constituencies the junto oligarchs had been stymied; if 46 of

---

[63] To Sir John Lowther, 6 January 1701/2. Cumb. R.O., Lonsdale MSS.

[64] Vernon to Shrewsbury, 8 November 1701. *Vernon Corr.*, iii, 159–62.

[65] Henry Blake to Wm. White, Sat. night. Marq. of Lansdowne, *Wilts Arch. and Nat. Hist. Mag.* (Devizes, 1932), xliv, 79.

[66] To Furley, 29 December 1701 Forster, *Shaftesbury Corr.*, p. 163.

[67] *A Letter sent to a Gentleman in Gloucestershire About Electing a New Parliament* (11 November 1701).

[68] Lady A. Pye to Abigail Harley, 29 November 1701. *H.M.C. Portland* iv, 27.

[69] Brandenburg dispatch, 9/20 December. B.M. Add. MSS. 30,000 E. f. 416 v.

[70] James Lowther to Sir John Lowther, 29 November 1701. Cumb. R.O., Lonsdale MSS.

[71] James Lowther wrote '...we doubt not by the Kings helping hand to have a great majority.' To Sir John Lowther, 25 November. *Ibid.*

[72] Vernon to Shrewsbury, 28 November. *Vernon Corr.*, iii, 159–62.

the 147 blacklisted members were not returned, 121 were, and few of these appear to have moderated their opinions.[73] The blacklist itself would soon be voted scandalous.[74]

Why had court and junto candidates not achieved greater success? To a large degree, of course, the answer lies in inertia. The previous election had occurred less than a year before. The spirit of the Kentish Petition exaggerated the change of spirit in the nation and was not even reflective of Kent, where there was no appreciable change of the representatives and both blacklisted members were again returned.[75] The addresses calling for the dissolution of the previous parliament, which the court took such delight in, were signed by many only for fear of court vengeance.[76] Many saw the junto's opportunistic nature symbolized in the snap dissolution. Some, indeed, might have looked to the triennial act where, although couched in ambiguous language, it was clearly implied that parliaments should last exactly three years or at least not nine months.[77] The reputation of the junto and its supporters left much to be desired. Was it necessary to have ministers who found their interest in the war's continuance? Had many not foreseen the junto spirit of 'No Peace without Spain'? Although no one openly opposed war with France, many had been half-hearted in their support. Even if war was necessary, need it be fought with the vast and hideously expensive land armies that the king would undoubtedly ask for? Many electors had evidently thought twice before voting for those who would vote such supplies and in the manner least noticeable to the subject.[78]

---

[73] See Feiling, *Tory Party*, p. 353.

[74] Thomas Smith to John Roades, 19 February 1701/2. *H.M.C. F. L. Wood*, p. 85.

[75] The matter is discussed in Cobbett, v, 1339.

[76] Certainly the elections would indicate this to be true in Worcestershire.

[77] See pp. 107–8. Admittedly the previous parliament might have lasted another session. A parliament of but *one* session had last occurred under James II.

[78] Cornwall and Abingdon, for example, had given their nominees specific directions of a country character. See esp.: *The Cornish Hug: or, the Wrestlers against the Government. Being Instructions Given of Lestwithel, on Wednesday the 10th of December 1701, by the High Sheriff of the County of Cornwall, In his own Name, and the Name of the Gentlemen and Freeholders of the said County, to the Honourable John Granville and James Buller Esqrs. who were then Chosen Knights for the said County in the ensuing Parliament* (1702).

RETURN TO WAR

Even if the whigs had done little more than hold their own in the
election, Sunderland believed that this would be adequate. Had not
the war spirit developed in the previous so-called tory parliament to
bring addresses of support to the king? Had not Somers weathered the
first two votes of the impeachment proceedings? Had not then the
junto many more friends even in the previous parliament than had
generally been supposed? The main fault in the king's ministerial policy,
Sunderland argued, was his dallying. He believed this less dangerous
for the fears it caused the whigs than for the hopes it occasioned the
tories. While malleable old tories might be continued in the ministry
no new ones should be brought in. The king should tell them openly
that the new parliament was called owing to past abuses. He advocated
a return to the methods of 1696—methods which king and junto knew
so well–to obtain the desired ends. Owing to the superior oratorical
skill of the opposition, court and junto must immediately establish
themselves as being superior in force in the new parliament.[79]

The first test of strength would be the Speakership. Sunderland appears
to have taken it for granted that Harley would not be re-elected.[80]
Most people, indeed, expected a great victory for the junto-court
alliance, whose candidate was again Littleton. In early December the
odds against Harley being re-elected were four to one. One reason for
this was fear that Harley would wreak vengeance on those who had
urged the dissolution.[81] Whip letters were sent out forecasting disaster
if Harley were elected: 'If wee lose the Speaker we shall lose everything
and England into the bargain. This is the last time that affords an
opportunity of exerting our selves.'[82] Another cause for the bad odds
was Harley's hesitation to stand.[83] Harley wrote in his memoirs that
the king had at least four different intermediaries approach him: the
duke of Somerset, Secretary Hedges, Lord Sunderland and Henry Guy.
He told them that it was impossible for him to accept court support as

---

[79] Advice to Somers, Hardwicke, *Miscellaneous State Papers*, ii, 457–61.
[80] *Ibid.*
[81] Stanley West to R. Harley, 6 December 1701. *H.M.C. Portland*, iv, 28.
[82] Charles Hotham to Lord Irwin, 13 November. Leeds Pub. Lib. TN/9
(Temple and Newsom MSS.). See too, Locke's letter to Peter King, 31 January 1701/2. Bodl. MSS. Locke C.40 ff. 100–1.
[83] Stanley West to R. Harley, 6 December. *H.M.C. Portland*, iv, 28.

'...the hands he [the king] had trusted himself into would not permit it.'[84] It was not then that Harley did not wish to be Speaker, but rather that he did not wish to be the court's Speaker. Subsequent overtures were rejected verbally and at last in writing. To avoid further requests Harley used the elections as a pretext to excuse himself from London. Despite the urgings of Godolphin and other friends, he returned only four days before the opening of parliament.[85] Godolphin was optimistic, believing that Harley would have more friends than was generally supposed.[86]

Godolphin was right. On 30 December 1701, Littleton was proposed by Lord Spencer and seconded by Jack Smith; Harley by the earl of Dysert and Henry St John. On the division, Littleton was shown to have had four friends too few. Harley was then elected without dissent.[87]

Why had Littleton lost? The election had occurred, as Harley's brother later observed, 'in the middle of Christmas',[88] when country members were likely to be at home in their counties. Oddly enough, attendance by country members was excellent, and this was thought by the placeman, James Lowther, to be the reason for Harley's success: 'We have certainly a majority of the whole house but we have 50 absent and they not above half that number.'[89] Harley's supporters had been very active. Thomas Coke received three letters urging him to come quickly to London. One of them was from Anthony Hammond, who believed that if Harley won, the prospect would be fair, but that if Littleton won, it would mean disaster. The greatest service to Harley would be for 'the gentlemen' to be up in time for the opening.[90] Perhaps it was 'the gentlemen' whom Harley had in mind when he cannily refused the crown's customary gift of silver plate after the previous dissolution.[91]

---

[84] 'Account of Robert Harley's Conduct'. B.M. Portland loan 29/165/3 f. 17.

[85] *Ibid.*, f. 18.

[86] Godolphin to Harley, 9 December 1701. *H.M.C. Portland*, iv, 28.

[87] *H.C.J.*, xiii, 645. The vote was 216 to 212.

[88] 'Harley Family Memoirs', *H.M.C. Portland*, v, 646.

[89] James Lowther to Sir John Lowther, 30 December 1701. Cumb. R.O., Lowther Corr.

[90] 19 December. *H.M.C. Cowper*, ii, 443. Two letters 18 December from Capt. H. Cartwright and Lord Scarsdale, *ibid.*; another of 22 December from Henry Tate, *ibid.*, p. 444.

[91] Brandenburg dispatch, 9/19 December. B.M. Add. MSS. 30,000 E. ff. 416 v.–417 r.

Heavy country attendance alone cannot account for Harley's victory. Lowther gives as further reasons:

> ...the Northern Members that are absent... [and] the people of our side that are chose for two severall places of which we have nine or ten and the others but two or three.[92]

It was an irony that the most extensive court victories had been those furthest from Westminster, and that court-junto enthusiasm had induced many candidates to stand for two places, for both circumstances weakened the court-junto alliance in the election of Speaker.[93] Court defections were a further cause of Harley's victory. Lowther found that 'Sir G. Rook and the Navy board are violently against Sir Tho. Littleton.' Shaftesbury was even more outspoken, putting the blame 'wholly' upon these 'fals servants'.[94]

The Brandenburg envoy was informed the previous June that even if parliament were dissolved because of conflict with the lords, a new parliament would have the same spirit.[95] To some, Harley's victory seemed the fulfilment of the prophecy.[96] Harley's opening speech called for unity,[97] but there was to be little of that during the brief remainder of the reign.

As court and country were so evenly balanced, the committee of elections assumed unprecedented importance. Although the court found

---

[92] To Sir John Lowther, 30 December. Cumb. R.O., Lowther Corr.

[93] In the winter, members from the North would generally appear to have been slow to arrive. James Lowther's uncle, John (Lowther of Lowther), Viscount Lonsdale, once gave Portland as reasons other than his poor health for failing to be in Westminster: 'The depth of the Winter...and the Longest Journey in the kingdome.' 13 December 1698. N.U.L. PwA. 829.

[94] To B. Furley, 6 January 1701/2. Forster, *Shaftesbury Corr.*, p. 165.

[95] Brandenburg dispatch, 24 June/5 July 1701. B.M. Add. MSS. 30,000 E. 291 v. and 292 r. Bonet based his view on conversations with various tory chiefs. *Ibid.*

[96] Bishop King, who had an impartial dislike of all English factions, except possibly the court, believed Harley's success to be the first of five reasons for the junto's being found 'too light tho' the Court and Artifice are thrown in to turn the scales'. Bp. King to Lord N.n. (copy), 20 January 1701/2. T.C.D. MSS. 1489.

[97] Tho. Johnson (member for Liverpool) wrote to Rd. Norris calling it the '...usual method (I suppose) to heal divisions.' *Norris Papers*, ix, 76. Harley was probably less guilty of hypocrisy in his speech than is usually assumed. If he was accused, among many others, of having been bribed by France, yet even Fuller, his notorious accuser, denied having made the accusation. W. Fuller to R. Harley, 23 February. *H.M.C. Portland*, iv, 34.

it easy to win a few tactical victories with regard to the timing of the hearing of elections, on the greater questions the country party soon put up a determined enough challenge.[98] In committee, the election of John Comyns at Malden had been upheld against the petition of Irby Montague after a fierce debate and a narrow division.[99] The court appeared determined to reverse the decision, and the country party just as determined to uphold it. The court lost by a vote of 226 to 208 after a three-hour debate.[100] A placeman explained that the reason for the court's loss again lay in overwhelming country attendance. It was, he wrote '...the fullest House that ever I heard of...There were severall brought in men's arms to vote. There was not one man that could get out of bed absent on the other side and we had several wanting.'[101] Lord Hartington was also unsuccessful in challenging Thomas Coke's election in Derbyshire which seems a relatively honest one. Despite the most ingenious plots to discredit him and his election, he remained seated.[102] Many elections were said to have gone' ...agt the pulse and mind of some great ones.'[103] If, however, the junto was unsuccessful in most of its attacks on the sitting country members it was at least capable of defending its own. Lord Ashburnham, for example, was unsuccessful in his attempt to unseat that 'ropemaker', John Mouncher, the member for Hastings, on his son's behalf. While the 'cuntey party' was said to have received his son's electoral petition by a majority of twenty-six votes the same night as the success over the Maldon petition,[104] he came

---

[98] The placeman, James Lowther, wrote: 'We carried yesterday [5 January] two Questions upon great Divisions relating to two Elections, they were both Party matters and a disappointment to the other side.' To Sir John Lowther, 6 January 1701/2. Cumb. R.O., Lonsdale MSS. See too, his letter of 8 January bringing similar good tidings. *Ibid.*

[99] Chas. Hulton to Geo. Kenyon of Peel (a clerk of the peace), 20 January. Lancs. R.O. DDke/9/100/8.

[100] Thomas Johnson believed the vote to be 228–210. To Rd. Norris, mayor of Liverpool, 27 January. Liv. Pub. Lib. MSS. 920 Nor./ii/246.

[101] James Lowther to Sir John Lowther, 27 January. Cumb. R.O., Lonsdale MSS.

[102] Capt. John Beresford wrote that an Isaac Potter (potter and plotter), had an ingenious tale devised. Aside from aiding in the distribution of bribes he claimed to have seen armaments for 250 horsemen in Coke's possession. 7 February *H.M.C. Cowper*, ii, 453. See too, *ibid.*, 448–53.

[103] [Thomas Legh, of Lyme or Ridge?] to [Peter Legh], 31 January. John Rylands Library, Legh of Lyme MSS., box 47.

[104] John Ld. Ashburnham to Capt. Millward, 20 January. East Sussex R.O., MSS. 843 f. 279 (Ashburnham MSS.).

to think it as well that there appeared to be little likelihood of it being heard that session. As his son's chances for success against Mouncher were diminishing in direct proportion to the reduction of country attendance, he thought it best to wait '...until the return of many of his friends who will come up againe next winter.'[105]

Throughout much of the winter, the great ministerial question also hung in the balance. Before the election, there were even a few tory gains in regard to some of the minor places.[106] At about the time the new parliament met, the king was making changes favourable to the junto whigs. Manchester became secretary of the southern department while Hedges, no friend to the junto, was dismissed from the northern department, being replaced by Vernon, the former southern secretary. At the treasury, Godolphin's vacant place was taken by Carlisle who had done so much to aid the junto's electoral campaigns in the north. The loss of the Speakership and the inauspicious opening to the proceedings in the committee of elections made the king hesitate in his plans to remodel the ministry. It had still not been decided to drop or revive the impeachment proceedings.

By the end of January the king was again moving towards a trimming policy, appointing the rather independent Somerset to the post of lord president. Nevertheless, it is a question as to how far he could have proceeded along these lines. 'The Trimmer' was dead and Shrewsbury abroad recovering his health. There appeared to be few signs that such country leaders as Harley had relented in their unwillingness to accept office. Such hesitancy combined with the use made of petitions to the king, the way the proceedings of the past parliament were accepted as precedents and the re-introduction of the commission of accounts (again said to be much abhorred by the court) made one observer believe that: 'It would seem to me from these and some other circumstances that the party [i.e., the junto] is too light tho the Court and Artifice are thrown into the Scales.'[107]

Certainly the junto was not strong enough to return to the methods of 1696. In regard to the question of war, however, there appears to have been very little opposition. Increasingly, country thinking was coming to support foreign engagements as essential to the public interest. The king, moreover, followed Marlborough's advice and

---

[105] *Ibid.* S. to s., 10 February and 7 March. *Ibid.*, ff. 425 and 444.
[106] Brandenburg dispatch, 25 July/5 August 1700. B.M. Add. MSS. 30,000 E. f. 213.   [107] Bp. King to N.n. 20 January 1701/2. T.C.D. MSS. 1489.

settled the degree of English commitment not upon his own authority
but with the advice and assistance of parliament.[108] In so doing, he
doubtlessly incurred country confidence in his plans. In late January
one observer noted '...there seems to be a very happy unanimity between the King Lords and Commons and both Landmen and Seamen
come in with great cheerfullness to make up the numbers of 40,000
Landmen and as many Seamen...' The essential taxes had in part
already been voted and the rest would soon be forthcoming.[109] It
appeared too, that most of the men to be raised would be English,
which would create employment for all able persons of all ranks, a fact
which in itself also helped to appease country sentiment.[110]

While many troops were voted, the king had desired even more.
Seymour appears to have employed a finesse which deducted 7,000 men
from what the court had hoped for.[111] The commons did not retreat
either from its position in regard to the Irish forfeitures, and petitions
censuring the practices of the Irish commissioners were swiftly condemned. Culpepper, the leader of the Kentish petitioners was again
committed while addresses against the proceedings of the old parliament
were censured. There were, moreover, resolutions effectually defining
an expanded power of the commons which received very little opposition from the court.[112] These were thought considerable victories by
many observers.[113]

Nevertheless, the court was to lose few purely defensive battles. The
attempted motion calling for censorship of those involved in presenting
petitions to the king for the dissolution of the previous parliament

---

[108] Marlborough wrote: '...if the king should be prevailed upon to settle
this [i.e., the number of troops England is to supply] by his own authority,
we shall never see a quiet day more in England; and consequently not only
ruin ourselves, for if King and parliament begin with a dispute, France will
give what laws she pleases.' To Sec. Hedges, 3/14 October 1701. Coxe,
Marlborough, p. 97. The king asked for advice in his opening speech and subsequently appeared to keep the commons informed. *H.C.J.*, xiii, 646-7,
657-64.

[109] Robt. Clavell to Bp. King, 20 January 1701/2. T.C.D. MSS. 1122/868.

[110] Tho. Smith to [John] Roades [Ld Irwin's Secretary], 17 Jan. Leeds
Pub. Lib. TN/9.

[111] Brandenburg dispatch, 7/17 February in Feiling, *Tory Party*, p. 357.

[112] Bp. King to N.n., 20 January 1701/2. T.C.D. MSS. 1489.

[113] *Ibid.* S. to Clougher, 7 March. *Ibid.* T. Johnson to Rd. Norris, 24
February. Liv. Pub. Lib. MSS. 920 Nor/ii/216. The eventual outcome was
rather ambiguous for some of the resolutions diminished, while others advanced, the power of the commons. *H.C.J.*, xiii, 767.

failed. It was only owing to fortuitous circumstances that the court was
kept from taking advantage of the loss.[114]

On the key question of reviving the impeachment proceedings, the
whigs had won the day. There were no doubts as to the importance of
the question: Sunderland had declared that if the whigs lost it, the
support gained in the previous election would be for nought.[115] But
they did not lose it. The court supporters from the North had at last
arrived. Although there was a majority of but 14 votes they had made
their point, for it was a full house—probably the fullest house ever—the
vote being 235–221; 456 members were present. There was reason then
in 'those victorious shouts' led by the young Robert Walpole after the
great division, and it was thought that following the vote "Mr Majority" would be a courtier thereafter.'[116]

How great a victory may the court be said to have gained by passing
the bill calling for the abjuration of the pretender? The objectors to
the bill did not force a division and one might well assume that many
country members were probably quite willing to have a bill which
would rid the opposition of the charge of Jacobitism. The oath which
was to be tendered to all members, office holders and clergy was made
obligatory by but one vote.[117] Feiling finds it '...remarkable that one of
Harley's closest Tory associates, Granville, was teller for the majority.'[118]
In fact it is not. The aid of such as Granville in making the oath compulsory prevented the court from having another national index of
Jacobite sympathizers with which to brand and proscribe the opposition.
Indeed, it was the whig extremists who wished it to be voluntary;
'...the tares are in our wheat...,' wrote Shaftesbury, who believed that
a voluntary association was the only way to remove them.[119] It would

---

[114] It was said that a timely adjournment was effected when Sir William
Strickland stood up to speak, fell down in a fit and needed to be carried out
by several members. Thomas Smith to John Roades, 19 February. *H.M.C.
F. L. Wood*, p. 85.

[115] Sunderland's advice to Somers, n.d. Hardwicke, *Miscellaneous State
Papers*, ii, 457–61.

[116] Estates General dispatch, 27 February/10 March. B.M. Add. MSS.
17,677 xx, f. 235. Horace Walpole to his bro. [Robert] Walpole, 28 February.
Camb. Univ. Lib., Cholmondeley Corr. 196.

[117] The vote was 188–187. *H.C.J.*, xiii, 687. James Lowther to Sir John
Lowther, 20 January. Cumb. R.O., Lonsdale MSS.

[118] Feiling, *Tory Party*, p. 357.

[119] Shaftesbury to B. Furley, 26 August 1701. Forster, *Shaftesbury Corr.*,
p. 150.

seem that another tory, Thomas Coke, moved that the abjuration oath be compulsory.[120] A pragmatic course of action was being pursued by many who had learned a sad lesson from the first voluntary association of 1696. The compulsory oath could be taken with a clear conscience, at least by the more sophisticated, as simply being necessitated by force. This is not to deny that the passage of the bill was in fact a court victory, but simply to state that it was a limited one. The high churchmen could take little solace in the fact that an amendment proscribing from office those practising occasional conformity, was lost by almost a hundred votes.[121] The attempt in the lords to exclude peers from the obligatory oath was not successful either.[122] As may be seen by the junto's desperation in hurriedly having the bill signed, or rather stamped by the king (he was too weak to sign it, being on his deathbed), it seems likely that the junto was simply providing itself with a safeguard rather than gaining a proscription licence. Even if William had lived on and taken Sunderland's advice to restore the junto fully, then 'Mr Majority' would probably have remained a courtier only in votes of supply. Certainly any hopes that there would be a substantial alteration in the acts of the revolution settlement or the commons control of finance were virtually still-born. The most that the court could wish for was to avoid a further diminution of its power. Most of the country party's aims had been fulfilled and there was little left to do but discuss the men most likely to ensure their continuance. While then the conflict at the close of William's reign appears in predominantly whig-tory terms, it was owing not to the country party's failures but rather to its successes; the country party had made the court largely subservient to its wishes.

---

[120] John Fisher to Thomas Coke, 21 March 1701/2. *H.M.C. Cowper*, iii, 2. Admittedly, it was believed that this might be prejudicial to him and was denied by his friends. *Ibid*. Nevertheless one might suppose that such a sophisticated and cynical action would not be suited to country consciences.

[121] The vote was 203–139. *H.C.J.*, xi, 750.

[122] 21 February. *H.L.J.*, xvii, 43.

Appendices

APPENDIX A

Party Revisited

In considering the political structure of the period, it has been argued that most of the important issues were fought on a court-country basis, that contemporaries usually spoke in these terms, and that the chief exception was in the fight over the offices: that is, when the question was one of men rather than of measures. Such whig and tory historians as Macaulay and Feiling have generally accepted this interpretation, although pardonably over-emphasizing the whig-tory dichotomy because of their interest in party continuity. Professor Walcott's four-party concept generally fits in well enough with this system too, providing one takes his genealogical factions as somewhat superfluous.

In a recent article, however, Dr H. G. Horwitz disagrees in a more significant way. He finds that between 2 per cent and 23 per cent of the members included in selected printed division lists of the reign changed sides when compared to a manuscript list thought to be of those who might support or oppose the ministry in 1698. He thus sees William's reign in much the same way as Dr W. A. Speck sees Queen Anne's, namely that there were '...a considerable number of members who voted consistently along [whig and tory] party lines' and only a surprisingly small number whose 'voting habits were irregular'. Horwitz states that '...in short, if any schematization of post-revolution parliamentary politics is to be adopted, a revision of Walcott's "compass"—a version in which "whig" and "tory" would now figure as magnetic poles—might well be recommended.'[1]

---

[1] 'Parties, Connections, and Parliamentary Politics, 1689–1714: Review and

But it might well not be, too, and the reasons are several. Generally forsaking confidential correspondence and the debates, Horwitz relies far too heavily upon division lists—good cows, but by no means sacred. This handicaps his efforts from the outset, for he tends to ignore the fact that *there were no divisions* over such crucial matters as abrogating the king's right to suspend statute or putting the dispensing power under parliamentary control. And how many dared support William's *initial* requests for a large standing army in peacetime consisting primarily of foreigners: or his prodigious bequest of crown lands to Portland and Albemarle? What of parliament's usual support for the commission of accounts and its refusal to allow the king to gain any sort of financial independence?

All of Horwitz's divisions, moreover, are recognized exceptions to the predominantly court-country character of the period; when there was no clearly defined country position, as in the first and last days of the reign when it was a question of men rather than of measures;[2] when the country party had triumphed to such a degree that it was rather a question of how to tie up the loose ends than anything more dramatic;[3] or when the court succeeded in branding opposition as treason, as it had during the year following the disclosure of the assassination plot when country fortunes were at an ebb.[4] Then, admittedly, the court usually carried all before it. Of the 569 members officially returned during the parliament, 538 were sitting between February 1695/6 and February 1696/7. By taking three division lists (two of a seemingly financial nature, the other quasi-constitutional) as well as that of those who *refused* the voluntary association (thus excluding the four-fifths who signed), one finds that 213 or almost 40 per cent voted consistently country, 235 or almost 44 per cent consistently court, 59

Revisions', *Journ, Brit. Stud.* (1967) vi, 45–67. See too, W. A. Speck, 'The Choice of a Speaker in 1705', *Bul. Inst. Hist. Res.* (1963), xxxvii.

[2] The letters given below are those employed by Horwitz, that is, a–h plus the manuscript list of 1698: (a) Supporters of the Sacheverell clause (d) Opponents of making William and Mary King and queen (g) The junto blacklist of 1701 (see list II, below) (h) 'A List of 223 Honest Gentlemen, who signalized themselves in the Defence of the Rights of the Commons of England in the Point of Impeachments.' The manuscript list of 1698 possibly regarding support and opposition to the ministry.

[3] (c) The king's supporters during the final stages of the disbandment crisis.

[4] (b) and (f) Voted for or against the court proposal to devalue the guinea to 22 shillings in March, 1696. (e) Refused to subscribe to the association.

or nearly 11 per cent voted inconsistently, while 31 or between 5 per cent and 6 per cent did not vote.[5] While the percentage of inconsistent and non-voters is small, the court's margin of victory is still smaller. Under different circumstances, the situation could be radically altered. The comparative unanimity of the commons against court proposals for a large standing army during the last session of this parliament needs no further discussion.

Nor are all of the reign's recorded divisions discussed. Two manuscript lists show a very different picture from Horwitz's theory of continuity. An opposition list of 1694, possibly of those favouring constitutional reform, indicates that almost as many voted consistently court in the recorded divisions of the subsequent parliament as voted consistently country.[6] A list of 1701, possibly of supporters for Harley's project for the succession and concomitant limitations, also demonstrates the fluidity of party; almost a third of the junto's blacklist are excluded, while a considerable number of independent whigs are included.[7] Although Horwitz makes a great deal of the fact that only two per cent of those refusing the association changed sides to support the court in 1699, he utterly ignores the obvious corollary; namely that virtually everyone

---

[5] In addition to the two aforementioned lists, the following were also employed in arriving at these results: those voting for or against the attainder of Sir John Fenwick on 25 November 1696 (this list is being dealt with by Mr Rawlins of the Institute of Historical Research, see below) those voting *pro* or *con* in what may have been a division over the creation of a royal (as opposed to a parliamentary) board of trade in early February 1695/6. The list may be roughly dated by the inclusion of Sir John Bushnall (returned in a by-election of 8 January 1695/6) and Wharton, who was created a peer on 6 February. The question of the creation of a parliamentary or royal board of trade virtually dominated the debates during the early days of the month. Those marked as doubtful are counted in the tabulating. I am indebted for knowledge of the existence of this list to Dr W. A. Speck. It is of interest that the voting records of the knights of the shire alone reflect similar proportions. Of these 97 members, 44 voted consistently country, 40 consistently court while 11 voted inconsistently and 2 did not vote. The lists may be found in my thesis 'The Country Party in the Reign of William III' (D.Phil., Oxon.) ff. 375–93 and are being examined by Dr Burton, Mr Rawlins and others in a forthcoming article dealing with the division lists of the 1695–8 parliament. [It has been impossible to obtain a preview as the proofs have been under considerable revision, but it is believed that neither list I nor list II (given below) will be mentioned.]

[6] About 40 voted court on two or more divisions and 45 consistently country. I am indebted for this computation to Dr Burton.

[7] See list II (below).

else in the house signed it. Perforce then, a very large percentage 'changed sides' in 1698, and this statistic is not to be found in his scientific findings (Table II).

Even this table, moreover, cannot hide the fact that over a fifth of the convention extremists were to 'change sides'. A tenth might be overlooked, but a fifth! A very significant fifth at that.[8] To those who must have whig equal court and tory equal country, perhaps this still will not be an obstacle; they might simply swallow hard and say that the country whigs had deserted their party. But to others it should have its effect, especially when one considers the slender majorities, the many others who supported them on major questions of the reign, and the fact that they supported the very principles which the junto whigs appeared to abandon.

It would be wrong to be purely destructive. Dr Horwitz's analysis shows that often when there was no strong country position, considerable regularity in voting did exist. And if in the closing days of William's reign court-country conflicts gave way to 'the rage of party', it must be remembered that this was a lesser storm, perhaps even a harbinger, albeit a ferocious one, of impending political stability for an island nation. Whig-tory divisions were signs of a willingness to count heads (the heads which counted) to avoid breaking them. It must be reiterated, however, that country principles could be said to be submerged then, or even in Anne's reign, only just below the surface, and they were always ready to tear the bottom from any ship of state failing to pay them sufficient heed.

LIST I: *Opposition in the Last Session of the Officers' Parliament.*

The following are included in what is possibly a partial listing of members likely to support the triennial bill in the event of a division during the 1694–5 sessions.[9] For a discussion of the matter, see above, pp. 111–13 and 51–2. I wish to thank the marquis of Downshire, for permission to print the list.

The following abbreviations are employed:

A A court clerk's list of 103 placemen in the summer-autumn of 1692. P.R.O., S.P. Dom., King William's Chest, 81/4. Printed in Browning *Danby*, iii, 184–7.

---

[8] See above, pp. 51–2.   [9] Berks. R.O., Trumbull Add. MSS. 13/68.

B Robert Harley's list of 97 members which is only mentioned in *H.M.C. Portland*, iii, 39, may be found in B.M. Portland loan 29/206 ff. 171–2.

C The non-juror Samuel Grascombe's list of 136 placemen, *c.* 1693. Bodl. Rawlinson MSS D.846 ff. 1–6.

X Those Grascombe no longer believed to be courtiers when he corrected his list during the last session of the 1690–5 parliament. *Ibid.*

D The 'D' which precedes twenty-nine names in this opposition list, probably means *doubtful*, that is, those who were not thought to be definitely voting for the issue(s) in question.

T Those *tories* thought to have voted against making the prince and princess of Orange king and queen in the convention parliament. *Somers Tracts*, x, 256–7.

S Those thought to have voted for the *Sacheverell* clause in the convention parliament. Oldmixon, *History of England under William and Mary, Anne and George I*, p. 36.[10]

The constituencies and dates of by-elections are added.

NAME	DATE OF RETURN (*in the event of a by-election*)	COUNTY, CITY, UNIVERSITY OR PLACE	PLACE AND VOTING RECORD
Sr. Humphrey Foster [Forster]		Co. Berks	
Coll. [Charles] Godfrey	26 Oct. 1691	Chipping Wycombe	
Sr. Thomas Lee		Aylesbury	S.
[Simon] Mayne	14 Feb. 1690	Aylesbury	D.
[Thomas] Christy		Bedford	D.
[Edmund] Waller		Agmondesham	
[Richard] Beake		Wendover	A.B.C.D.
[James] Chase		Great Marlow	A.B.C.
[John] Backwell		Wendover	A.C.D.
Sr. William Whitlocke		Great Marlow	A.C.X.
Sr. Robert Cotton		Co. Cambridge	T.
[Russell? or Francis? Roberts[11]]	28 Nov. 1693	Co. Cornwall or Bodmin	
Edward Finch		Univ. Cantab.	A.C.X.
[Henry] Boyle	21 Nov. 1692	Univ. Cantab.	D.
Sr. John Mainwaring		Co. Chester	S.
Sr. Rob. Cotton of Cheshire		Co. Chester	A.B.C.S.

[10] Indebtedness is expressed for the last computation to Dr Ivor Burton.
[11] T. if Francis. Not counted.

Sir Thom. Grosvenor		Chester	D.
Bernard Granville		Launceston	B.
Lord Henry Hyde	15 Nov. 1692	Launceston	C.
Sir Bourchier Wrey		Liskeard	A.T.
Sir Bevil Granville		Lostwithiel	A.B.C.
Charles Godolphin		Helston	A.B.C.T.
[Samuel] Travers		Grampound	B.C.
Shadrach Vincent		Fowey	C.
Sir Joseph Tredenham		St Mawes	A.B.T.
[John] Tredenham	9 April 1690	St Mawes	A.C.X.
Sr. George Fletcher		Co. Cumberland	
[Christopher] Musgrave		Carlisle	C.
Sir Edw. Seymour		Exeter	A.B.C.X.T.
Christopher Bale		Exeter[12]	A.B.T.
[Henry] Seymour[13]		Totnes	T. (?)
Thomas Colson [Colston]	14 Dec. 1692	Totnes	D.
John Granvile		Plymouth	
Sr. George Hutchins		Barnstaple	A.C.X.
Sr. Joseph Herne		Dartmouth	A.B.C.
[Edward] Nicholas		Shaftesbury	A.B.T.
[William] Cullyford		Corfe Castle	B.C.
[William] Lambton		Co. Durham	T.
William Tempest		Durham	
[George] Morland		Durham	T.
Sir John Gise [Guise]		Co. Gloucester	A.C.S.
[William] Cooke		Gloucester	T.
John Howe		Cirencester	S.
Paul Foley		Hereford	S.
L[ord] [Thomas] Coningsby		Leominster	A.B.C.
[John Dutton] Colt		Leominster	A.B.C.S.
Young Mr [Thomas] Foley	5 June 1691	Weobley	D.
Tho. Foley		Co. Worcester	S.
His Son [Thomas Foley Jun.]	21 Nov. 1694	Stafford	D.
[Ralph] Freeman		Co. Hertford	
Coll. [George] Churchill		St Albans	A.C.
Sr. William Cooper		Hertford	S.
Caleb Banks	27 Oct. 1691	Rochester	C.T.
Sr. John Banks		Queenborough	C.T.
Coll. [Robert] Crawford		Queenborough	A.B.C.
Coll. [James] Stanley		Co. Lancs.	B.C.
Fitton Gerrard	23 Feb. 1693/4	Clitheroe	
Mr [Edmund] Webb		Cricklade, Wilts.	A.C.
Thomas Preston		Lancaster	

[12] Returned in by-election later than division for making William and Mary king and queen.

[13] Probably Henry, as Edward would probably be called 'Young Mr Seymour' or the like as with the Foleys. Counted.

Sr. Christopher Greenfield		Preston	C.
Sr. Edward Chisenall	5 Dec. 1690	Preston	T.
L[ord] Castleton		Co. Lincoln	A.B.C.
[Hon. Peregrine Bertie]			
Mr Vice Chamberlain		Preston	
His Brother [Hon. Philip]			
Bertie	6 Dec. 1694	Stamford	
[Hon. ?] Charles Bertie		Stamford	C.X.T.D.
Sr. Stephen Fox	9 Nov. 1691	Westminster	A.C.
Sr. Walter Clarges		Westminster	D.
Sr. William Pritchard		London	
Sr. Sam Dashwood		London	A.B.C.
Sr. Tho. Vernon		London	
Sr. Jo[hn] Fleet	2 Mar. 1692/2	London	D.
[Thomas] Blofield		Norwich	A.C.
[Daniel] Bedingfield		King's Lynn	D.
[George] England		Great Yarmouth	S.
[Samuel] Fuller		Great Yarmouth	
Baptiste May		Thetford	A.C.
Sr. Rob. Howard		Castle Rising	A.B.C.S.D.
Gilbert Dolben		Peterborough	T.
Coll. [Henry] Mordant	2 Jan. 1691/2	Brackley	B.C.
Thomas Andrews		Higham Ferrers	
[John] Parkhurst		Co. Northampton	A.D.
[Robert] Fenwicke		Morpeth	T.
George Nicholas	24 Nov. 1692	Morpeth	B.C.
Sr. Fran. Blake		Berwick-on-	
		Tweed	S.
Sr. Scrope Howe		Co. Nottingham	B.C.S.
Mr [Sir Ralph?] Carre of			
Newcastle		Newcastle	T.
Heneage Finch		Univ. Oxon.	D.
Henry Bertie		City Oxford	T.
Sr. Edward Norris		City Oxford	D.
Sir Tho. Littleton		New Woodstock	A.B.C.S.
[Thomas] Wheate		New Woodstock	C.
Sr. Robert Dashwood		Banbury	
[Bennet] Sherrard		Co. Rutland	
[Edward] Kynaston		Co. Salop	T.
[Hon.] Andrew Newport		Shrewsbury	T.D.
Coll. Titus	14 Jan. 1690/1	Ludlow	D.
Sir Will Forrester		Wenlock	A.B.C.D.
[George] Weld		Wenlock	T.
John Sandford	25 Sept. 1690	Minehead	T.
John Hunt		Ilchester	T.
Marquesse of Winchester		Co. Southampton	A.B.C.S.
L[ord] William Pawlett		Winchester	A.B.C.S.
Sr. Charles Wyndham		Southampton	

Sr. Benjamin Newland		Southampton	T.
[Charles] Duncomb		Yarmouth	A.B.C.
[Richard] Holt		Petersfield	
E[arl] Ranelagh		Petersfield	A.B.C.T.
[Thomas] Dore		New Lymington	B.C.T.
[Francis] Gwyn		Christchurch	B.C.T.
[Michael] Biddulph		Tamworth	
Sr. Samuel Barnardiston		Co. Suffolk	D.
[Henry] Poley		Eye	T.
Sr. Robert Davers		Bury St Edmunds	T.
[Thomas] Felton		Orford	A.B.C.
Sr. Hen[ry] Johnson		Aldeburgh	T.
William Johnson		Aldeburgh	T.
Sr. Francis Vincent		Co. Surrey	
John Arnold		Southwark	S.
Tho[mas] Howard		Bletchingly	A.B.C.S.
Sir Rob. Clayton		Bletchingly	A.B.C.S.
Sr. Jo. Parsons		Reigate	
[John] Parsons		Reigate	
[Morgan] Randyll		Guildford	D.
Sr. John Thompson		Gatton	C.X.S.
Sr. Will Thomas		Co. Sussex	
Tho. May		Chichester	
Major[John] Perry		New Shoreham	
Dr [John] Radcliffe		Bramber	
[William] Bromley		Co. Warwick	D.
[Richard] Hopkins		Coventry	
L[ord] Digby		Warwick	T.D.
Sr. Christopher Musgrave		Co. Westmorland	T.
[William] Cheyne[14]		Appleby	T.
Sir Charles Raleigh		Downton	
[Maurice] Bocland		Downton	S.D.
L[ord] Fitzharding	20 April 1691	Hindon	C.
John Methuen		Devizes	A.B.
Goodwin Wharton		Malmesbury	
[George] Booth	3 Feb. 1691/2	Malmesbury	A.B.C.
[Charles] Fox		Cricklade	A.B.C.T.
Sr. Jonathan Raymond		Great Bedwyn	
Thomas Neale		Ludgershall	A.C.
Sr. Jo[hn] Ernle[y]		Marlborough	T.
L[ord] Fairfax		Co. York	A.B.C.
Sr. Jo[hn] Kaye		Co. York	
Rob. Waller		York	C.
John Ramsden		Kingston-on-Hull	

[14] Returned in by-election after vote for making William and Mary king and queen.

John Hungerford	28 April 1692	Scarborough	
Sr. Jonathan Jenings		Ripon	A.B.C.T.
Sr. Henry Goodricke		Boroughbridge	A.B.C.
Sr. Will[iam] Strickland		Malton	S.
[William] Palmer		Malton	S.
[Thomas] Frankland		Thirsk	A.B.C.
[Christopher] Tankard		Aldborough	A.B.C.T.
Sr. Jo[hn] Austen		Rye	D.
[Robert] Austen		Winchelsea	A.B.C.S.D.
Sr. Charles Sedley		New Romney	
[John] Brewer		New Romney	C.
Sr. Philip Butler [Boteler]		Hythe	
[Thomas] Papillon		Dover	S.
Thomas Bulkeley		Beaumaris	
L[ord] Bulkely		Co. Anglesey	
[Richard] Vaughan		Carmarthen	
Sir Richard Middleton		Co. Denbigh	T.
Edward Brereton		Denbigh	T.
Sr. Roger Pulleston		Co. Flint	
[Thomas, or Bussy] Mansell[15]		Cardiff	
Sir Jo[hn] Wynne		Co. Merioneth	
Sr. Will[iam] Wogan		Haverfordwest	A.C.T.
[Robert] Harley		New Radnor	S.

TABULATION

Total placemen		*Placemen in opposition list*	
A.B.C. (inc. in all lists)	$59 - 9 (x) = 50$	A.B.C.	$30 - 1 (x) = 29$
A. (only)	$14 = 14$	A.	$2 = 2$
A.B. (only)	$8 = 8$	A.B.	$4 = 4$
A.C. (only)	$20 - 7 (x) = 13$	A.C.	$8 - 4 (x) = 4$
B.C. (only)	$25 - \text{nil} (x) = 25$	B.C.	$7 - \text{nil} (x) = 7$
C. (only)	$31 - 2 (x) = 29$	C.	$12 - 2 (x) = 10$

Those placemen sitting in the last session of the 1690–5 parliament:

All placemen		*Opposition placemen*	
A.B.C.	$-x. = 50$	A.B.C.	$-x. = 29$
A.C.	$-x. = 13$	A.C.	$-x. = 4$
B.C.	$-x. = 25$	B.C.	$-x. = 7$
C.	$-x. = 29$	C.	$-x. = 10$
Total	$= 117$	Total	$= 50$

Thus 42 per cent of the opposition listed are placemen.

---

[15] T. if Thomas, S. if Bussy, not counted as T. or S.

Early list: Those placemen included in the early list also listed as place-
            men in the last session:

All

A.B.C. —x. and A.C. —x. = 63

Opposition

A.B.C. —x. and A.C. —x. = 33

Thus 52 per cent of the placemen on the earlier list are in opposition.

Later lists: Those placemen only included in the latter lists sitting in the
            last session:

All

B.C. —x. and C. —x. = 54

Opposition

B.C. —x. and C. —x. = 17

Thus only 31 per cent of the newer placemen are in opposition

LIST II: *Divisions in the* 1700/1 *Parliament*

The first of the two lists of the 1700/1 parliament is similar to that of
1694 in demonstrating the fluidity of party in William's reign. It was
composed early in the life of the parliament and might be one of those
who had concurred in Harley's election as speaker and were likely to
support his project for the succession with concomitant limitations.[16]
That as many as 229 should be included shows considerable bipartisan
support, as does the list's very mixed composition which includes not
only such opposition leaders as Harley, Harcourt, Hammond and Howe
and many placemen including Sir Thomas Littleton and James Lowther,
but the then comparatively independent whig, Robert Walpole.
Members of such junto families as the Russells, Whartons and Mont-
agues are excluded and so too are Sir Edward Seymour and Sir Christopher Musgrave.

---

[16] The list might be one of those who supported Harley's candidacy as
speaker save for the omission of such friends as Sir Christopher Musgrave
and Sir Edward Seymour as well as the inclusion of Richard Gulston who was
elected in a by-election of 21 February, eleven days after Harley's election.
No one is included who was elected after that date and Gilbert Heathcote
was expelled the next day. It seems quite probable that the list was prepared
as the house went into committee over the problem of the succession and
the placing of additional limitations upon the prerogative in late February.
Considering the size and composition of the list there seems little likelihood
that it could have been drawn up for any other purpose. See p. 212.

The second list is the black list of those variously supposed to have supported the impeachments of the junto minister or the proceedings taken against the Kentish petitioners. 112 or over two-thirds of the 164 names[17] are also included in the earlier list, but the smaller number shows quite clearly the more limited appeal of an attack upon men as well as measures.

Abbreviations:

H Included in the bi-partisan list of February 1700/1 which is possibly one indicating support for Harley's project for the succession. B.M. Add. MSS. 28091 (Osborne Papers)

B Included in the black list of those variously supposed to have supported the impeachment or the gating of the Kentish petitioners. Various printings, the one employed is James Drake, *Some Necessary Considerations Relating to all future Elections of Members to Serve in Parliament* (1702), pp. 23–8.

BEDFORD
Lord Edward Russell
Sir William Gostwick, knt. and bart.
Samuel Rolt, esq.
William Spencer, esq.

BERKS
Sir Humphrey Forster, bart. H
Richard Nevill, esq. H
Symon Harcourt, esq. HB
Sir Owen Buckingham, knt.
Francis Knollys, esq. H
William Jennens, esq. HB
Thomas Renda, esq. HB
John Lord Viscount Fitzhardinge H
Richard Topham, esq. H

BUCKS
Goodwin Wharton, esq.
William Lord Cheyne, Viscount Newhaven HB

Sir John Garrard, bart.
John Drake, esq. *vice* Sir John Garrard, bart. deceased.
    By-election 19 February 1700/1
Sir Samuel Garrard, bart., B *vice* William Lord Cheyne, who elected to serve for the county of Bucks
    By-election 10 March 1700/1
Sir Thomas Lee, bart.
James Herbert, esq. HB
Sir Richard Temple, bart., of Stow, county Bucks
Sir Edmund Denton, bart., of Hillesdon, county Bucks
Charles Godfrey, esq.
Fleetwood Dormer, esq.
Sir James Etheredge, knt. HB
James Chase, esq. H
John Backwell, esq. HB
Richard Hampden, esq.

---

[17] 166 names if one counts the Mitchel listed for Kent and the Seymour for Sussex. Neither name, however, appears in the returns for those counties (Sir Edward Seymour is blacklisted in the Devon entry).

CAMBRIDGE

John Lord Cutts, Baron of Goran in Ireland H

Sir Rushout Cullen, bart.

Henry Boyle, esq.

Anthony Hammond, esq. HB

Sir John Cotton, bart. H

Sir Henry Pickering, bart. H

CHESTER

Sir John Manwaring, bart.

Sir Robert Cotton, knt. and bart. H

Sir Henry Bunbury, bart.

Peter Shakerley, esq. HB

CORNWALL

Hugh Boscawen, esq.

John Specott, esq. H

Richard Edgcumbe, esq., *vice* Hugh Boscawen, esq., deceased
By-election 25 June 1701

Russell Robartes, esq.

John Hoblyn, esq. HB

Francis Robarts, esq.

John Tregagle, esq. B

Thomas Wentworth, *alias* Watson, esq., *vice* Francis Roberts, esq., who elected to serve for Tregoney.
By-election 21 March 1700/1

Sir William Coryton, bart., of West Newton Ferrars

Robert Rolle, esq., of Stevenstone, county Devon H

Henry Manaton, esq., of Harwood, county Cornwall HB

Dennys Glynn, esq., of Glynn, county Cornwall

John Williams, esq., of Bodinneck, county Cornwall

John Granvill, esq. HB

Sir William Scawen, knt. H

Francis Scobell, esq. HB

Charles Godolphin, esq. HB

Sidney Godolphin, esq. HB

The Hon. Henry Hide, commonly called Lord Henry Hide HB

William Cary, esq. H

William Bridges, esq. H

Henry Darell, esq.

Francis Godolphin, esq. eldest son of Sidney Lord Godolphin HB

Sir Henry Seymour, bart., of Langley HB

James Kendall, esq., of Killigarth, county Cornwall

John Mountsteven, esq., of Lancarffe, county Cornwall HB

Sir John Molesworth, knt. and bart.

John Buller, jun., esq.

George Booth, esq., *vice* John Buller, jun., esq., deceased
By-election 18 April 1701

William Beaw, Ll.D. B

Sir Richard Vivian, bart. B[18]

Francis Stratford, esq. HB

John Prideaux, esq., of Souldon HB

Samuel Trefusis, esq.

Alexander Pendarves, esq. HB

John Specot, esq.

Henry Flemming, esq.

Daniel Eliot, esq., *vice* John Specot, esq., who elected to serve for the county of Cornwall
By-election 2 April 1701

James Praed, esq.

Benjamin Overton, esq.

Sir Joseph Tredenham, knt. HB

John Tredenham, esq. HB

James Buller, esq., of Shillingham, county Cornwall

Alexander Pendarves, esq., of Roskrow, county Cornwall

Thomas Carew, esq., of Barly, county Devon, *vice* Alexander Pendarves, esq., who elected to serve for Penryn.
By-election 22 March 1700/1

Francis Robarts, esq. H

Hugh Fortescue, esq.

Hugh Fortescue, esq.

---

[18] Return amended by Order of the House, 20 March 1700–1; the name of Anthony Row, esq., erased and that of Sir Richard Vivian, bart., substituted.

Henry Vincent, esq. H

Sir John Hawles, knt. Solicitor General, *vice* Hugh Fortescue, esq., who elected to serve for Tregony. By-election 4 March. 1700/1

CUMBERLAND

Richard Musgrave, esq. H

Wilfrid Lawson, esq.

Philip Howard, esq. H

James Lowther, esq. H

William Seymour, esq. B

George Fletcher, esq. B

DERBY

William Marquess of Hartington, eldest son of William Duke of Devonshire

John Lord Roos, eldest son of John Earl of Rutland

James Cavendish, esq., younger son of William Duke of Devonshire

Sir Charles Pye, bart.

DEVON

William Courtenay, esq., of Powderham Castle, county Devon HB

Samuel Rolle, esq., of Heanton, County Devon HB

William Stawell, esq. H

Richard Duke, jun., esq. H

Nicholas Hooper, esq., serjeant-at-law B

Arthur Champneys, esq.

Sir Rowland Gwynne, knt.

Peter Kinge, esq., of the Temple, London

William Cowper, esq., *vice* Sir Rowland Gwynn, knt., who elected to serve for the county of Brecon By-election 7 March 1701

Frederick Herne, esq. HB

Nathaniel Herne, esq. HB

Sir Edward Seymour, bart. B

Sir Bartholomew Shower, knt. HB

Sir William Drake, knt. and bart., of Ash, county Devon

Sir Walter Yonge, bart., of Eastcott, county Devon

William Harris, esq.

Thomas Northmore, esq. B

Charles Trelawny, esq. HB

Henry Trelawny, esq. HB

Courtenay Croker, esq.

Martyn Ryder, esq.

Lord Edward Russell, son of William Duke of Bedford, deceased

Charles Spencer, esq., son and heir of Robert Earl of Sunderland

Thomas Bere, esq.

Francis Gwyn, esq. HB

Thomas Coulson, esq. HB

DORSET

Thomas Strangwais, esq. HB

Thomas Freke, esq. HB

Alexander Pitfield, esq.

William Gulston, esq.

John Bankes, esq. H

Richard Fownes, esq. HB

Nathaniel Napier, esq. HB

Thomas Trenchard, esq. H

Robert Henley, esq. H

Joseph Paice, merchant

Sir William Phipard, knt.

William Joliffe, esq.

Edward Nicholas, esq. HB

Thomas Chafin, esq. HB

Thomas Erle, esq. H

George Pitt, esq.

Sir Edward Ernle, bart., *vice* the Hon. Thomas Earle, esq., who elected to serve for Portsmouth. By-election 5 March 1700/1

Henry Thyne, esq. HB

Charles Churchill, esq. HB

Maurice Ashley, esq.

Michael Harvey, esq. B

DURHAM

William Lambton, esq., of Lambton, county Durham HB

Lionel Vane, esq., of Long Newton, county Durham H

Charles Mountagu, esq., citizen and alderman of Durham

Thomas Conyers, esq. HB

ESSEX

Sir Charles Barrington, bart. HB
Sir Francis Masham, bart.
Sir Thomas Cooke, knt. HB
Sir Isaac Rebow, knt.
Sir Thomas Davall, knt., Recorder of
  Harwich HB
Dennis Lyddell, esq. H
Irby Montague, esq.
William Fytche, esq. HB

GLOUCESTER

John Howe, esq. HB
Sir Richard Cocks, bart.
Sir William Daines, knt.
Robert Yate, esq.
James Thynn, esq. B
Charles Coxe, esq. B
William Selwin, esq. H
John Bridgman, esq.
Richard Dowdeswell, esq.
Edmund Bray, esq., of Barrington

HEREFORD

Sir John Williams, knt.
Henry Gorges, esq.
Thomas Foley, esq., of Stoke Edith B
James Brydges, esq. HB
Thomas Lord Coningsby, Baron of
  Clanbrazell, in Ireland, a Privy
  Councillor
Edward Harley, esq. B[19]
Henry Cornwall, esq. H
John Birch, esq.

HERTFORD

Ralph Freeman, jun., esq. HB
Thomas Halsey, esq. HB
Charles Caesar, esq. HB
Thomas Filmer, esq.
Richard Goulston, esq., *vice* Thomas
  Filmer, esq., deceased HB
  By-election 21 February 1700/1
George Churchill, esq. H
Joshua Lomax, esq.
John Gape, jun., esq., *vice* Joshua

Lomax, esq., whose election was
declared void B
  By-election 19 March 1700/1

HUNTINGDON

John Dryden, esq.
John Proby, esq.
Charles Boyle, esq.
Francis Wortley, esq.

KENT

Sir Thomas Hales, bart.
Thomas Meredith, esq.
George Sayer, esq.
Henry Lee, esq. B
Sir Robert Marsham, knt. and bart.
Thomas Bliss, esq. HB
Robert Crawford, esq. H
Thomas King, esq. H
Sir Joseph Williamson, knt.
Sir Clowdisley Shovell, knt. H

LANCASTER

James Stanley, esq.
Richard Bold, esq. B
Thomas Stringer, esq.
Christopher Lister, esq. H
Robert Heysham, merchant B
Roger Kirkby, esq.
Sir William Norris, knt.
William Clayton, esq. B
Thomas Legh, esq., of Ridge, county
  Chester HB
Thomas Brotherton, esq., of Gray's
  Inn, county Middlesex HB
Edward Rigby, esq.
Henry Ashurst, esq., Attorney Gen-
  eral for the County Palatine of
  Lancaster
Sir Roger Bradshaigh, bart.
Orlando Bridgman, esq.

LEICESTER

John Verney, esq. HB
John Wilkins, esq. HB
Sir William Villiers, bart., of
  Brookesby, county Leicester

---

[19] Return amended by Order of the House, 3 April 1701; the name of
John Dutton Colt, esq., erased, and that of Edward Harley, esq., substituted.

Laurence Carter, jun., esq., of le
Newark, near Leicester н

LINCOLN
Charles Dymocke, esq. н
Sir John Thorold, bart. н
Edmund Boulter, esq. в
Sir William Yorke, knt.
Thomas Baptist Maners, esq. н
Sir William Ellis, bart., of Nocton,
county Lincoln н
William Cotesworth, esq., of London
Thomas Vyner, esq., of Topholme,
county Lincoln нв
Sir John Bolles, bart. нв
Sir Thomas Meres, knt. н
William Cecill, esq., of Burghley,
county Northampton нв
Charles Bertie, esq., of Uffington,
county Lincoln нв

LONDON AND MIDDLESEX
Hugh Smithson, esq. в
Warwick Lake, esq. нв
Sir Robert Clayton, knt., alderman н
Sir William Ashhurst, knt., alderman
н
Sir William Withers, knt., alderman
Gilbert Heathcott, esq. н
Sir John Fleet, knt., alderman, *vice*
Gilbert Heathcote, esq., expelled
the house.
By-election 20 March 1700/1 в
James Vernon, esq.
Thomas Crosse, esq. нв

MONMOUTH
John Morgan, esq.,
Sir John Williams, bart. н
John Morgan, merchant of London

NORFOLK
Roger Townsend, esq. н
Sir Jacob Astley, knt. and bart. нв
Thomas Howard, esq.
Robert Walpole, esq. н
Robert Cecil, esq., *vice* Thomas
Howard, esq., deceased
By-election 30 April 1701
Sir John Turner, knt. н

Sir Charles Turner, knt. н
Robert Davey, esq. нв
Thomas Blofield, esq. нв
Sir Joseph Williamson, knt., of Cob-
ham Hall, county Kent
Edmund Soame, esq., of Deerham
Grange, county Norfolk в
Thomas Hanmer, esq., of Euston
Hall, county Suffolk, *vice* Sir
Joseph Williamson, knt., who
elected to serve for Rochester
By-election 19 March 1700/1
George England, esq. н
Samuel Fuller, esq. н

NORTHAMPTON
Sir Justinian Isham, bart. нв
John Parkhurst, esq.
Charles Egerton, esq. н
Harry Mordant, esq.
Thomas Ekins, esq. в
Christopher Montagu, esq.
William Thursby, esq.
Thomas Andrew, esq., *vice* William
Thursby, esq. deceased
By-election 21 February 1700/1
Sidney Wortley, *alias* Montagu, esq.
Gilbert Dolben, esq. нв

NORTHUMBERLAND
Ferdinand Forster, esq. н
William Howard, esq. н
Ralph Grey, esq.
Samuel Ogle, esq.
William Howard, esq.
Sir Henry Belasyse, knt. н
Sir Richard Sandford, bart., *vice*
William Howard, esq., who elected
to serve for the county of North-
umberland.
By-election 31 May 1701
William Carr, esq. н
Sir Henry Liddell, bart.

NOTTINGHAM
Sir Thomas Willoughby, bart., of
Woolaton, county Nottingham н
Gervase Eyre, esq., of Rampton,
county Nottingham н

John Rayner, esq. HB
William Pierrepont, esq. H
Sir George Markham, bart. H
Robert Sacheverell, esq. B[20]
John Thornhagh, esq. H
Sir Willoughby Hickman, bart. H[21]

OXFORD
Sir Robert Jenkinson, bart. HB
Sir Edward Norreys, knt. HB
Charles North, esq. B[22]
Heneage Finch, esq. HB
Sir Christopher Musgrave, bart.
William Bromley, esq., of Bagington, county Warwick, B. *vice* Sir Christopher Musgrave, bart., who elected to serve for the county of Westmorland.
By-election 21 March 1700/1
Thomas Rowney, esq. HB
Francis Norreys, esq. HB
James Bertie, esq. HB
Sir Thomas Littleton, bart. H

RUTLAND
Sir Thomas Mackworth, bart. HB
Richard Halford, esq. B

SALOP
Sir Humphrey Briggs, bart., of Haughton, county Salop
Robert Lloyd, esq., of Aston, county Salop
Charles Mason, esq., of Rockley, county Salop
George Walcott, esq., of London
Sir Edward Acton, bart., Recorder of Bridgnorth HB
Roger Pope, jun., esq., alderman
Sir Thomas Powys, knt. HB
William Gower, esq.

John Kynaston, esq., of Hordley, county Salop H
Richard Mitton, esq., of Horlston, county Salop
Sir William Forrester, knt.
George Weld, esq. H

SOMERSET
Sir John Trevelyan, bart.
John Hunt, esq. H
William Blathwayt, esq. H
Alexander Popham, esq.
John Gilbert, esq.
George Balch, esq.
Sir Philip Sydenham, bart.
James Anderton, esq. B
Sir Thomas Travell, knt.
Sir Richard Newman, bart.
Alexander Lutterell, esq.
Sir James Banke, knt. H
Henry Portman, esq.
Edward Clarke, esq.
Sir Francis Warre, bart., B *vice* Henry Portman, esq., who elected to serve for Wells
By-election 17 March 1700/1
William Coward, serjeant-at-law, Recorder of Wells H
Henry Portman, esq. HB

SOUTHAMPTON
Thomas Jervoise, esq. B
Richard Chaundeler, esq.
John Smyth, esq., Chancellor and Under Treasurer of the Exchequer, one of the Lords of the Treasury, and a Privy Councillor
Francis Sheppherd, esq., of London
Edward Viscount Cornbury
William Ettricke, esq., of the Middle Temple, London HB

---

[20] Return amended by Order of the House, 10 June 1701; the name of George Gregory, esq., erased, and that of Robert Sacheverell, esq., substituted.

[21] Return amended by Order of the House, 15 April, 1701; the name of Thomas White, esq., erased and that of Sir Willoughby Hickman, bart., substituted.

[22] Double Return of the same date; that by which John Dormer, esq., was returned was taken off the file by Order of the House.

Thomas Dore, esq.

Paul Burrard, esq.

John Lord Cutts, Captain and Governor of the Isle of Wight

Samuel Shephard, sen., esq.

Henry Greenhill, esq., *vice* John Lord Cutts, who elected to serve for the county of Cambridge
By-election 3 March 1700/1

James Worseley, esq., of Pilewell, county Southampton

Thomas Hopson, esq., of Weybridge, county Surrey H

Ralph Bucknall, esq.

Richard Markes, esq.

Thomas Erle, Major General of the Forces, and Governor of Portsmouth H

Sir George Rooke, knt., one of the Lords Commissioners of the Admiralty H

Roger Mompesson, esq., Recorder of Southampton B

Mitford Crowe, merchant

Anthony Sturt, esq., of Hickfield HB

John Pitts, esq., of Crows Hall

Lord James Russell

Richard Woolaston, esq.

Lord William Pawlet

George Rodney Bridges, esq.

Henry Homes, esq.

Anthony Morgan, esq.

STAFFORD

Henry Pagett, esq. H

Edward Bagott, esq.H

Richard Dyott, esq. H

William Walmisley, esq.

Sir John Leveson Gower, bart. HB

Rowland Cotton, esq.

John Chetwynd, esq. H

Thomas Foley, jun., esq. HB

Sir Henry Gough, knt. HB

Thomas Guy, esq.

SUFFOLK

Sir Samuel Barnardiston, bart. B

[Lyonel] Earl of Dysert in Scotland
HB

Sir Henry Johnson, knt. HB

William Johnson, esq.

Sir Robert Davers, bart. HB

John Hervey, esq.

Sir Charles Blois, bart. HB

Robert Kemp. esq.

Spencer Compton, esq.

Sir Joseph Jekyll, knt., serjeant-at-law

Joseph Martin, esq.

Sir Charles Duncomb, knt. HB

Sir Edmund Bacon, bart. HB

Sir Edward Turner, knt. HB

Sir Gervase Elwes, bart.

Sir John Cordell, bart. B

SURREY

Sir Richard Onslow, bart.

John Weston, esq. HB

Sir Edward Gresham. bart.

John Ward, esq.

Thomas Turgis, esq.

Maurice Thompson, esq. H

Morgan Randyll, esq., of the parish of St Martha, county Surrey

Denzil Onslow, esq., of Pirford, county Surrey

Sir Theophilus Oglethorpe, knt. HB

George Woodroffe, esq.

Sir John Parsons, knt. HB

Stephen Hervey, esq.

Charles Cox, esq.

John Cholmley, esq.

SUSSEX

Henry Lumley, esq. H

John Miller, esq. B

John Cooke, esq.

Edmund Dummer, esq.

Thomas Stringer, esq.

Thomas Owen, esq., of Gray's Inn

Francis Conway, esq., *vice* Thomas Stringer, who elected to servef or Clitheroe, county Lancaster.
By-election 18 March 1700/1

Sir Thomas May, knt., of Raughmare, county Sussex.

William Elson, esq. B

John Conyers, esq. B

Mathew Pryor, esq. B
Henry Yates, esq.
Henry Cowper, esq. B
Thomas Pelham, esq.
Sir Thomas Trevor, knt. Attorney General H
John Lewknor, esq., of Westdean, county Sussex
Lawrence Alcock, gent.
Nathaniel Gould, esq.
Charles Sergison, esq. H
Sir John Fagg, bart.
Sir Edward Hungerford, knt. of the bath
Sir Robert Fagg, bart., *vice* Sir John Fagg, bart., deceased
By-election 4 March 1700/1
Charles Goring, esq., *vice* Sir Robert Fagg, bart., whose election was declared void. B
By-election 16 April 1701

WARWICK
Sir John Mordant, bart., of Walton de Vile, county Warwick HB
Sir Charles Shuckburgh, bart., of Shuckburgh, county Warwick H
Sir Christopher Hales, bart. B
Thomas Hopkins, esq.
Sir Henry Gough, knt.
Thomas Guy, esq.
Francis Grevile, esq. HB
Sir Thomas Wagstaffe, knt. HB

WESTMORLAND
Henry Grahame, esq., of Leavens, county Westmorland HB
Sir Christopher Musgrave, knt. and bart., of Hartley Castle, county Westmorland B
Gervase Pierpoint, esq. H
Wharton Dunch, esq., of Pusay, county Berks

WILTS
Sir George Hungerford, knt. B

Richard How, esq. H
Francis Stonehouse, esq.
Charles Davenant, Ll.D. HB
Walter Long, esq.
Walter Hungerford, esq.
John Lord Mordant B
Walter White, esq.
Edmond Dunch, esq., of East Wittenham, county Berks
Sir Stephen Fox, knt., of Whitehall, county Middlesex H
Sir Francis Child, knt. HB
Francis Merewether, esq. B
John Eyre, esq.
Carew Rawleigh, esq.
William Ashe, esq. H
Edward Ashe, esq.
Sir James Howe, bart. B
George Morley, esq.[23]
Edmund Webb, esq. H
John Webb, esq. H
Edward Pauncfort, esq.
Samuel Shepherd, jun., esq.
Richard Earl of Ranelagh
John Jeffryes, esq. HB
William Harvey, esq.
Charles Mompesson, esq.
Robert Eyre, esq., Recorder of Salisbury
Sir Thomas Mompesson, knt., of the Close of Sarum
Charles Fox, esq., of Whitehall, *vice* Sir Thomas Mompesson, knt., deceased
By-election 9 July 1701
Robert Bertie, esq. HB
Richard Lewis, esq. H
John Gauntlett, esq. H
Thomas Phipps, esq. B
Henry St John, jun., esq. HB
Henry Pinnell, esq. B

WORCESTER
William Walsh, esq. H
Sir John Pakington, bart. HB

[23] Return amended by Order of the House, 13 May 1701. The name of Reynalds Calthorp, esq., erased, and that of George Morley, esq., substituted.

Salwey Winnington, esq. HB
Thomas Foley, esq.
Charles Cocks, esq.
Philip Foley, esq., *vice* Thomas Foley,
    esq., deceased B
    By-election 25 February 1700/1
Sir James Rushout, bart.
John Rudge, esq.
Thomas Wylde, esq.
Samuel Swift, esq. B

YORK
Thomas Lord Fairfax, Baron of
    Cameroon in Scotland
Sir John Kay, bart. H
Robert Monckton, esq. H
Cyrill Arthington, esq. H
Sir Michael Warton, knt. H
Ralph Warton, esq.
Sir Henry Goodrick, knt. and bart.,
    a Privy Councillor H
Sir Bryan Stapylton, bart. H
Sir Robert Bedingfield, knt. B
Anthony Duncomb, esq. HB
Sir William St Quintin, bart.
William Maisters, merchant
Robert Byerley, esq. H
Christopher Stockdale, esq. H
Sir William Strickeland, bart.
William Palmes, esq.
Sir William Hustler, knt. H
Ralph Milbank, esq. H
Sir John Bland, bart. HB
John Bright, esq. H
Thomas Yorke, esq.
James Darcy, esq. H
John Aislaby, esq. H
Jonathan Jenings, esq. H
Arthur Viscount Irwin, in Scotland
Sir Charles Hotham, bart.
Sir Godfrey Copley, bart. HB
Sir Thomas Frankland, bart. H
Sir William Robinson, bart. H
Edward Thompson, esq.

CINQUE PORTS
Sir Charles Hedges, knt. H
Mathew Aylmer, esq. H
John Pulteney, esq.

Peter Gott, esq.
Sir Philip Boteler, bart. H
John Boteler, esq.
Sir Charles Sedley, bart.
John Brewer, esq.
Sir Robert Austen, bart.
Joseph Offley, esq.
Sir Henry Furnice, knt.
John Taylor, esq., of Bifrons, county
    Kent
John Mitchell, esq., *vice* Sir Henry
    Furnice, knt., expelled the House
    By-election 7 April 1701
Sir William Thomas, bart.
William Londes, esq. H
Thomas Newport, esq.
Robert Bristow, jun., esq.,

WALES
ANGLESEY
Richard Lord Viscount Bulkeley H
Conningsby Williams, esq., of Pen-
    mynyth, county Anglesey

BRECON
Sir Rowland Gwynne, knt.
Sir Geoffrey Jeffreys, knt., of Saint
    Mary Axe, London HB

CARDIGAN
Sir Humphrey Mackworth, knt. HB
John Lewis, esq., of Coedmore,
    county Cardigan

CARMARTHEN
Sir Rice Rudd, bart.
Richard Vaughan, esq., of Derwith,
    county Carmarthen H

CARNARVON
Thomas Bulkeley, esq., of Dinas,
    county Carnarvon H
Sir John Wynn, knt. and bart. H

DENBIGH
Sir Richard Myddleton, bart. H
Edward Brereton, esq. H

FLINT
Sir John Conway, bart. H

Thomas Mostyn, esq.

GLAMORGAN
Thomas Mansell, esq., of Britten
    Ferry
Sir Edward Stradling, bart. H

MERIONETH
Hugh Nanny, esq.
Richard Vaughan, esq., *vice* Hugh
    Nanney, esq., deceased
    By-election 29 April 1701

MONTGOMERY
Edward Vaughan, esq.
John Vaughan, esq. H

PEMBROKE
Sir Arthur Owen bart.
William Wheeler, esq.
Sir John Phillipps, bart.

RADNOR
Thomas Harley, esq. B
Robert Harley, esq., of Brampton
    Castle, county Hereford HB

Membership in the Commission of Accounts

Dec. 1690	Dec. 1690	Apr. 1694	*Votes Received* March 1694/5	Feb. 1695/6	*Membership in Parliament before 1690*	*Voting Record and Remarks**
Sir Mathew Andrews	119				(4, 5, 7)	Sach, C.O., S.A., F.R.B.T, F.D.G., F.F.A.
Robert Austen	129				(2, 3, 4, 7)	Sach. (By provision of 15 Feb. 1690/1 was excluded as a commr. of the admiralty), C.O., S.A, F.D.G., F.R.B.T.
Sir Samuel Barnardiston	104				(2, 3, 4, 5)	Opp. to James II in country, S.A., C.O., A.D.G., A.R.B.T., A.F.A.
Sir Thomas Clarges	178	131	183		(1, 2, 3, 4, 5, 6, 7)	T. Died 4 Oct. 1695.

* See table of abbreviations below.

| *Dec. 1690* | *Votes Received* | | | | *Membership in Parliament before 1690* | *Voting Record and Remarks** |
	Dec. 1690	Apr. 1694	March 1694/5	Feb. 1695/6		
Sir Peter Colleton	97				(5,7)	Sach. Died 24 March 1693/4.
Paul Foley	178	134	Vote not recorded (F. Gwyn recd. 142 but was disq.)	238	(3, 4, 5, 7)	Sach., C.O.,S.A. Speaker, March 1694/5–98.
Robert Harley	90	145	192	243	(7)	Sach., C.O., S.A., A.D.G., A.R.B.T., A.F.A.
Sir Benjamin Newlands	118				(2, 3, 4, 5, 6, 7)	T.
Sir Robert Rich	211				(6, 7)	C.O., S.A., A.D.G., A.R.B.T. Sach. (By provision of 15 Feb. 1690/1 was excluded as a commr. of the admiralty). S.A., F.D.G., F.R.B.T., F.F.A.
Apr. 1964						
Sir Edward Abney	121					S.A, F.D.G., F.R.B.T., F.F.A.
Sir Thomas Pope-Blount		134				
Sir James Houblon	110 (also casting vote)		141		(3, 4, 5, 7)	Sach., S.A., F.D.G., F.R.B.T, F.F.A. Not a member of parliament
Charles Hutchinson	122	142				Died 3 Nov. 1695.
March 1694/5						
Henry Boyle			172	228	(7)	Sach., C.O., S.A., A.D.G., A.R.B.T., A.F.A.

Dec. 1690	Votes Received Apr. 1694	March 1694/5	Feb. 1695/6	Membership in Parliament before 1690	Voting Record and Remarks*
Sir John Thompson		140		(6,7)	Sach, C.O., S.A., F.D.G., F.R.B.T. Called to upper house as Baron Haversham.
William Bromley			200	(6,7)	C.O., R.A., A.D.G., A.R.B.T., A.F.A.
Sir Thomas Dyke			185	(6,7)	Opp. to James II in parlt., R.A., A.D.G., A.R.B.T., A.F.A.
John Granville			227	(6,7)	C.O., R.A., A.D.G., A.R.B.T., A.F.A.
Francis Gwyn			185	(2,5,7)	Sach, C.O., R.A., A.D.G., A.R.B.T., A.F.A.

Abbreviation Employed:

Membership in the commons before 1690:

(1) 1660, Convention (2) 1661, Cavalier (3) 1679, First Exclusion (4) 1680, Second Exclusion (5) 1681, Oxford Parliament (6) 1685, James II (7) 1688/9.

Opp. to James II (in parlt.) in the country. Those not sitting in the convention parliament who are listed as being in opposition to James II in 1685 (in parliament) in the country. (Browning, *Danby*, iii, 152–63).

Sach.   Favoured the *Sacheverell* clause in the convention (*Ibid.*, 164–72).

T.   *Tories* opposed to making William and Mary king and queen (*Ibid.*)

C.O.   Listed on (*constitutional?*) *opposition* list of December 1694. (Berks, R.O., Trumbull Add. MSS. 13/68. See appendix A.)

S.(R.)A.   *Signed (Refused)* association (Browning, *Danby*, iii, 187–213). See Appendix A.

F.(A.)D.G.   For (*Against*) *devaluation of guineas* (Samuel Grascombe, *An Account of the Proceedings in the House of Commons in Relation to the Devaluation of Guineas* (1696), pp. 10–16).

F.(A.)R.B.T.   For (*Against*) *royal board of trade* (B.M. Portland loan 29/31/1). See Appendix A.

F.(A.)F.A.   For (*Against*) *Fenwick attainder* (B.M. Add. MSS. 40608). See Appendix A.

APPENDIX C

The Act of Settlement: The Timing of Further Limitations Upon the Prerogative

An Act for the further Limitation of the Crown and better Securing the Rights and Liberties of the Subject: (12 and 13 William III, c. 2).

c.3. Further provision for securing the Religion, Laws and Liberties of these Realms.

AND whereas it is requisite and necessary that some further Provision be made for securing our Religion Laws and Liberties from and after the Death of His Majesty and the Princess Ann of Denmark and in default of Issue of the Body of the said Princess and of His Majesty respectively Be it enacted by the Kings most Excellent Majesty by and with the Advice and Consent of the Lords Spirituall and Temporall and Commons in Parliament assembled and by the Authority of the same.

[From the wording the clauses would appear to take effect:

1 *THAT whosoever shall hereafter come to the Possession of this Crown* shall joyn in Communion with the Church of England as by Law established

On William's death

2 *That in case the Crown and Imperiall Dignity of this Realm shall hereafter come to any Person not being a Native of this Kingdom of England* this Nation be not obliged to ingage in any Warr for the Defence of any Dominions or Territories which do not belong to the Crown of England without the Consent of Parliament.

On Anne's death (if d.s.p.).

3 *That no Person who shall hereafter come to the Possession of this Crown* shall go out of the Dominions of England Scotland or Ireland without Consent of Parliament.

On William's death

282

From the wording the clauses would appear to take effect:

4 *That from and after the Time that the further Limitation by this Act shall take Effect* all Matters and Things relating to the well governing of this Kingdom which are properly cognizable in the Privy Councill by the Laws and Customs of this Realme shall be transacted there and all Resolutions taken thereupon shall be signed by such of the Privy Councill as shall advise and consent to the same.
On Anne's death (if d.s.p.).

5 *That after the said Limitation shall take Effect as aforesaid* no Person born out of the Kingdoms of England Scotland or Ireland or the Dominions thereunto belonging (although he be naturalized or made a Denizen (except such as [are*] born of England Parents)) shall be capable to be of the Privy Councill or a Member of either House of Parliament or to enjoy any Office or Place of Trust either Civill or Military or to have any Grant of Lands Tenements or Hereditaments from the Crown to himself or to any other or others in Trust for him.
On Anne's death (if d.s.p.).

6 That no Person who has an Office or Place of Profit under the King or receives a Pention from the Crown shall be capable of serving as a Member of the House of Commons.
At once.

7 *That after the said Limitation shall take Effect as aforesaid* Judges Commissions be made Quam diu se bene Gesserint and their Salaries ascertained and established but upon the Address of both Houses of Parliament it may be lawfull to remove them.
On Anne's death (if d.s.p.).

8 That no Pardon under the Great Seal of England be pleadable to an Impeachment by the Commons in Parliament.
At once.]

    * Interlined on the roll. Italics added.

Select Bibliography

I. MANUSCRIPT SOURCES

A. England

Berks:

County Record Office.
Trumbull Additional Manuscripts.
The following of this deposit were useful:
68/13 Contains a division list of 1694.
125   Trumbull's Diary which is of some use for understanding Trumbull's problems with the court in 1696 and 1697.

98   Brydges Correspondence, contains a few letters regarding the 1698 election.
130   A few notes on proceedings in the 1700/1 parliament.

Cambridge:

Cambridge University Library.
Cholmondeley (Houghton) Manuscripts.
Correspondence, 15–200, consists primarily of letters to Walpole and a few to his father.

Chester:

City Record Office.
Mayor's Letters.
Includes letters from Peter Shakerley, M.P., to the mayor, aldermen, and citizens of Chester.

Cumberland:

1. *County Record Office (Carlisle).*
Lonsdale Collection.
The collection contains several very large deposits of papers relating to the Lowthers of Whitehaven.
(1) Uncatalogued Lowther correspondence, bundled and boxed in roughly chronological order, contains over a hundred important political letters from a placeman, James Lowther, to his father, Sir John, between the years 1698 and 1702 while the former was a member for Carlisle and sometime (from 1698) clerk of the deliveries of the ordnance. Sir John was himself a member for Cumberland between 1698 and 1700, but, as the letters bear witness, was usually busy with his coal and shipping interests in Whitehaven.
(2) Lonsdale Misc. Unsorted Correspondence, include a few letters of electoral interest from diverse correspondents to Sir John Lowther of Whitehaven from 1695–1700.
(3) Lonsdale bound volume of original letters are written mostly to Sir John Lowther of Whitehaven, covering the period, 1692–7.
(4) Letter Books of Sir John Lowther of Whitehaven include copies of some political letters sent between the years 1694 and 1701. Unfortunately many are in shorthand.
(5) Aside from the Lonsdale collection there are a few letters of interest in a boxed collection called simply, 'Unsorted Seventeenth Century Manuscripts', which include a few letters and manuscripts, pamphlets of political significance.

2. *Cockermouth Castle.*
Leconfield Estate Documents.
Includes letters of various agents and friends of the duke of Somerset to and from his grace or his secretary, Charles Heron.

Derby:

Chatsworth (Derbyshire).
Chatsworth Manuscripts, in the possession of the duke of Devonshire.
(1) Although largely printed in Foxcroft, *Halifax*, the notebook of George Saville, Marquis of Halifax, provides some interesting comments from 1687–1691. This is also the case with the Halifax Collection, Group A (Halifax Memoranda) which contains a justification of the opposition.
(2) The Whildon Collection.
Letters to James Whildon, auditor at Hardwicke Hall from Jos. Whildon and Aaron Kniton, the duke of Devonshire's steward in London. Contains 347 items, mostly estate papers but occasional remarks are worthwhile.
(3) Finch-Halifax Manuscripts.
Five boxes, largely of letters arranged in a roughly chronological order, contain correspondence from Nottingham, Heneage Finch and Sir John Banks, bart. They throw a good deal of light on politics in Oxford University and Surrey during the last half of William's reign.
(4) Chatsworth MSS., 1st series.

The papers of the Cavendish family, which yield little of value that is not already printed in Lady Russell's letters.

Dorset:

County Record Office (Dorchester)
J. M. Lane Papers. Includes letters to Sir John Trenchard from William Blathwayt, Henry, Lord Capell and others, 1693–1694/5. There are also some of Trenchard's draft letters.

Durham:

University of Durham, Prior's Kitchen.
Baker Baker Papers. These papers contain a few letters regarding the problems of apologists of the glorious revolution.

Gloucester:

1. *County Record Office.*
Lloyd-Baker Manuscripts, Sharp papers, boxes four and five, include some political correspondence of Archbishop Sharp. These papers are on restricted loan from Col. Lloyd-Baker.
DpA/D1799 (Dyrham Park Archives), Blathwayt Family papers, correspondence. Includes some political correspondence to the placeman, William Blathwayt, between 1695 and 1700/1, while he was member for Bath.

2. *Hardwicke Court.*
Lloyd-Baker Manuscripts, in the possession of Col. Lloyd-Baker. Although very little of political interest remains at Hardwicke for this period, box 27 of the Lloyd papers contains a large collection of interesting sermons.

Hereford:

1. *County Record Office.*
Brydges Collection.
(1) Brydges unsorted collection, consists mostly of estate papers but contains occasional letters of political importance which are usually addressed to Francis Bridges sometimes regarding the Hon. James Brydges, M.P.
(2) A81, E31 (Brydges Collection, Calendared Correspondence), contains little of value.
(3) B47/A (Records of Robert Price, personal and relating to his legal profession) contains a few electoral letters.
(4) The Foley Estate Papers, contain little political information.
(5) The Harley Estate Papers, are also of little value.
(6) The Cowper Estate Papers, are roughly catalogued and of little value.

2. *Brampton Bryan*
Harley Estate Papers at the estate office, in the keeping of Christopher Harley, contain some letters of political interest from 1683 to 1693.

Hertford:

County Record Office.
Cowper (Panshanger) MSS.
Cowper family papers, include only a little of value for this period.

Lancaster:

1. *County Record Office (Preston).*
DDKE/6, DDKE/9 (Kenyon Papers, Parliament, Correspondence). Includes letters to Roger and George Kenyon, both of Peel. This collection complements those reported by the Historical Manuscripts Commission (4th Report, Appendix, Part IV (1894)) which still remain at Gredington.

2. *Liverpool Public Library.*
920/NOR1, 920/NOR2 (Norris Papers). Several hundred letters primarily addressed to Richard Norris, alderman, mayor and M.P. for Liverpool from Thomas Norris of Speke and Sir William Norris, bart. Only part of this collection was printed by the Chetham Society (vol. ix, 1846).

3. *John Rylands Library (Manchester).*

(1) The original biographical notes on members of parliament by W. D. Pink which include many corrections.
(2) Legh of Lyme Manuscripts, boxes 47, 48, 52, 55, 57, 61, 65 and 66. Includes a few letters from the earl of Derby, William Banks and others to Peter Legh of Lyme which touch on parliamentary proceedings.

Leicester:

County Record Office.
Finch Manuscripts, box 5, bundle 22, contains some of Nottingham's political correspondence between 1694 and 1706.

London and Middlesex:

1. *British Museum.*
Loan 29 (Portland Manuscripts).
The first deposit, formerly at Welbeck and reported extensively in the Historical Manuscripts Commission reports on the Portland manuscripts, leaves out or merely alludes to scores of letters of the Harley's which are of considerable value. See especially, loan 29/184 to loan 29/190, which cover the years 1687–1701/2 (bound volumes).
The second deposit includes sixty boxes, largely of letters arranged by correspondent to either Sir Edward Harley (loan 29/73–29/88), Edward Harley (loan 29/70–29/71), or Robert Harley (loan 29/125–29/166). Of special importance is the 'Account of Robert Harley's conduct with reference to the Revolution and succession' (Box 163, folder 3). It is a fair copy in a clerk's hand with corrections in Harley's hand. Although written in the third person, there are occasional slips into the second. It seems surprisingly fair and accurate.

It may be noted in passing that from the signatures which appear on the manuscripts slip on the inside of the boxes, no more than one or two others have been through all of the above, although perhaps some looked at them while standing at the circulation desk. This method obviates the necessity of them being checked and thus allows one to receive more than three boxes a day (which is most helpful as most of the letters fall outside William's reign). Loan 29/31 contains a division list probably regarding the royal board of trade. Additional Manuscripts.

5124 (Collection of Dutch State Papers).

6703 (Manuscript Transcripts of Diverse Political Pamphlets and Tracts).

7060, 7070, 7074, (George Stepney (the envoy) correspondence).

7080 (Letters from the Hon. Andrew Newport (M.P. Shrewsbury) to the Hon. Richard Newport (M.P. Salop)). Unfortunately the letters are somewhat superficial.

15397–15398 (*Monumentum Britanicum ex Autographis Romanorum Pontificum ...*). Transcripts from the papal registers relating to England, Scotland and Ireland which are so general as to be of little use.

15895 (Hyde Correspondence and Official Papers). Correspondence of the earl of Rochester.

17677 HH-XX (not VV) (Netherland Transcripts). Reports of L'Hermitage to the Estates-General.

21494 (Southwell Letters and Official Documents).

22193 (Strafford Manuscripts).

28053 and 29588 (Finch Manuscripts).

28070 (Anne-Godolphin Letters).

28091 (Osborne Papers) contain what appears to be a 1700/1 list of supporters either for Harley as speaker or his programme for the succession.

28070 (Godolphin Manuscripts).

28876–88 (Ellis Manuscripts).

29594–5 (Finch-Hatton Papers).

30000 A, B, C, D and E (Transcripts of the Dispatches of Frederic Bonet, resident in London for Frederic III, elector of Brandenburg, first king in Prussia and first king of Prussia).

32520–24 (North Manuscripts).

32681 (Sydney Correspondence).

34355 (Montague-Blathwayt Letters, 1695–7).

34095–6 (Official Letters and Newsletters to Sir William Dutton Colt). Newsletters cover the period from May 1691 to May 1692.

40621 (Correspondence and Papers of the Harley family) is of value for the period 1688–1690.

40771–5, 40781 (Vernon Papers). The first group consists mostly of letter drafts while 40781 are Vernon's notes on privy council proceedings.

Stowe Manuscripts

222 (Hanover Papers).

Landsdowne Manuscripts.

1012, 1034 (Kennet-Blackwell Correspondence).

2. *Dr Williams's Library.*
Roger Morrice, 'Entering Book, being an Historical Register of Occurences'. Three volumes. Volume three covers the period from April 1677 to April 1691. Morrice was a Presbyterian clergyman (ejected 1662) with views similar to the younger Hampden or the third earl of Shaftesbury, who was nonetheless an astute if biased observer of parliamentary affairs.

3. *Public Record Office.*
S.P. 8/14–S.P.8/15.
State Papers Domestic, King William's Chest. Includes some material which was missed in the calendar.
30/24 (Shaftesbury Papers). Includes a life of the third Lord Shaftesbury by his son.
31/3 (Baschet Transcripts on reports of French envoys).

4. *Historical Manuscripts Commission.*
Finch Papers, in various stages of being calendared. Volume four, in galley proof, covers the year 1692. Volume five, in manuscript, covers the year 1693. These volumes consist mostly of naval letters to and from Nottingham.

Northampton:

1. *County Record Office.*
Isham Manuscripts. Includes letters to Sir Justinian Isham (M.P. for Northampton or Northamptonshire for most of William's reign) from his brother, John and others.
Finch-Hatton Correspondence, includes a few letters of interest for 1701.

2. *Althorpe.*
The Halifax Manuscripts, in the keeping of Earl Spencer, K.G.
(1) Correspondence. A large collection of letters mostly to the first and second Marquises of Halifax from Francis Gwyn, Robert Harley, Nottingham, Lord Weymouth, Col. Granville and others. They are kept in ten large cardboard boxes.
(2) Bound volume containing two manuscripts, one for an election pamphlet, the other an 'Original journal by the (1st) Marquess of Halifax of his Conversations with King William III'.

(3) Boughton House.
The Shrewsbury papers, in the possession of the duke of Buccleuch and Queensberry, are only partially printed in the three volumes of G. P. R. James, *Vernon Correspondence* (1841). Over 150 letters mostly from Vernon to Shrewsbury are deleted (see bibliographical appendix), scores of which are of considerable importance in understanding conflicts between court and opposition between October 1696 and October 1700.

Northumberland:

County Record Office (Newcastle).
1. Blackett (Matfen) Manuscripts is an unsorted collection which contains a few political comments for the period 1696–9.
2. ZSw 27/4 (Swinburne Papers).

Nottingham:

Nottingham University Library.
PwA (Letters to and other papers of William Bentinck, first earl of Portland.
A most important collection which includes letters from Sunderland, Shrewsbury, Montague, Guy, Somers and many others. A very few of the letters are
printed in R. Kenyon, *Sunderland* and a very large number in N. Japikse,
Correspondentie. As, however, Japikse was interested more in letters relating
to European rather than purely domestic affairs, a large number remain
unprinted (as may be seen in his collated index in the second volume, pages
798–828). Of these, there are at least fifty which are of considerable importance
in understanding court and country conflicts between 1690 and 1700.

Oxford:

1. *Blenheim Palace.*
Marlborough Manuscripts, in the muniments room, contain only a few letters
of any importance for William's reign.
The first volume of the Sunderland letter books in the palace library, contains
some letters from Somers to the earl of Sunderland during 1698 and 1699. Of
greater importance are the extensive comments on parliamentary proceedings
made by John Methuen, Lord Chancellor of Ireland, in letters written from
January to June 1698 during one of his not infrequent absences at Westminster, when member for Devizes, Wiltshire. The recipient, as may be easily
deduced from internal evidence, was the earl of Galway, one of the joint lord
justices of Ireland.

2. *Bodleian Library.*
Additional Manuscripts. A. 191, Letters to Burnet.
Ballard MSS. 7, 8, 9, 10, 11, 12, 13, 15, 21, 23, 24, 35, 38, 39, 45 and 48 contain
a number of political letters for the beginning and end of William's reign,
many of which are addressed to Dr Charlett, fellow of Trinity College, Oxford.
Carte Manuscripts: 79, 230 and 233 contain a few letters giving information
about the political attitudes of the Whartons.
228 (Newsletters), are unfortunately shallow; 130, is a bound volume which
includes a number of important letters with detailed comments on parliamentary proceedings from 1691 to 1698/9, written to the duke of Beaufort
from Robert Price, while a member for Weobley.
Manuscript English Letters C. 54.
Letters to Sir Robert Southwell from his agent Philip Madoxe at Whitehall
(1688–90) are of little value.
Manuscript film, 296–7. (Newsletters to Sir Richard Newdigate in the
possession of the Folger Shakespeare Library, Washington, D.C.) covers the
period 10 January 1688 to 11 June 1706, but are unfortunately rather shallow.
The Lovelace Collection of Locke MSS. c:5, 6, 7, 8, 11, 16, 18, 22, 23, 24, 40.
A number of political letters remain in the above collection to or from John
Locke between 1695 and 1700/1 which are not to be found in B. Rand, *Locke
Corres.* (1927) or T. Forster, *Shaftesbury Corres.* (1830).
Montague Manuscripts, D. 1, contains a few papers of Charles Montague.

North Manuscripts, b.1 (The Papers of William, 6th Baron North), contains a few political papers for William's reign.

Rawlinson Manuscripts, A77, A139, A179, C735, D41, D836, D846 and D1079. A79 contains manuscript copies of the history of exchequer bills (1697) and observations of the commission of public accounts (*c.* March 1690/1). J401, J404, J405, J fol. 3 and J fol. 13 give additional information on political figures educated at Oxford who wrote minor works during William's reign. Rawlinson letters 98 and 104.

Smith Manuscripts, 149 (Diary of Thomas Smith), contains information dealing with the convention parliament.

Tanner Manuscripts 21, 22, 23, 25, 26 and 27 contain a few important political letters which remain unprinted. They are addressed to Archbishop Sancroft and cover the early years of William's reign. Some of those to Thomas Tanner or Humphrey Prideaux for the later years are also of some value.

3. *Codrington Library, All Souls.*
Manuscripts 158a and b.
'An Abstract of the Debates Orders and Resolutions In the House of Commons, wch are not printed in their votes. Collected by N.[arcissus] L.[uttrell] during his attendance therein as a Member.' MSS. 158a, extends from 6 November 1691 to 4 November 1692 and MSS.158b, from 4 November 1692 to 7 November 1693. The abstract is almost four times as inclusive as the debates reported in Grey, *Debates*, vol. x, or Cobbett, *Parliamentary History*, vol. v, for the same period. (The abstract contains about 175,000 words, while the debates reported for the same period in either of the latter two works are under 47,000 words.)

Salop:

County Record Office.
Attingham Collection.
Includes only a few letters for this period but some of these are of outstanding importance for the 1690 election.

Somerset:

County Record Office (Taunton).
Clarke Correspondence, containing a few letters of Edward Clarke, M.P., to the borough of Taunton.

Stafford:

William Salt Library (Stafford).
1. D.1721/3/291 (Bagot Family Manuscripts) contains some interesting election letters.

Surrey:

Reigate Corporation.
Somers papers.
A folder of letters to Somers, some dealing with elections.

Sussex:

East Sussex County Record Office (Lewes).
MSS. 840–3 (Ashburnham MSS.). Letterbooks of John, 1st lord Ashburnham, covering the period from 1695 which contains some interesting electoral
material for William's last parliament.

Westmorland:

1. *County Record Office (Kendal).*
DRY (Le Fleming Papers). There was some political material left out of the
Historical Manuscript Commission report on the S.H. Le Fleming manu-
scripts (12th Report, Appendix, Part VII (1890)).
A second deposit from Rydal of unsorted Le Fleming papers also supple-
ments the report, although there are only a few letters of note.

2. *Levens Hall*
Bagot Manuscripts, in the possession of Oliver Bagot, Esq., contain some
important political correspondence largely to Col. James Grahme of Levens
Hall, which was omitted from the Historical Manuscripts Commission's
report on Capt. J. F. Bagot's manuscripts (10th Report, Appendix, Part IV
(1885)). The letters remain in four tin boxes and are arranged in alphabetical
order by correspondent.

Wilts:

Longleat.
Thynne Papers, in the possession of the marquis of Bath, includes correspondence of Seymour, Nottingham, Abingdon, Winchelsea and others with
Thomas (Thynne), 1st Viscount Weymouth. The following bound volumes
seem most important: xii, xiii, xiv, xv, xvii and xix.

York:

Leeds Public Library.
TN (Temple and Newsom Manuscripts): 9 (correspondence) contains
political correspondence to Lord Irwin in 1701; LA/5 (Aire and Calder Navigation papers).
DB204/3/221. Manuscript of Thomas Wilson, eighteenth-century Leeds anti-
quarian.

B.   Wales

Anglesey:

Plas Newydd, Llanfairpwll.
Paget Manuscripts in the keeping of the marquis of Anglesey includes thin
notes on parliamentary proceedings from 12 March 1700/1 to 17 April 1701,
as well as Jacobite manuscript tracts.

Caernarvon:

1. *University College of North Wales (Bangor).*
Penrhos Manuscripts i, ii, v, vii, include letters of Humphrey (Humphreys), bishop of Bangor and later of Hereford (1701–12).
2. *Vaynol.*
Sir William Williams's papers were largely destroyed by fire. Sir Michael Duff is helpful in supplying recollections of their contents.

Cardigan:

National Library of Wales (Aberystwyth).
(1) Brogyntyn Manuscripts include letters to Sir Robert Owen from Sydney Godolphin, Owen Wynn and others.
(2) Wynnstay Manuscripts include letters from Robert Harley and Sir William Williams to the son of the latter.
(3) Chirk Castle Manuscripts include letters from Robert Harley and Robert Wynne to Sir Richard Myddleton.
(4) Pemrice and Margam Manuscripts contain letters to Sir Thomas Mansell, bart., from his son, Bussy and others.
(5) Mostyn Manuscripts.

C. Scotland.

Edinburgh:

Public Record Office.
Two manuscript tracts are of interest:
GD/25/13/95, Anon., 'Memorial to the Members of the Court Party' (*c.* 1701). It contains the argument that Scottish courtiers are to be patriots before being courtiers.
GD/26/13/95, Thomas Bease, 'England's oversights being some considerations humbly offered to this present parliament by which we may discover the excellent use of Dutch spectacles for all blear-eyed Englishmen, by a true lover of the English Interest'. Deals with forces sent to Ireland and naval precautions for securing Ireland from the French fleet.

D. Ireland

Dublin:

1. *Public Record Office.*
Wyche Correspondence (1634–1766), 1st series, includes letters from Maurice Annesley and Sir William Russell to Sir Cyril Wyche in 1700 and 1701 while Wyche was one of the elected commissioners for Irish forfeitures and a member of the Irish privy council.
2. *National Library of Ireland.*
Orrery Correspondence and Papers includes a few letters of interest from Henry Boyle to the countess of Orrery.

3. *Trinity College Library.*
(1) Manuscripts 749 (Clarke Correspondence), includes letters to George Clarke, secretary for war for King William's forces in Ireland, 1690–1, from Thomas Clarges, William Blathwayt, R. Yard, Geo. Felding and others often giving valuable information regarding parliamentary affairs.

Two collections, largely of letters to, or copies of letters from, William King, while bishop of Derry, present a generally hostile view of the English country party. The bishop, while firm to England, was as patriotic an Anglo-Irishman as his sometime friends, Molyneux and Swift, and for a time might be said to have been the leader of the Irish country party.
(2) Manuscripts 1122 (Lyons Collection).
Letters from Geo. Tollet (sometime secretary to the commission of accounts and Bishop King's law agent in London), Sir Robert Southwell and others to Bishop King. The Historical Manuscripts Commission in the appendix of the second report, pages 231–62, published only about a dozen of the hundreds in the collection, about fifty of which throw considerable light on English parliamentary proceedings.
(3) Manuscripts 1489 (Bishop King's Letterbooks, 2 vols.). These volumes cover the period 1699–1702/3.

E.   United States

Chicago:

University of Chicago Library.
Miscellaneous English Manuscripts includes in a bound volume: 'A Collection of all the Secret Poems and Lampoons wrote during the Reigne of the Late King William.'

New York:

1. *New York Public Library.*
Hardwicke Manuscripts 33.
Includes some remarks on the convention parliament and a few biographical notes concerning Somers which remain unpublished.
2. *Pierpont Morgan Library.*
Miscellaneous English Autograph Collection.

II.   PRINTED SOURCES
(The place of publication is London unless noted otherwise).

A.   *Official Documents*

Accounts and Papers, vol. xvi, part 1 (Members of Parliament). (1878.)
Calendar of State Papers, Domestic Series, of the Reign of William and Mary: William III. W. J. Hardy and E. Bateson ed. (1895–1937).
Calendar of Treasury Books, W. A. Shaw ed., vols. viii–xvii (1923–39).

Journals of the House of Commons, vols. x–xiii.
Journals of the House of Lords, vols. xiv–xvii.
Statutes of the Realm (folio edition), vols. vi–vii (1819–20).

B. *Reports of the Historical Manuscripts Commission.*

Report on the Manuscripts of the Earl of Ancaster (1907).
Report on the Manuscripts of Capt. J. F. Bagot. 10th Report, Appendix, Part IV, pages 331 and following (1885).
Report on the Manuscripts of the Marquis of Bath, at Longleat (1904–8). Vols. i and iii.
Report on the Manuscripts of the Duke of Buccleuch, Montague House, Whitehall (1903). Vol. ii, part ii.
Report on the Manuscripts of Earl Cowper, at Melbourne. 12th Report, Appendix, Part III (1888–9). Vols. ii–iii.
Report on the Manuscripts of the Earl of Denbigh. 7th Report, Appendix IV, pages 196 and following (1879).
Report on the Manuscripts of Alan George Finch (1957).
Report on the Manuscripts of F. J. Savile Foljambe of Oberton. 15th Report, Appendix, Part V (1897).
Report on the Manuscripts of Mrs Frankland-Russell-Astley (1900).
Report on the Manuscripts of Lord Kenyon. 14th Report, Appendix, Part IV, pages 187 and following (1894).
Report on the Manuscripts of S. H. Le Fleming. 12th Report, Appendix, Part VII (1890).
Report on the Manuscripts of F. W. Leyborne-Popham, Esq. (1899).
Report on the Manuscripts of the Earl of Lonsdale, at Lowther Castle. 13th Report, Appendix, Part VII (1893).
Report on the Manuscripts of the House of Lords. 12th and later reports (1889–1962).
Report on the Manuscripts of the Duke of Portland. 13th and later reports (1893–1931). Vols. ii–v, vii and x.
Report on the Manuscripts of Reginald Rawdon Hastings, Esq. Vol. ii (1930).
Report on the Manuscripts of the Earl of Onslow. 14th Report, Appendix, Part IX, pages 458 and following (1895).
Report on the Manuscripts of the Marquis of Ormonde. New Series, Vol. viii (1920).
Report on the Manuscripts in Various Collections; Report on the Manuscripts of F. L. Wood. Vol. viii, pages 1 and following (1913).

C. *Other Original Correspondence and Diaries including Compilations.*

'Correspondence of James Brydges and Robert Harley, Created Earl of Oxford', edited by Godfrey Davies and Marion Tinling, *Hunt. Lib. Quart.* (San Marino, Calif., 1938), i, 457–72.
Bishop Burnet's History of his Own Time (with notes by Swift, Dartmouth, Onslow and Hardwick). 6 vols. (Oxford, 1833).*
* *Supplement to Burnet's History of My Own Time,* edited by H. C. Foxcroft (1902).

*State Papers and Letters Addressed to William Carstares, confidential secretary to
K. Williams...To which is Prefixed The Life of Mr Carstares*, edited by J.
McCormick (Edinburgh, 1774).

Cobbett's Parliamentary History of England (1809). Vol. v.

Court and Society from Elizabeth to Anne, edited from the Papers at Kimbolton
by William Drogel Montague, duke of Manchester (1864). Vol. ii.

Memoirs of Mary, Queen of England, edited by R. Doebner (1886).

The Diary of John Evelyn, edited by E. S. De Beer (Oxford, 1955). Vols.
iv–v.

*Miscellaneous State Papers from 1501 to 1726 from the Collection of the Earl of
Hardwicke*, edited by Philip (Yorke), second earl of Hardwicke (1778). Vol.
ii.

*The Diary of John Hervey, First Earl of Bristol, with Extracts from his Book of
Expenses, 1688–1742* (Suffolk Green Books, Wells, 1894).

The Letter Books of John Hervey, First Earl of Bristol (Suffolk Green Books,
Wells, 1894).

'Lord Halifax and the Malmesbury Election in 1701', edited by A. L. Browne,
Wiltshire Archaeological and Natural History Magazine (Devizes, December
1936), xlvii, 500–3.

*The Correspondence of Henry Hyde, Earl of Clarendon and of his Brother, Laurence
Hyde, Earl of Rochester; with the Diary of Lord Clarendon from 1687 to 1690...*,
edited by S. W. Singer (1828). Vol. ii.

Correspondence of the Family of Hatton, edited by E. M. Thompson. Camden
Society Publications, New Series, xxiii (1878).

*Historical and Political Memoirs Containing Letters Written by Sovereign Princes,
State Ministers, Admirals, and General Officers, etc. From Almost all the Courts
in Europe, Beginning with 1697 to the end of 1708*, edited by C. Cole (1735).

Debates in the House of Commons, 1667–1694, collected by the Hon. Anchitel
Grey, Esq. (1763). Vols. ix–x.

*The History and Proceedings of the House of Commons from the Restoration to the
Present Time*, published by R. Chandler (1742–4). Vols. i–iii.

*The History and Proceedings of the House of Lords from the Restoration in 1660 to
the Present Time*, published by E. Timberland.

The Harcourt Papers, edited by E. W. Harcourt. Vol. ii. (No correspondence
is to be found in William's period in this second volume although there
are a few biographical points made in the beginning which are of interest.)

Der Fall des Houses Stuart, und die Succession des Hauses Hanover, edited by Onno
Klopp (Vienna, 1877–81). Vols. v–x (Dispatches of the Austrian envoy).

*The Leven and Melville Papers, Chiefly Addressed to George, Earl of Melville,
Secretary of State for Scotland*, edited by W. L. Melville, Bannatyne Club
(Edinburgh, 1843).

*The Lexington Papers, or, some Account of the Courts of London and Vienna at the
conclusion of the Seventeenth Century...*, edited by the Hon. H. Manners-
Sutton (1851).

A Brief Historical Relation of State Affairs..., by Narcissus Luttrell (Oxford,
1857). Vols. i–v.

Memoirs of John, Duke of Marlborough, with His Original Correspondence, edited
by William Coxe (1818). Vol. i.

A Selection from the Papers of the Earls of Marchmont in the Possession of the Rt. Hon. Sir George Henry Rose..., edited by G. H. Rose (1831). Vol. iii.

Authentick Memoirs of the Life and Conduct of her Grace, Sarah, Late Dutchess of Marlborough, edited by George Caldecott (1744).

Memoirs of the Life of Charles Montague, Late Earl of Halifax (2nd edition, 1716).

The Norris Papers, edited by T. Heywood for the Chetham Society Publications. Vol. ix (1846).

Letters of Humphrey Prideaux, sometime Dean of Norwich to John Ellis, sometime Under-Secretary of State, 1674–1722, edited by E. M. Thompson, Publications of the Camden Society, new series (1875. Vol. xv.)

A Selection from the Papers of the Earls of Marchmont, edited by G. H. Rose, 3 vols. (1831).

Correspondence of Charles Talbot, Duke of Shrewsbury, edited by W. Coxe (1821).

Original Letters of Locke; Algernon Sidney and Anthony Lord Shaftesbury, Author of the 'Characteristics', edited by T. Forster (1830).

Verney Letters...of the Eighteenth Century from the Manuscripts at Claydon House, edited by Margaret Maria, Lady Verney (1930). Vol. i.

Letters Illustrative of the Reign of William III from 1696 to 1708 Addressed to the Duke of Shrewsbury, by James Vernon, Esq., edited by G. P. R. James. 3 vols. (1841).

Correspondentie van Willem III en van Hans Willem Bentinck, edited by N. Japikse. Rijks Geschiedkimdige Publicatien, kleine series, xxiii, xxiv, xvi–xviii (The Hague, 1927–37).

Letters of William III and Louis XIV and of their Ministers...1697–1700, edited by Paul Grimblot. 2 vols. (1948).

'Correspondence of some Wiltshire Politicians *c.* 1700', edited by Lord Landsdowne, *Wiltshire Archaeological and Natural History Magazine* (Devizes, December 1932), xlvi. 64–85.

D.   *Contemporary Pamphlets.*

The collections of the Bodleian and the British Museum have been employed extensively, although many are included in *The Harleian Miscellany*, T. Park, ed., 10 vols. (1808–13), or Sir W. Scott, ed., *The Somers Collection of Tracts*, 13 vols. (1809–15).

Index